ICSA Study Text

Development of Strategy

ICSA Study Text

Development of Strategy

Mark Wearden

The Governance
Institute

First published 2019
Published by ICSA Publishing Ltd
Saffron House
6–10 Kirby Street
London EC1N 8TS

Typeset by Patricia Briggs

British Cataloguing in Publication Data
A catalogue record for this book is available from the British Library.

ISBN   978-1-86072-753-5

Contents

How to use this study text

This study text has been developed to support the Development of Strategy module of the ICSA's qualifying programme and includes a range of navigational, self-testing and illustrative features to help you get the most out of the support materials.

The text is divided into three main sections:

◆ introductory material
◆ the text itself
◆ reference material.

The sections below show you how to find your way around the text and make the most of its features.

Introductory material

The introductory section includes a full contents list and the aims and learning outcomes of the qualification, as well as a list of acronyms and abbreviations.

The text itself

Each part opens with a list of the chapters to follow, an overview of what will be covered and learning outcomes for the part.

Every chapter opens with a list of the topics covered and an introduction specific to that chapter.

Chapters are structured to allow students to break the content down into manageable sections for study. Each chapter ends with a summary of key content to reinforce understanding.

Features

The text is enhanced by a range of illustrative and self-testing features to assist understanding and to help you prepare for the examination. You will find answers to the 'Test yourself' questions towards the end of this text. Each feature is presented in a standard format, so that you will become familiar with how to use them in your study.

These features are identified by a series of icons.

The text also includes tables, figures and other illustrations as relevant.

Reference material

The text contains a range of additional guidance and reference material, including a glossary of key terms and a comprehensive index.

Stop and think

Test yourself

Making it work

Case study

Worked example

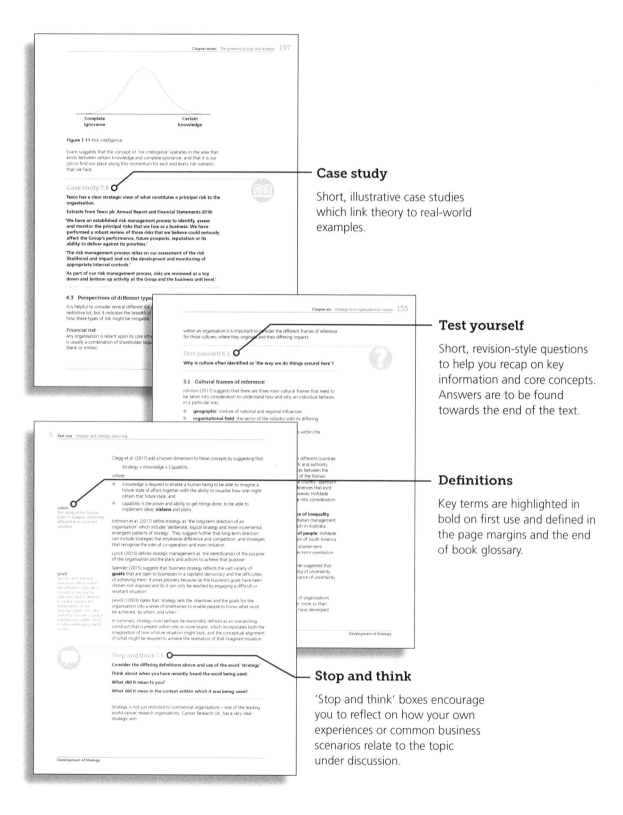

Chapter seven The governing body and strategy   197

Figure 7.11 Risk intelligence

Evans suggests that the concept of 'risk intelligence' operates in the area that exists between certain knowledge and complete ignorance, and that it is our job to find our place along this momentum for each and every risk scenario that we face.

Case study 7.8

Tesco has a clear strategic view of what constitutes a principal risk to the organisation.

Extracts from Tesco plc Annual Report and Financial Statements 2018:

'We have an established risk management process to identify, assess and monitor the principal risks that we face as a business. We have performed a robust review of those risks that we believe could seriously affect the Group's performance, future prospects, reputation or its ability to deliver against its priorities.'

'The risk management process relies on our assessment of the risk likelihood and impact and on the development and monitoring of appropriate internal controls.'

'As part of our risk management process, risks are reviewed as a top down and bottom up activity at the Group and the business unit level.'

4.3   Perspectives of different types

It is helpful to consider several different risk restrictive list, but it indicates the breadth of how these types of risk might be mitigated.

Financial risk

Any organisation is reliant upon its core infra is usually a combination of shareholder (equ (bank or similar).

Case study

Short, illustrative case studies which link theory to real-world examples.

Chapter six Strategy and organisational culture   155

within an organisation it is important to consider the different frames of reference for those cultures, where they originate and their differing impacts.

Test yourself 6.1

Why is culture often identified as 'the way we do things around here'?

3.1   Cultural frames of reference

Johnson (2017) suggests that there are three main cultural frames that need to be taken into consideration to understand how and why an individual behaves in a particular way.

◆ **geographic**: mixture of national and regional influences
◆ **organisational field**: the sector of the industry with its differing

Test yourself

Short, revision-style questions to help you recap on key information and core concepts. Answers are to be found towards the end of the text.

---

6   **Part one** Strategy and strategic planning

Clegg et al. (2017) add a human dimension to these concepts by suggesting that

Strategy = Knowledge + Capability

where

◆ knowledge is required to enable a human being to be able to imagine a future state of affairs together with the ability to visualise how one might obtain that future state, and
◆ capability is the power and ability to get things done, to be able to implement ideas, **visions** and plans.

Johnson et al. (2017) define strategy as 'the long-term direction of an organisation' which includes 'deliberate, logical strategy and more incremental, emergent patterns of strategy'. They suggest further that long-term direction can include strategies that emphasise difference and competition, and strategies that recognise the roles of co-operation and even imitation.

Lynch (2015) defines strategic management as 'the identification of the purpose of the organisation and the plans and actions to achieve that purpose'.

Spender (2015) suggests that 'business strategy reflects the vast variety of **goals** that are open to businesses in a capitalist democracy and the difficulties of achieving them. It arises precisely because (a) the business's goals have been chosen not imposed and (b) it can only be reached by engaging a difficult or resistant situation'.

Levicki (2003) states that 'strategy sets the objectives and the goals for the organisation into a series of timeframes to enable people to know what must be achieved, by whom, and when.'

In summary, strategy could perhaps be reasonably defined as an overarching construct that is present within one or more brains, which incorporates both the imagination of how a future situation might look, and the conceptual alignment of what might be required to achieve the realisation of that imagined situation.

vision
The ability of the human brain to imagine something different from a current situation

goals
Specific and definable outcomes which enable identification of progress towards achieving the objectives and, if defined in such a manner, the achievement of the strategic intent; the outline useful to consider a goal as something tangible which is either achieved (scored) or not

Stop and think 1.1

Consider the differing definitions above and use of the word 'strategy'.

Think about when you have recently heard the word being used.

What did it mean to you?

What did it mean in the context within which it was being used?

Strategy is not just restricted to commercial organisations – one of the leading world cancer research organisations, Cancer Research UK, has a very clear strategic aim.

Definitions

Key terms are highlighted in bold on first use and defined in the page margins and the end of book glossary.

Stop and think

'Stop and think' boxes encourage you to reflect on how your own experiences or common business scenarios relate to the topic under discussion.

About the author

Mark Wearden, MSc FCCA FCIS, delivers consultancy projects through MBS Governance a private strategy consultancy, which he has run for the past 23 years, following 12 years in International Banking as an analyst, and 8 years in Industry as a finance director.

In addition to his client-focused consultancy, Mark is an experienced Non-Executive Director and an Audit Committee Advisor. He undertakes director and board mentoring, a range of academic work, and delivers public workshops, seminars and lectures for professional bodies, together with 'in-house' programmes for client organisations.

Mark is the strategy examiner and an assessor for ICSA final level exams, and a member of the judging panel for the ICSA annual reporting awards. He stepped down this year after two years as Chairman of the ACCA Global Forum on Governance, Risk and Performance.

Throughout his career, Mark has worked extensively with directors and senior managers from a wide range of different type and size of organisation, from FTSE 100 down and back again, giving him a challenging insight into the minds of the directors of corporate Britain. Mark specialises in strategic analysis and challenge, aligned with board and director evaluation.

Mark's areas of interest are 'governance thinking', 'risk and reporting', 'financial analysis', 'supply chain challenge' and exploring the dichotomy that frequently exists between theory and practice.

Acknowledgements

Figures 8.7 and 13.4 Copyright © December 2013 by the International Integrated Reporting Council ('the IIRC'). All rights reserved. Used with permission of the IIRC. Contact the IIRC (info@theiirc.org) for permission to reproduce, store, transmit or make other uses of this document.

Extracts from Financial Times articles in case studies 1.6, 3.5, 4.5, 7.2, 9.4, 9.6, 10.1, 11.1, 11.3, 12.3, 12.5, 13.5, 13.6, 15.3 © *The Financial Times*, www.ft.com

Figure 1.5, Figure 8.2 © Maccoby, Michael, *Strategic Intelligence*

Figure 1.6 © Argyris, Chris, *Overcoming Organizational Defenses*

Figure 2.1, 4.3, 6.6, 8.3, 10.2 © Johnson et al., *Exploring Strategy 11th edition*

Figure 2.3, 3.3, 5.6 © Senge, Peter

Figure 2.4, 12.11 © Mintzberg, Henry

Figure 2.5, 2.7, 14.6, 15.7 © Pettigrew, Andrew and Whipp, Richard

Figure 2.6, 14.2 © Martin, Roger

Figure 3.1 © Adair, John

Figure 3.2 © Covey, Stephen

Figure 4.5, 7.5 © Lynch, Richard

Figure 4.6, 5.4, 10.5, 10.7, 10.8, 13.3 © Porter, Michael

Figure 5.1 © Grant, Robert, Contemporary Strategy Analysis

Figure 5.2 © Carter, Steve, Renaissance Management

Figure 5.6, 8.5 © McKinsey & Company, https://www.mckinsey.com/

Figure 6.2 © Schein, Edgar

Figure 6.4, 12.9 © Handy, Charles

Figure 6.5 © Deal, Terrence and Kennedy, Allan

Figure 6.7 © Grinyer, Peter and Spender, J.C.

Figure 6.8 © Renaissance Management 1999

Figure 8.4 © Campbell, Andrew

Figure 8.6 © BAE plc, https://www.baesystems.com

Figure 8.8 © Berenschot 1998

Figure 9.1 © Bagley, Constance

Figure 9.3 © Carroll, Archie

Figure 9.4 © ClearlySo Ltd, https://www.clearlyso.com/

Figure 9.5 © Hamel, Gary

Figure 10.4 © Ansoff, H. Igor

Figure 12.7 © Bartlett, Christopher and Ghoshal, Sumantra

Figure 13.7, 13.8 © Dess, G., Lumpkin, G., & Eisner, A.

Figure 13.10 © Kaplan, Robert and Norton, David

Figure 14.3 © Balogun, Julia & Hope Hailey, Julia

Figure 14.4 © Robbins, Stephen and Judge, Timothy

Figure 14.5 © Lewin, Kurt

Figure 15.1 © Belbin, Meredith

Figure 15.2 © Luft, Joseph and Ingham, Harry

Figure 15.4 © Mintzberg, Henry; Ahlstrand, Bruce and Lampel, Joseph

Figure 15.5 © Beer, Michael et al.

Figure 15.6 © Kotter, John.

Acronyms and abbreviations

AI	artificial intelligence
AIM	Alternative Investment Market
BCG	Boston Consulting Group
BPR	business process re-engineering
BRIC	Brazil, Russia, India, China
CAGE	cultural, administrative, geographic, economic
CEO	chief executive officer
CFO	chief financial officer
CGMA	Chartered Global Management Accountant
CIC	Community Interest Company
CMA	Competition and Markets Authority
CRM	customer-relationship management
CSR	corporate social responsibility
EBITDA	earnings before interest, tax, depreciation and amortisation
EQFM	European quality framework management
ERP	enterprise resource planning
ESG	environmental, social and governance
FRC	Financial Reporting Council
HACCP	hazard analysis and critical control points
HR	human resources
IBE	Institute of Business Ethics
IIRC	International Integrated Reporting Council
IMF	International Monetary Fund
IoD	Institute of Directors
IoT	internet of things

KPI	key performance indicator
LSE	London Stock Exchange
MINT	Mexico, Indonesia, Nigeria, Turkey
NED	non-executive director
NHS	National Health Service
PESTEL	political, economic, socio-cultural, technological, environmental and legal
SBU	strategic business unit
SOARR	situation, opportunity, action, result, reflect
SWOT	strengths, weaknesses, opportunities and threats
USP	unique selling point
VRIN	value, rarity, inimitability and non-substitutability
VRIO	value, rarity, inimitability and organisational support
VUCA	volatile, uncertain, complex and ambiguous

Introduction

Throughout the next 15 chapters, a wide range of differing aspects of strategy as a theoretical subject will be explored. As this is also a very practical subject, there is a strong emphasis on not just being able to understand concepts and theory, but in being able to apply them in the real and challenging world that we live in. Strategic thinking is required by company secretaries and governance professionals, by the organisation they work for, and to enable all of us to deal with the challenges that we face every day of our lives. In essence, strategy is about decision-making.

We start at a very precise moment in time – now, this very second. At this point we can, in our imagination, freeze time and everything around us; we can just stop and think about why we are where we are in the journey through our lives. We can look back and understand why our lives are the way they are. We can analyse ourselves and understand why we have made certain decisions that have brought us to this very moment in time.

This is the starting point for our development of strategy, by understanding now, and this will be called the 'today' point throughout this text. We can then think about what lies ahead, the 'future'. This might be the next few minutes or hours, or it might be a few years, or across the remainder of our lives. As you will discover, we have to accept that very little about the future is certain, therefore we are dealing with aspiration and hope. The key strategic word for this is *vision* – this implies that we can see something in our minds, we can visualise how something in the future might be, or needs to be, different from today.

Throughout this text students will be encouraged to stop and think about the different aspects they are studying, and apply these aspects to themselves, their organisations and the world around them. Students are encouraged to always start with simple straightforward and logical thought patterns before trying to apply them to the complexities that are often caused by those around us. This last comment gives students the next clue to understanding why the development of strategy is so important for us and our organisations.

The challenge

If it was just you, or just me, or just any one individual, then achieving our vision could be relatively straightforward – we could remain single-minded in the pursuit of our goals. However, we are surrounded by other human beings, each with their own particular vision, which might be similar to ours, but can never be exactly the same, because each person has a unique 'today' point from which they are starting. The development of strategy requires us to plot a route through the challenges and forces of the single and cumulative human brains around us. The management of an organisation is concerned with trying to achieve goals and **objectives** through the combination of people and process. This combination is our start and end point, with the final two chapters considering the dynamics of changing processes and changing people.

We need to recognise that strategy is a science but also an art – we can plan a logical route, but we also need to be creative to find our way through the obstacles we face. The late Peter Drucker, an Austrian-American consultant and management thinker, suggested that organisations do not exist for their own sake, but to fulfil a specific social purpose, and to satisfy a specific need of society or community, with management being the drivers of the organisation. He suggested some core principles:

objectives
A range of criteria which identify and clarify differing aspects of the vision and mission–objectives are often aligned with the acronym SMART.

◆ Management is about human beings.

◆ It deals with the integration of people in a common venture.

◆ There is a need for a commitment to common goals and shared values, which need to be set and exemplified by management.

◆ Management must allow the organisation and each of its members to evolve, as needs and opportunities change.

◆ Management must:
  – establish the purpose and mission of an organisation
  – make work productive and employees effective
  – manage social impact and responsibilities.

The world around us

The development of our strategy, personal and organisational, needs to take place within the realities of the world in which we live. This is sometimes referred to as a VUCA world – volatile, uncertain, complex and ambiguous. The term originated from the end of the original Cold War, the geopolitical tension that existed between the US and the USSR, but the financial crises of 2007 and the subsequent years of austerity and financial uncertainty could equally attract this acronym. This concept has been tempered by a growth across the same period of time of a much higher level of societal expectation and concern with the world as a place to exist. This is evidenced by the growth of corporate social responsibility (CSR) expectations and the increased investor interest in reporting on environmental, social and governance (ESG) aspects of an organisation and its strategy.

The concept of uncertainty is not new in strategic thinking, nor restricted to strategic thinking. As already suggested, very little beyond our 'today' point can be stated with 100% certainty – we live our lives based around our expectations of what is likely to happen. This can be illustrated by considering the relationship between what we know and what we don't know.

In February 2002, Donald Rumsfeld, US Defence Secretary (Rumsfeld, 2011) was asked about the likelihood that the Iraqi government were supplying terrorist groups with weapons of mass destruction. His comment was:

◆   There are known knowns; things we know that we know.

◆   There are known unknowns; things that we know we don't know.

◆   But there are also unknown unknowns; things we do not know we don't know.

These considerations need to be included in our thinking as we approach our consideration of how to best develop our strategy. Nassim Taleb describes the unknown unknowns as 'black swans', suggesting that:

The black swan exists, but is highly unusual and therefore lies beyond expectation, and outside conscious awareness (Taleb uses the word *outlier* to describe this).

◆   The appearance of a black swan will cause an impact upon a situation and will affect the conscious awareness of people involved.

◆   The black swan event will later be explained, by those affected and others, in a manner that suggests that its likelihood was already known (Taleb's phrase here is *retrospective predictability*).

As we approach our consideration of strategy, we need to always be thinking from a 'black swan' perspective. What might be out there that could impact our strategic plan or totally change our vision and mission?

The Fourth Industrial Revolution

The industrial and commercial world within which we operate is described as entering the Fourth Industrial Revolution, a technological revolution that will fundamentally alter the way we live, work and relate to each other. It is suggested that its scale, scope and complexity will be unlike anything that people have ever experienced. Precisely how it will evolve is an unknown unknown, but it will involve all aspects of our lives.

The First Industrial Revolution mechanised production through the use of water and steam power; the Second used electricity to create mass production; the Third used electronics and information technology to automate production. The Fourth is blurring the lines between physical, digital and biological spheres, causing:

◆ disruption to jobs and skills

◆ the need for greater innovation and enhanced productivity

◆ greater inequalities among people

◆ agility in governance

◆ breakdowns in security

◆ enhanced risks to data through cyber crime

◆ business disruption

◆ technology fusion

◆ challenges to ethics and perceived societal norms.

We will not be studying any of these in significant depth, but they form an important backdrop to the environment where we are developing our strategy.

Placing strategy in context

Throughout the text there are case studies from the *Financial Times* together with a selection of extracts and examples from a range of different companies. The appendix contains a brief introduction to each of the companies that have more than one reference within the text. It is important to constantly consider how you can apply your developing knowledge to your own environment and that of your own and other organisations.

While the syllabus and the text contain all of the academic knowledge required for this subject, students are encouraged to bring the subject to life through regular reading of the business pages of a major newspaper. The use of many extracts from the *Financial Times* is deliberate, as it contains, on a daily basis, excellent examples of all aspects of how strategy is developed and put into practice within a wide range of different types of organisation.

Core focus

Make sure you stop and think about each different aspect of this subject.

Keep it simple and apply it to your own daily personal and commercial life.

Enjoy the study and make use of it in your strategic interactions with those around you.

Part one

Strategy and strategic planning

Introduction

The first part of this text introduces the meaning and purpose of
strategy and strategic planning. It is important to recognise that
the concept of the starting point of 'today' is a fixed and known
point, which can be analysed and understood. Our approach
to strategy will be based around how we perceive the need or
desire to change what is happening now to something different.
Strategy is therefore how we focus on our vision of the future.

Overview

Chapter 1 focuses on how and why we need to be able to use
different approaches to our development of strategy. It recognises
the individuality of each human being who plays a role in this
process and suggests how and why we are able to make decisions.

Chapter 2 explains the difference between rational strategy,
an approach which is detailed in its planning, and emergent
strategy, an approach which allows strategic change to be at least

partly driven by the differing forces which surround us and our organisations. We will consider the importance and the impact of these forces.

Chapter 3 defines the importance of leadership within the development of strategy. It then considers a number of core models and structures, including using a SWOT (strengths, weaknesses, opportunities and threats) analysis to analyse an organisation, the need to consider the supply-chain of the organisation and the need for and benefit of taking a systems-thinking approach.

Learning outcomes

At the end of this part, students will be able to:

- understand and define 'strategy' and many of its associated terms;
- differentiate between the realities of 'today' and the unknown nature of the future;
- discuss the five Ps of Mintzberg – plan, pattern, position, perspective and ploy;
- consider the different business levels where strategy is developed;
- comment in depth on the difference between rational and emergent strategy;
- understand that strategy is influenced by a wide range of human behaviours ;
- consider why a learning organisation approach can enhance strategic thinking;
- demonstrate an understanding of different leadership approaches to strategy;
- understand how to use a SWOT analysis to analyse an organisation;
- discuss the use of systems thinking within an organisation;
- consider the different roles that are required to develop and challenge strategy; and
- understand the significance and importance of the company secretary and governance professional role in the development of strategy.

Chapter one
The nature of strategy and planning

Contents

1. Introduction

This chapter will define a number of core terms that will be used throughout the text. It is important to understand the context and the application of these terms. In the world of business, many such terms are used on a regular basis, often without people thinking about their true meaning. It is important for the company secretary and governance professional to understand the real meaning and be able to challenge the use of such terms when appropriate.

This chapter introduces:

◆ the meaning and purpose of strategy

◆ an understanding of the distinction between planning and strategy

◆ the core terms associated with the development of strategy

◆ an understanding of strategic planning

◆ the characteristics of strategic decisions

◆ several different perspectives of strategy

◆ an initial concept of some of the themes in different chapters.

In order for company secretaries and governance professionals to apply strategic principles, the importance of objectivity, and the ability to stand back and consider all sides of a situation, play a large part in the making of effective strategic decisions.

Case study 1.1

Consider the breadth of area covered by the six stated strategic drivers of Tesco plc.

Extract from Tesco plc Annual Report and Financial Statements 2018:

'Our six strategic drivers will create long-term value for all of our stakeholders

- **a differentiated brand**
- **reduce operating costs**
- **generate cash from operations**
- **maximise the mix**
- **maximise value from property innovation**
- **innovation'**

strategy
The combining of knowledge and capability in the perception of a future outcome.

As we progress through this text, we will be considering all of these aspects of **strategy** and more, so it is important to start to consider strategy from different perspectives.

Contrast the Tesco statement with that of BAE plc, which is put more succinctly but covers just as wide an area of consideration.

Case study 1.2

Extract from BAE plc Annual Report and Financial Statements 2017:

'Our strategy is comprised of five key long-term areas of focus that will help us to achieve our vision and mission. This strategy remains relevant and consistent. We have updated our Group strategic framework to reflect our renewed focus on becoming a stronger company, able to win and grow in a tougher competitive market'

organisation
Formal usage: a group of people with a particular purpose and focus.
Informal usage: used interchangeably with the word company.

Tesco and BAE are very different companies. Tesco has a short strategic operation cycle – buying from suppliers and selling to consumers, often with date-sensitive products. BAE contract with their customers for the manufacture and supply of technology and products which might take many months or years to complete.

Take note that both companies have a similar breadth of strategic focus. The timeframe of strategy is very relevant, but needs to be considered in the context of the individual operational cycle of each **organisation**.

2. The meaning of strategy

2.1 Distinguishing between planning and strategy

Our very existence as human beings requires us to plan on a perpetual basis. Every morning at the start of the day we will have some concept of what we plan to do for the rest of that day; that concept might be described as our strategic intent. Our **planning** may have started earlier than this by having an alarm set to ensure that we wake up at an appropriate time to allow us to fulfil our planned activities for that day. Usually, our plans will extend beyond the next 24 hours, so we will have an idea of what we might intend to do during the next week or month, or an even longer period.

> **planning**
> The bringing together of objectives, goals and actions in a cohesive and comprehensive manner to enable the realisation of the vision while maintaining the ethos of the mission.

Often the words 'plan' and 'strategy' are used interchangeably, but it is important to recognise that, although they are intrinsically linked, there is an important distinction between the two concepts.

The word 'plan' has four slightly different dictionary definitions:

1.   a detailed scheme or method for attaining an objective
2.   a proposed, usually tentative idea for doing something
3.   an outline or sketch
4.   to have something in mind as a purpose.

The concept of planning is therefore a combination of objective, goal, and anticipated route; an explicit idea, or sometimes a statement, which identifies a number of distinct facets that we expect to encounter, or complete, on our journey into the future.

The word 'strategy' has two core dictionary definitions:

1.   the art or science of the planning and conduct of a war
2.   a particular long-term plan for **success** especially in politics or business.

> **success**
> Notionally, the achievement of goals and objectives, the fulfilment of the plan, the realisation of the strategic vision; however, the concept of success must always be aligned with the particular expectations of the person or persons who are assessing whether or not the strategy, plan, objectives or goals have been achieved.

In reality, there are as many definitions of strategy and strategic planning as there are books on the subjects; a simple search on Amazon will reveal in excess of 100,000 such texts. The following examples are being used to illustrate the breadth of the subject.

A strategy will under normal circumstances precede a plan, and a strategy may contain several different plans. Pettigrew and Whipp (1991) suggest that there are three key elements behind any strategic decision:

◆   Context: the environment within which the strategy operates and is developed.

◆   Content: the main **actions** of the proposed strategy.

◆   Process: how the actions link together or interact with each other as the strategy unfolds (this may be described as the plan).

> **actions**
> The steps that are required to be undertaken to enable the achievement of goals and objectives.

Clegg et al. (2017) add a human dimension to these concepts by suggesting that:

Strategy = Knowledge + Capability

where:

◆ knowledge is required to enable a human being to be able to imagine a future state of affairs together with the ability to visualise how one might obtain that future state; and

◆ capability is the power and ability to get things done, to be able to implement ideas, **visions** and plans.

vision
The ability of the human brain to imagine something different from a current situation.

Johnson et al. (2017) define strategy as 'the long-term direction of an organisation' which includes 'deliberate, logical strategy and more incremental, emergent patterns of strategy'. They suggest further that long-term direction can include strategies that emphasise difference and competition, and strategies that recognise the roles of co–operation and even imitation.

Lynch (2015) defines strategic management as 'the identification of the purpose of the organisation and the plans and actions to achieve that purpose'.

goals
Specific and definable outcomes which enable identification of progress towards achieving the objectives and, if defined in such a manner, the achievement of the strategic intent: it is often useful to consider a goal as something tangible which is either achieved (scored) or not.

Spender (2015) suggests that 'business strategy reflects the vast variety of **goals** that are open to businesses in a capitalist democracy and the difficulties of achieving them. It arises precisely because (a) the business's goals have been chosen not imposed and (b) it can only be reached by engaging a difficult or resistant situation'.

Levicki (2003) states that 'strategy sets the objectives and the goals for the organisation into a series of timeframes to enable people to know what must be achieved, by whom, and when.'

In summary, strategy could perhaps be reasonably defined as an overarching construct that is present within one or more brains, which incorporates both the imagination of how a future situation might look, and the conceptual alignment of what might be required to achieve the realisation of that imagined situation.

Stop and think 1.1

Consider the differing definitions above and use of the word 'strategy'.

Think about when you have recently heard the word being used.

What did it mean to you?

What did it mean in the context within which it was being used?

Strategy is not just restricted to commercial organisations – one of the leading world cancer research organisations, Cancer Research UK, has a very clear strategic aim.

Case study 1.3

Extract from Cancer Research UK Annual Report and Financial Statements 2017/2018:

'Cancer Research UK's vision is to bring forward the day when all cancers are cured from the most common types to those that affect just a few people. Our ambition is to see 3 in 4 people surviving cancer by 2034.'

Think about the focus of the Cancer Research strategy in comparison to that of Tesco and BAE.

2.2   Key terms related to strategy

We have already started to use a number of strategic terms without providing a simple definition for use within the context of both this text and the practical application of these concepts within differing organisations. The following list of definitions can be viewed initially as interpretive and then gradually, as your understanding and consideration of the development of strategy expands, you will be able to both interpret and apply these concepts within a wide range of practical organisational situations. These are not finite or prescriptive definitions – you should not simply learn and repeat them verbatim, but always consider the meaning within the context of the situation that faces them: the strategic challenge.

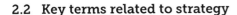

- Strategy: the combining of knowledge and capability in the perception of a future outcome.
- Vision: the ability of the human brain to imagine something different from a current situation.
- Mission: the ethos, beliefs and **values** which enable the forming of a vision.
- Objectives: a range of criteria which identify and clarify differing aspects of the vision and mission – objectives are often aligned with the acronym SMART which is discussed later in this text.
- Goals: specific and definable outcomes which enable identification of progress towards achieving the objectives and, if defined in such a manner, the achievement of the strategic intent: it is often useful to consider a goal as something tangible which is either achieved (scored) or not.
- Action(s): the steps that are required to be undertaken to enable the achievement of goals and objectives.
- Planning: the bringing together of objectives, goals and actions in a cohesive and comprehensive manner to enable the realisation of the vision while maintaining the ethos of the mission.
- Review: a process by which any aspect of the strategic journey is considered to enable an evaluation of progress and/or fulfilment: a plan

values
Beliefs and principles which drive our decision making, our opinions and our attitudes.

will often include a pre-emptive review process to ensure that progress is considered at key points.

◆ Iteration: a repetition of a process or action, usually to either clarify a previous outcome or to apply a slightly different set of criteria to be able to assess the impact of such change.

◆ Success: notionally, the achievement of goals and objectives, the fulfilment of the plan, the realisation of the strategic vision; however, the concept of success must always be aligned with the particular expectations of the person or persons who are assessing whether or not the strategy, plan, objectives or goals have been achieved.

◆ Risk: any situation or decision where there is more than one possible outcome, and such outcomes can be visualised and ranked against likely probability.

◆ Uncertainty: any situation or decision where there is more than one possible outcome, but it is not possible to visualise all possible outcomes.

◆ Control: a step or measure taken or implemented to attempt to reduce or mitigate perceived risks or uncertainties.

◆ Values: beliefs and principles which drive our decision-making, our opinions and our attitudes.

◆ Paradigm: the perspective, view or vision held by one or more human brains at any particular point in time.

Stop and think 1.2

Review all of the terms defined above. Most of them are in common usage within any organisation. Consider how and when they are used either within the organisation you work for, or alternatively type them into a business search engine to find the many different uses.

In this first extract from GSK plc, we see a more people-based focus of strategic aims, this is partly due to the nature of their business, but also their organisational culture. The concept of culture will be considered in depth in Chapter 6.

Case study 1.4

Extract from GSK plc Annual Report and Financial Statements 2017:

'Our purpose: To help people do more, feel better and live longer.

Our goal: To be one of the world's most innovative, best performing and trusted healthcare companies.

Our strategy: Bring differentiated, high-quality and needed healthcare products to as many people as possible, with our three global businesses, scientific and technical know-how and talented people.

Our values and expectations are at the heart of everything we do and form an important part of our culture.

Our values: Patient focus; Transparency; Respect; Integrity

Our expectations: Courage; Accountability; Development; Teamwork'

3. Strategic planning

Having differentiated between the concepts of strategy and planning, it is important to recognise that they are closely aligned as a process within the development of strategy. The purpose of such alignment is to enable a comprehensive structure which encompasses the wide range of different attributes of the process as identified in the definitions above. The definitions themselves give some idea as to their relationship with each other, but the complete process is best illustrated in the following diagram.

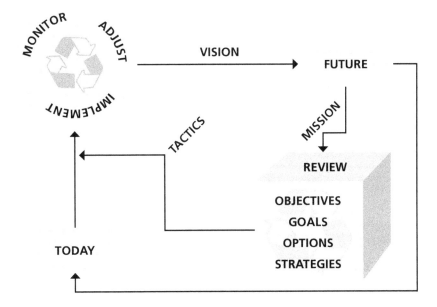

Figure 1.1 The strategic journey
© Mark Wearden

3.1 Today and future

This diagram will be discussed more fully and frequently referenced through the text as it sits at the heart of the process of the development of strategy within any organisation. It can be simplified into an initially more accessible form as in Figure 1.2. The first requirement is to understand the starting point, defined simply as TODAY and representing the status quo of any situation that we find ourselves within.

The simplified version of the strategic journey in Figure 1.2 is used to highlight the gap that exists between TODAY and FUTURE. Life is lived in that gap based around the strategic decisions we make at TODAY. This diagram should be kept in mind as we progress through the many different dimensions of the development of strategy. Figures 1.1 and 1.2 sit together and will be referred to as either the 'strategic journey' or the 'core strategy model'.

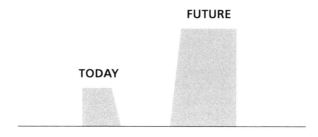

Figure 1.2 Simplified strategic journey
© Mark Wearden

This TODAY position is a moment fixed in time; the very moment when you are reading this sentence is your TODAY point. In an organisational context this could be a very defined date, such as the end of a financial year when a balance sheet would be required to show the alignment of the assets and liabilities of an organisation. The important concept to retain from a strategy perspective is that the TODAY position is a point at which time can be frozen, and it is possible to understand everything that contributes to that exact position, while also being able to look backwards and understand the rationale for why that position exists.

Stop and think 1.3

Consider your TODAY point and make yourself a few notes on one side of a piece of paper.

How do you feel about this subject – Development of Strategy?

What has brought you to this point in your life?

What are your strengths?

What are your weaknesses?

Imagine you are looking at yourself from a distance. How would you be described? What sort of person are you? Is your view the same as that of the observer?

The simple model then requires the visualisation of the FUTURE as an unknown and unrealised reality; we know we will get there but we have no idea what it will really look like. To be precise, there are certain aspects of the way that the world works, such as day turning to night and then again back to day, that we can feel a certainty about, but within that important and quite limited framework everything else that we anticipate will happen to us as an individual or our organisation can only ever be an expectation, a guess, an estimation, or prediction, based upon where we stand in our certain knowledge of our TODAY point.

Stop and think 1.4

Re-read the notes you made in Stop and think 1.3 above.

What would you like to change?

What do you think will have changed in 12 months' time?

Turn the piece of paper over.

Write down your vision.

The third dimension of the model is how to move from TODAY to the FUTURE. The simple model in Figure 1.2 illustrates a simple straight-line connection across the base. At this stage of consideration, this is the best we can do, we know that TODAY and FUTURE are linked but the route is not yet determined. We can only visualise how we move across this chasm. We need to realise that to make that move, individually or as an organisation, we have to understand where we are starting from and where we hope we are heading.

RISK is an inevitable consequence of viewing the world from a model such as this. The minute we leave the safety of the TODAY position, and head towards the FUTURE, we are surrounded by risk. The only certainty that we have in life at any point is TODAY.

risk
Any situation or decision where there is more than one possible outcome, and such outcomes can be visualised and ranked against likely probability.

The fixing of a TODAY point in the consideration of strategic change is to secure a determined known reference point from which to start our strategy and move forward into the FUTURE.

However, as soon as we leave that TODAY point, the parameters may change; in reality TODAY is a constantly moving dimension of time.

Test yourself 1.1

Clarify the relationship between knowledge, capability and strategy.

3.2   Boundaries and parameters

In the development of strategy, it is important for any organisation to fully understand the boundaries and parameters of the starting point, the route and even the perceived vision. This might sound restrictive, but it will ensure that the strategic thinking is based in reality. As we progress further through this text, we will be considering in depth how we can analyse the external (macro) environment, together with the internal (micro) environment. These are important considerations for anybody involved in strategic development, either from an organisational perspective or for each of us as individuals when we consider our own career path.

The boundaries of our strategy suggest the limits beyond which we are not able to operate. For example:

- A firm of accountants is unlikely to cross a boundary that required it to begin a manufacturing process.
- The four companies already referred to above – Tesco, GSK, BAE, Cancer UK – each have clear boundaries of operation.
- As individuals, students will have boundaries which define the type of organisation where they are already working and where they are prepared or not prepared to work.

The parameters of our strategy suggest the aspects which need to remain constant. For example:

- A firm of accountants will have parameters suggesting the expected level of return and the likely client mix that they expect to maintain within their strategic development.
- Large organisations will each have a set of parameters which define the way in which they need to define and develop their businesses; think, for example, of the difference between the parameters that differentiate the operational objectives of Tesco and Cancer UK.
- Individuals will have parameters which define the expectations of their career path, such as salary progression, income level required to meet commitments such as a mortgage etc.

As we plan and develop our strategy, we may anticipate that certain boundaries and/or parameters may need to change to enable the realisation of our objectives. It will be important for us to be able to plan the route from today to the future as we perceive it, and to benchmark our anticipation of required change.

The nature of strategic planning is to establish an anticipated route such as that illustrated in Figure 1.3, which illustrates an anticipated movement from A to B across a one-year period. At the point of creation this is simply a line on a graph, but it forms our line of expectation or benchmark based around our beliefs at point A.

gap analysis
The comparison of actual performance or events with projected or desired performance or events. The analysis is required to understand the gap between actual and projected/desired.

In juxtaposition, Figure 1.4 reflects the position looked at retrospectively having arrived at point B. The objective has been achieved, but the route has been different as illustrated by the dotted line.

The purpose of benchmarking in the development of strategy is to enable an understanding of why reality is almost always different from anticipation. This is often referred to as '**gap analysis**' or 'exception analysis' and will become an important part of our strategic thinking as we progress through this module.

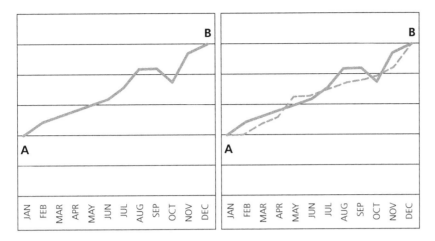

Figures 1.3 and 1.4 Anticipated vs actual journey from A to B
© Mark Wearden

If one were to now be planning the next 12 months with point B as their today position, they would need to understand why the route from A to B differed from their original expectations. They would achieve this by analysing and understanding the various gaps between the original fixed line of anticipation and the dotted line of reality.

3.3 Success

If we start our development of strategy on the basis that we intend to achieve something in the future that differs in some way from today, then it is important that we understand how we will realise whether or not we have succeeded. The problem with the term 'success' is that it will be perceived differently by different people.

If our strategy includes precise goals, then it will be clear to all whether or not these goals have been achieved (scored). If we have a more generic vision of what the future needs to look like, and this is aligned with objectives which have not been clearly defined then it will be natural to be able to state, when we reach the future, our strategy has been successful.

Behind this concept, our brains have matured during this period of time and we have therefore adapted to the changing circumstances around us, the changes in the today position. How success is perceived at the starting point may be quite different from how it is perceived at the endpoint. This re-emphasises the importance of having benchmarks – so that we can measure achievement against expectation.

Test yourself 1.2

Suggest three significant differences between the strategic dimensions of 'today' and 'future'.

4. Characteristics of strategic decisions

When we are considering the development of strategy, we are discussing the making of decisions at the TODAY point which we hope will influence, impact, and potentially change the FUTURE to reflect our expectations. Every time a human being makes a decision, that decision is based upon all of their learning to that point in their lifetime, and will be influenced by the principles that they hold and the situation within which they find themselves.

4.1 Types of decision

There are a number of different types of decision and there is a core difference between an irreversible and a reversible decision.

An irreversible decision means that there really is no going back – for example:

◆ I get on a train, the doors close – I have to wait until the next stop.

◆ I have pushed the fire alarm button and the bell is now ringing.

A reversible decision allows you to go back to the original starting point and rethink – for example:

◆ I get in my car, I shut the door – I can open it again, or set off, then stop wherever is safe and open the door again.

◆ I switch on a light, I can switch it off again.

An *experimental*, *staged* or *subjective* decision is one that 'tests the water' and maybe gives us time before taking an irreversible or reversible decision – for example:

◆ I get in my car, switch it on to see if I have enough fuel – as a result of that decision I can then either leave on my journey, or go to get some fuel.

◆ I walk into a lecture room with six light switches, I can make a series of experimental staged or subjective decisions before I settle on the optimal lighting for the lecture I am about to deliver.

This level of subliminal detail will be a major influence on our ability to decide; we need to always be aware of the potential consequences and impact of our decision making.

The following is a series of questions which can be used to examine our intent when considering the cause and effect of our decision-making:

◆ *Why* must I make a decision?

◆ *Who* will my decision affect?

◆ *Where* do I look for help to inform my judgement?

◆ *What* is my personal objective in this situation?

◆ *When* is my deadline?

◆ *How* can I judge the outcome of my decision?

It is useful to consider what the decision is intended to resolve. Here are some possibilities of how to approach this – but note that the development of strategy in any organisational context can and will cover all of these and more:

◆ situations which need to improve or change

◆ complexities which need managing

◆ issues which need tackling

◆ difficulties which need to be overcome.

4.2   Timeframe of a decision

Part of our consideration of the type of strategic decision we are making will be to consider the length of time that exists between the known point of today and the anticipated point of the future. Directors of the **company** are legally bound to ensure that the organisation is a 'going-concern'. At a simple level, this means that the organisation has sufficient assets to cover its liabilities for the next 12 months. This can act as a useful strategic dynamic for short-term decision-making.

company
Formal usage: a limited liability company formed under Companies Act legislation. Informal usage: any structured organisation.

This timeframe of expectation was increased in 2014 for directors of companies with shares quoted on the London Stock Exchange (LSE) with the introduction of the concept of the longer-term viability of an organisation. Such companies are now required, in the annual report and accounts, to discuss the length of time over which the viability of the organisation has been assessed, why that timeframe is an appropriate length of time, and how the viability is justified. You can see that this requires a significant concept of time when making strategic decisions.

It is important to always consider the immediate impact of a strategic decision; any change that this might require within an organisation; the anticipated longer-term impact of that strategic decision; and the potential timing of impacts that may occur during the journey. All of this is anticipatory, given that strategy is to a greater or lesser extent a process of attempting to deal with the **uncertainty** that exists beyond today.

uncertainty
Any situation or decision where there is more than one possible outcome, but it is not possible to visualise all possible outcomes.

Stop and think 1.5

What is your personal timeframe horizon?

When does your personal strategy suggest that you will qualify with ICSA: The Governance Institute?

How long after that do you anticipate it will be before you are seeking greater responsibility within an organisation?

4.3   Scope of a decision

Company secretaries and governance professionals will also need to consider the operational scope and parameters of their strategic decisions.

In Chapters 3 and 4 we will consider the impact of our strategic decisions upon the micro and macro aspects of the external environment.

In Chapter 5 we will consider the use of our resources and competencies. How well is our strategy aligned with utilising what we already have as a resource, and how far do we need to change, adapt and expand those resources to enable us to fulfil our strategic objectives?

Our considerations of these aspects of strategic decision-making are often referred to as the *strategic fit* – are we dealing with something that is already within our comprehension, or are we embarking upon a strategic journey which requires the development and expansion of existing resources and competencies.

4.4   Values and expectations

mission
The ethos, beliefs and values which enable the forming of a vision.

In section 2.2 above it was suggested that values form part of the underlying principles behind the **mission** of an organisation. These values will be a combination of the beliefs and expectations of the people who originated and or continue to lead the organisation, and will also be an accumulation of the practices and actions that have developed within the organisation across its history. Cumulatively this is often referred to as the *culture* of the organisation. The impact of this upon the development of strategy will be discussed further in Chapter 6.

Think, for example, about the strategic values that need to be associated with an organisation like Cancer Research UK.

Case study 1.5

Extract from Cancer Research UK Annual Report and Financial Statements 2017/18:

'The strategy focuses on four key objectives: preventing cancers; diagnosing cancer earlier; developing new treatments; and making cancer treatments more effective for each patient'.

4.5   Strategic change

Think back to the simple TODAY: FUTURE diagram in section 3.1. If we have some understanding of what it is that we are trying to achieve with our decisions, we will be able to consider more comprehensively who and what will be affected or influenced by our decisions.

We need to realise that strategic decisions will have an ethical impact, and this will be discussed in greater detail in Chapter 9. We also need to also recognise that change is often difficult for an organisation and for the people within that organisation, areas which will be discussed in greater detail in Chapters 14 and 15.

4.6   Complexity and the development of strategy

If you consider all of the characteristics that have already been suggested, it will be clear that the development of strategy is not a simple process and requires a depth and breadth of organisational understanding to allow genuine participation in the process. As a Chartered Secretary or Chartered Governance Professional sitting at the board table with other executive and non-executive directors, it is important to be able to take a holistic view of the strategic decisions that are being discussed, and to be able to challenge the potential and likely partisan perspectives of other people. The following list is just a starting point of the aspects of strategic development where they need to feel confident in their considerations:

◆   the uncertainty of the operational environment

◆   continuing rapid changes in technology

◆   the intricacies of multinational trade

◆   the incomprehensible nature of many decisions made by others

◆   differing styles of leadership

◆   the complexity of an individual human brain, and the inevitable challenges that are created when two or more brains (people) start to work together.

There is no shortcut, or tick-box approach to the development of strategy. Each strategic decision needs to be considered within its particular context, and the people and organisational parameters that surround it.

5. Perspectives of strategy

This section contains four different perspectives of strategy from four leading strategic thinkers and academics. These are not the only perspectives that are relevant to the consideration of strategy in this module, but they do represent a breadth of consideration of the topic of strategy and help to position a number of key dynamics that we will explore further. It is important to consider and understand each of these perspectives to enable you to challenge your later considerations from different dimensions. The four perspectives are:

◆   Mintzberg – 5Ps theory (2008)

◆   Spender – four paradigms (2015; adapted by Mark Wearden)

◆   Maccoby – *Strategic Intelligence* (2017)

◆   Argyris – inference and control (1990).

5.1   Mintzberg – 5Ps theory (2008)

Mintzberg is intrigued by the influential nature of the word 'strategy' and contends that all too often it is used by people who have only one perspective and are determined to view strategy in a one-dimensional manner. The referenced text *Strategy Safari* is based around a consideration of ten different 'schools' of strategy. Underpinning each of these is a five-fold definition of the word and the concept of strategy (the 5Ps). Mintzberg uses the fast food chain McDonald's as an example for some of his theory, and this has been expanded below to suggest McDonald's references for each of the five aspects (italicised):

◆ **Plan**: the theory recognises that planning in some way sits at the very heart of strategy, giving a direction or course of action, or an attempt to define a route to get from here to there. However, it also suggests that very often this aspect of strategy is only ever forward-looking, and that people are more comfortable discussing what they actually did rather than what they intended to do; no surprise here, most people live in the real world. *The number and geographical spread of McDonald's outlets is based around a plan to attract customers in convenient locations.*

◆ **Pattern**: the theory suggests that strategy is perhaps better considered as a pattern, a manner of behaving across a period of time. It recognises that human beings generally like to work and behave in a comfortable and familiar way, and therefore an organisation (which is only a collection of human beings) is likely to also develop a familiar pattern in its behaviour. *The very nature of how McDonald's outlets works epitomises the concept of the word pattern with regard to strategy; part of the attraction is the familiarity and the known.*

◆ **Position**: the theory suggests that strategy also requires an understanding of position – there is a right time and right place. *Although the core of a McDonald's menu is very similar and familiar (pattern) across the world, there will also be specific offers and products positioned to attract customers in a particular location; this may be based upon nationality, or may be based upon a particular national or international event.*

◆ **Perspective**: the theory recognises that strategy does not just happen by chance and therefore a perspective is always required. This implies the need for the person or people charged with the development of strategy to be able to step back, mentally or physically, outside the organisation, and look at the organisation and its strategy from one or more perspective. *McDonald's introduced the Egg McMuffin having been able to recognise the need to change position from providing essentially meat products to align their strategy to a wider perspective.*

◆ **Ploy**: finally, the theory suggests that strategy may also be a ploy, a deliberate and intended move to thwart the competition and maintain a competitive edge. *Different McDonald's outlets have different levels of profitability – sometimes they have been opened in areas where it is unlikely that high volumes will be achieved. However, simply by being there, the strategic ploy will prevent competitors from opening and will also prevent potential customers from seeking an alternative.*

Test yourself 1.3

Why is it important to establish benchmarks as part of the development of strategy?

5.2 Spender – four paradigms (2015; adapted by Mark Wearden)

Spender is interested in considering strategy from the starting point of the question 'what are we going to do now?'. He suggests that the development of strategy involves frequent change in identity, intention and context, sometimes making it sensible to adapt goals rather than sticking to a rigid end vision. He suggests that there are four basic **paradigms** from which we approach these questions, and these are summarised under four headings – which could be perceived as moving from a static approach to strategy to a more eclectic approach. These are:

paradigm
The perspective, view or vision held by one or more human brains at any particular point in time.

1. **Goals**: a scientific approach to strategy suggests that the strategist is considering objectively the nature and context of an organisation together with the logical cause and effects of the relationships of the people involved within such an organisation. It is necessary to consider both internal and external relationships, and in the belief that people are always rational presume that X will always happen because of Y. This allows the strategist to focus on the goal while not necessarily recognising the changing environment around them. The example given by Spender is that of Kodak and their failure to adapt to the rapidly encroaching digital environment which surrounded them.

2. **Judgement**: a recognition of inevitable change in environment, together with the realisation that people are not always rational can lead the strategist to recognise that gaps do exist in any plan or structure. These gaps enable people who make wise decisions to end up with good results, and vice versa; and the recognition that in the middle many people simply muddle through. Spender suggests that mergers of organisations often fall into this territory, where presumptions are made about the value of the differing organisations which in the end prove to be unjustified.

3. **People**: having recognised and accepted that people are not always rational, it is then possible to change to a people-centric approach to strategy, recognising that the role of the strategist is often to persuade others to change their expectations and therefore be able to promote the strategic objectives being pursued. People are perceived as malleable in this paradigm and Spender suggests this is why it is possible, for example, for companies to sell diamond-studded mobile phones.

4. **Flexibility**: paradigms A, B and C assume that the strategist has stable goals and objectives, and that their intention in the development of the strategy is to ensure that the vision is realised. Paradigm D recognises that the developers of any strategy, themselves being human, are also malleable and therefore have the ability to adapt and change the original intentions. Spender uses Bill Gates at Microsoft as a good example of this paradigm – the original vision of creating and selling packaged software rapidly needed to change to the point where everything produced by Microsoft became web-based, and then helped to change that environment for other users and strategists.

Stop and think 1.6

Apply Spender's paradigms to your organisation.

5.3   Maccoby – *Strategic Intelligence* (2017)

Maccoby suggests that the concept of strategy, as planning towards an advantage or desired end, needs to be aligned with the concept of intelligence, our ability to consider and understand. He suggests that we need to be able to develop our intelligence to consider strategy from four dimensions:

◆   **Foresight**: in anticipation of what can be perceived as likely to happen that can change our intentions.

◆   **Visioning**: a recognition of the need to continually improve processes, products and services to fulfil the aspirations of our customers.

◆   **Partnering**: a recognition that we need to work with others; in particular that working with customers and suppliers may strengthen our strategic perspective.

◆   **Motivating**: the need to inspire others to share our vision and therefore to help implement our strategy.

Maccoby illustrates this in the diagram shown in Figure 1.5.

Figure 1.5 Strategic Intelligence
© Maccoby, 2017

5.4 Argyris – inference and control (1990)

The fourth perspective is a particular concept developed by Chris Argyris (1923–2013), an American business theorist, thought leader and academic from Harvard Business School. Argyris had a particular interest in organisations from a systems perspective and how people behaved and learned lessons in the way they planned, ran and then changed organisations. The aspect of his thinking that we will apply to the development of strategy is a concept called the 'ladder of inference'.

Argyris used his 'ladder' to consider how the brain enables us to take any action, from the simplest to the most complex. His explanation is that the brain moves through a series of stages (steps on the ladder) based around the initial observation (through all of our senses), with the assimilation of data and then the iterative sorting and selection which enable us to take a specific action. This is illustrated below. As a concept this has been developed and discussed by a number of other authors such as Peter Senge (Senge, 2006) and Roger Martin (Martin & Riel, 2017).

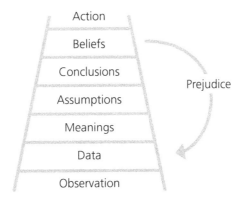

Figure 1.6 Ladder of interference
((Argyris, 1990) adapted by Mark Wearden)

A key learning from the use of the 'ladder of inference' model is that the penultimate stage before we take action – known as the 'belief stage' – combined with the result of the action itself, will then inform the earlier stage of 'data filtration', which allows us to retain what we perceive as relevant for our ongoing approach to life (our attitude).

This process can be described as the basis of prejudice or bias within the brain. The word prejudice tends to be used with negative connotations, but we require this action of prejudice for every aspect of our behaviour as a human being – if we take the example of stopping our vehicle at an unexpected red light, our prejudice will mean that we apply the brake quickly in the belief that this will enable the car to stop in sufficient time.

If we are able to recognise these prejudices (positive and negative) within ourselves, this will help us in our development of strategy and reduce the number of **iterations** required during the development process.

In Chapter 4 we link this concept to our ability to find the optimal combination of knowledge and imagination in our strategic thinking and planning.

control
A step or measure taken or implemented to attempt to reduce or mitigate perceived risks or uncertainties.

iteration
A repetition of a process or action, usually to either clarify a previous outcome or to apply a slightly different set of criteria to be able to assess the impact of a change.

Test yourself 1.4

Write a short sentence about each of Mintzberg's five aspects of strategy (the 5Ps).

6. Levels of strategy and planning

The final consideration in this opening chapter is the different dimensions of the levels at which we are pitching the development of our strategy:

◆ the level of planning will determine the strategic timeframe; the accuracy with which we are able to determine the surrounding parameters; and often the nature of the people who are involved and affected; and

◆ the level of strategy will determine the breadth of involvement in consideration of the strategy, and therefore the roles and expectations of the people involved within its development.

The degree to which an organisation tangibly splits and/or recognises these different levels will be closely aligned to the size and nature of the organisation; the expectations of **stakeholders**; the complexity of the supply chain; and the manufacturing requirements (if any).

stakeholder
A person or organisation that has an interest or involvement (a stake) in another organisation and can both affect or be affected by that organisation.

6.1   Levels of planning

The core driver of the level of planning required, often referred to as the *planning horizon*, will be the immediacy that is required for the anticipated task or change. The horizon is the time which elapses between the making and the executing of the plan:

◆ to fulfil today's production output will require a short-term plan – usually referred to as an *operational* plan;

◆ to ensure cohesion among the different parts of an organisation will require a medium-term plan – usually referred to as an *intermediate* plan; and

◆ to achieve the wider business objectives of an organisation, and its stakeholders, will require a longer-term plan – usually referred to as a *strategic* plan.

The further that the planning horizon stretches into the future, the greater the potential for a wide impact from the plan, and the greater the level of uncertainty. The further we move from today, the less we can be certain about the changing characteristics of the parameters that surround our strategic intent.

Operational plans are accomplished and overseen by each individual employee of an organisation, at whatever level they might be operating within a hierarchy.

Intermediate plans are generally overseen by people with some aspect of management responsibility, working together to bring cohesion to the impact of strategic change. The intermediate plans are accomplished through a shorter-term operational plan.

Strategic plans are generally developed by directors and senior managers, people with organisation-wide accountability and authority, and will be realised through subsequent intermediate and then operational plans.

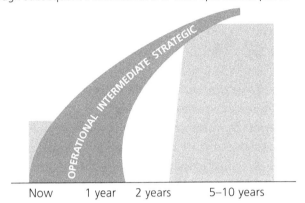

Figure 1.7
© Mark Wearden

Although we recognise these different levels of planning, it is important also to recognise their inter-connectivity and reliance upon each other. An effective strategic plan will establish the parameters within which intermediate and then operational plans can be formulated and fulfilled, leaving sufficient flexibility for all of us working each day at the operational level to be able to make the decisions which affect the immediate requirements of an organisation.

6.2 Levels of strategy

While the planning dimension is driven by the perceived timeframe of the strategic development, the strategy dimension is driven by the depth and breadth of the business structure for both initiation and impact.

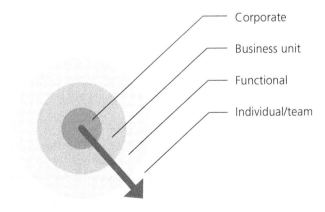

Figure 1.8
© Mark Wearden

The *corporate* level of strategy development sits at the centre of the diagram, and the organisation, driving all other strategic dimensions within the organisation. It will be closely aligned with the concept of governance within an organisation – this will be discussed further in Chapter 7. It will include, but not be restricted to:

resource
A source or a supply from which a benefit can be produced.

- identification and oversight of organisational purpose and focus
- financial infrastructure; funding of the organisation
- long-term viability and short-term liquidity
- understanding and achievement of stakeholder objectives and requirements
- recognition and building of required **resources**
- supply-chain relationships – customers, suppliers and other core partners
- environmental and legal awareness and compliance (e.g. health and safety)
- recruitment and succession planning for all key managerial roles.

The *business unit* level of strategy development is fed directly by the corporate level. It will include, but not be restricted to:

market
A group of customers with similar needs who are prepared to compete with each other for the satisfaction of that need.

- achievement of medium-term goals and objectives as derived from the corporate strategy
- development of sustainable competitive advantage within focused **markets**
- building of sustainable customer and supplier relationships
- monitoring of markets and customers, identifying changes and opportunities.

The *functional* level of strategy puts the strategic intent of the business unit decisions into action. It will include, but not be restricted to:

- identification and oversight of the appropriate timeframes and methods for the delivery and monitoring of short to medium term operational goals – this can be anything from the immediate to a few months
- where, when and how to market and promote the product or service being offered
- the detailed requirements of the manufacturing or production cycle
- the monitoring and control of day-to-day financial and liquidity requirements
- a human resource strategy which ensures the recruitment of the appropriate skill-levels, and required number of people at each level across the organisation
- the development, production and monitoring of key performance indicators (KPIs) for communication back through the strategic levels to ultimately keep those empowered with corporate strategy appropriately informed to enable the iteration of their strategic thinking – in line with the full strategy model at Figure 1.1.

The *individual/team* level of strategy is where the real day-to-day work takes place and where most of the key decisions are made. This is the make-or-break point for the effective running of an organisation against a developed strategy.

If an individual has clarity of purpose and parameter, passed down through the different levels of strategy, then they are able to operate effectively and strategically. If not, the problems begin, as we shall explore at various points throughout this text.

Strategic drive needs to be communicated from corporate through to individual:

> 'this is what we would like you to achieve'

Strategic challenge needs to be communicated from individual through to corporate:

> 'this is how we have achieved it, or why the strategic parameters will not allow achievement'

Consider the strategic impact of the new chair described in Case study 1.6. Think about the impact that his approach of 'acting first and talking second' would have at different functional levels within the organisation.

Case study 1.6

Extract from 'Liberty adopts a stop-go strategy', FT.com, 23 November 2018 (www.ft.com/content/e6219ea2-cc7d-11e8-8d0b-a6539b949662):

'When Liberty Media closed its $8bn acquisition of Formula One in January last year, the US company made an immediate shift at the top. The new owner shunted aside the former chief executive who had run the global race car series for four decades, replacing him with a media industry veteran who became the group's new chairman.

More changes were expected. The new regime spoke of tackling waning interest from TV audiences by making races more competitive, limiting spending by dominant teams to make the outcome of races less predictable, and making race car engines simpler, cheaper and louder. There was a desire to sign more multimillion-dollar deals with new sponsors, attract millennial viewers by securing digital streaming deals and launch new Grands Prix in the US and beyond.

Almost two years on, the most ambitious of these plans are yet to get off the grid.

The new Chairman says: "There's a reality to getting things done. It was about a year ago we finally got an organisation in place to pursue the initiatives we've talked about — motorsport initiatives or commercial initiatives." Insisting that a lack of flashy announcements does not reflect inactivity behind the scenes. "This is a sport that seemed to, in the past, like to talk first and then act second and I think business is probably more productive when you act first and then talk second," he says. "Realistically, I've been around long enough to know growing anything or building anything is not easy, You don't win every battle, but I think we're winning more than we're losing. I think we're making headway."'

Stop and think 1.7

Consider the implications of not being able to deliver the expected strategic objectives on time and in budget. Think about what is needed to drive continued credibility and integrity for disappointed stakeholders who believe 'they could do it better themselves'.

Chapter summary

- This chapter introduces the purpose and meaning of strategy and planning and to many of the important words and terms that are associated with this subject.

- The ability to always be able to look at a situation, a plan or a vision from a 'today' perspective is a fundamental part of the development of strategy. Every time company secretaries and governance professionals consider their strategy, they need to look with a renewed pair of eyes, and ask what has changed since they last looked.

- The strategic journey takes them from 'today' towards the 'future' through the process of the daily operation of an organisation (implement, monitor, adjust). This drives the visions, the ability to see a different way to operate, and then creates the iterative review process.

- The purpose of developing a strategy to move from the realities of today towards the vision of the future is to create a map, or a benchmark. This will help in our strategic planning and will also act as a checkpoint along the way, and when we believe the journey has been completed.

- Mintzberg introduces the idea of different ways to view the development of strategy – plan, pattern, position, perspective, ploy (the 5Ps). The purpose of such 'modular' thinking is to help the human brain identify differing characteristics within each strategic situation.

- We need to understand why we think in the way that we think, and be able to understand, consider and challenge the way that others think.

- At the outset, the development of strategy within an organisation requires a time dimension and an understanding of the level at which the strategy is being visualised.

- A company secretary and governance professional needs to be able to step back and look at the organisation as a whole, understanding the realities and drivers of 'today' while listening to and themselves considering how and why the 'future' can and may need to be different.

Chapter two
Strategic management

Contents

1. Introduction

Chapter 1 considered and reviewed the language and meaning of strategy and strategic planning, together with a range of the parameters and characteristics which influence and affect strategic decision-making. Towards the end of the chapter, some specific models and positioning of strategy were introduced to enable a recognition of the breadth of the subject, and its all-encompassing nature within an organisational environment.

To move beyond the certainties of *today* we are all naturally involved in strategic thinking and strategic planning.

This chapter will consider a further range of strategy models, most of which have originally been developed by academics or practitioners to explain or promote a particular situation or set of organisational perspectives. At this early stage of the consideration of the development of strategy it is helpful to realise that all strategic and business models are developed at a 'today' point by whoever is the developer. They only have the ability to work with what they know and therefore although their model may be brilliant and relevant at the time for one or more focused situations, this relevance can very rapidly change, and we need to always think widely about how to make such models relevant to us, today.

This chapter begins by considering two core aspects of strategy development:

◆ **Rational strategy**: change that evolves as a result of the working through of a strategic plan.

◆ **Emergent strategy**: change that evolves without a rational plan, or as a result of the changes in the parameters that have helped in the construction of a rational plan.

Towards the end of the chapter we will begin to consider other aspects of strategy development that affect our strategic planning, such as:

◆ the type and sectoral context of an organisation

◆ the prevailing economic conditions.

The strategic approach of BAE plc was introduced in Chapter 1. The extract in Case study 2.1 shows how they see their strategic impact as being wider than just the company itself.

Case study 2.1

Extract from BAE plc Annual Report and Financial Statements 2017:

'We manage a balanced business of products and services, employing world-class skills in technology and engineering to meet our customers' current and future needs. We use these capabilities primarily in the defence sector but, where appropriate, extend our reach into related and adjacent commercial market areas. We develop the skills necessary to supply our customers by a commitment to apprenticeships, graduate training and life-long learning.'

2. Rational strategy

2.1 Principles of the rational view

Strategy does not just happen – it requires management by people. The rational view of strategic management is based upon the presumption that the people undertaking the strategic management will always act in a logical, structured and proactive manner.

Although we might feel inclined to immediately discount this logical view of human nature, it is important that we use it as a base point to understand both the nature of strategic management and how other views of strategy have developed. To enable us to explore and understand a plethora of different perspectives of strategy and strategic management, it is essential to recognise our starting point.

This could be aligned with the development of strategy in itself where it has already been suggested that at least part of the success or otherwise of strategic development originates from the understanding of the *today* point.

What is it that we know and can understand about where we are starting from, and therefore how do we develop the iterations required to turn the alignment of status quo and vision into practical implementation within the organisation?

The presumption is that we are setting out to achieve one or more objectives. Ansoff (1990) suggested that organisations are 'purposive', that they have an intent to achieve something. He further suggested that an objective was a means by which success or failure could be identified, and split these objectives into four different categories:

- **Economic**: the efficient use of available resources to convert inputs into outputs, giving the opportunity to measure this quantitatively – as a result of 'x' input we achieved 'y' output.

- **Non-economic**: the ability to satisfy the expectations of stakeholders this can be both quantitative and qualitative.

- **Self-renewal**: the building of an organisation through reinvestment.

- **Flexibility**: sufficient latitude in the prescribed plan to enable an organisation to survive and manage different forces.

Stop and think 2.1

Reflect upon your own organisation and differentiate between the economic objectives and the non-economic objectives.

Having already accepted that the future is by definition unknown, we are clearly making plans in conditions of *partial ignorance*, and Ansoff suggests that a strategy is the *linking thread* that exists within the organisation enabling management to provide guidance. The parameters that exist around this *thread* are therefore fundamental to the success or otherwise of the organisation.

There are a number of core attributes that are normally attached to the thinking behind rational strategy:

- a rational strategy will be created at the top of an organisation, by the leaders and/or those who have accountability for an organisation;

- a rational strategy starts with the entirety of an organisation, before it can be broken down into smaller constituent parts; and

- a rational strategy will contain conscious choices that have been made concerning the length of the plan, the levels of risk, opportunities and threats offered by the environment, and the realistic availability of resources (this particular perspective was promulgated by Drucker (1968)).

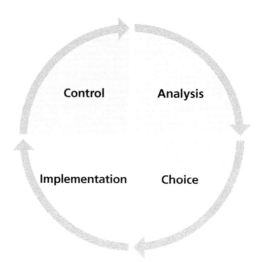

Figure 2.1 Aspects of strategic management (Johnson, 2017)

Johnson et al. (2017) report that strategic management needs to include, but also differentiate between, the day-to-day *operational* (shorter term) decisions made by managers and the process often undertaken by the same managers of making *strategic* (longer-term) decisions. They suggest that strategic management has four core aspects:

◆ **Analysis**: the collection and interpretation of appropriate data to enable the understanding of reality, resource and expectation.

◆ **Choice**: the evaluation of the strengths and weaknesses of different potential options arising from the analysis, and the ability therefore to establish a method of how to choose a preferred option.

◆ **Implementation**: the ability to put the chosen option into action. Refer back to Figure 1.1 of Chapter 1 – the strategic journey – 'implementation' is represented by the transition from the planning iterations into the operational circle.

◆ **Control**: the establishment of a method of monitoring outcomes of each stage of the process of strategic development (this could be described as being able to measure how far the real position has moved from Ansoff's theoretical thread).

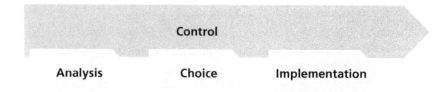

Figure 2.2 Strategic management amended

The Johnson categories do not necessarily follow a straight and logical path, in reality the four elements are interrelated and will constantly inform each other, although perhaps a more rational perspective might be achieved by changing the diagram from Figure 2.1 to Figure 2.2, whereby control is seen as a constant influence and requirement throughout the strategic development and management process.

Test yourself 2.1

Identify the four methods suggested by Ansoff that can be used to identify the success or failure of a strategy.

2.2   Evolution of the rational view

Many strategists and writers on strategy have used the concept of 'rational strategy' as their starting point, and then added their own particular nuance to the simplicity of a logical approach. These different perspectives are always seeking to explain why human beings do not behave in a rational and logical manner and therefore why rational strategy can only ever be a starting point for the benchmarking of an eventual outcome.

We will now briefly consider a number of different perspectives of the rational approach; the list is neither exclusive nor prescriptive, and the intention is not to provide a list of writers and options to be learned and regurgitated, but to suggest that each person, and each organisation, needs to be prepared to consider, challenge and place their own strategic development within a range of different contexts. These are:

◆ crafting and intuition
◆ competition
◆ the learning organisation
◆ chaos theory
◆ limitations of the rational model.

Crafting and intuition

◆ In *The Mind of the Strategist*, Ohmae (1982) discusses the development of strategy in a range of Japanese companies suggesting that human traits of creativity and obsession were as important as a rational and logical approach in the formation of strategy. He suggests that this combined approach better informed the analysis of available data and the making and implementation of strategic choices.

◆ In *The Age of Unreason*, Handy (1989) suggests that planning is as much based on intuition as on analysis; although he also recognises that our human intuition derives from what he calls the wheel of learning, a constant cycle of theory, test, reflection, question, theory, test.

◆   The human brain allows us at one and the same time to be dealing with what purports to be a logical direct line of thought while at the same time imagining what may lay either side of that line and therefore reshaping and or redirecting that line. This we may describe as intuition, defined as *the ability to understand something instinctively, without the need for conscious reasoning*.

Competition

◆   Porter (1980) considered the competitive markets within which organisations operated and suggested that the underlying rationality of their strategic development was often geared to enabling an advantage over the various competitive forces. These aspects of Porter's work will be considered in greater detail later in the text.

◆   Peters and Waterman (1982) added to the work of Porter producing a comparison of leading companies with a look at the individual ingredients that enabled the distinction for particular companies – the concept of *excellence*.

The learning organisation

This consideration of the manner in which strategies are developed, and the deviation from the stability of a rational model recognises the significant influence played by different individuals within an organisation. Further, there is a recognition that this might be one or more individuals bringing their own individuality to play, but with increasing evidence that when such individuals become aligned in their vision it is possible to describe the organisation itself as a learning organisation.

The organisation is perceived not as some distinct or indistinct entity, but as a group of individuals, bringing together a range of core competencies, and working and learning together.

◆   Pedler et al. (1997) developed a set of practical tools for an organisation to determine and understand its learning capabilities. Their starting point was a recognition that any organisation (*at its today point*) is a combination of the ideas of the people involved, the stage that the organisation (*as a collection of people*) has reached in its life-cycle, and the wider economic and cultural contexts in which both the organisation and its people exist.

◆   Senge (1990) in his bestseller *The Fifth Discipline* considers the development of an organisation, and the ultimate success or otherwise of its strategic management, from a fivefold perspective, each building upon the previous perspective. At the foundation is the concept of individuality, which Senge describes as *personal mastery*. This concept will be picked up again later in the text, so at this early stage it is worth considering how it applies to you, your organisation, and the organisations that have been mentioned thus far.

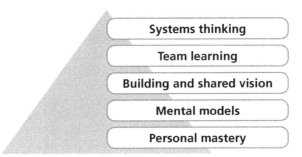

Figure 2.3
((Senge, 1990) adapted by Mark Wearden)

Case study 2.2

Extract from Tesco plc Annual Report and Financial Statements 2018:

'Our business is organised around three pillars

Customers: Tesco exists to serve customers – listening to them and acting on what is most important, however they choose to shop with us.

Product: We build close and mutually-beneficial relationships with our supplier partners, to source the best possible products that meet and anticipate customers' needs.

Channels: To bring the best products to customers we work through a range of channels – from small shops to large shops, and our online business.'

Stop and think 2.2

Think about yourself, your knowledge and your learning to TODAY.

What would you admit to as 'personal mastery'?

What do you feel totally in control of – personally and within your organisation?

The work of Argyris (1990) on how the human brain develops an understanding of all that surrounds it, and therefore ultimately a strategic approach, is at the foundation of the concept of *personal mastery* as discussed by Senge.

Consider how the Senge model might be applied to Tesco plc, given their three pillars.

Where does the 'personal mastery' become relevant? Consider how many different types of people at different levels are involved in such an organisation, and the difficulty of aligning strategic goals with differing behaviours.

Chaos theory

The concept of chaos evolves in what is known as the VUCA world in which we live – 'volatility, uncertainty, complexity and ambiguity', an acronym which resulted from the end of the Cold War and was derived from US military vocabulary. Later in the text the wider influence of chaos on the development of strategy will be discussed, but at this stage it is sufficient to recognise that all is not as it may seem at first glance, and that the most logically formulated rational strategic plan will be subject to VUCA forces before the plan is concluded.

Limitations of the rational model

Much of what has already been discussed in this section will be perceived as identifying a range of limitations of the strategic thinking and development included in the rational model. These concepts, together with others, were best summarised in the challenges laid down by Mintzberg (1994):

◆ Data: it is difficult to gather, control and structure the required level of data to enable the formulation of a rational plan in the first place, thus making the starting point impossible to contain.

◆ Routine: rational plans very often form a recurrent part of a planning process, often in an annual cycle, but an organisation cannot allow itself to wait 12 months before addressing problems.

◆ Inertia: once a rational plan is established people are unwilling to question it; this can also lead to an obsession with performance against the plan rather than a readiness to cope with uncertainty.

◆ Politics: the rational plan ignores the 'political' environment and 'power struggles' that exist within most organisations.

Mintzberg raises a number of questions concerning the fundamental fallacies that exist within the concept of rational plans from his perspective. These can be summarised as:

◆ How can intuitive judgement be reduced to a logical and rigid sequence of steps?

◆ How can planning be divorced from doing – ultimately it is the people who perform the action on a regular basis and will have a better concept of the optimal way to perform that action?

◆ As the differing strengths and weaknesses of people (at an individual and a team level) are only really discovered while tackling actual problems, why is so much time spent in the pre-emptive consideration of theoretical strengths and weaknesses?

◆ In a rapidly changing world environment, how is it possible to forecast anything other than the immediate future (and even that is susceptible to change)?

3. Emergent strategy

3.1 Principles of the emergent view

By considering the various aspects of the evolution of, and challenges to, the rational view of the development of strategy, it can be seen that Mintzberg and others (1985) were working towards a view which suggested that strategy development is a continually moving and evolving process, rather than something which is static and takes place as a single process.

The use of the word 'crafting' hints towards this continual change and Mintzberg developed this concept using the image of a potter's wheel. In his later publication *Strategy Safari*, Mintzberg further developed the following diagram to explain his concept of *emergent strategies*.

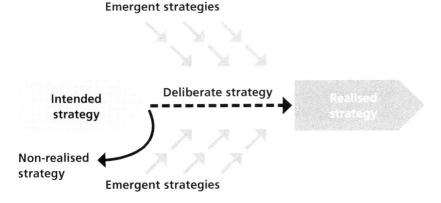

Figure 2.4
((Mintzberg, 2008) adapted by Mark Wearden)

All strategy is initiated through the type of rational intention that has been discussed above. Mintzberg describes this as *intended strategy*. This progresses in two different directions:

- Some of the intentions will not succeed, these are referred to as non-realised strategy. For example: a company changes its strategy after market research shows there is no demand for their planned product or service.

- The rest follow the deliberate strategy route to eventually become realised strategy. For example: a company has a strategy to introduce an additional service for its customers, this is well received by customers and rapidly becomes part of the core process.

However, during the route from *intended* to *realised*, the deliberate strategy will often come under significant influence from *emergent strategies*. For example, the relatively recent move by all motor manufacturers to hybrid and/or electric cars is the result of emergent pressure from consumers and governments – the new environmental strategy has had to emerge rapidly.

3.2 Evolution of the emergent view

What causes the *emergence* of different strategic ideas or the alteration of a strategic requirement?

◆ **People**: someone leaves or joins the organisation or the team; someone changes their mind or opinion about an existing process.

◆ **Direct organisational events**: a customer fails to buy; a supplier fails to supply; a piece of significant machinery breaks down; people go on strike.

◆ **Indirect wider economic and other external events**: taxation or interest rates change; there is a change in government.

Further ahead in this text, we will consider all of these events in much greater detail. In broad terms, we will refer to direct events as the *micro environment* and indirect events as the *macro environment*. These and other emerging dynamics and forces will always influence the eventual shape and realisation of strategy.

However, you will have realised why it is important to have a thorough understanding of the intended strategy, the rational strategy, and the *today* point. If we don't recognise where we are starting from, how will we recognise anything different?

Mintzberg was always firm in the view that few, if any, strategies were purely deliberate or exclusively emergent. Across his various publications he has developed many structured lists of attributes around the subject of strategy (often referred to as taxonomies of strategy).

Mintzberg produced a non-exhaustive list of the differing degrees of deliberation and emergence that can influence and be contained within a strategy (1985).

Type of strategy	Summary of Mintzberg	Practical examples
Planned	Explicit and deliberate with tight control and little room for variation from the intended course	An engineering company needs to source a new piece of machinery, and for it be working within six months to satisfy the demands of a customer.
Entrepreneurial	Commences with intention and vision, but will be subject to the vagaries of the mind of the entrepreneur	A software company is producing an 'app' to compare different online shopping websites.
Ideological	Driven by strong beliefs and/or culture with the intent to influence or structure conformance to ideals; deliberate and formulaic, but subject to the views of the leaders	A political group decides it needs to triple its membership within the next two years.

Umbrella	Broad boundaries within which a range of different types of strategy may exist; ultimate intent being built around commonality of vision, but open to many emergent influences	In the UK, government strategies for the National Health Service (NHS) would fall under this category (irrespective of political party) – the ultimate strategic objectives are clear, but the enormity of the structure will encompass many different strategic routes to achieve those objectives.
Process	Expectation that a particular route will be followed within certain 'process' boundaries, but allowing people some flexibility of operation within the boundaries	The use by different organisations of a piece of accounting software. The process required to achieve the end strategic result (a set of accounts in line with accounting standards) will have been structured within the software, but there will be flexibility in the mode of operation within different organisations.
Unconnected	A breakaway from the norm by part of an organisation, initially emergent, but likely to form its own deliberate structure to enable the 'break' to happen	A clothing manufacturer decides to create a weekly online fashion news subscription publication. The strategy is emergent, but those in charge of the new venture will need to establish deliberate strategies to initiate their route to success. Although there might be areas of crossover, these are largely two different strategic ventures with different dynamics and routes to customer sale.
Consensus	Strategy from discussion and agreement between two or more people; by its nature this is largely emergent	Read Case study 2.3 below on Ocado, this is a good example of consensus strategy.
Imposed	An autocratic imposition of the required end result but often with flexibility to enable different approaches to successful achievement of the goal	A good example given by Clegg et al. (2017) is the imposition of a budget cut imposed on a national government by the International Monetary Fund (IMF). For the recipient government the strategy is emergent but will require them to initiate a deliberate strategy to achieve the strategic objective.

Table 2.1
((Mintzberg, 1985) adapted by Mark Wearden)

Case study 2.3

Ocado was launched as an online trading concept by three former merchant bankers in January 2000, initially trading as the online business partner of Waitrose plc January 2002. When the company first started, the founders ran every part of the business themselves. They had a mutual belief in the future potential of online sales and built their strategy around their mutual vision and their combined views and expertise. Their strategy was deliberate in intent – to earn the right to a material share of the growing online market for food retail; but emergent in realisation with many changes of strategic direction needed along the route thus far. Their website in 2018 stated:

'The grocery market has evolved out of recognition over the last 60 years, from small, local retailers to sprawling, out-of-town hypermarkets. Each "channel shift" in the market has taken over 50% of customers to the new, dominant format – and it's happening again now.

The relentless growth of online shopping is powered by improved technology, faster broadband and better mobile devices – and a significant increase in uptake of all three. Traditional supermarkets face a difficult dilemma: invest in online, and cannibalise themselves; or don't invest, and risk losing customers and market share.

Ocado is different. As the UK's only "pure play" online grocery operator, and the world's largest dedicated online grocery supermarket, our business was built for this channel shift – to benefit from, and to lead the online revolution.'

The strategic journey of Ocado has required the ability to react to a wide range of emergent forces. The strategic focus was rational and clear in the minds of the three founders, but by working so closely with one retailer at the outset, they found that their own ideas had to merge with the ideas of their strategic partner and their strategy had to evolve. This led to them freeing themselves from a sole partner arrangement and developing a much wider but still focused offering of home delivery for online sales, now offering their own direct online sales.

Stop and think 2.3

Which types of strategic direction or structure do you work within?

How do they feel to you as an individual?

How much can you influence the emergence of change?

It is important to recognise that all people within an organisation will be actively involved in an organisation that genuinely embodies the concept of emergent strategy. The best people to comment upon, challenge and help to redesign required change are those who are dealing with the day-to-day operations. It is always important to remember the distinction between the different timeframes of strategy and planning discussed towards the end of Chapter 1.

There are a plethora of different models and developments of the concept of emergent strategy that could be considered, but for the purpose of this text, we will include two further models which take and develop the concept of emergent strategy; one from the same time as Mintzberg was writing about emergent strategy, one from a more recent approach:

◈ context, content and process

◈ integrative thinking.

Context, content and process

Pettigrew and Whipp (1991) purport that all strategic change takes place within a threefold context as a result of the inextricable linkage that exists between strategic change and competition; these aspects are seen as joint and inseparable processes which occur at multiple levels across time. Our first reference to this work here identifies the attributes of their threefold approach, our second reference in section 5 below will clarify the perceived levels of strategic change.

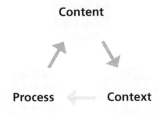

Content

Process **Context**

Figure 2.5
((Pettigrew & Whipp, 1991) adapted by Mark Wearden)

◈ The *content* of the planning process requires a strategic vision, a strategic plan and an implementation plan. These will identify how and why certain products and/or markets have been chosen; the underlying objectives and assumptions; a range of targets; and methods of evaluation success.

◈ The *context* will consider the people, the organisational culture, the internal and external politics, the resources available, the performance rewards for the stakeholders involved.

◈ The *process* will consider the available and required leadership, the identity of the change managers, the communication routes required, change impact analysis (people and system) and a projection of the perceived route to deliver the strategy.

They recognise that this threefold process is a continual momentum from the outset to completion, driven by people and their idiosyncratic brains at all stages. Lynch (2015) relates this structure to the introduction of small motorbikes into the market-place by Honda:

◆ Strategy content: Honda used small machines as an entry point followed later by its launch of larger machines.

◆ Strategy context: the historical dominance of the US manufacturers initially led to the failure of Honda's prescriptive entry strategy, but the industry's relative weakness in the small market provided an opening for Honda.

◆ Strategy process: the strategy was developed through a combination of luck, product performance and management persistence in the face of initial difficulties.

Integrative thinking

In his book *The Opposable Mind* Roger Martin (2007) introduces the idea of 'integrative thinking'. This is a methodology that is analogous to 'systems thinking' but allows us to focus on the way that the brain as a system deals with the other systems which surround us, and within which we have to operate. Martin identifies certain characteristics of the integrative thinker which form a useful starting point for the strategic challenges which face us:

◆ Models which exist in the brain are not reflecting totality, they are simply the best that we have at that moment in time.

◆ The brain has the ability to hold and reflect upon conflicting models of, or approaches to, a particular situation. These are to be leveraged rather than feared.

◆ Better models do and will exist that have not yet been discovered by us.

◆ The brain of the integrative thinker is able to overlay an existing model with a perceived better model and allow them to morph into a new 'best that we have' structure.

◆ The brain will enjoy the complexity and confusion that exists while looking for an optimal understanding.

◆ An integrative thinker will ensure that they dedicate sufficient time to enable the first five challenges, but also recognises that this inevitably becomes an iterative process.

Martin talks about the need for wisdom, using the context of Confucian thinking which suggests that wisdom has three core attributes – reflection, imitation and experience. Additionally, that the brain requires a sensitivity, this being a capacity to distinguish between conditions that are similar but not exactly the same.

He models integrative thinking as shown in Figure 2.6.

◆ Salience: what features are seen as important for achievement of the vision?

◆ Causality: how do people make sense of what they are seeing?

◆ Architecture: what order is required for the practical tasks involved?

◆ Resolution: How will I know when I achieve the vision?

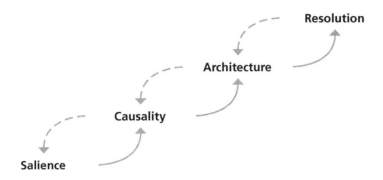

Figure 2.6
((Martin, R., 2007) adapted by Mark Wearden)

This is taken further by Martin and Riel in *Creating Great Choices* (2017) where they align the concepts of the opposable mind with the Argyris' 'ladder of inference' (1990) (discussed in Chapter 1 above) and develop a concept of strategic challenge of one or more brains faced with a multiplicity of options along a route with frequent new emergent forces appearing.

Stop and think 2.4

Reflect upon your brain and its ability to think in an integrative manner. How do you determine what is right and wrong about a situation or a person? How can you judge whether a vision is realistic or idealistic, what are your benchmarks?

Test yourself 2.2

Briefly define what is meant by 'rational strategy' and give an example.

4. Rational versus emergent strategy, and other models of strategy

It is clear that there is no one method for the development of strategy. All strategies are likely to have a mixture of rational, emergent and many other influences. Lynch (2015) expresses a number of concerns about the nature of the people and the organisation in the consideration of emergent strategy.

Lynch suggests that the people who are accountable and/or in charge of an organisation will have agreed their strategic plans (rational) and are unlikely to simply sit back and allow the operational managers to adapt and amend the strategy (emergent). Both perspectives need to be included, the 'bigger picture' of the ultimate stakeholder expectation but tempered by the practical operational realities of the day-to-day.

Any organisation only has finite resources, these must be utilised in a structured manner (rational) and cannot be allowed simply to be consumed as the need demands (emergent).

The timeframe and length of a strategy will have a significant impact on the interaction of rational and emergent thinking. A short-term strategy will have more chance of remaining within rational boundaries, whereas a longer-term strategy will inevitably be more affected by emergent strategies (not least the evolution of human minds). However, it is also important that there are rational boundaries for a longer-term strategy to ensure that a core focus is maintained and there is an eventual satisfaction of the strategic objectives, even if these have been reframed as a result of emerging forces.

Lynch also suggests that rational decision making based upon evidence is more likely to be successful than hunches and personal whims. In contrast, Albert Einstein, although not specifically talking about strategy, suggested that:

'Imagination is more important than knowledge'

The reality behind this is that it is essential for the knowledge to be present (a thorough and deep understanding of *today*), to enable the imagination to explore different possibilities of the unknown *future*.

The world is never static, so it follows that the development of strategy must also never be static. Every book on strategy has its own model or its own skew on the traditionally accepted academic approaches to strategy. The rest of this section contains a non-exhaustive, non-exclusive range of approaches to the development of strategy, some of which have already been mentioned. Each offers something slightly different, but each, in its turn, evidences the truism that strategic management has to always be a continuous and emerging process of change. In most instances there is only one citation and or example of the particular perspective, and this is sufficient to broaden the mind in the consideration of emergent strategy. The approaches covered are:

- complexity and chaos theory
- institutional theory
- the ecological view
- the relationship between strategy and objectives
- human behaviour and strategic choice
- incrementalism
- competitive structures
- co-operation and networks
- game theories
- innovation and knowledge-based theories.

4.1   Complexity and chaos theory

Although often referred to as a joined approach to the theory of emergent strategy, it is important to be able to differentiate between the two different aspects – complexity and chaos.

Complexity derives from the recognition that any organisation exists on a day-to-day basis due to the interaction of different aspects of the systems that coexist within that organisation – this is aligned to systems theory and the recognition that the complexity is rarely due to the different attributes within a system, but almost always linked to the relationships between the attributes. Even so, these relationships, if complex, can be ordered and structured.

Chaos derives from the relationship between the system and the people who operate within that system. While the system can be structured and defined, the irrationality of human behaviour can always introduce the risk of chaos.

Stacey (1995) suggests that strategy is significantly affected by the dynamics of an organisational system, this being characterised by positive and negative feedback as the system evolves away from the equilibrium towards unpredictable long-term outcomes.

Another aspect of this linkage of complexity and chaos is sometimes referred to as the 'butterfly effect' – a term ascribed to the meteorologist Edward Lorenz in 1972, with his associated image of a hurricane in one part of the world having been caused by a butterfly flapping its wings in another part of the world. In strategic systems theory it is possible to understand within an organisational context how a small decision or action from an individual can ultimately have a high-level non-linear impact within the organisation.

4.2   Institutional theory

All organisations operate within an environment that is populated by a range of differing institutions, and a complex web of institutional behaviour. The influence, restriction and drive of these differing institutions on the development of strategy needs to be understood and taken into consideration.

Institutionalisation may be sector based, for example there is significant ongoing discussion about the dominance of the UK audit and accountancy market by virtually replica practices within the 'big four' accountancy firms. Institutionalisation will also be based around culture, geography and economic structures, for example the different reporting requirements and expectations of individual stock exchanges in different countries.

An organisation has the choice of adapting its strategy to the surrounding institutional behaviour or attempting to challenge and change the perceived common behaviours.

Test yourself 2.3

Briefly describe what is meant by 'emergent strategy' and give an example.

4.3 The ecological view

Ecologists would argue that any organisation will evolve its own ecosystem, operating within the institutional structures that surround it. Part of their argument is that development is, by its nature, incremental and will lead to one of three outcomes – a change to the perceived norm; an adaptation to the surrounding structures; or the decline of the organisation.

Iansiti and Levien (2004) take this concept further by suggesting that each member of a business ecosystem will ultimately share the fate of the network as a whole, regardless of individual strength. In their article they use Wal-Mart and Microsoft as examples of organisations that have recognised this ecological perspective of strategic development and developed their own individual infrastructures from the perspective of their own interests, but also to lead the overall development and health of other individual business ecosystems.

4.4 The relationship between strategy and objectives

Some writers on strategy believe that it is not possible to separate the strategy itself from the objectives that it is trying to achieve.

This text has already discussed the need to establish intended outcomes of strategic management, and has referred to these outcomes as 'objectives'. The presumption thus far has been that our wider strategic vision can be segmented into one or more focused objectives.

In his book *The Concept of Corporate Strategy*, Kenneth Andrews (1987) takes an alternative perspective and suggests that the strategic objectives of an organisation are revealed through the decisions that are made through plans that are implemented within the organisation. He suggests further that this practical action within an organisation will determine ultimately its output to differing stakeholders. His view assumes that an organisation is consistent in its manner of decision-making, and that these decisions will determine the strategy, rather than the other way around.

4.5 Human behaviour and strategic choice

It will already be apparent that a significant difference between rational strategy and emergent strategy is the concept of behaviour. This suggests that when we develop strategy, we need to be aware of the potential for different individual behaviour and response We will need to consider how those behaviours may or may not alter when individuals work together. Johnson et al. (2017) suggest that planning as a human concept will significantly influence the direction of both strategic thinking and strategic outcome.

The approach can be split into four phases – in each phase it is important to recognise the interaction between individual and group behaviour:

◆ Recognition: an individual will recognise a particular strategic problem; as soon as that individual recognition is shared with others the organisational drivers start to take effect.

◆ Diagnosis: the identified strategic problem will be diagnosed by one or more individuals; their conclusions are likely to differ based around their differing levels of experience. This original concept from Johnson might be challenged by the introduction of artificial intelligence into the diagnostic phase of strategic decision-making.

◆ Alternative solutions: there is rarely only one answer to a strategic problem, so individuals will severally and jointly develop alternative approaches to resolve a problem, these could be based around historic evidence or experience, or at the other end of the scale might be an attempt to try something new.

◆ Selection and action: the alternative solutions will need to be screened and ultimately one or more individuals will select a solution and then implement change.

4.6 Incrementalism

In his consideration of emergent strategy, Mintzberg (*Strategy Safari*, 2008) suggests that a key component of effective emergence is that of a 'learning school' where the drive is description rather than prescription. The people involved within the strategic development process continually ask and challenge how strategies are actually formed within an organisation, with a focus upon understanding the practical actions involved within strategic outcome, rather than the process of formulation.

We have already used the term incrementalism, and the concept that strategy will often develop in an incremental manner. There have been two distinct academic approaches to this concept.

An early provocative attempt to challenge the concept of ordered rational strategy was provided by Charles Lindblom (1959) in his article 'The Science of "Muddling Through"', the title in itself suggesting his belief that strategy was not a neat controlled process but a messy one in which the strategists (or in his specific case, governmental policymakers) try to cope with the new world which is too complicated for them. This was a concept of an emergent, incrementalist strategy which suggested that organisational change was based around reactive consideration of outcome rather than the moulding of a preconceived vision. This has been referred to as 'disjointed incrementalism'.

As an alternative approach, James Brian Quinn (1980) described a process of 'logical incrementalism'. The process of strategic development is seen as a 'continuous, pulsing dynamic', suggesting that although there will always be a reactive nature to the development of strategy it need not be as irrational as that suggested by Lindblom; the nature of those empowered with the controllable organisation will provide the structure and parameters to enable an appropriate level of incrementalism set against an underlying logic to align the various strands of the organisation.

4.7 Competitive structures

There is significant discussion of the influence and strategic impact of the competitive environment within which an organisation operates in Chapters 3 and 4 of this text. However, it is worth recognising in this consideration of different attributes of emergent strategy that competition will have a significant influence on both the development of the strategy and the strategic outcomes.

Ohmae (1982) suggests that 'a good business strategy is one by which a company can gain significant ground on its competitors at an acceptable cost' recognising that all organisational strategy needs to be assessed by the potential for competitive success. He suggests that successful strategic development relies upon the recognition and interplay of a strategic triangle referred to as the 'three Cs':

- Customers: those who will fund our organisation as the result of a successful business cycle.
- Competitors: those who will seek to take our customers, or those whose customers we wish to attract.
- Corporation: the organisational structure itself and how it is designed to operate within the various competing environments where it is situated.

Porter (1980) suggests that competitive strategy is the 'taking of offensive or defensive actions to create a defendable position within an industry and therefore being able to generate a superior return on investment'. There are three core aspects of Porter's thinking around competitive structures:

- There is a difference between the development of strategy and the effectiveness of an operation – the former being conceptual, the latter being based in reality.
- Competitive strategy requires an organisation to recognise how it is differentiated from its rivals.
- The achievement of a sustainable strategic position in a competitive environment will require an organisation to recognise that it cannot be all things to all people and that it will need to live with inconsistencies in the ability to include trade-offs within its business model – as an example, the airline discount companies such as Ryanair and easyJet are able to offer very low-priced seats, but the trade-off for price is the level of service and facilities that can be expected by a customer.

4.8 Co-operation and networks

The concept of a strategic network is a recognition by an organisation, as its strategy emerges, that there will be players in the competitive field with whom it is sensible to co-operate, and/or network, to enable mutual benefit. This can sometimes be more beneficial than spending time and resources in attempting to thwart the competition. The development of a strategic network can often build a supply chain and sourcing efficiency into the respective operations of organisations that are otherwise in competition. An example of this would be food retailing within the UK, where many small shops operate jointly on a network basis; and even at the larger end of the retail sector Tesco plc announced in 2018 that they will be working strategically with the large French retailer Carrefour to develop a sourcing network.

It is important for any organisation to recognise the breadth and depth of the economic and political network within which they operate, and therefore, when appropriate, to identify competitors, and others, within the network with whom it might be beneficial to co-operate strategically.

4.9 Game theories

The influence of game theory on the development of strategy is important, and we need to understand the different perspectives that can be taken by viewing strategic development as part of a competitive game. A basic understanding of this will help to frame the many different perspectives of strategy that will be considered through this syllabus; passing reference will also be made to 'game theory' throughout the text.

Game theory is often aligned with two differing but connected approaches:

◆   Mathematical game theory can be applicable where there is only a limited range of clear outcomes for a particular scenario and differing values can be associated with each potential outcome – you may have already come across the concept of standard deviation which is closely linked to this mathematical approach.

◆   An alternative approach is often referred to as 'war gaming' as its origins lie in the positioning of different players within a military scenario to determine a range of moves and counter moves. In this instance, there are no predefined outcomes, but the intention is to consider the move and likely reaction of and impact upon differing players.

Within the context of strategic thinking, game theory is usually referred to from one of four potential outcomes – lose:lose; win:lose; lose:win; win:win – the last of these having become common business terminology for the aspired outcome of a negotiation. The reality, however, is often that the person purporting that an outcome is win:win can see for themselves at least a modest advantage and therefore strategically their real intention is a win:lose outcome.

Stop and think 2.6

When were you last involved in a game theory type scenario?

What was the outcome?

How did you feel – win or lose?

4.10 Innovation and knowledge-based theories

In their book *The Knowledge-Creating Company*, Nonaka and Takeuchi (1995) discuss the need for managers to recognise the difference between tacit knowledge and explicit knowledge in their ability to be innovative in their strategic thinking.

Knowledge is seen as the ability of the human brain to consider, contemplate and utilise refined data, together with perception, learning and experience. Knowledge is always a human activity which is often facilitated and encouraged by an organisation.

Tacit knowledge is that which we know implicitly (inside ourselves) and for which there is normally a combination of intangible and tangible evidence.

Explicit knowledge is that which we know formally where there is always tangible evidence.

Nonaka and Takeuchi suggest that there are four processes in play, interacting in a dynamic manner, to enable knowledge to be converted into action. These processes could be interpreted as follows:

- **Socialisation**: the implicit sharing of tacit knowledge either verbally or experientially – 'I think this should happen because'.
- **Externalisation**: the conversion of tacit knowledge to explicit knowledge through deeper analysis and application, through metaphor or real-life experience – 'if you don't believe me have a look at how this happens'.
- **Combination**: the formal transfer of knowledge from one person to another in some form of codified manner – 'if you take this MBA course you will join a group of people with similar knowledge'.
- **Internalisation**: the need for a human being to take explicit knowledge back into tacit form – 'having completed this task, go away and think about the implications of what you have done'.

These concepts could be aligned with incrementalism, but in this case, it is the gradual building of the knowledge of the brain which is incremental, and in turn will affect the strategic thinking and development in an incremental manner.

5. Organisational contexts

Strategic thinking is an essential part of everyday life for each individual and each type of organisation.

Consider how, as an individual, you start your day, each day. You will wake up with a plan in your mind of what you intend to do between the point of waking up, to the next time you need to go to bed. If it is a day of significance, then the strategic planning will have pre-empted the day, possibly even interrupting your sleep. If it is just a normal day, then much of your strategic planning will be subliminal and you will be able to carry out journeys and tasks based around previous experience.

Stop and think 2.7

Consider the different levels of strategic planning required between:

1. **waking up and heading to an airport for ten days' holiday**

2. **waking up and catching the normal train to work**

3. **waking up for a relaxing day at home.**

All strategic thinking is ultimately only an extension of these simple concepts, and as with much of corporate and organisational life it is often useful to bring things back to first principles – What are we trying to achieve? Why are we trying to achieve it? What is the required timeframe?

In this section we will consider briefly the different types of organisational structure that exist together with some of the strategic influences which may affect these organisations.

Case study 2.4

The phrase often associated with some organisations as being 'not-for-profit' immediately leads many people to assume that money will not be a core strategic driver in such an organisation. This could not be further from the truth.

Consider a local hospice trust established as a 'not-for-profit' organisation and registered as a charity, with a focused strategic output of delivering care for the terminally ill. Think about the monetary flows in such an organisation; the strategy has to be designed to generate funds to be used for the strategic objectives. Although the structure is 'not-for-profit' the organisation needs to ensure that its income regularly exceeds its expenditure to help deliver a strategic sustainability.

Arguably, all organisations need to exist with a profit motive, income needs to exceed expenditure. The real strategic difference is how the excess of income over expenditure is utilised in the interests of stakeholders (the concept of stakeholders will be considered further in Chapter 3).

As you consider each of these different types of organisation and those below, try to visualise the operational context of each organisation at a simplistic level – what is it trying to achieve, and who is it trying to achieve it for? Company secretaries and governance professionals encounter many different types of organisation; each organisation, despite its differences, will have a common strategic goal – long-term sustainability for its stakeholders.

- **Sole trader**
  - The strategic objectives and strategic planning will be based upon the expectations of the individual, although set within the operating parameters of financial, legal and environmental constraints.

- **Partnerships**
  - The strategic objectives and strategic planning will be based upon the expectations of the partners, set within the operating parameters of financial, legal and environmental constraints.

- **Limited companies**
  - The strategic objectives and strategic planning will be based upon the expectations of the shareholders, set within the operating parameters of financial, legal and environmental constraints – and in particular the wider stakeholder expectations as required from the directors in **Companies Act** 2006 s172 and associated sections.

Companies Act
UK Companies Act 2006 together with its subsequent amendments. The phrase may also incorporate earlier UK Companies Act legislation.

- **Private companies versus public companies**
  - The shares of a *private company* are not traded publicly, and, within the restrictions of the constitution of that company, will normally only be traded between existing shareholders; the strategic objectives will be defined by those shareholders.
  - The shares of a *public company* are traded on a public stock exchange – there will therefore be a much wider and more diverse group of shareholders, including institutional investors (those who invest funds on behalf of others such as pension funds and insurance companies) and retail investors (individuals who decide to invest in shares); the strategic dynamics are therefore significantly more diverse.

- **Multinational corporations**
  - A multinational corporation is any organisation operating in more than one geographical market – this could be from a product sale perspective and/or an operating site location perspective.
  - Different geographical markets will have different legal and environmental expectations, and although the strategic control will normally be based in one country, the cultural and operating expectations of all other countries will need to be considered from a strategic planning perspective.
  - There has been much public debate in recent years over the appropriate legal and ethical treatment and taxation of funds generated in one country by a company resident in a different country.

- Although normally such organisations would be considered as being within the private or public limited company structure, it would be reasonable to suggest that partnerships such as the 'big four' accounting firms are also multinational corporations.

◆ **The public sector and the third sector**

- Public sector organisations are those operating on behalf of, or as an adjunct to, national or local government, and will include organisations such as schools and hospitals. Funding is usually directly received from national or local public funds.

- Third sector organisations exist within the operational dynamic that exists between traditional business and the public sector; they are generally voluntary, non-profit making and often charitable organisations reliant on the accumulation of private energy and resource for the greater public good.

- Strategic planning within the public and third sector can sometimes prove problematic, with a disconnect often appearing between the ethical and social aspirations of the organisation and the need for strategic drivers to ensure achievement of focused objectives and longer-term sustainability.

- Strategic choice is often more limited in such organisations.

◆ **Professional service organisations**

- These organisations will usually have a formal structure of either partnership or limited company as described above (or the conjoint of a limited liability partnership).

- A particular service (e.g. accountancy, law, company secretarial support etc.) is offered to a wide range of potential clients; the strategic planning must either therefore be focused broadly or with a particular parameter of clients in mind.

◆ **Membership organisations**

- A membership body will have a formal legal structure in line with one of the above formats, but will exist for the particular benefit, support and development of the like-minded aspirations of its members.

- Particular examples would be organisations such as an accountancy body, the National Trust in the UK, and of course ICSA: The Governance Institute.

- The strategic direction of such organisations will require an alignment between those who run the organisation itself and those who are the underlying members of the organisation; as such organisations grow in size the potential diversity of individual member aspiration can lead to a strategic disconnect.

Stop and think 2.8

Consider the similarity and likely differences between the strategic drivers for each of the above types of organisation.

Try to differentiate between the different types of vision, mission and objectives that might be applicable, as discussed in Chapter 1.

6. Economic conditions

6.1 Stability and growth conditions

The economic conditions of the environment within which any type of organisation is operating will need to be taken into consideration in any strategic planning, particularly in longer-term plans. The economic dynamic will be considered many times and in many different ways throughout this text, but at this stage it is important to consider the different strategic impact of two broadly opposite sets of conditions:

◆ Periods of stability and growth: Organisations will be able to take a longer term and more developmental strategic perspective, allowing appropriate levels of time for the development of products, and the market testing of innovative ideas. While profit and operating margins will clearly be important, it will be possible to develop strategic plans which enable a far more incremental approach to longer term success. The operating environment will be more confident, supportive and willing to accept short-term failures for the betterment of sustainable long-term success if this is well communicated at all levels and throughout the process of change.

◆ Periods of instability, recession and austerity: In the VUCA world it would be reasonable for strategic planners to build in an expectation of instability. Since the financial crisis of 2008, and the subsequent austerity measures and recession across much of the Western world, strategic planners have been forced to consider a series of much shorter-term dynamics to enable longer term viability.

Test yourself 2.4

Suggest the relationship that exists between complexity and chaos in strategic planning.

6.2 Content–context–process

As a final brief consideration of the importance of economic conditions, and how they influence the development of strategy, we return to the content–context–process model of Pettigrew and Whipp (1991) illustrated in Figure 2.6 and their suggestion that this structure needed to always be viewed within a multi-dimensional framework. They extended their thoughts to the more detailed model in Figure 2.7.

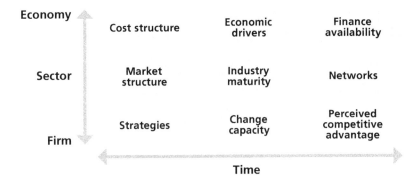

Figure 2.7 Detailed content-context-process model
((Pettigrew & Whipp, 1991) adapted by Mark Wearden)

The horizontal time axis suggests that the sectoral and national conditions within which a firm operates are unstable, they perpetually change with time. As an example, competitive advantage only really exists for a transitory period of time while the competitors are trying to 'catch up'.

The vertical axis recognises that all organisations operate within a three-dimensional context. This consists of the organisation itself, the sector that it operates within and the wider economy.

In Chapter 4 we will reconsider the sector (micro) and economy (macro) dimensions further.

The level of strategic flexibility within the organisation itself will be driven significantly by its economic position. Where does it sit on the economic dynamic that exists between perfect competition and monopoly?

Perfect competition	Monopolistic competition	Oligopoly	Monopoly
Large number of sellers	Many sellers	Few sellers	One seller
Homogeneous product	Differentiated product	Restricted choice	Unique product

Table 2.2 The economic dynamic
© Mark Wearden

An organisation in perfect competition with a homogenous product will almost inevitably begin a process of differentiation by publicising its culture or ethics to those who consume or who are affected by its deliverables, it needs to make its product more distinct.

An organisation with a monopoly or near-monopoly will know that the competitors are working to impact upon their control and will likewise need to have a clear view of differentiation.

Most organisations do not work at either extremity but are somewhere within this dynamic; strategically it is important to recognise the direction of travel from a micro (product) and macro (whole business) perspective. Is the strategic direction towards separation or towards participation?

Chapter summary

- ◈ This chapter focuses on the important differences that exist between rational strategy and emergent strategy.

- ◈ The detailed planning and levels of expectation that are involved in rational strategy are aligned by Ansoff as analysis, choice, implementation and control.

- ◈ While the academic and (in some organisations) practical application of a rational model is structured and logical, it is important to remember that strategy will come under internal and external forces. Further that 'today' will become the 'future' and the originating principles of our strategy may need to change.

- ◈ Mintzberg developed the realisation that much of strategy is actually emergent. Even if we start with a rational, and fully worked approach, the forces that surround us and our strategy will cause it to be 'crafted' like the clay on a potter's wheel.

- ◈ Pettigrew and Whipp devised a threefold understanding of emergent strategy showing a constantly moving relationship between content, context and process. Through the iterations of this process strategy can be implemented and objectives achieved.

- ◈ A number of the forces and influences that cause the emergence of altered strategies were introduced, such as chaos, complexity, game theory and network relationships. These and many of the other aspects mentioned in this chapter will re-occur through the text. Many of the concepts in this chapter form the basis of the study of the development of strategy.

- ◈ A company secretary and governance professional must understand the plethora of different dimensions that sit behind the development of strategy. Often, in the boardroom and other meetings, it is important to be able to review the origin of the ideas being discussed, the natural organisational movement from rational to emergent strategy.

Chapter three
Developing strategy

Contents

1. Introduction
2. Strategic leadership
3. Systems and strategy
4. People and strategy
5. Strategic actions

1. Introduction

To complete the consideration of the fundamentals that are needed to understand the development of strategy, this chapter will begin a consideration of the practical requirements for the development of strategy within an organisation. Chapters 1 and 2 considered the meaning, language, purpose and a number of different approaches as to how and why strategy exists and is an essential requirement for any organisation.

It is always people rather than organisations that devise, formulate, plan and implement strategy. It is a human need and desire to move from the 'today' position into the 'future' – life does not stand still, we live an existence which requires both mental and physical momentum.

This chapter will consider the following four further areas of fundamental background to enable students to better challenge and develop their knowledge of:

◆ Leadership: the role of leadership within the development of strategy, and the attributes that are required to be an effective leader.

◆ Systems: the visualisation and evolution of an organisation as a system that requires analysis, understanding, input and iterative challenge.

◆ People: the people involved in the system and its leadership.

◆ Actions: the fundamental actions that are required to maintain momentum.

Case study 3.1

Many organisations make bold claims about the central and strategic significance of the people within their business – consider the following from BAE.

Extract from BAE plc Annual Report and Financial Statements 2017:

'At the heart of our business are the people we employ and the talent we build from apprentice to boardroom'

2. Strategic leadership

2.1 The meaning of, and the need for, leadership

Strategy does not just happen by itself – it requires people and their brains, and in anything other than the smallest groups of people leadership is required. As we start to develop our understanding of how strategy actually happens within an organisation, it is important to be able to place that strategy, and strategic thinking, within the context of the type and style of leadership that is taking place.

At one extreme of the classic leadership dynamic is an autocratic leader who will dictate and drive the strategic direction. At the other extreme, a participative leader will work with others for a combined decision on direction.

The basic dictionary definition of 'leadership' is 'the action of leading a group of people or an organisation, or the ability to do this'. This is a good place to start, but needs more focus and refinement when considering how to develop strategy within an organisation.

This is one of many such definitions that could have been used, and at the heart of all of them is what Maccoby (2017) describes as unarguable, that a leader is *someone with followers*. If there are no followers, there is no one to lead, and even if you are in a position of significant authority you cannot be classed as a leader. Consider the world of politics across the world, the varying levels of leadership that are displayed, and how quickly the fortunes of those 'leaders' can rise or fall based upon the reaction of the followers.

Transmit this concept into an organisation and consider the impact that different types and styles of leadership can have upon long-term strategic direction. To be effective, leaders need to have the ability to change how people think, as well as to influence what they do. Leaders will often need to develop a belief in the minds of the people who are following that an organisation can actually change. The final two chapters of this text will consider further a range of aspects of change in relationship to strategy. At this point we will consider a number of aspects of strategic leadership.

This text will consider three differing perspectives of strategic leadership to focus on the strategic thinking required for the day-to-day world of a Chartered Secretary and Chartered Governance Professional. John Adair (1979) talks about 'action centred leadership', suggesting that really effective leadership comes at the centre of the triangulation of individual, group and task.

Individual

Task   **Group**

Figure 3.1
((Adair, J., 1979) adapted by Mark Wearden)

Every leadership decision will emanate from one of these three aspects, and the effective leader will be able to take decisions to ensure that all three perspectives are satisfied appropriately.

It is useful to also be able to differentiate between transformational leadership and transactional leadership, and the attributes of the respective leaders.

A *transformational leader* will focus on the building of the strategic vision, the creation of identity and empowerment and the development of an appropriate culture (discussed further in Chapter 6). The original inspiring entrepreneur behind an organisation is often a transformational leader, such as Steve Jobs at Apple. The people and organisational impact are clear to see, but a large gap can be created when that personal leadership of transformation is no longer part of the organisation, especially if much of the operation relied upon it.

A *transactional leader* is generally more concerned with making sure that the operational flow is appropriate to enable the strategy to be achieved. The term 'transaction' refers to the motivation of followers by the exchange of reward for performance. The leadership of Fred Goodwin at RBS plc before the 2007 financial crisis could be identified as transactional; the bank was seen as a series of high-profile operations with significant levels of reward for success. Problems which occur in the longer-term strategic vision are often caused by unachievable goals or **hubris**.

hubris
Excessive pride or self-confidence.

Successful strategic leadership requires a combination of both transformational and transactional leadership; it also requires both autocratic and participative leadership. The real sign of a truly successful strategic leader is their ability to encompass a range of different styles as required in the ever-changing world around them.

Stop and think 3.1

Draw a horizontal 4 x 6 matrix for use as we progress through this section of the text.

People	Qualities	Style	Skills	Principles	Learning

In column 1 (people) write down the names of three people who you think of as strategic leaders.

In column 2 (qualities) identify three key leadership qualities that they possess.

In column 3 (style) identify whether they are generally more transactional or more transformational leaders.

Columns 4, 5 and 6 will be used later in this chapter.

2.2 Models of leadership and organisation

Essential skills

An article in the *Harvard Business Review*, based upon work with more than 20,000 executive leaders, suggested that there are six key skills that are required for a successful strategic leader. Even though each of these skills is often considered in isolation, it is only when a strategic leader is sufficiently resolute and flexible to be able to apply all six skills at once that they have the ability to genuinely lead.

The original article identifies the skill, refers to an example from the research, and then suggests methods for leaders to improve their ability in each particular skill. This text restricts itself to two brief comments against each of Schoemaker's suggested leadership skills. Leaders should:

◆ Anticipate
  – the need for constant vigilance, honing the ability to consider potential changes within the business and ambiguous threats and opportunities on the periphery of the business
  – the ability to scan the environment for signals of change, in particular an alert awareness to the business and behaviour of customers and rivals.

◆ Challenge
  – a perpetual questioning of the status quo, challenging own and others' views in a desire to understand and appreciate divergent opinions
  – the ability to identify, and dispel where appropriate, assumptions that are made about the organisation and its environment.

◆   Interpret
   –   the process of assimilating complex and conflicting information viewed in the context of previous strategic decisions
   –   the ability to analyse, challenge and synthesise ambiguous data.
◆   Decide
   –   the driving of strategic action after a robust and appropriate consideration process
   –   the ability and confidence to identify the appropriate decisions, or partial decisions required to move from consideration into action.
◆   Align
   –   the bringing together of differing stakeholder expectations
   –   the ability to communicate through using the appropriate channels with internal and external stakeholders, identifying, understanding and addressing their concerns.
◆   Learn
   –   the promotion of a culture of organisational enquiry to ensure that all participants in the strategy process understand why some strategies succeed and some fail
   –   the ability to understand and help others to understand. This will help to ensure that strategy is designed in full cognisance of the outcome of previous strategic decisions, realising that learning is a continuous process.

Stop and think 3.2

Using your matrix from Stop and think 3.1: in column 4 (skills) identify which of these six essential skills the leaders possess.

Case study 3.2

Tesco is keen to emphasise the strategic importance of the 'colleagues' working within the company and their longevity of development within the company.

Extract from Tesco plc Annual Report and Financial Statements 2018:

'I would like to pay tribute to every colleague at Tesco. I firmly believe that the retail industry, and Tesco in particular, have an important role in helping people to develop fulfilling and successful careers. Almost a quarter of our most senior leaders began their careers in stores and, as I travel around our business, I am constantly impressed by the calibre and experience of the colleagues I meet, from a very diverse range of backgrounds. Tesco is a powerful engine of social mobility and creating opportunities for colleagues to get on in their careers is a focus for us at every level of our business.'

Principle centred leadership

In his book *The Seven Habits of Highly Effective People* (1989), Stephen Covey suggested:

> 'The basic task of leadership is to increase the standard of living and the quality of life for all stakeholders'

In the context of the development of strategy, this can be seen to epitomise what is required from effective strategic leadership. It recognises the need for change, it recognises that what is required is an improvement on the 'today' position, and it recognises that there will be a range of stakeholders.

The reason for including this as an example of a model of strategic leadership is, however, that Covey then expanded his thoughts on leadership in his next book, *Principle-Centred Leadership* (1992). This suggests four core dimensions that are required to be an effective leader: security, guidance, **power** and wisdom. These can each be aligned with our concepts of strategic thinking, and are simplified in the diagram and comments below.

power
The ability of an individual or organisation to persuade, induce or coerce others into following a certain course of action.

Figure 3.2
(Covey, *Principle-Centered Leadership*, 1992) adapted by Mark Wearden)

1. **Security**
    –   A strategic leader will need to be secure in their own knowledge and their ability to lead others.
    –   As a principle, a strategic leader must maintain their own professional ability and integrity through relevant continual learning and the ability to find a safe route through the conflicting views of others.

2. **Guidance**
    –   Other people will look to a strategic leader for guidance. As suggested above, the nature of being a leader is to have followers, and those followers will need to be helped in finding the right path forward.
    –   As a principle, a strategic leader must develop the ability to

communicate with the different parties who will be looking to them for guidance and have sufficient breadth of awareness to guide others in the optimal strategic direction.

3. **Power**
   - Being seen by others as a guide will give the strategic leader significant power over the lives and path of other people (all stakeholders as Covey suggests).
   - As a principle, a strategic leader must learn how to use that power for the benefit of the individual, the team and the task (this can be linked to the John Adair concept in Figure 3.1) as the strategic leader will be influencing all three.

4. **Wisdom**
   - The real strength of this Covey concept comes from the recognition that wisdom is a fundamental part of being an effective strategic leader. Followers will assume that the leader is making the right decisions for the right reason; if they do not believe this, they will cease to follow; the integrity has been lost.
   - As a principle, a strategic leader must find the time to think before acting and therefore bring their wisdom into their strategic decision making.

Stop and think 3.3

Use your matrix from Stop and Think 3.1: in column 5 (principles) identify which of the principles your selected leader(s) exhibit most clearly, and then consider the need for wisdom in strategic leadership.

Test yourself 3.1

Suggest why Adair's threefold action-centred leadership model is useful in the driving forward of strategy.

The learning organisation
At the outset of his book *The Fifth Discipline*, Peter Senge (2006) recognises that a learning organisation is only possible because an organisation is in itself just a number of people, each on their own personal strategic journey. People by their nature are inquisitive, starting the process of learning from the point of birth and continuing this throughout their lives until the point of death.

The following summary is an introduction to the five-fold approach to achieve systemic thinking, developed in particular by Senge. This will provide sufficient detail for the purposes of your studies and an oversight understanding of how systems thinking is aligned to strategic leadership.

The learning organisation is built from five cumulative stages, and is best viewed as an increasing model.

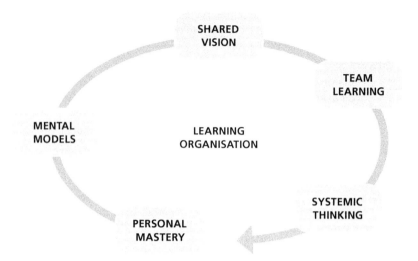

Figure 3.3 The learning organisation
((Senge, 2006) adapted by Mark Wearden)

1. **Personal mastery**
   - The starting point for the development of a learning organisation is a recognition of the individuals who work within the organisation. Each individual should be encouraged to utilise and develop their own particular, unique skill set to the point where they develop a personal mastery of their specific areas of expertise.
   - The strategic leader will need to encourage the development of each person to their own level of potentiality.

2. **Mental models**
   - As each individual develops a personal mastery of their specific areas of focus and expertise, so they need to be encouraged to develop mental models. This requires the ability to visualise a combination of the 'today' and the 'future' with regard to each aspect. What does it look like now, and what could it look like in the future?
   - These mental models can be very varied, and the individual should be encouraged to explore and model in their mind anything which is remotely practical; and even perhaps what seems impractical. This approach will stretch the mind of the individual and stretch the potential for the organisation by encouraging individuals to build a holistic vision which can be explained to others.
   - The strategic leader will delight in enabling others to begin to develop diverse mental models.

3. **Shared vision**
   - An organisation will never make progress if all it consists of is a number of highly motivated individuals; even if these individuals have been

encouraged to develop a personal mastery which has then been enhanced by the visualisation of mental models.

- Each individual needs to be encouraged to develop their communication ability to share their vision and their mental models with others. This will not just happen by chance. This organisational learning needs capturing from the individuals and sharing.

- The sharing process can be just between those individuals who are on this learning path, but more usefully from an organisational development perspective it is good at this stage to involve a wider group of people. Firstly, it will embed the mental models within a wider reality. Secondly, it will encourage others to also begin to develop their own mastery and mental models.

- The strategic leader will facilitate the sharing process through workshops and other such events, and ensuring the involvement of all appropriate stakeholders.

4. **Team learning**

- Having begun to share the vision, or more correctly to share a range of very often quite disparate visions, a natural process of team learning will emerge. Individuals who have developed a personal mastery of a particular area or skill will quite often be challenged through the sharing and explanation of their vision, and their initial lack of comprehension of others.

- This team learning stage, with regard to any subject, can be exciting, challenging, and often emotional at the same time. If an individual becomes determined to succeed in their own personal mastery, imagine how much stronger this desire for success will be from a team of people with a shared vision.

- The strategic leader needs to establish the boundaries and ensure that action follows.

5. **Systemic thinking**

- The final stage in the evolution of a learning organisation approach is the emergence of systems thinking. Senge calls this stage 'systemic thinking', which implies a more constant interrogative approach now being taken by the empowered group team.

- The strategic leader will need to bring together the individual, team and task to focus on strategic outcomes. There is a further discussion in section 3.5 below.

Stop and think 3.4

Using your matrix from Stop and think 3.1: in column 6 (learning) consider the people's strategic leadership from a learning organisation perspective – how near to systemic thinking does their strategic leadership move?

Case study 3.3

GSK use their scientific baseline for measuring their strategic direction, driven by their learning culture.

Extract from GSK plc Annual Report and Financial Statements 2017:

'Our ambition is to drive a high-performance culture, putting science at the heart of GSK, remaining true to our values and our purpose: to help people do more, feel better, live longer.'

Test yourself 3.2

Identify the six skills that Schoemaker suggests are needed for successful strategic leadership.

3. Systems and strategy

What do you think of when you read or hear the word 'system'? The Oxford English Dictionary (OED) provides a wide and disparate range of potential meanings, but with a common underlying theme of 'order' or 'structure':

> system
> - A set of things working together as parts of a mechanism or an interconnecting network; a complex whole.
> - A set of principles or procedures according to which something is done; an organised scheme or method.
> - The prevailing political or social order, especially when regarded as oppressive and intransigent.

The word 'system' is noted by the OED as one of the top 1,000 words in most common use within the English language. This frequency of use, or misuse, is in itself one of the causes of confusion. When a word has such a multiplicity of meanings and is in such frequent use, it leads to presumption within the human brain.

Systems thinking, and systems theory, is used to underpin a range of different academic and practical challenges, but in today's 21st century world it is estimated that 99% of people hearing the word 'system' would assume the involvement of computers, when in reality computers are merely a facet of both the word and the meaning.

As a starting point for your thinking, try the following exercise.

Stop and think 3.5

Take a typical day and start to build a list of all of the systems that surround our existence.

For example:

1. **the system within the alarm clock that wakes me**

2. **the system which controls my electric kettle**

3. **the network system of the utility companies enabling water, gas and electricity to reach my house.**

Each one of these can justifiably be categorised as a system, and each of these has been developed, and continues to change through the strategic leadership of the very different people involved within keeping the system active.

The development of strategy requires us to *stop*, *pause* and *think*.

Amidst increasing levels of complexity, and constant change, how is intelligent, viable and sustainable strategy developed? This section will suggest a few further tools to help in our quest. Remember that all such models need the application of wisdom to ensure that they are being tailored to fit a particular set of circumstances – rarely can we simply apply a textbook tool or model directly into a workplace scenario.

As a further reminder of our core starting point, we are looking to move from the known position of *today*, across the chasm of the unknown, towards our vision of the *future*.

3.1 Building a SWOT analysis of 'today'

One of the core tools in use to acquire a better understanding of the realities of the today position is referred to as a SWOT analysis. By identifying, considering and challenging the interaction of strengths, weaknesses, opportunities and threats we are able to ensure that we have a comprehensive understanding of why today looks like today, why the business is performing in the way that it is performing, why people behave in the way they behave. Each of these four aspects of an organisation, both singly and combined, are often an invaluable checkpoint, on the basis that today is always an exact reality, and that it will have changed since the last time it was reviewed.

The SWOT analysis is normally portrayed in the form of matrix, although it is possible simply to list out the various elements. The advantage of using matrix is the visual impact of seeing different aspects aligned against each other, as suggested in the figure below.

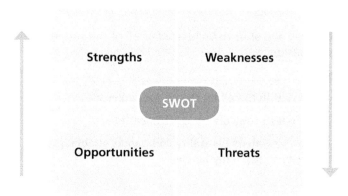

Figure 3.4 SWOT analysis
© Mark Wearden

The strengths and weaknesses of an organisation are predominantly based around the internal drivers, whereas the opportunities and threats are predominantly based around external drivers. The arrows at either side suggest the likely direction of travel – if an opportunity is taken it can become a strength, if a weakness is not resolved it can become a threat.

Many organisations simply use this model to identify and recognise these different four aspects of their status quo, but the real advantage of developing a comprehensive and vibrant SWOT approach to business analysis and **review** is to understand:

review
A process by which any aspect of the strategic journey is considered to enable an evaluation of progress and/or fulfilment: a plan will often include a pre-emptive review process to ensure that progress is considered at key points.

- how the *strengths* are able to combat the weaknesses and avoid them becoming *threats*
- how the optimal strategic *opportunities* can be identified and be turned into *strengths* within the organisation
- how the *strengths*, either existing or through realisation of opportunity, can be used to mitigate the *threats*.

It is common to find that any particular aspect of an organisation can appear in one or more boxes of the matrix, and sometimes all four boxes. An example could be the liquidity of an organisation at a given moment in time:

- cash in the bank could be seen as a *strength*
- delayed payment of cash to suppliers could be seen as a *weakness* (even though this results in a higher bank balance)
- the ability to borrow cash in a low interest rate market could be seen as an *opportunity*
- the risk of a customer who owes cash (a debtor) going into liquidation could be seen as a *threat*.

These four scenarios will always exist in juxtaposition at any given moment in time.

To compile and effectively use a SWOT analysis, there are a few simple rules:

◆ Ensure that the analysis is focused and brief – it is often good to restrict each segment to an equal maximum number of aspects, either five or nine are good benchmarks.

◆ Each point should be restricted to a relatively small number of words. This means that the point has to have been considered before including it in the analysis.

◆ Relative positioning within the matrix, particularly with regard to strength and weakness, can be important.

◆ The completed analysis should be used for debate, challenge and brainstorming within the organisation.

◆ There is a need for timely and recent data and information.

◆ There should be a consistent approach each time the SWOT analysis is undertaken and communicated.

3.2 Basic environmental considerations

In our development of strategy, we will recognise quickly that we are able to control internal aspects of our organisation (the *strengths* and *weaknesses*) far more readily than we are able to control the external aspects (the *opportunities* and *threats*).

Chapter 4 will expand our thinking about the external environment to consider different ways of analysing and considering the impact upon our strategy. At this stage we simply need to understand the difference between the micro-environment and the macro-environment, both of which will influence our strategic thinking:

◆ The *micro-environment*, often called the near environment, is external to the organisation but is relatively close, and is often seen as something that should be considered closely in our strategic thinking.

  – To use the example of liquidity again, if we needed additional cash in our business and interest rates were low as suggested in the SWOT analysis above, we should be able to negotiate an appropriate loan with our bank assuming we have the wherewithal to meet their terms and conditions. This is an external structure and force, but the basic dynamics will be within our negotiating control.

◆ The *macro-environment*, often called the far environment, is external to the organisation but is much further away than the micro-environment, and usually outside our direct control.

  – To continue the example of liquidity, a major financial crisis, a central bank deciding to significantly increase interest rates, the increasing of taxation on customers, or other such events would be outside our control but could have a significant impact on the business.

3.3 Resource consideration

As we develop our strategy, we need to always be taking a realistic position based around the resources that are currently available, or those that we believe we can obtain. It is important to ensure that we base our strategic thinking around reality rather than an unachievable vision. This is often referred to as determining an appropriate 'operational fit'.

The resources that we require will form the input to our operational flow and are identified in the next section on supply chain thinking as people, capital, material and knowledge.

Although listed in separate sections, all of these aspects are required to work together within a development of organisational strategy. A common mistake that organisations make is to use one such tool or model in isolation.

It should now be apparent that the use of the SWOT is effectively looking at the resources that are available and their respective strengths and weaknesses, while also identifying external influences upon these. All of these greatly influence the overall supply chain of the organisation.

3.4 Supply chain thinking

To think strategically, one must be able to understand and assess the strategic significance of the three underpinning aspects of an organisational supply chain: *inputs*, *transformation* and *outputs*.

Figure 3.5 Supply Chain
© Mark Wearden

Inputs are separated into four categories with key strategic questions:

◆ **People**
- Who are the key decision-makers, who do we rely upon, who are the initiators?
- Is it clear how the cost of people (very often the largest single operational cost of an organisation) is used to drive strategic value within the supply chain?

◆ **Capital**

  – Is the short-term working financial position sustainable and what can challenge it?

  – Is the longer-term strategic financial structure appropriate for the organisation?

◆ **Material**

  – Which suppliers are fundamental to the existence as a viable organisation?

  – Do we build strategic relationships with suppliers to ensure inbound supplies?

◆ **Knowledge**

  – Where does the strategic thinking and planning power reside, who are the real thinkers?

  – Is appropriate use made of the brains of the people within the organisation?

Transformation is the point of strategic differentiation from the competition. Every organisation that is successful has its unique selling point (USP). This is how an organisation is differentiated from its competitors, and from the marketplace as a whole. Everyone will know immediately what is meant by an 'iPhone' or a 'Mac' or the name 'Nike' or 'Starbucks'.

It is suggested here that the USP of any organisation is a transformation process; the organisation has the ability to take its inputs and transform them into outputs which can then be sold to either a customer or a consumer.

The consumer is at the extreme end of a supply chain, ultimately using the product or service. A customer is simply the next link within a supply chain; that customers' customer might be the consumer or might be yet another customer.

◆ What does the transformation look like, how will the customer or consumer recognise the benefits and purpose?

◆ Who are the key people involved?

◆ Which aspect of the 'inputs' is fundamental to achieving the USP?

◆ Does the organisation's strategy recognise how it builds sustainability into its USP?

Outputs to the customer or consumer end of the supply chain are the ultimate drivers of value and successful delivery of strategy. Whatever it is that is created through the transformation of the inputs, we need to have a clear vision of who the product or service is aimed at.

The requirement and expectations for directors of listed and other large companies to issue a longer-term viability statement will require an awareness of the strategic answers to customer-based questions. If an organisation does not know who will buy its products or services, how can it assert viability?

There is a close relationship between 'supply chain thinking' and the 'today'–'future' model. If the strategic direction of an organisation is being led effectively, then the supplier base should form part of the known aspects of 'today'; the 'future' is our aspiration to satisfy the customer; the transition is the 'route' between the two.

If you build these basic conceptual models into your thinking, you will find it easier to apply and challenge the range of specific scenarios and more complex concepts that we will be considering in the remaining chapters of the text, and the strategic decisions that face you every day, as your plans have to change.

Test yourself 3.3

A pharmaceutical company employs a team of expert scientists to create a new drug. Suggest briefly why this team, jointly or individually, might appear in each of the four aspects of a SWOT analysis.

3.5   Systems thinking

Through this section different approaches to viewing an organisation as a system have been considered. This final section of this part will take a more academic view of what it takes to make a system work efficiently. There is a close relationship between this concept and the systemic thinking aspect of the 'learning organisation' referred to above from Peter Senge's book *The Fifth Discipline* (2006).

The fundamental nature of any system is that, at any moment in its existence, it is a structure which is definable, with a presumed modus operandi, a recognisable external parameter, an initiating force to enable it to operate, and an anticipated outcome or range of outcomes.

Any system will have a number of constituent parts, and O'Connor and McDermott (1997) suggest that 'a system is an entity that maintains its existence and functions as a whole through the interaction of its parts'.

This helps us when we start to interrogate what is really meant by a 'system'. It is clear that there are three core constituents to a system:

- the whole
- the parts
- the connections between the parts.

This is close to an understanding of the basics of mathematics which uses symbols (numbers), relationships between the symbols (incrementation) and operators which affect the symbols (+, −, ×, / etc.). Each of these three aspects (symbols, relationships and operators) can then have properties which affect them jointly and severally. These principles are not just the basis of mathematics, but also the basis of all computing.

This leads us to a comprehension that a system as an entity must, in some way, rely upon the way that the parts work together, and hence our first foray into one of the differentiators of a systems thinking approach.

In the world of mechanistic thinking, driven by Aristotelian logic (syllogism), effect is a straight-line result of cause:

> 1 + 1 will equal 2; the whole will always be the sum of the parts.

In the world of systems thinking:

> 1 + 1 might equal 2, but then it might equal 3 or 1 or something totally different when placed in context; the whole will always be greater than the sum of the parts (in perspective rather than necessarily size).

Stop and think 3.6

I am asked to write a short report for stakeholders explaining the rationale for the values of the organisation. I think about it and write the report.

I understand what I have written and why – Aristotelian logic.

I present the report to the directors and allow open discussion. To my surprise, there are many views different to my own view, and through debate we arrive at a different report to be sent to our stakeholders.

Why is the whole greater than the sum of the parts?

The practical approach towards systemic analysis recommended in this section will enable you to analyse any type of system within an organisation, from a small structured process to a much larger complete business structure. As professionals, we often need to be able to make a rapid assessment of many different aspects of an organisation. We have to recognise the realities of the today position, and at the same time be able to visualise the risks as the organisation moves towards the future. We need to understand how the system is working. This will better enable us to really understand why the system goes wrong, when it inevitably does go wrong. This is the basis of 'management by exception' and 'gap analysis':

- It will enable a focused and disciplined method to describe the business 'models' which sit above and behind the system.
- If you are required to produce a business model for your annual reporting, or for internal purposes, this methodology will focus your mind.
- In a wider context, it is a methodology which can significantly help in the writing of a board paper or other report, and also help in the building of a coherent presentation.

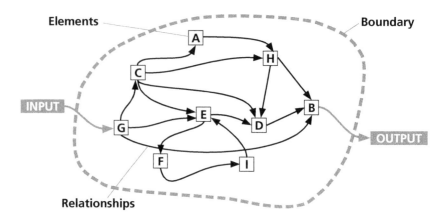

Figure 3.6 A system structure
© Mark Wearden

Stage 1: draw the boundary
The boundary represents the extremities of the system or structure that we are going to consider. It is necessary to recognise this boundary, and to recognise:

◆   what stimulates action within the boundary – the *input*
◆   what is the intended result of the activity that takes place within the boundary – the *output*.

Stage 2: identify the elements
These are the core facets within any system boundary; they may be people, they may be documents; they may be processes; they may be questions that need answering before continuing. It is useful to use a one or two-word descriptor for each element.

Stage 3: establish the relationships
It is then important to consider the positioning of, and the linkages between, the elements.

The diagram in Figure 3.6 suggests only a potential set of relationships:

◆   note the importance of curved arrows, rather than straight arrows
◆   note that linkages can be iterated
◆   note that we may need to force our brain to rethink some of the earlier concepts before reaching our output.

Case study 3.4

Determining the boundary

A company will have many different levels of systems thinking. In each of the following two scenarios a system of elements and relationships would need to operate effectively.

Macro boundary	Micro boundary
You are a director on the board of a FTSE100 company. The government requires you to comply with a range of new statute law. This could be seen as the *input*; the *output* would be the tangible proof through reporting and practice that your organisation operates within the law. The directors need to understand not just the *input* (the requirement) and the *output* (the reporting), but also to have assured themselves that the perceived and portrayed output is genuine.	The board of directors have asked the audit committee to review and consider a particular aspect of risk regarding payment of expenses. The *input* is now the detail of the board request; the *output* will be the report on that particular aspect of risk applicable regarding the payment of expenses back from the audit committee to the full board of directors.

Apart from the clarity of thinking that it delivers, the purpose of a systems diagram, such as Figure 3.6, is to allow systemic analysis when 'things go wrong'. When there is a problem in the operation of the system, it is possible to use the systems diagram to consider which of the relationships is failing. It is unlikely that the model, or business as a whole is at fault, it is very likely that there is a disconnect, or incorrect relationship between two or more elements.

In the following example from the UK rail industry, it is clear that those involved in the planning had lost sight of all of the relevant connections between the various parts of the railway network, as a holistic system.

Case study 3.5

Extract from 'UK rail service disruption', FT.com, 20 September 2018 (www.ft.com/content/803d57b8-bc27-11e8-94b2-17176fbf93f5):

'Severe disruption to train services after timetabling changes on lines operated by Govia Thameslink Railway and Northern was caused by an "apparent gap" in responsibility and accountability for managing systemic risks, according to the industry regulator.

The Office of Rail and Road said that during preparation for introducing new timetables in May, the industry had placed engineering and planning concerns ahead of serving passengers. "That was made worse by the poor information train operators provided when disruption happened".

The study found that problems caused by delays to electrification schemes by Network Rail were magnified by attempts to make up time. The report also said the Department for Transport and the regulator did not sufficiently question assurances they received from the rail industry on the risk of disruption stemming from the timetabling changes.

The transport secretary told the BBC "The reality is it is not about ownership, it's about the pressure on the system. I'm not going to point fingers at individuals today, it's a system problem, it's the way the whole industry works, that's what the review says."'

4. People and strategy

This brief section helps to identify and consider the differing roles that we would normally see within an organisational structure for people who are involved in the development of strategy.

Despite the common belief that strategy must be led from the top, we have already suggested that the development of strategy involves more than just the directors or managers of the business – they may formulate strategy, but rarely do they become engaged in its direct achievement.

The following sections, together with further references later in the text, suggest a common perceived framework. Every organisation is slightly different in its structure, and its mixture of people and roles, so there are many crossovers in the way this will appear in different contexts. The best that can be achieved from a generic perspective is to establish a set of parameters or benchmarks for the anticipated involvement of different people in the development of strategy.

4.1 Strategy from the top

The board of directors of an organisation are appointed by the shareholders and/or stakeholders to ensure that the business is run operationally with the intention of achieving the strategic objectives desired by those owners. In the UK, Companies Act 2006 s172 gives each director a duty to strive towards the 'success' of the company. This has to therefore mean that each director is in some way involved with the establishment and oversight of strategy within the organisation. This forms part of what is generally known as governance of an organisation.

Chapter 7 will give a far more detailed consideration of governance, the leadership of strategy and the roles of different people and stakeholders; in these initial considerations of how strategy is developed, it is sufficient to suggest that there will be some differentiation between the establishment and oversight of strategy (governance) and the day-to-day delivery of the strategic objectives (operation). In small organisations these aspects are generally carried out by the same people, but in larger organisations there are often two quite distinct groups of people, but with the common denominator of a chief executive officer (CEO), a person who will normally have a dual accountability within the organisation.

Lynch (2015) suggests that:

> 'Strategic leadership is the ability to shape the organisation's decisions and deliver high value over time, not only personally but also by inspiring and managing others in the organisation. That leadership begins with the top management team – chief executive officer, other leading directors and, in large companies, the leading divisional directors'

In many organisations the CEO is seen as the chief strategist with ultimate responsibility and ownership of all strategic decisions, and full accountability for its success or failure. It is certainly true that a significant percentage of time will be spent by all CEOs in the formulation and delivery of strategy. Montgomery (2008) suggests that 'a CEO must be the steward of a living strategy that defines what the firm is and what it will become', but of course the CEO is only ever a person with the same time/resource constraint as all other people.

There is significant danger to any organisation when its strategy is too closely aligned, on a personal level, with the character and work of the CEO. Success in such circumstances can lead to significant overconfidence. The strategic viability of the organisation is then perceived as being aligned entirely to the person of the CEO. While in small private companies this is very difficult to avoid, in a large public company, investors may often be led to buy or sell shares based around the character of the CEO rather than the successful operation (or otherwise) of the organisation.

Case study 3.6

Cancer Research UK places significance on strategic leadership skills throughout the organisation.

Extract from Cancer Research UK Annual Report and Financial Statements 2017/2018:

'Creating inspiring leaders and exceptional talent across the Charity is key to what we do. We are focused on nurturing and developing our employees and have launched a core development programme for all covering skills critical to our success. We provide our leaders with regular feedback through our Manager Insight Survey, and we have refreshed our manager development programme as well as providing specific tailored development to our most senior leaders.'

At a wider level, the risk of top-down strategy is epitomised well in the Chinese saying, 'The fish rots from the head'. Garratt (2010) uses this saying as the title of a book in which he discusses how ultimately the success or failure of strategy will depend upon the performance and/or leadership of the board of directors and senior management in an organisation.

The significance of the board of directors and its various roles in the formulation and oversight of strategy will be discussed further in Chapter 7.

4.2   Strategy from within

Throughout an organisation, many people with management responsibility will also contribute to the development of strategy. Very often people within the organisation are only viewed as being accountable for the working out and implementation of strategy. The reality, of course, is that the day-to-day decisions that are required in any organisation mean that people are constantly having to react to the internal and external forces that surround them. The decisions that they make may be guided by the strategic parameters established by others, but the direct impact of their decisions will inevitably influence strategic outcome, and therefore strategic direction of an organisation.

The suggestion here is that anybody within an organisation who has some aspect of decision-making within their role is also contributing in some way to the strategy of the organisation. While there is not the time to formally involve all people within the strategic development process, appropriate communication structures and a culture of inclusion will ensure that a wide range of differing views are heard by those with the ultimate responsibility for the longer-term development of strategy; this type of culture will be discussed further in Chapter 6 below.

The deliberate involvement of people can bring some immediately apparent advantages:

◆   people working within the organisation have a much greater knowledge of the day-to-day pressures of the operation

◆   people will find workable solutions to ensure a task is achieved

◆   people are always working at the latest 'today' position as opposed to the point where an original strategy was established

◆   people will bring momentum to the strategic success of an operational activity

◆   people will be more motivated to help when they recognise that the development of the strategy has involved others who are directly involved in and understand the requirements.

The downside of allowing too much strategic involvement from within the organisation can be:

◆   a lack of understanding of a wider strategic vision from within the organisation

◆   a lack of confidential information that is required to understand the longer-term vision

◆   the risk of negative and inappropriate reaction to short-term operational and task failure.

Different departments and influencers within an organisation will be able to contribute at particular points to the effective development of strategy:

◆   The finance department will have a key role at the outset of the development of a strategy in ensuring the appropriateness of required funding, will also act as a useful sense checker as the strategy involves, and finally will be able to provide a financial measurement of success based around key performance indicators.

◆ The human resources (HR) department will need to ensure that the appropriate people are in place at the outset of the strategy and throughout the life of the strategy, ensuring that appropriate succession plans are in place so that strategic failure is not caused by lack of appropriate people and knowledge. HR can be a useful source of people being available to objectively listen and react to feedback.

◆ External consultants or experts may be required on an ad hoc basis to supplement existing employees to satisfy particular, or complicated short-term requirements both in the initial formulation of a strategy and potentially at key points throughout its evolution.

◆ The company secretary and other governance professionals can play an important part in the strategy process, dependent upon how the position is formulated and viewed within a particular organisation. Research commissioned by ICSA: The Governance Institute in 2014 suggested a number of key roles for the company secretary:

  – the provision of an independent link between directors, chair and the chief executive

  – the objective facilitation of information gathering and the alignment of different interests

  – the observation of directors and others within meetings, identifying areas of weakness and training need

  – the building of an independent oversight and history of strategic successes and failures.

4.3   Conflicts of interest, the 'agency problem' and information asymmetry

Conflicts of interest

If we consider the range of different personalities that we have identified as being involved in the formulation of strategy within an organisation, it is understandable that there will often be conflicts of interest within an organisation.

This might be as simple as people quite justifiably taking diametrically opposed views of a particular opportunity situation, or it might be an individual seeking to gain personally from influencing a strategic decision in a particular direction.

In the UK the expected behaviour and duties of directors of limited companies with regard to conflicts of interest are covered substantively within Companies Act 2006.

Declared conflicts are managed usually through using a control mechanism such as a register of conflicts and managing the conflict itself. Should there be a conflict of interest, it does not mean that the person with that conflict cannot be involved in the process, it means that the conflict itself has to be managed.

Conflicts such as those involving family members or business associates or people with personal stakes are usually manged by the person with the conflict not being permitted to be involved in the decision making of that particular aspect.

Agency

One area for further consideration within the context of Development of Strategy is known as the *agency* problem. This perceived and actual problem is derived from the representative roles that are often taken by decision-makers within an organisation, and the fact that their personal beliefs may be in conflict with the role that they are expected to fulfil.

Does a director act primarily in their own interests or in the interests of the owners of the company? Further, in a large public company, is it possible to assume that there is a common ownership interest?

Worked example 3.1

Two executive directors within a company have no ownership of shares in the company. Their contractual remuneration consists of a market-aligned base salary together with the potential to earn a significant bonus each year based upon achieving certain financial targets within each financial year.

Many of the strategic plans, order lines, production processes and operational activities run across a number of financial years.

The natural human drive will be to maximise performance within each year to satisfy their remuneration targets and expectations, even if those in-year targets do not necessarily satisfy the longer-term strategic expectations or opportunities.

The resolution to the scenario above is to ensure that remuneration is more closely aligned with longer-term strategic objectives. The reality is that there will often be a disconnect between the mindset, needs and expectations of an individual strategic influencer, and those of other stakeholders. Organisations need to recognise this reality and seek to develop strategy to avoid the risk of conflicted individual influence whenever possible.

Asymmetry

One further aspect of conflict is known as information *asymmetry* and reflects the differing levels of information, and therefore knowledge, that are available to different players within the development of strategy.

A board director will usually have a wide knowledge and awareness of the ultimate strategic objectives of the organisation, but will often be lacking in an awareness of the short-term day-to-day decisions that are required to enable the progression of an operational activity.

A shift leader in a busy factory will have a keen awareness of what is required to fulfil the expectations of the operational output from the shift, and how best to motivate the team to fulfil that short-term objective. Unless they also have some other involvement within the organisation, it is unlikely that they will be able to place the direct operational objective of an individual shift within the context of the wider strategic objectives of the organisation.

At any stage within the 'game' of evolving strategy within an organisation, individual players will have an awareness of the information they need to know to fulfil their immediate objectives – this does not mean that they will have the same level of information as other players in the game.

4.4 Initial stakeholder considerations

In Chapter 7 there will be a wider consideration of how to determine and fulfil the varying expectations of stakeholders, but here we will briefly consider the principle of being a stakeholder and the influence that will be brought by core stakeholder groups upon the strategic development process:

- What does it mean to be a stakeholder in an organisation?
    - The term 'stakeholder' implies the input of a 'stake' (an interest, an investment, an involvement of some sort) into the organisation. If the involvement was purely philanthropic then there would be no expectation of any return, but the nature of holding a 'stake' implies the expectation of some sort of return or counter-action from the organisation in response to the involvement.
- Owners as stakeholders
    - Expect the organisation to fulfil their ownership objectives, such as profit or market-share;
    - may have a financial investment and therefore will expect a financial return (an owner buying shares will be anticipating a dividend and/or an increase in share price);
    - may have a range of other expected success factors which will need to form part of the strategic vision such as an environmental or societal benefit.
- Employees as stakeholders
    - Expect remuneration in line with their contractual terms, together with a range of other potential employment benefits;
    - invest their time, knowledge and efforts in the organisation to achieve their return;
    - as already discussed, the diversity of employees, and their varying needs, abilities and expectations will have a significant influence in strategic planning and development.
- Customers as stakeholders
    - Expect their product or service requirements to be fulfilled by the organisation;
    - rely upon the organisation to fulfil their contractual expectations through investing belief in the ability of the organisation to deliver, and then ultimately paying for the product or service they have received;

- – the need to fulfil customer expectations has to form a core part of strategic planning; without a customer there is no organisational purpose.
- ◆ Other supply chain stakeholders
  - – Expect satisfaction from the organisation based around the differing input; suppliers of raw material will expect to be paid in accordance with their contract, a bank will expect to receive interest for a loan payable at a pre-agreed date, the government will expect to receive taxation as it falls due;
  - – each different supply chain stakeholder will have a different stake within the organisation;
  - – the ability to satisfy each of these stakes and their contractual obligations needs to be taken into consideration as the strategy is developed.

5. Strategic actions

The phrase 'strategic action' is broadly used to define any and all activities that follow from the planning and development of strategy. At the start of Chapter 1 strategies was defined as a combination of knowledge and capability – the knowledge allows us to imagine and visualise the future, the capability gives us the power and ability to implement our ideas and plans.

Much of the rest of this text concerns the structures, forces, tools and implications of taking strategic action. As with the development of the strategic plan, at each stage of action we need to have clarity as to what it is that we hope we will achieve. This could be defined under three headings:

- ◆ Improvement: something that we intend to do more effectively.
- ◆ Innovation: something different that we need to do, usually involving an improvement in technology or systems.
- ◆ Improvisation: something where we need to interpret what is happening and react accordingly.

To set the rest of the text in the context of this chapter, it will be useful to briefly outline a number of core strategic actions.

5.1 Analysis

A significant amount of students' study and learning, together with a material amount of the time they spend working, in whatever role they find themselves, will either deliberately or inadvertently be spent in strategic analysis.

- ◆ Analysis can be *formal* and part of a defined process within the development of strategy.
  - – One might need to understand the full extent of a current marketplace before they decide whether it is a realistic opportunity for their organisation.

◆ Analysis can also be *informal* and require immediate attention.

– Yesterday's output was 10% below expectations – what has been the cause of this?

You can see that both of these examples will have a strategic impact upon the organisation, and both will require that same analytical brain activity. When viewed as a single isolated activity, the approach to the required analysis can seem quite straightforward, however in an organisation many strategic analyses are required on an ongoing basis, both formal and informal. Most organisations will have a project control function which can be as simple as a spreadsheet on which project priority is established and all required future strategies can be controlled and managed.

The process of deciding how to allocate appropriate resource to such analytical activities becomes a core part of the strategic plan. If this need is ignored, it is likely to cause long-term damage to the strategic development of the organisation. However, the reverse is also true – if too much time and resource is spent purely on analysis rather than action, then equal long-term damage is likely to follow, other opportunities can be lost and unrecoverable costs incurred.

Throughout this text there are a plethora of tools and structural models designed to help in the analysis process but remember that these always need using within the context of a particular scenario. They will have been originally developed to resolve or challenge a particular set of organisational circumstances and will need adjusting and reconsidering in the light of a different set of circumstances – even within the same organisation.

5.2 Determining strategic direction

The long-term strategic direction of any organisation will consist of a number of related parts:

◆ the vision of the future (as already discussed in Chapters 1 to 3) which needs to be built into a range of differing organisational forces and influences

◆ the limitations and opportunities offered by the external environment in alignment with the internal capabilities (discussed in Chapters 4 and 5)

◆ the culture, ideology and governance of the organisation (which will be discussed in detail in Chapters 6 to 9)

◆ the ability to choose alternative routes (Chapters 10 and 11)

◆ the control and management of the strategic direction (Chapters 12 and 13)

◆ the management and implementation of change (Chapters 14 and 15).

The strategic direction taken by an organisation will involve a plethora of decisions about how the organisation wishes to develop over time. If the ultimate strategic vision is relatively short-term (less than five years) the direction is likely to be reasonably visualised at the outset, even if inevitably it is altered during the journey. In a longer-term vision, anything other than long-term contractual performance criteria, perhaps based around perceived manufacturing or delivery time, will be very hard to define with any precision.

The strategic direction will be based around a number of different criteria, not least measures which will determine the success or failure of the vision; these of course can be personal and will alter from person to person.

Eisenhardt (1990) suggested that there are a number of helpful guidelines for managers with regard to their strategic direction:

◆   Managers should always consider building a number of simultaneous alternatives to enable both contrast and criticism; as with many other such situations within corporate life there should always be at least two alternatives to consider.

◆   In a fast-moving environment, it is important that real-time information is captured and its impact upon the strategic direction is considered, monitored and recorded.

◆   The strategic leaders need to look for the views of advisers and specialists – this will bring an external unbiased consideration of the situation.

◆   The objective should be consensus, but at times it is necessary for the person, or people who have ultimate responsibility to take decisions to enable the strategic direction to be maintained; and for those decision-makers to take accountability for the strategic impact.

5.3   Mapping of strategy, route and resource

As we leave the known facts of 'today' and head into the unknown territory of the 'future', we need to have a map of the route we intend to take across the chasm of change that faces us. We will consider the subject of strategy mapping in greater detail in Chapter 11.

Stop and think 3.7

At this point, place this into context – imagine you live in London but need to go to a five-hour meeting in Manchester starting at 10am.

You can define your today position – you know where you are now, you can plan your intended route and mode of transport, you can leave at the required time. If you are going by train, you will have an anticipated schedule; if you are driving, you will have either looked at a map or be reliant upon your satellite navigation system; in each case you will have pre-planned how long you anticipate your journey will take, you know the resources that you require and you can set off upon your journey from the known territory of today into the future meeting at 10am.

Without going into a plethora of unnecessary detail, it is easy to imagine how rapidly your map and your anticipated route can be changed – weather, delays, roadworks etc.

Take the above analogy and place it into a corporate context. At least part of the purpose of studying the subject of strategy is to enable you, the Chartered Secretary and Chartered Governance Professional, to be ready to map the route, identify the resource, understand the anticipated destination, anticipate risks along the route, and then to be prepared to alter everything based upon the impact of external and internal forces.

5.4   Optimising communication

We need to consider communication from two perspectives – the *individual* and the *organisation* (a collection of individuals).

The individual

There has been significant medical research into the way in which the human brain works and communicates. This has particular significance today in the attempts to enable the reproduction of such functionality through computer driven artificial intelligence and robotics. This has often been represented by medical research as the difference between left and right brain thinking.

- **Left brain thinking** being the normal day-to-day logical, subconscious reactions which allow us to function in our day-to-day lives.
  - Someone who tends to just accept things as they are, could be described as having a dominant left-brain attitude.
- **Right brain thinking** being the lateral, creative abilities which lie within each of us.
  - The type of person who is always challenging could be described as having a dominant right-brain attitude.

Of course, in neither case, does that exclude us from regularly using both perceived sides of the brain. That is required to be a human being, otherwise we would never be able to deal with the unexpected.

The way in which we are perceived by others as using our brains will influence our behaviour, and therefore we move into a constant iteration – we behave in a certain way, that is perceived in a certain way, we react and therefore behave in a slightly different way, and this continues. Refer back to Chapter 1 and the brief consideration of the 'ladder of inference' originated by Chris Argyris (1990).

As an individual human being, we will receive a multiplicity of incoming communication – our brains will deal with what is relevant to us at that point and store the rest.

The organisation (a collection of individuals)

As soon as we move away from a single brain, we have to deal with a multiplicity of different 'ladders of inference' and of differing left/right brain approaches.

All of our consideration of strategy, planning, strategic management and the process of developing strategy becomes a futile individual act unless we are able to communicate the vision, the starting point and the route. Unless people understand the strategy, it is unlikely that it will ever be achieved.

Stage 1 – reality

◆ Every human being will interpret received communication in their own unique manner.

◆ Established behaviour is hard to change (refer to Chapters 14 and 15).

Stage 2 – core elements

It is necessary for an organisation to develop a strategy towards the communication process itself. Thatcher (2006) suggested that this has four core elements.

◆ **Focus**: what are we really trying to achieve – specifics rather than generalities?

◆ **Impact**: what difference will it make?

◆ **Media**: how do we ensure the right people have the right level of information?

◆ **Engagement**: how do we get people working together?

Consider the closeness of this approach to that of the learning organisation as previously discussed.

As part of its communication strategy, an organisation will need to employ different techniques to deal with different types of message and different behavioural traits of people. Some common approaches are:

◆ **Strategy workshops**

   – An intense and dedicated period of time to allow focus from participants.

   – Participants should not just be the 'top team' but any key player of influencer.

   – Often these are better held away from the organisation to enhance the levels of focus.

   – These can be ad hoc to deal with particular issues, or built into a strategic development programme.

   – They can be invaluable to develop a team learning approach, and to enhance mutual, cross-functional understanding.

   – The commitment of the sponsors must be clear (the senior team, the owners, the customer – whoever is ultimately supporting the project) – members of the workshop will engage far more readily with something which is credible and has integrity.

◆ **Strategy projects and project teams**

   – Develop focused groups for whole or partial strategic tasks.

   – Use a cross-functional approach – never restrict the team to just like-minded people or there will be no challenge.

   – Ensure the parameters of the project, or sub-project are clearly communicated.

    – Do not allow empire-building by dynamic dominant individuals.

◆ **Holistic business case justification**

    – Every strategic project will have a whole-business impact – ensure that the intended impact is clear.

    – The strategic plan must be holistic and cover all business dimensions.

    – The strategic needs must be clearly identified with a transparent awareness of the perceived issues of 'today' and the anticipated issues of the 'future'.

    – Required resources need to be clearly identified, together with their sourcing.

    – The business case needs supporting with personal integrity and auditable data.

    – The meaning of success should be clear, together with likely measures of progress.

Test yourself 3.4

Give three reasons why the particular skills of a company secretary and governance professional can make a significant contribution in the development of strategy.

Chapter summary

◆ This chapter emphasises the importance of effective leadership in the development of strategy.

◆ Leadership is seen as making effective decisions while taking into consideration the individual, the group and the task that has to be completed. This approach is attributed to John Adair.

◆ An effective leader needs to be driven by principles and find the ability to have wisdom in their leadership. This wisdom is the ability to ignore natural bias and use all of the iterative learning at a particular moment in time to step back and reconsider.

◆ The chapter explored in full the five stages of development in a learning organisation and stressed the importance of understanding these stages in the development of effective strategy. It needs to be driven by, understood by, owned by and challenged by the people involved in the organisation.

◆ The core tool of a SWOT analysis introduced with some thoughts on how this tool can be implemented in practice, realising that aspects of an organisation may appear in more than one of the quadrants.

◆ The organisation needs to be segmented into the various 'system' aspects of its supply chain, recognising the links, the different elements and the key drivers.

◆   The need for systemic thinking and systemic analysis was identified to help in our challenge of what we are really trying to achieve with our strategy. Which parts of the system really need to be changed? It is unlikely to be all of it.

◆   The differing roles of people within the organisation and within the strategy development process need to be understood. The company secretary and governance professional can and will be expected to play a key role in this process. The uniqueness of their position often means that they are one of the few people whose role is not conflicted by the strategic challenge, and their objectivity can prove invaluable in the strategic challenge.

Part two

Understanding the external environment

Introduction

The second part of this text takes the core strategic concepts identified within Part one and considers them from two different perspectives. Firstly, from the differing forces of the micro and macro environment. Secondly, from the need to identify the mixture of capabilities and competencies that reside within the organisation to enable the driving of competitive advantage within the external environment.

Overview

Chapter 4 differentiates between the far (macro) environments which an organisation is unlikely to be able to influence, and therefore must just react, and the near (micro) environments where the organisation may have some influence. Two core models for the consideration of strategy are introduced – PESTEL (political, economic, socio-cultural, technological, environmental and legal), and five forces.

Chapter 5 will help students to understand the relationships that exist between resources, capabilities and competencies, and how the optimal alignment can lead to competitive advantage, and the delivery of stakeholder value.

Learning outcomes

At the end of this part, students will be able to:

◆ understand the different operating environments of an organisation;

◆ demonstrate the relevance of undertaking a PESTEL analysis of an organisation;

◆ consider the varying impact of the five forces identified by Michael Porter on organisational positioning;

◆ understand the importance of human influence, opinion and reputation within all aspects of the development of strategy;

◆ demonstrate how resources fuel the capabilities that are needed within any organisation;

◆ comment on how the capabilities can be aligned with competence to drive competitive advantage;

◆ understand different types of competitive advantage and their different organisational impacts; and

◆ demonstrate the need for the company secretary and governance professional to have a holistic understanding of how and where strategy is derived.

Chapter four
The external environment

Contents

1. Introduction

Part one of this text considered the generic concepts which need to be applied to begin to think strategically. It introduced thinking about the forces of 'today', why and how we and our organisations exist, the recognition of our knowledge at a 'today' point, and the need to be able to understand how we have arrived at 'today'. This has been considered in alignment with the reality that most of the future is unknown, and therefore that our development of strategy requires the use of the brilliance of the human brain to create a vision of what we would like the future to look like, based around a starting point of our knowledge of today.

This chapter will begin to consider the development of strategy from a more focused organisational perspective. The same underlying principles that have already been considered will apply, but students will now need to consider strategy in the context of the real-world working environment.

In the introduction to this text as a whole, we briefly considered the VUCA – volatile, uncertain, complex and ambiguous – world in which we live, and in which all of our organisations have to develop, plan and drive their strategy. We know that Taleb's black swans (Taleb, 2010) of the 'unknown unknowns' will one day appear on our organisational radar. While we do not know what they will look like or their potential impact, in our development of strategy we need to have a generic plan of how we will deal with their inevitable emergence.

Case study 4.1

Using the knowledge gained so far in this text and keeping in mind the strategic purpose of GSK and Tesco, consider their 'far' and 'near' operational environments while working through this chapter. Before continuing, consider the similarity and difference between these statements from their respective annual reports.

GSK	TESCO
'By understanding our operating environment and having a clear strategy, against which we measure performance and manage risks, we deliver long-term value for shareholders and society.'	'The strategic drivers are designed to create sustainable value for our four stakeholders in our business: customers, colleagues, supplier partners, and our shareholders.'

2. Analysing the operational environment

Irrespective of the type of organisation that we are considering from a strategic or an operational perspective, it is essential that we consider the breadth and depth of the environment within which an organisation exists. At its simplest level, any organisation is fulfilling a need that exists to bridge a gap between an originating supplier and an ultimate customer.

All organisations have a common business model.

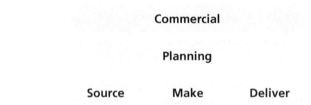

Figure 4.1
© Mark Wearden

◆ We source our knowledge or raw material.

◆ We make or create something using that knowledge or raw material.

◆ We deliver this transformed product or service to a customer.

◆ This structure is only enabled by:
  – planning – strategic consideration of what we hope to achieve
  – commercial reality – how are we going to survive – profitability and funding.

Unless we are the originating source, or the ultimate consumer, we are part of a chain. Even in small businesses this chain can become quite complex; consider how complex these chains can become in large multinational businesses.

Figure 4.2
© Mark Wearden

This type of structure is usually referred to as a supply-chain, and from a strategic thinking perspective it is essential that we are able to determine, as far as possible, the structure of the supply-chain within which an organisation functions and where the organisation is positioned within that chain.

Chapter 3 introduced the concept of supply chain thinking. Chapter 5 will consider further the internal supply-chain of an individual organisation and consider how we can start to analyse its strengths and weaknesses from both a 'today' and 'future' perspective, and therefore help to ensure that we are framing our strategic thinking within appropriate parameters. Chapter 10 will consider aspects of influence from a 'distance' perspective using the CAGE (cultural, administrative, geographic, economic) framework.

This chapter will focus on several related but different methodologies that have been designed to enable us to consider the uncertainties of the immediate environment within which we operate our businesses. One of the major problems with strategic thinking is the plethora of risks and uncertainties that we are faced with on a daily basis. These could be categorised into a number of areas:

◆ Environmental influences: in today's corporate world these are often recognised through the approach of the organisation to corporate social responsibility (CSR). There is a prevailing view that an organisation needs to consider its use of resources and how it will, at least, replace such usage for future generations. CSR is discussed in more detail in Chapter 9.

◆ Technological influences: the speed and complexity of technological development appears to continue at an exponential rate of change. Consider the current technological ability of your mobile phone; this far exceeds the technological ability that was used to run large businesses only 20 years ago. As part of any strategic planning process we need to allow for the uncertainties of technological advance. At the forefront of our mind should be the increasing use of, and potential for, artificial intelligence (AI).

◆ Human influences: as human beings we are naturally competitive, although each individual will have their own level of competitiveness. The work of behavioural scientists suggests that an individual focus on a particular task or direction can in itself be skewed by a wide range of external influences. If we were to consider that an organisation is only ever a collection of individuals, working in cohesion, then any strategic development needs to consider and allow for the vagaries of human behaviour.

The following example of Star TV shows how the alignment of environment, technology and people can change the original strategic plan of an organisation.

Case study 4.2

Updated by Mark Wearden from an original article by Ghemawat 2001:

In 1991 Star TV was launched to broadcast readily-available, low-cost American and English television programmes to the newly rich Asian elite, who could afford to subscribe, but also who represented an attractive advertising market opportunity. Through satellite technology the constraints of geographic distance would be overcome. In 1995 News Corporation bought Star from its founders believing in a strategic earnings opportunity. Following continual financial losses, the business was split into three in 2009 and now is a successful Asian TV service showing a mixture of local and imported material.

Consider why the environmental and human influences forced a change in strategic direction despite the success of the technological structure.

The process of analysis requires us to follow a logical path of consideration, while allowing for the reality that our own brain may also lead us down unexpected routes. It is generally recognised that analysis requires a continual iteration of the following actions to enable us to eventually arrive at a decision or a conclusion, you may wish to refer back to 'the ladder of inference' in Chapter 1:

Assessment of data

→ Application of meaning

→ Consideration of information

→ Challenge against our existing knowledge

→ Restructuring of our opinions, and adjustment of our knowledge

As we consider the development of strategy within an organisation, it is important that we are aware of how our brain is affected by and reacts to the range of different stimuli that surround us.

Stop and think 4.1

Consider the organisation that you work for. What does the supply chain model look like?

◆ **Source: what is the earliest starting point in the process?**

◆ **Make: what differentiates your organisation?**

◆ **Deliver: who is the ultimate consumer of your output?**

2.1   Recognising the boundaries

We need to be able to clearly identify the boundaries within which we operate.

These boundaries can be identified as a series of increasingly large layers (Johnson et al., 2017) which surround an organisation. Johnson illustrates these as follows.

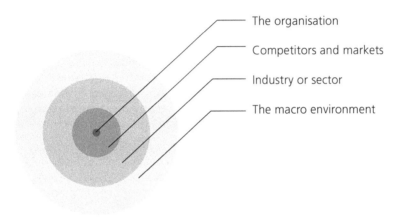

The organisation

Competitors and markets

Industry or sector

The macro environment

Figure 4.3
((Johnson, 2017) adapted by Mark Wearden)

At the centre of this structure is the *organisation* itself, and much of this Development of Strategy text and module is based around how best to explore the organisation and its strategic direction. This chapter suggests that, before considering the organisation itself in detail, it is important for us to recognise the differing influences of the boundaries which surround it.

The second level is denoted by Johnson as *competitors* and *markets*, and the third level as *industry* or *sector*. These two levels could be considered as part of the micro or near environment. Directors and managers will have some level of ability to influence these layers and the impact that they have upon an organisation. The level of influence will diminish the further away from the centre one moves. However, there will only be limited, if any, control available within this micro environment.

By the time we reach Johnson's *macro environment*, control and influence have been replaced by the need to respond. In strategic planning and strategic analysis, it is important to recognise these forces, and to understand the potential impact upon the organisation.

Remember that boundaries can be fluid across a passage of time. Based around its strategic decisions, and within certain operational parameters, an organisation has the ability to influence and change the positioning of the boundaries that exist within the first three circles of the Johnson model. It is only the macro environment where an organisation has very limited, if any, powers of influence.

Test yourself 4.1

Identify the difference between environmental, technological and human influence on strategic thinking.

2.2   Macro thinking – the 'far' environment

The biggest single problem with macro thinking, faced by the directors of any organisation, is the sheer distance of the far environment, and the seeming lack of ability to be able to influence or control the various external forces at play within that environment. These forces are sometimes referred to as 'megatrends', significant changes which can be slow to form but which have significant impact; an example would be the changing age of populations in different countries with its resultant impact upon the available workforce.

As with all such strategic thinking, the problem is lessened through deeper understanding and analysis. While much of macro thinking is to do with the forces with which we have to deal, it is possible from a strategic thinking perspective to manage, mitigate and plan for a range of possible outcomes.

At the oversight level it is possible to differentiate between the changeability and the predictability of these differing environmental dynamics. Lynch (Lynch, 2015) using the work of Ansoff (Ansoff & MacDonnell, 1990) describes these dynamics as the turbulence in the environment and this creates a useful image for strategic thinking.

Changeability is defined as the degree to which the external environment is likely to change – e.g. there is always likely to be a low level of changeability within the market for basic food products such as bread or milk; whereas there is a higher level of changeability within the potential use of artificial intelligence.

Predictability is defined as the degree to which such changes can be predicted – e.g. there is a low level of predictability in the potential timing of the development of drugs to combat a major illness such as Alzheimer's; whereas there is a higher level of predictability with the likely consumer acceptance of new electronic gadgets as they become available in the marketplace.

Stop and think 4.2

Think about the organisation that you work for. Imagine you are sitting at the board table helping to develop the strategy for the next ten years of the business. Look out across a ten-year period and try to differentiate for yourself any environmental changes that you believe are predictable and compare these to the potential changes that may impact the organisational environment.

PESTEL

An important and frequently used model for the analysis and deeper interrogation of the macro environment is known by the acronym PESTEL, standing for:

- political
- economic
- socio-cultural
- technological
- environmental
- legal.

Use of this popular model forces the consideration of these six different perspectives of the far environment. There are a number of different methods for the use of PESTEL, but most frequently it is first presented within a tabular structure, often with additional narrative, or an additional column, to further expand the points available with particular reference to the organisation that is being considered.

Remember that the use of this model is primarily as a checklist to force the brain to consider different environmental perspectives. There is no preconceived prioritisation between these six aspects, and although any organisation can consider each of the aspects, the depth and breadth of the analysis and interrogation will be determined by the organisation itself and the wider environment within which it and its sector is operating.

After an initial consideration of the underlying purpose of each aspect below, this text then uses a tabular format to highlight the key areas of PESTEL and suggest how they might apply to, by way of example, Tesco plc.

Political

The political element requires the consideration of the influence and role that government, or governments, might play in the wider operational marketplace. In many countries the state, represented by the government, can be an owner, a customer, a supplier, and often a regulator of business. The health and education of people is largely determined by political influence and levels of changeability or predictability might form a significant part of macro strategic considerations.

◆   A good example is the defence sector, where in many countries the government will be involved in all aspects and will have a major influence in the far environment of any other organisation working in that sector.

◆   Another example might be the airline industry, where government will ultimately have the regulatory responsibility for determining the appropriate levels of air safety, in terms of flight volume and airport capacity within their own geographical location but while also being a customer and a supplier (a National Air force) in the same marketplace.

Economic

Although the economic elements will often derive from a particular political objective or stance, it is important that an organisation is able to determine the specific macroeconomic factors that will influence its strategic future, while recognising that politics and economics are often inextricably linked.

The common forces that would be considered under this heading would be the impact of interest rates, currency exchange rates, inflation rates and other economic growth rates from the country where the organisation is based; and also the impact and influence that may be experienced from the economic considerations and decisions of other countries.

◆   A multinational company such as BP plc will always have to consider the potential impact of currency exchange rates in its strategic thinking. The variety of differing economic environments within which they operate would need to be challenged by concepts of *changeability* and *predictability*. There is no easy answer, but the consideration of these aspects will bring a greater depth to strategic planning.

◆   A company with a high level of financial gearing – i.e. where its longer-term infrastructure funding has been derived from borrowing (debt) rather than from shareholders (equity) – would need to consider seriously the impact of a rise in interest rates, and the resultant impact of higher interest cost to the organisation leading to a reduction in net profitability.

Socio-cultural

This element has often been referred to simply as 'social', but the wider term 'socio-cultural' more correctly recognises not just the social forces at play but also the significant influence of culture and changing cultural attitudes. Culture has also been recognised as a key driver in the governance of an organisation and will be discussed in greater detail in Chapter 7 of this text.

This element concerns centrally the impact of changing demographics within a region or a country and the differing levels of wealth distribution among the population.

◆   **Demographics**: many western countries have an increasingly ageing population, at least in part as a result of increased longevity, and this can provide both an opportunity and a threat within the private and public sector. A particular socio-cultural force affecting strategic thinking is the increasing expectation of services and care that will be required for the elderly demographic against the resultant diminishing supply of younger people within the workforce. This aspect also requires consideration of population geography, and an organisation must ensure that it is basing its key operations in an area where appropriate levels of skill and expertise may be attracted into the workforce and management.

◆ **Wealth distribution**: western civilisation has seen an increasing concentration of wealth in the hands of fewer people. This has had a constraining effect on certain areas of consumption, but with an increase in demand for luxury goods in other areas.

Changes in cultural attitude are both driven by demographic change, and in turn can drive demographic change. The use of technology is a good example of this: the rapid growth of mobile phone technology and the drive to an immediacy of response as required by social networking has led organisations to seriously consider the potential reputation impact that can be caused through people anywhere knowing what has just happened through constant global news updates. The personal impact that this has had on many individuals, for example phone hacking by the media, has led to an ethical and cultural demand for greater restrictions, protection and enhanced security.

Technological
The technological element infiltrates most aspects of the way we live our lives today. However, when trying to analyse the macro environment, it is important to consider a number of specific forces that are at play within the environment where we are attempting to develop an organisation.

◆ **Technology push or market pull**: in our strategic thinking, are we anticipating the use of technology to help us to drive effective business solutions, or are we being forced down a particular route by either customer or supplier, or have we have failed to keep our hardware or software current and leading edge?

◆ **People skill divergence**: have we recognised as a strategy the likely need for higher skilled, technologically aware people within an organisation, recognising a future point where the structure of many jobs may well be undertaken through robotic mechanisms? This will impact the socio-cultural perspective.

◆ **Diffusion**: have we considered the process and likely timing of the spread (diffusion) of the use of technology within the differing boundaries that we are considering? Remember that it took 28 years from origination to the point where 50 per cent of the US population owned a television set; whereas it took approximately half this time for the same diffusion with mobile phones.

We also need to be aware of the plethora of potential new influences from within the world of technology such as biotechnology, nanotechnology, 3D-printing technology and the invention of new materials such as graphene. Remember that the impact is likely to be not just upon the organisation itself and the different levels of boundary, but also upon the ultimate customers and consumers; as an example, the longer term viability of the core printing industry has been hit significantly by the use of online resources.

Environmental

This element is sometimes referred to as 'ecological' rather than 'environmental', but the impact and focus in terms of our strategic thinking is identical. There has been a strong focus in recent years on how an organisation tackles its CSR. This ranges from the requirement to comply with laws covering areas such as waste disposal to increasing narrative reporting requirements from companies whose shares are publicly traded. As we plan a strategy for our organisation, there are a number of very specific areas that we need to take into consideration in terms of the macro economic impact and requirement. An organisation can suffer both financial and reputational damage as a result of its handling of its wider operating environment. For example:

◈ **Sustainability and stewardship**: what damage is being done to natural resources, and how can we show that our longer-term impact is either positive or neutral?

◈ **Global warming**: how will the arguments surrounding this topic, and its potential impact, affect our strategic plans? Remember that this may be a tangible impact, but also an intangible impact based upon the changing attitudes of people throughout the world.

◈ **Public conscience**: although this might be included under the socio-cultural aspect, there are potentially specific supply and demand implications that could arise from our strategic planning.

The environmental perspective can be challenging from the predictability and changeability perspectives, but remember that we can only ever base our thinking and planning around a breadth of understanding of 'today's' position, combined with a realistic and honest anticipation of the range of possibilities that may lie ahead.

As an example, BP plc suffered both financial and reputational damage as a result of the following incident.

Case study 4.3

The Deepwater Horizon oil spill (also referred to as the BP oil spill/ leak, the BP oil disaster, the Gulf of Mexico oil spill and the Macondo blowout) is an industrial disaster that began on 20 April 2010, in the Gulf of Mexico on the BP-operated Macondo Prospect. This was considered to be the largest marine oil spill in the history of the petroleum industry and estimated to be 8% to 31% larger in volume than the previous largest spill. The US government estimated the total discharge at 4.9 million barrels (210 million US gallons; 780,000 m3). After several failed efforts to contain the flow, the well was declared sealed on 19 September 2010. The strategic impact of the damage continues to this day.

Legal

The final element of PESTEL covers a very wide range of legal aspects that exist within the macro environment. The directors, managers and company secretaries of an organisation are entrusted with developing strategic plans on behalf of the owners. They need to have a strong knowledge and awareness of existing legislation within the wider environment and take into consideration the trends and likely development of legal expectations. Of all the macro elements, the legal and regulatory landscape is the one where an organisation is most likely to have to respond and comply rather than have any influence or impact. The exception to this would be where the organisation is of such size or market significance as to be able to lead a legal challenge, and influence change, on behalf of others.

Some of the specific legal areas which need considering from a macro perspective are:

◆ labour and employment laws

◆ environmental protection legislation and consumer regulation

◆ finance, taxation and reporting requirements

◆ ownership, merger and competition law.

Worked example 4.1

Example of a short PESTEL analysis of Tesco plc

External influences	Factors to consider	Issues for Tesco plc to consider
Political	Foreign trade regulation	→ Current and new non-UK subsidiaries/suppliers
		→ Brexit risks and opportunities
	Competition and monopolies	→ Ownership of local stores and launch of direct competition to discounter entry stores
		→ Market position and monopolisation of geographic areas
Economic	Taxation	→ Complexity of the UK tax systems and continuing talk of reform
		→ Potential increase in employer NI requirement
	Interest rates	→ Impact on consumer spend
		→ Impact on current and future debt funding

Socio-cultural	Lifestyle change	→	Consumer taste trends
		→	Influence of the media
	Education levels	→	Greater product and provenance awareness
		→	Government intervention on healthy eating – e.g. sugar
Technological	Internet availability	→	Online ordering and order fulfilment
		→	In-store technology – automatic check-out
	Privacy of personal data	→	Holding of consumer data
		→	GDPR (EU General Data Protection Regulation) and cyber security implications
Environmental	Packaging	→	Media focus on plastics and other materials
		→	Consumer purchasing trends and expectations
	Food miles	→	Local sourcing, freshness and shelf-life
		→	Risks of 'slave-labour' or bribery in supply chain
Legal	Employment law	→	Zero hours contracts, gender and pay diversity
		→	Pension obligations
	Product safety	→	Traceability of product and due-diligence defence
		→	Supply chain health and safety

The table in worked example 4.1 is a worked outline example of a PESTEL analysis, using Tesco plc. These aspects and comments are neither prescriptive nor exclusive but are intended to give an indication of two aspects within each element which might be considered from the macro environment perspective. It is worth noting that many of these are current at the time of compilation. Remember that all such strategic modelling is immediately valid when it is completed, but can quickly become out-of-date and so needs regular refreshing – the five-year plan problem was discussed in earlier chapters.

Stop and think 4.3

What are the PESTEL influences on your organisation?

2.3   Forecasting and scenario planning

Strategic planning is faced with significant diversity and complexity as evidenced in the PESTEL model, combined with the fact that the use of PESTEL will be based around the depth of our understanding of 'today', and the anticipation of an unknown 'future'. The result is a speculative exercise, but then that is the same for all forecasting and budgeting exercises. At the best, we are establishing benchmarks to help us in our visualisation of the future, and to further challenge our considerations as we work into the future.

Remember that these benchmarks are based around the parameters that we have established today, the point where we have put together the plan, so we need to be conscious of the range and number of variable parameters that we introduce into our forecasts, together with our end-point focus. The maxim 'less is better than more' can be useful in this context.

Johnson (2017) introduces a useful model where he contrasts the differences between the following:

◆ **Single point forecasting**: the focus being one single figure or result; *this is where we are able to forecast with a degree of certainty both a starting point and the route from today to a future defined end point.*

◆ **Range forecasting**: the focus being a range of possibilities; *this is where there is a relatively high level of risk involved along the route, the diversity of end-point possibilities will be determined by the levels of risk that we perceive at the today; sometimes we are also able to assign probabilities to the potential outcomes.*

◆ **Alternative futures forecasting**: the focus being a defined number of potential fixed-point outcomes; *this will be where we recognise there are a recognisable range of likely results from our strategy, but that the end result will be dependent upon decisions or events along the route.*

To use single point forecasting, an organisation needs to have resolute confidence about the future, but even this will be based around certain starting parameters which may in reality change across the passage of time.

In any other form of forecasting we are required to consider a range of different scenarios, and therefore the interaction of a complexity of changing parameters. One of the problems with the flexibility of today's technology, and the use of a spreadsheet such as Excel, is that we are able to provide a range of apparently coherent forecasts with relative ease.

To build an effective analysis of a range of different potential future scenarios, it is important first to understand and identify the key parameters that are likely to change in the future, and how these parameters interact with each other. This is taking the concepts of changeability and predictability into a third dimension.

A useful image to have in mind when considering this type of scenario planning is that of a Rubik's cube. Imagine that each of the six distinct colours is a changeable parameter. Each of these parameters is then separated into a number of separate aspects (nine squares), and the whole then works in a three-dimensional way. This requires the ability to consider how to enable the interaction of these different parameters to achieve the end objective. This is no different to everyday scenario planning in most organisations.

An interesting set of scenario planning dimensions was developed by Ringland (Ringland, 2014) to challenge the strategist to contemplate what really matters within a particular organisation. In the following table, these dimensions have been aligned with the type of question that a scenario planner ought to be asking, together with some 'trigger' words which should be in the mind of the planner.

Dimension	Questions	Trigger words
Vital issues	◆ What is critical for the future as we currently perceive it?	Data and knowledge
Positive outcome	◆ What does the best possible outcome look like? ◆ What difference would it make?	Utopian impact
Negative outcome	◆ What does the worst possible outcome look like? ◆ What difference would it make?	Dystopian impact
Internal systems	◆ What are the culture, structure and process drivers within the organisation? ◆ What might need to change?	Reality and obstacles
Key learnings	◆ What have we learned from previous strategies?	Experience
Key decisions	◆ What are the urgent actions needed to begin the process of strategic change?	Immediacy
Personal dimension	◆ What would I like to influence to make a real difference? ◆ What can I do to make a real difference?	Ego and reality

Table 4.1: Scenario planning dimensions
((Ringland 2014) adapted by Mark Wearden)

Stop and think 4.4

Imagine your organisation as a Rubik's cube, and then hold the dimensions in Table 4.1 in your head at the same time.

What are the real key driving parameters that will impact upon your strategic plans?

Test yourself 4.2

Discuss briefly the potential strategic impact of each of the factors of a PESTEL analysis.

2.4 Micro thinking – the 'near' environment

We return to the different boundaries which surround our strategic planning process. So far, we have only considered the extremity of the boundaries, the macro environment, the area that we have little ability to influence or control. We now turn to the two middle rings in the boundary model included in Figure 4.3 above.

Although the model has 'competitors and markets' and 'industry or sector' as differentiated boundaries, they are both usually referred to as the micro thinking, or 'near' environment dimension and we will treat them as requiring the same type and level of interrogation and consideration within the strategic planning process.

The term 'near' environment implies the forces and influences which will impact the daily lives of our business, but which are not part of the business itself. Although often we will be forced to react to such forces, because they are within relatively close proximity, we are able to more readily include their potential impact within our strategy. Beyond that, because our organisation in itself forms part of both of these areas, we are sometimes able to influence and change the structure and the impact within a particular area.

Case study 4.4

In early 2000, the Royal Bank of Scotland Group (RBS) succeeded in a takeover of National Westminster Bank (NatWest); at this point NatWest was approximately twice the size of RBS. This was the biggest takeover in UK history. Prior to the takeover, RBS had been the recipient of market and economic forces from its larger competitors. After the decision, the 'near' environment was significantly changed, not only for RBS but also for the banking and finance sector.

Economics dynamic
When thinking about the micro environment, it is important to start from an economics dynamic.

Figure 4.4
© Mark Wearden

A *monopoly* exists where there is no competitive rivalry. In the UK, monopolies at an organisational level are restricted and controlled by the Competition and Markets Authority. When one company acquires another, its relative market strength and power over the consumer is determined and can be restricted or restrained. Monopolistic strength, however, can exist within a particular service (e.g. Facebook or Microsoft). Buyers are forced to take the price at which the product or service is being offered by the monopolistic provider.

An *oligopoly* exists where there is a high concentration of a defined number of players. An example would be the top four professional accountancy firms – although many other accountancy firms exist, the top four have significant market strength and reputation. Another example would be the sale of petrol and diesel through garages – even including the fuel stations established by high-street retailers, there are only a small and defined number of players. There is always a risk of cartel pricing within such oligopolies.

There is a significant risk of hyper-competitiveness where only a few players exist. This can often be cut-throat and threaten overall business longevity for one or more players.

Perfect competition exists where there are many competitors providing similar and largely undifferentiated products or services. Buyers will make their decision on price or other points of differentiation.

A recognition of where an organisation is positioned at a particular point in time is an important starting point for strategic considerations; whatever the business is attempting to achieve in the future it is certain that its positioning along this dynamic will change. Where does the organisation currently sit? Is it at the monopolistic end of the dynamic, with the ability to set prices within the 'near' environment; or is it at the other end of the dynamic being forced to take the prices that the market dictates?

There are other similar parameters which will enable us to consider further the starting point for strategy:

- In the 'near' environment, is the organisation considered to be a rule maker or a rule follower?
- Is the strategy being developed as a result of foresight, or to enable the organisation to combat competition?
- Is the strategic thinking of the directors and other leaders aimed at redesigning the micro-environment, or restricting itself to enable it to operate within the current environment?

Business lifecycle

Having considered the economic positioning of an organisation, our next consideration within the micro environment needs to be the concept of business lifecycle. The hypothesis, supported by many management thinkers and academics is that an industry, or segment of an industry will go through four basic phases of change:

Introduction ➜ Growth ➜ Maturity ➜ Decline

There is a natural curve for these phases which plots market volume against time, but without attempting to add any numerical scale to each axis in the generic model.

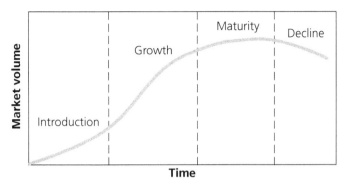

Figure 4.5
((Lynch, 2015) adapted by Mark Wearden)

Consider the different requirements from a strategic planning perspective during each of these phases:

◆ Introduction
  – High level of strategic planning
  – Need to decide on market aim – small share vs large share
  – High prices available, but with higher per unit overheads, therefore lower profitability
  – Competitors will be showing moderate interest
◆ Growth
  – Continued focus on strategic planning, anticipation of maturity levels
  – Consolidation of market positioning
  – Potential for good profitability as long as costs are contained
  – Competitors showing significant interest
◆ Maturity
  – Strategic planning for volume maintenance and anticipation of decline
  – Maintenance of market share
  – Prices and profit margins are likely to decrease as the market matures
  – Competitors focused on product differentiation
◆ Decline
  – Strategic planning for either the next growth phase, or new products or markets
  – Minimisation of loss of volume
  – Potential for losses unless costs can also be reduced in line with volume
  – Competitors will be assessing their own position, potentially leading to opportunities

Although the concept of lifecycle phases is tried and tested, and generally reflects reality, it is important that the various phases are not seen as inevitable. Different organisations, different consumers and different products can bring significant variability. Although the general trend may often apply, the timing of the phases can vary greatly, and the overall pattern may be significantly more disjointed with periods of growth and decline occurring in a number of iterations before any final maturity of market is reached.

Case study 4.5

Extract from article in *Financial Times*, 9 February 2018 (www.ft.com/content/e5ff4578-0cc5-11e8-839d-41ca06376bf2):

'The UK is one of the world's largest video game markets by consumer revenues, with more than £4bn spent on games in 2016. It has become a hub for the companies that make the games, some 2,182 such businesses. The industry has proved challenging for some of these companies. A number have struggled to replicate the success of early hits, while older businesses have had to contend with a rapid shift away from traditional boxed software to online gaming. A host of smaller listed companies reflect the mixed fortunes of the sector.

Frontier Developments, a Cambridge based company has a reputation for geeky, indie games with lasting appeal, and has seen its market value increase more than sevenfold since it listed on Aim in 2013, with a 75 per cent rise in revenues and 6 -times increase in pre-tax profits. Tencent, the world's largest gaming company, bought a 9 per cent stake in Frontier last July as part of its attempt to expand in Europe and the US. Frontier expects Tencent will help it reach more customers in China, the world's largest gaming market, and the company will expand into Chinese-language games. Frontier commented "This deal gives us a very strategic partner".

Game Digital was once a high street stalwart but after its previous incarnation, Game Group, fell into administration in 2012, the retailer has struggled to pay down debt and reinvent itself for a new era. Shares in the group dropped to a record low last June after it said it had failed to sell as many Microsoft Xbox and Sony PlayStation consoles and games as expected and suffered supply shortages of the new Nintendo Switch consoles. Sports Direct bought more than a quarter of its shares a month later, in a move to help it expand into the "esports" market, where celebrity players play the latest games in front of thousands of spectators. The company highlighted in its annual report the impact social media has had on the industry by altering the way people interact, commenting "some of these changes continue to provide challenges to our business, but they also provide significant opportunities".

Gfinity is the UK's main esports event organiser. It is best known for its massive competitive tournaments which it hosts in partnership with companies such as Microsoft and Activision Blizzard at a permanent arena in London. The events are frequently streamed by broadcasters such as the BBC and BT Sport. Gfinity floated on Aim at the end of 2014 but has not yet managed to turn its popularity into profitability. Losses have increased by almost two-thirds as the company has invested in future growth and new gaming franchises.'

Contemplate the marketplace described in the above article, consider how difficult it must be to formulate strategic plans within such a fast-moving 'near' environment. Have this in mind as you read the next section about Porter's five-forces model.

Test yourself 4.3

Suggest briefly why it is important to consider, at an early stage of the development of strategy, the position of an organisation on the economics dynamic.

Porter's five forces

In this text there are a number of different models and thinking-concepts that have emanated from, and been influenced by, the work and writing of the Harvard Business School professor Michael Porter, together with some direct references to his core industry modelling. The five-forces model is one of these. Developed originally in 1980 (Porter, 1980) it recognises the key forces and positioning of any organisation that is operating within a competitive market place.

Originally developed and designed to be used to analyse aspects of the micro environment, like many such models, its underlying logic can be used for a much wider breadth of strategic analysis, including looking inwardly to enable an individual organisation to challenge its own particular market strength and market positioning.

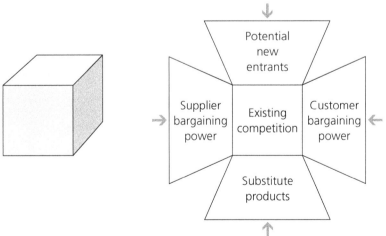

Figure 4.6
((Porter, 1980) adapted by Mark Wearden)

To enable a practical use of five forces, the optimal approach is to first define the boundaries of the model.

On the left-hand side of Figure 4.6 is a simple diagram of a cube. This cube represents the boundaries of the structure to which we wish to apply the five-forces model. These boundaries could encompass competition and rivalry; they could include the industry or sector; they could potentially include a wider environment; or they could include just the organisation itself.

On the right-hand side of Figure 4.6, we have lifted the lid off the cube and are able to investigate it and therefore see the constituent five parts conceived by Porter. At the very centre is the 'today' sphere of operation with all of its inherent forces. This current competitive and economic position is then surrounded by four potential future forces of change.

◆   The horizontal forces are based around the dynamics of the supply-chain of operation. All organisations exist within such a supply-chain, as a pivot between supplier and customer.

◆   The vertical forces are based around the dynamics of the competitive marketplace, with a recognition that there are alternative products or services, and also, in a successful marketplace, there will be the potential for new competition.

These five forces will interact with each other and affect the whole marketplace, or in our 3D cube thinking, they will affect the dynamics that exist within the cube, and also potentially the dimensions of the cube itself.

This becomes even more complex if you consider the cube as a Rubik's cube, but that is outside the scope of Porter's original concepts discussed below; but try to consider how and why the five-forces model can have such a practical application in real world strategic thinking.

Stop and think 4.5

Before considering the detail of the Porter five-forces structure, take the diagram in Figure 4.6 and populate the five sections with some thoughts about the 'near' environment operational sphere of your own organisation.

Today
Existing competition (first force)
At the centre of the five-forces model is the rivalry that exists between the current players. This has already partly been considered in the economic dynamic discussed above. The greater the number of players, the greater the rivalry and therefore a lower level of certainty exists. There are a number of specific aspects which define the interaction with the existing competition.

◆   Relative strength, and skew of strength, of the players in the arena. Is it dominated by one or two, or are there a number of equally strong players?

◆   The rate of growth or decline in the marketplace. This could be related to the angle of the curve in the lifecycle model.

◆   How easily are the varying products of different players differentiated? Are we dealing with a homogenous product or service, or are there subtle differences which enable one product or service to be preferred to another?

◆   The level of fixed costs that are required to enable a player to exist. This will affect minimum pricing levels.

◆   The ease with which a player can or cannot exit the marketplace. Divestment of high levels of investment, or the potential for large redundancy costs will influence the level of potential fluidity.

Supply-chain
Supplier bargaining power (second force)
The term 'supplier' would include everything that is required to enable the production and delivery of a product or service. This includes tangibles such as premises, raw materials, labour, utilities and packaging; it would also include intangibles such as knowledge, information and expertise. The bargaining power of the supplier will be influenced by:

◆   Number of potential suppliers. If there is only a small pool of suppliers and it is difficult to change supply, the supplier will hold the power. If there is a large pool of suppliers, then the supplier power is reduced.

◆   Reliance upon the production expertise of a particular supplier or suppliers will again place the power in the hands of those suppliers, and they will be more towards the price-maker rather than price-taker end of the economic dynamic. It would be at its most extreme if there was no alternative supply available.

◆   If operating margins are low, and therefore supplier cost is a material percentage of ultimate sales price, then a relatively small change in supplier cost could affect the overall profitability of an organisation. A supplier will be aware of this and may be able to use it to their advantage when negotiating terms of trade.

◆   In a long and convoluted supply-chain, the supplier themselves may be dependent upon one or more other suppliers, and this can lead to a complexity of power and control within the supply-chain.

The potential ability of the supplier to undertake the next stage of the supply-chain process themselves would enable them to enhance their own profit margin but would also move them into the potential new entrant category of the five-forces model.

Organisations that have developed highly reputed branded products, such as BMW or Microsoft are largely able to dictate their supply into the market. If they are your supplier, and you are their customer, they hold the power through the strength of their brand and reputation.

Customer bargaining power (third force)

Customers are those who buy directly from us and therefore fund our ongoing operation and organisation through their purchases. However, unless they are themselves the end consumer, they are likely to be in an equally pivotal position, with the end consumer ultimately making the decision to fund the entire supply-chain. The power of the customer, in many cases is a mirrored reflection of the power of the supplier and will be influenced by:

◆ Number of potential buyers. In a marketplace with many buyers, the customer bargaining power will be low. In a marketplace with only one, or a very defined number of buyers, the bargaining power will be high. The concepts of the economics dynamic of supply and demand explain the rationale behind this.

◆ The bespoke nature of the customer requirement. If a customer requires a specific design and delivery of a product or service, then the customer's bargaining power will be reduced as it is likely that they will have a limited number of potential sources, therefore placing the economic power in the hands of the supplier.

◆ The same ability to 'make' rather than 'buy' clearly exists at this end of the supply-chain as well.

◆ If the customer is in turn a supplier to the end consumer, then their bargaining power will be restricted by all the above but also be influenced by the bargaining power of the end consumer. Many high-street retailers base their price around what they believe a consumer is willing to pay, or as a means of attracting business. A few years ago, a loaf of bread could be bought for 20p, which was well below its production price, but used by the retailers as a means of attracting customers, the bread was positioned at the back of the store requiring customers to walk down the aisles first and be tempted by other products. This is strategic planning in action to take advantage of and recognise customer desire.

critical mass
Holding a controlling or majority share or influence in any market, product or service.

Large companies with a significant market share in, and access to a market place (often referred to as a **critical mass**) will hold the bargaining power with smaller suppliers. Examples are companies such as Dixons Retail Group plc for the electronics retail sector and Rio Tinto plc for the mining sector.

Marketplace dynamics
Potential new entrants (fourth force)

In any market which is, or appears to be, profitable, the threat of new entrants is always a possibility. At the monopolistic end of the economics dynamic there will always be others wanting to attempt to enter the market and gain market share with its resultant profitability. The ability of others to enter the marketplace will be based around the barriers that are placed in front of them.

Porter identified the existence of some significant barriers:

◆ *Economies of scale*: in any business based around volume of production or sale, a potential new entrant must have a degree of certainty that they can gain market share rapidly to enable the financial and operational viability of their business.

◆ *Product differentiation*: existing players are there for a reason and have built their profile and reputation to enable them to survive within the marketplace. A potential new entrant would need to find a point of differentiation (unique selling point (USP)) to enable them to successfully compete. If the product is currently patented by another competitor this will produce a further barrier to entry.

◆ *Capital requirement*: the cost of entry will vary according to the level of production sophistication and technology required to enter the marketplace. Funds need to be readily available to commence the production or service.

◆ *Customer persuasion*: customers who are satisfied with their current supplier will need a reason to change. In the case of a large and potentially complex structure, such a change may be very difficult to deliver.

◆ *Government policy*: legal restraints on competition, combined with consumer protection may deter potential new entrants.

◆ *Organisational strength*: if the existing player or players are financially and commercially strong, then the potential retaliation from these players may deter new entrants because of their existing supplier and consumer relationships.

An example of a significant barrier is the dominance of Microsoft in the field of operating software. This makes it very difficult for a new entrant to achieve any significant market share.

Substitute products (fifth force)
The potential threat of substitution exists in different forms:

◆ Direct alternative: this could occur if a supplier is able to find an alternative product which is attractive to either the imagination or the price point of the customer. Customers are only loyal to specific products as long as it suits their current and future needs.

◆ Different branding: this might enable a product which in reality is similar, or identical, to become a potential substitute for the customer.

Examples of substitute products include:

◆ the move to laptops instead of desktop computers
◆ the move to e-cigarettes instead of tobacco
◆ the move to aluminium instead of steel.

Worked example 4.2

Five-forces analysis of Tesco plc

This example suggests how the five-forces structure could be used to give an overview of the forces affecting Tesco plc.

Five-forces factor	Relative pressure being exerted	Issues for Tesco plc to consider
Existing competition	CONSTANT pressure from competition to perform well within the oligopoly and maintain market share	→ Oligopoly of high market share players → High pricing pressure → Risk of being market leader with largest market share → Relative profitability pressure → Stock market performance → Media expectations → Recent infiltration and taking of market share by overseas discount retailers
Supplier bargaining power	LOW pressure from suppliers other than for specialist products	→ Range of large and small suppliers → Large suppliers will have some influence over Tesco → Tesco will have significant influence over smaller suppliers → Payment terms will be important → Continuity of delivery will be a significant requirement for Tesco – they do not want empty shelves
Customer bargaining power	Perceived HIGH pressure from end customers for continual low prices – perceived because, in reality customers buy core commodities on more than just price	→ Need to continue to maintain customer base, and prevent desertion to smaller discount retailers → Important to have/maintain sensible mix of product and price range, tempting customers with price in some areas, while tempting with quality or provenance with higher margin products
Potential new entrants	LOW pressure from further potential entrants due to high costs of entry HIGH pressure from recent entrants, using existing overseas cost infrastructure	→ Immediate risk from recent new entrants to UK market – Lidl and Aldi – has been handled so far → Need for awareness of market share creep to discounters and other → Pressure of being number 1 – either maintenance of position or decline

Substitute products	MEDIUM pressure for bulk of product range	→	Need for frequent re-invention
	HIGH pressure for changing branding and commodities to drive market and pricing differential	→	Reliance on supplier base for bearing of cost of development and innovation
		→	Need to stay ahead of (and often try to lead) customer trends and preferences

Stop and think 4.6

Compare the five-forces worked example 4.2 with the earlier PESTEL analysis example in Case study 4.3.

◆   **Consider the different purposes, and the different boundary levels that are being challenged.**

◆   **Think how different the content of each model would be for GSK plc – there will be many similarities, but also differences.**

◆   **Think how each of these models would look for your organisation.**

◆   **Ensure you are confident in how to use both of these core analytical models.**

Market segmentation

Johnson (2017) introduced the idea of market segmentation which recognises the differences that exist between different groups of customers, and that customers have differing needs, expectations and ways of behaving.

It builds on the concept of strategic groups, these are organisations within the same market place that have similar strategic characteristics and are following similar strategies. The characteristics will be different from other strategic groups in the same *sector*. As an example, in the food retail sector there is a clear differentiation between:

◆   large supermarket chains who rely on selling large volumes of a large range of products at lower prices, and base their model around maximum potential footfall and shop size;

◆   small corner shops who rely on their geographical convenience to a much smaller consumer market, but can charge higher prices for this convenience; and

◆   specialist focused shops such as a butcher, a delicatessen, or bakery which rely upon gaining a reputation for their niche product range and personal service, and again can charge higher prices than a large supermarket.

Another aspect of the strategic group concept is to recognise the individuality of the different types of consumer who will use such groups. Johnson summarises this in his market segmentation table below.

	Consumer markets	Industrial / organisational markets
Characteristic of people / organisation	Age, gender, ethnicity	Industry
	Income	Location
	Family size	Size
	Life-cycle stage	Technology
	Location	Profitability
	Lifestyle	Management
Purchase / use situation	Size of purchase	Application
	Brand loyalty	Importance of purchase
	Purpose of use	Volume
	Purchasing behaviour	Frequency of purchase
	Importance of purchase	Purchasing procedure
	Choice criteria	Choice criteria
		Distribution channel
User's needs and preferences for product characteristics	Product similarity	Performance requirements
	Price preference	Assistance from suppliers
	Brand preferences	Brand preferences
	Desired features	Desired features
	Quality	Quality
		Service requirements

Table 4.2
((Johnson, Whittington, Scholes, Angwin & Regner, 2017) adapted by Mark Wearden)

3. Behavioural forces and game theory

Consider again the boundary structures that we have been discussing so far in this chapter. As we put together our strategic plans, we are having to consider not just a range of different time dimensions, but also the depth and breadth of the environment within which we are operating. The underlying strategic challenge is that the environment is constantly changing, and therefore we need to recognise this in our handling of the strategic vision. Strategic planning needs to be fluid.

The macro environment forces recognised through a structure such as PESTEL, and the micro environment identified through Porter's five forces, help with our perception of the challenges that lie ahead. The common denominator across all aspects of time and environment is *people*. It is people and their decisions and behaviour that will impact upon and challenge our decisions; it is people and their decisions and behaviour that will underpin all aspects of our deepening consideration of the development of strategy.

We therefore need to consider briefly the competing behavioural forces that we will have to deal with:

◆ The human psyche: this topic is outside our current study of strategy, other than to have an awareness of the impact of ethics and morals on our decisions; we will consider this further in Chapter 9.

◆ The reliance upon technology for an increasingly wide range of tasks is already leading to the growth of a workforce who base decision upon computer output, rather than upon their own root decisions. With the growth of Artificial Intelligence this will only increase, and the potential impact of this will be considered across the following chapters.

◆ The impact of the media, aligned with the instant communication speed enabled by social networking and similar use of internet technology, forces a speed of decision making which has not previously existed within society. The perceived need for immediacy of response may in some circumstances lead people to make decisions which are often counterintuitive to logical expectation.

◆ The 'making of law' risks becoming re-active to the perceived abuse of norms that have previously relied upon moralistic behaviours. We will consider examples of this in the areas of corporate governance and corporate social responsibility.

The recognition that certain organisations who operate within the 'public interest' have become 'too big to fail'. Resulting in the evolution of an organisation, where rather than following the lifecycle concepts above, its progress may be manipulated by governments and others.

Case study 4.6

The first US bank that was classed as 'too big to fail' was Bear Stearns. It was worried that its failure would destroy confidence in other banks. So in 2008, the Federal Reserve lent $30 billion to JPMorgan Chase to buy the failing investment bank.

However in the same year, a bailout was not given to the investment bank Lehman Brothers. This meant that they filed for bankruptcy. By the following Monday, the Dow had dropped 350 points. This led to wide-spread panic, with lending almost stopping entirely. While not the entire cause of the financial crisis of 2008, Lehman Brothers going bust and the panic that ensued helps to illustrate that some organisations truly are too big to fail.

Game theory suggests that the consideration of strategy is best viewed by stepping back and allowing the brain to consider the different players (organisations and people), potential routes across the void, and the eventual possible outcomes win : draw : lose. It requires an exploration and visualisation of the interaction between an organisation and the other players in the environment who are impacted by events, and the impact of such decisions as they are made.

There is a recognition that when people, as those responsible for developing strategy in an organisation, make a choice that is perceived to be the optimal strategy for the organisation itself, this will have an immediate implication for all other players within the game. Further, that the behaviour of others, and their decisions as a reaction to 'our' initial decision, will impact upon our original perceptions of the anticipated playing out of the game.

Game theory, as a concept, appeared in the 1940s, but has only relatively recently been associated with strategic decision-making. One of the reasons for this is that the increasing complexity of decisions, based around the diversity of operational environments is difficult to model from a straight line mathematical perspective. There is a recognition that enhanced forms of game theory will enable planners to consider potential options without insisting upon strict mathematical analysis. This will be considered further in later chapters.

Stop and think 4.7

Think about the operation of your organisation as a game being played out on a board in front of you.

◆   **What are the rules?**

◆   **Who are the players?**

◆   **What defines success?**

Test yourself 4.4

Write one short question that you could use with an organisation to identify the impact of each of Porter's five forces.

Chapter summary

◆   This chapter considers how and why it is important to understand the different boundaries of operation that exist for an organisation. These boundaries must be initially assessed at the 'today' point to enable the consideration of how potential changes within the boundaries might affect strategic planning.

◆   The 'far' or 'macro' environment describes the wider world of organisational operation. Leaders of an organisation must be able to identify how and when the people, and the operation itself, might need to adapt to encompass changes in the 'macro' environment. These changes will, by their nature, almost always be reactive. It is unusual and unlikely that an organisation will be able to influence or affect changes in the 'macro' environment.

◆ The PESTEL model is a useful tool to help differentiate between the various aspects of the 'macro' environment.

◆ The 'near' or 'micro' environment describes the operating gap that exists between the organisation itself and the 'macro' environment. Johnson's model splits this into two – competitors/markets and industry/sector, with the latter being seen as more distant than the former. It is important to understand the influences and challenges that will exist within the 'micro' environment, and that an organisation can often influence this environment by its presence.

◆ The five-forces model from Porter is a key tool with which to analyse the impact of the different forces within the 'micro' environment.

◆ Models such as PESTEL and Porter's five forces have been originally designed for specific purposes, but the thinking behind the models can be widened and applied to a much wider range of circumstances. The company secretary and governance professional needs to develop the ability to view such models as practical, thinking tools which can be applied to situations that are evidenced in everyday organisational life.

◆ In addition to organisational factors and drivers, it is necessary to have some understanding of the human psyche and the impact that human nature and human behaviour will have on the development and working through of a strategic plan.

◆ A company secretary/governance professional needs to be able to assess organisational potential and behaviour, within the context of the 'macro' and 'micro' aspects, and the pressures of the operational environment. This understanding can then be used to challenge and refine the development of strategy.

Chapter five
Strategic capability and competencies

Contents

1. Introduction

The first part of this text, Chapters 1, 2 and 3, considered the nature of strategy, how it developed and some of the key dynamics that we need to take into consideration. Chapter 4 set the organisation within the wider context of its differing external boundaries and considered a number of the forces that enable and restrain the moulding and shaping of the organisational strategy, and its day-to-day operational activities.

The underlying presumption is that an organisation needs to be able to build a sustainable competitive advantage, within the context of the macro and micro forces that it exists and operates within. The development of strategy needs to recognise the capabilities and competencies that exist currently within an organisation, and then to consider how these need to evolve and change as part of the realisation of the perceived vision.

Stop and think 5.1

An organisational capability is the potential to achieve an outcome.

An organisational competence is the ability to apply and utilise a capability.

Strategic capabilities are both *common* and *unique* within organisations.

Common, because there will be a plethora of different capabilities which will be required by all organisations. These can be assessed, benchmarked and considered, to help us to understand why one organisation is more successful at a generic activity than another. An example might be financial planning which is a common required activity.

Unique, because every organisation has a unique mixture of individuals, each with their own unique capabilities. When these are combined, they will give any one organisation different capabilities to any other organisation, and these are very often hard to replicate. An example might be a pharmaceutical company where one of the directors is a world-renowned specialist in research into a particular disease.

This is often referred to as a 'resource-based strategy'. Using this concept does provide the ability for an organisation to recognise, detail and apply its various and differing resources. However, it fails to recognise that the manner in which resources are applied and utilised by different unique individuals is what will really drive the real capabilities of the organisation.

In his book *Contemporary Strategy Analysis* (1998) Grant illustrated the relationship between originating resources and the application of these resources. Suggesting that these combined with external industry factors will enable the formation of a strategy that will lead to competitive advantage for an organisation.

Figure 5.1
((Grant, 1998) adapted by Mark Wearden)

Case study 5.1

In planning their strategy, Honda took a broad view of the needs of the market and the competencies that they could bring to the customer base.

Adapted from *Competing on Capabilities: The New Rules of Corporate Strategy* (Stalk, Evans, & Shulman, 1992):

Having accepted that Honda's core competencies in engines and trains gave them distinct advantage in car, motorcycle and generator businesses, it is important to recognise that it is broader skills that will transform key business processes into strategic capabilities and lead to competitive success.

Innovative designs of products and the way in which they were manufactured were not the only factors which underpinned Honda's success.

The company's ability to train and support its dealer network with operating procedures and policies for merchandising, selling, floor planning, and service management was equally important – summarised as the Honda expertise in the 'dealer management process'.

The process of identifying and building competencies and capabilities is seen as a top-down process with the CEO and senior management playing a key role. Competitive advantage is found in the resources and skills inside the company rather than finding weaknesses in the external environment.

Knowledge, skills and resources need to work together to drive the strategic capabilities.

Stop and think 5.2

As part of your breadth of consideration of how strategy is developed, compare the Honda alignment of knowledge, skills and resources to your own organisation. Alternatively find another similar example from today's business pages.

2. Sources of strategic capability

2.1 Resources

As suggested in the diagram from Grant (1998) above it is useful to identify the resources that are available to a particular organisation before assessing its capabilities and its competencies. These can be classified under a number of generic headings and will often underpin core understanding and analysis of an organisation. These resources will always be assessed at a snapshot moment in time, for instance through the use of a SWOT (strengths, weaknesses, opportunities and threats) analysis, and other than the most tangible of physical resources they are likely to change on a frequent basis through the operational iterations of the organisation.

◆ Tangible resources

   – The financial resources of an organisation are tangible because funds need to be readily available, when required. This will include the short-term working capital required for the payment of employees, suppliers and others in cash, and also the longer-term infrastructure finance achieved through the funding of either shareholders (equity) or financial institutions (debt).

   – The physical resources of the organisation will include land and buildings, machinery, vehicles and arguably also the spare production capacity that exists within the tangible infrastructure.

◆ Intangible resources

   – Technology is viewed as an intangible resource because it exists within and throughout an organisation and can cover a multitude of different aspects and potential. However as opposed to a tangible asset, its value can be subjective.

   – The culture of the organisation is discussed in detail in Chapter 6 of this text, but as an intangible resource it could be defined as the way in which people within the organisation behave towards other people (internal and external) together with the perception of how the other resources within the organisation are being utilised.

Case study 5.2

Tesco could see an opportunity to expand their offering to a wider supply-chain market and enhanced their overall capabilities through acquiring a food-service focus company, Booker.

Extract from Tesco plc Annual Report and Financial Statements 2018:

'**The combined Tesco and Booker business allows us to bring together the retail and wholesale expertise of our two businesses, and access new opportunities for growth. Together we employ over 310,000 colleagues in the UK, serve 117,000 independent retailers, 441,000 catering businesses, 641,000 small businesses, and work with over 7,000 suppliers. Through our merger, we will bring benefits to customers, suppliers, colleagues and shareholders'.**

◆ Human resources

   – A key resource for any organisation is the individual and combined skills of its employees, together with the current and historic knowledge which underpins its purpose and operation. This is an example of the intrinsic value that an organisation can have as an asset. The difficulty arises when attempts are made to ascertain the value of this asset.

    – The means of working within the organisation, and the communication channels which enable a holistic understanding of the strategic purpose (or otherwise) are a key aspect of the human resource. The manner in which people work together, and the understanding of teamwork will often be a key determinant of efficiency and effectiveness within an organisation.

    – The motivation that exists within employees is seen as a core resource. In his book *Renaissance Management* Carter (1999) categorises this into four areas based around the interaction of attitude and energy exhibited by people within the work environment; he portrays the following image of an organisation that exists with a combination of: players, spectators, cynics and the walking-dead. He argues that in their development of strategy, leaders need to have an awareness of the balance of these different aspects of human response. This will help in recognising the people changes that are required to achieve strategic success.

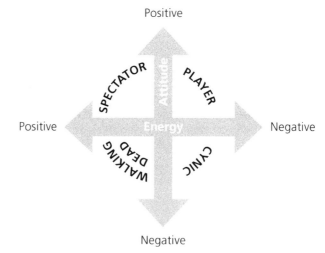

Figure 5.2
((Carter, 1999) adapted by Mark Wearden)

Stop and think 5.3

Look around your workplace and try to identify the different aspects of motivation identified by Carter above.

2.2　Capabilities

Organisational capability is the potential to use one or more resources of the organisation, individually or jointly, to achieve a specific outcome. At the macro level, capability could be seen as the ability of the organisation to utilise its resources to achieve its larger strategic vision. At the micro level, the same concept would apply but within the achievement of a specific organisational or operational task.

Lynch (2015) defines 'organisational capability' as 'the skills, structures and leadership of the organisation behind all its assets together and allow them to interact efficiently'.

Kay (1993) suggests that it is the distinctive capabilities of an organisation's resources that will enable it to develop and fulfil its strategy, while retaining a position of competitive advantage. He argues that the organisational environment consists of a series of contracts and informal relationships between the organisation, its stakeholders, and the various parts of its supply chain. He identifies three core capabilities that are required:

◆ The architecture requires an organisation to design and maintain a network of internal and external relationships.

◆ The reputation requires an organisation to monitor, understand, maintain and build the manner in which it is viewed by its stakeholders.

◆ The innovative capability requires an organisation to be prepared to develop and exploit boundary-stretching ideas.

We could therefore suggest that the capabilities of the organisation need to be understood from three aligned perspectives:

◆ Organisational: how the infrastructure, and its leadership, enable the utilisation of the resources.

◆ Potential: how differing resources are stretched, and their utilisation is maximised.

◆ Challenge: how the current accumulation of resources has arisen, in particular the human resources, and what is required to achieve the strategic objectives.

Case study 5.3

In his book *The Opposable Mind*, Martin (2007) discusses the concept of integrity of thinking and suggests that human capability can be best realised through the development of:

◆ **sensitivity: the capacity to distinguish preconditions that are similar but not exactly the same**

◆ **skill: the capacity to carry out an activity so as to consistently produce the desired result.**

The example he uses is of a chef having the sensitivity to distinguish between the different stages of cooking a steak, while also having the skill to consistently produce a steak cooked to the same level of individual required perfection.

In developing successful strategy, we need to be able to understand the strengths and weaknesses of the different parts of our plan, while at the same time ensuring that the end customer or consumer will be satisfied and buy or require the product or service.

Stop and think 5.4

Consider the interaction of sensitivity and skill described by Martin.

While you might not be a chef, you will have aspects of your work which require the same requirements as cooking a piece of fine steak.

Think about how well you handle such situations.

It is suggested that the role of company secretary and governance professional frequently requires the ability to make finite distinctions while delivering consistent quality.

2.3   Core competencies

The ability to demonstrate competence requires the appropriate resources combined with the capability to utilise and apply those resources.

Organisational competence could be seen to describe how well (or not) an organisation is able to perform its required activities.

Competence is therefore variable rather than fixed and will frequently change based upon the rationality or irrationality of human behaviour.

A core competence could therefore be defined, at any particular moment of time, as the ability of an organisation to align its resources and its capabilities in the satisfaction of stakeholder, and in particular customer, expectations. This concept is considered further in the next section.

2.4   Achieving competitive advantage

The achievement of a sustainable competitive advantage is assumed to be one of the core methods of adding value within an organisation. In a commercial organisation the value will usually be recognised through a mixture of quantitative measures, such as market share. In a non-commercial organisation the value is more likely to be identifiable through qualitative measures, such as the focused delivery of charitable aid to intended recipients.

In his book *Competitive Advantage* (2004), Porter suggests that there are two basic types of competitive advantage:

◆   **Cost advantage**: where the organisation is able to deliver a greater level of profitability and financial benefit when compared to its competitors.

◆   **Differentiation advantage**: where the organisation is able to deliver a product or service that is distinct from that of its competitors.

It is important to make a distinction between the normal day-to-day operating level of an organisation (which allows it to survive within its economic environment), and those aspects of an organisation which are harder, or impossible, for competitors to imitate or obtain, such as the reputation of a key individual.

The term normally associated with the normal operating level is *threshold capabilities*. This describes the alignment of resource and capability which enables an organisation to meet stakeholder requirements and expectations, fulfil focused strategic objectives and goals and maintain its economic position within a marketplace, without advancing or declining against its competitors.

The term normally associated with a distinctive differentiation between an organisation and its competitors is core competencies. This describes the particular alignment of resource and capability which enables an organisation to have a unique product, service or reputation which enables it to either maintain or gain a leading market position. As suggested by Porter this could be from a cost or differentiation perspective, or both.

Case study 5.4

Tesco has seen the expansion of its capabilities and competencies through its acquisition of Booker. The following quotation suggests a new strategic plan is emerging.

Extract from Tesco plc Annual Report and Financial Statements 2018:

'Work is already well underway to unlock the substantial synergies that are now available to the combined Group (of Tesco and Booker). Bringing together knowledge and skills from across retail and wholesale is both allowing us to trial innovative new concepts and to move faster with existing strategies'.

Test yourself 5.1

Differentiate between a strategic capability and a strategic competence, giving an example in each case.

3. Understanding, achieving and sustaining competitive advantage

Arie de Geus suggests in his book *The Living Company* (1999) that:

'the ability to learn faster than our competitors … may be the only sustainable competitive advantage'.

What he is recognising here is that each organisation needs to take seriously, as part of its development of strategy, the nature and structure of the resources of the organisation, and in particular the need for a continuous learning approach to allow the organisation to evolve.

Think back to the 'ladder of inference' from Argyris discussed in Chapter 1. As human beings, we continually learn and develop our approach to decision-making and our interaction with other human beings through our a breadth of experiences as we mature. An organisation needs to capture and enable the individual and team learning, but also recognise that the organisation itself also has the capability of changing its behaviour as it continues to progress on its strategic journey. An example would be the moves being made by many organisations to radically reduce the use of plastic packaging.

Lynch (2015) suggests that competitive advantage is derived from the interaction of a number of core operational aspects:

- **Differentiation**: the recognition of an organisation's unique features or attributes, often represented through branding.
- **Low costs**: the ability to source resources at a lower level of cost than competitors (e.g. bulk purchasing power).
- **High performance or technology**: the alignment of particularly skilled people, patented products and leading-edge technology which are hard to replicate.
- **Quality**: actual or perceived differentiation from the customer perspective.
- **Service**: going above and beyond customer expectation.
- **Culture, leadership and style**: the dynamic and charismatic bringing together of employees in a way which differentiates the organisation from its competitors. An example would be Google with its relaxed office designs which reflect a different type of experience for the type of staff that Google wish to recruit. Google has also found that this helps to stimulate a creative approach to the strategic objectives.

He suggests the following principles which can underpin competitive advantage in different types of organisation.

High-technology business	Service business	Small business	Market leading manufacturer
Technical excellence	Reputation for quality of service	Quality	Low costs
Reputation for quality	High quality and training of staff	Prompt service	Strong branding
Customer service	Customer service	Personalised service	Good distribution
Financial resources	Well-known name	Keen prices	Quality product
Low-cost manufacturing	Customer-oriented	Local availability	Good value for money

Table 5.1

((Lynch, 2015) adapted by Mark Wearden)

When appropriate, an organisation is able to achieve competitive advantage through the building of strategic alliances within its supply chain. These might be formal or informal and can lead to significant cost advantage. Many organisations have found that they can create an agile and more focused approach by removing layers of unnecessary management that have often been built over many years. Recognition of where a task is best controlled in the supply chain can add value to all participants.

◆ **Horizontal integration allows competing organisations to work together to procure a greater critical mass from their suppliers.** An example would be the recent sourcing alliance developed between Tesco plc and the French retail chain Carrefour to enable more effective purchasing and the maintenance of low prices to the end consumer.

◆ **Vertical integration allows an organisation to work with its suppliers or customers to create a more efficient and competitive end-to-end supply chain.** An example would be the vendor-management techniques used by large packaging companies and their customers. Mutual efficiency is gained through the supplier planning a cost efficient large production run, based upon the known requirements of a customer, but the customer requesting and paying for packaging as it is consumed within its own operation; the stock of packaging is managed by the vendor (the supplier).

Case study 5.5

The growth of 'vendor management' has enabled the suppliers (the vendors) of particular high-volume commodities to plan production processes to optimise cost, volume and timing.

In its approach to maximise supply chain efficiency, DS Smith (provider of corrugated packaging) states:

'Under pressure to boost efficiency and cut costs, our customers have shortened lead times and decreased inventories. With tighter supply chains it is more important than ever to master the art of getting our products from the manufacturing mill to the customer's premises. Rapidly, the supply chain is becoming electronic, open, integrated and global. DS Smith has responded by becoming exceptionally proactive and reliable. Working closely with our customers, our Supply Chain Services are cutting call lead times, improving quality and assuring supply, while reducing the impact of transport on our environment.'

Source: www.dssmith.com/paper/offering/services/supply-chain-services.

3.1 The VRIN or VRIO framework of competitive attributes

It has already been suggested that the strategic approach to the achievement and sustaining of competitive advantage will require the recognition of competitive value of the resources and capabilities of the organisation.

Jay Barney (1991) developed a framework to enable an organisation to identify and consider the significance of its competitive attributes. Initially this was known as the VRIN framework (value, rarity, inimitability and non-substitutability) and was then amended to VRIO (value, rarity, inimitability and organisational support) by Barney in a later development of his work.

Value

The *value* of the resources and capabilities of an organisation will be determined by the ability of the organisation to address opportunities or threats, and also the provision of a perceived value to customers. The questions to be asked will include:

◆ Are we able to use the resource or capability to exploit an opportunity in the micro or macro environment?

◆ Are we able to use the resource or capability to remove a threat from the micro or macro environment?

◆ Do our resources and capabilities provide a perceived or actual value to our customers, how can we maintain and develop this?

◆ Does the mix of our particular resources and capabilities give us a cost advantage over the competition?

Rarity

The *rarity* of the resources and capabilities of an organisation will deter or prevent competition. The questions to be asked will include:

◆ How easily could a competitor obtain a similar or better resource or capability, for example the particular skills and reputation of an individual?

◆ Is the rarity of this resource or capability sustainable into the future or will competitors be able to replicate this and destroy our competitive advantage?

◆ How firmly is our strategy aligned with this particular rare capability or resource, and will this restrict our ability to adapt to changes within the environment?

Inimitability

The *inimitability* of the resources and capabilities of an organisation will define its position in the market at any particular moment in time. The main question to be asked is:

◆ Is the accessibility to an inimitable resource or capability by a competitor sufficiently prohibitive or impossible?

Johnson (2017) identifies three different criteria around the inimitability of resources and capabilities:

◆ **Complexity**: the recognition that the development of internal or external linked activities or processes can provide a unique position of competitive advantage, often by providing more than just the core product or service.

◆ **Causal ambiguity**: the inability of competitors to discern and understand the causes which underpin the competitive advantage of a particular organisation. This ambiguity can be caused by their inability to understand a particular characteristic of the process, product or service, or likewise an inability to understand the precise nature of an organisation's activities and processes.

◆ **Culture and history**: the combination of 'taken for granted' activities within an organisation with evolution of the resource, knowledge and capability across the history of the organisation can lead to a process which is impossible for a competitor to imitate.

Stop and think 5.5

Identify an activity or process within your own organisation that gives a competitive edge.

Consider it from the perspective of 'inimitability'.

What prevents competitors from delivering the same activity or process?

Non-substitutability
The *non-substitutability* of the resources and capabilities of an organisation will prevent a competitor achieving the same strategic objective or goal. The questions to be asked are:

◆ Are we confident that an alternative product or service cannot be sourced by a customer, or replicated by a competitor?

◆ Can the individual or combination of resources and capabilities be matched by a competitor using a substitute?

The N then changed to O:

Organisational support
In his later development of his work, Barney decided that the concept of non-substitutability was too closely aligned with that of inimitability and therefore changed his fourth attribute to *organisational support*. This change also recognised the increasing expectation by customers of ongoing support and sustenance for the product or service. If an organisation is able to offer a particular package of support that this can lead to competitive advantage, this has been recognised by many technology companies in the provision and support of their software packages.

Case study 5.6

BAE has an approach to strategy which seeks to develop VRIO products and services. This gives the company its competitive edge.

Extract from BAE plc Annual Report and Financial Statements 2017:

'We search for new ways to provide our customers with a competitive edge across the air, maritime, land and cyber domains. We employ a skilled workforce of 83,200 people in over 40 countries and work closely with local partners to support economic development by transferring knowledge, skills and technology.'

4. Assessing strategic capability

Given the importance of strategic capabilities, it is useful for an organisation to be able to determine the interaction of capabilities within its particular structure and culture. As with many other areas of strategic consideration, there is no one right model that can and will apply to all circumstances and all organisations. The assessment methods detailed below are neither finite nor prescriptive. Each one of them may be applicable to a given set of organisational circumstances, but equally it might be useful on occasions to use more than one method to provide a breadth of understanding.

For the purposes of this examination, it is important to understand the principles that sit behind each model and consider how and when they might be applied within a real world context. Many of these models reappear a number of times throughout this text, as there is significant crossover and correlation between the different topics.

Test yourself 5.2

Identify two different types of competitive advantage.

4.1 Supply chain analysis

Chapter 3 considered the importance of viewing an organisation from a supply chain perspective using this diagram.

In the context of strategic capability and competence, it is clear that the *inputs* within the supply chain will form the resources that have been discussed earlier in this chapter. The *transformation* process represents the capability of the organisation, and its individuals, to apply and use these resources to create a distinctive unique selling point (USP).

Figure 5.3 Supply chain
© Mark Wearden

The competence of the organisation and competitive advantage being evidenced by the ability to complete the supply chain by delivering goods or services to the customer or consumer. The final proof of the capability and competence of the supply chain is actually the point at which the customer or consumer pays for the goods or services and therefore funds the entire supply chain.

This model can be used to assess the resources required; the capability of the organisation to apply those resources; and the competence of the organisation to utilise the resources and the capability to deliver an effective business model with sustainable competitive advantage.

Test yourself 5.3

Summarise briefly the four different aspects of a VRIO framework.

4.2 Value-chain analysis

Michael Porter (2004) uses a similar if slightly different approach to understand the sequential process of value creating activities that exist within an organisation, and as a means of identifying the resources and capabilities required to enable a competent organisation to deliver competitive advantage.

Porter separates the structure of the organisation into *primary activities* and *support activities*:

◆ **Primary activities**
  – **Inbound logistics**: receipt, storage, stock control and transportation of the material resources required for the business operation.
  – **Operations**: the transformation of the raw materials into the final product or service, including manufacturing, packaging testing and quality control.

Figure 5.4 Value chain
((Porter, M., 2004) adapted by Mark Wearden)

- **Outbound logistics**: storage and stock control of finished products together with the transportation of these products to the customer; in the case of a service rather than a product this process would include the means and location of the delivery of the service.
- **Marketing and sales**: the means through which consumers and customers are made aware of the product or service and are able to purchase it, including the selling process itself, the administration of the sales and associated advertising.
- **Service**: the enhancement addition of value to a product or service, such as installation, repair, training, spares, or ongoing support and consultation.

◆ **Support activities**

- **Procurement**: the processes used for acquiring the resources required for primary activities.
- **Technology development**: the range of technological activities that enable a continuity of throughput within an organisation and any required specific handling and protection of a product or service flows through the organisation.
- **Human resource management**: recruitment, managing, training, developing, rewarding of people across the organisation, including the ability to ensure that appropriate skill levels exist at core strategic points within the operational flow.
- **Firm infrastructure**: the formal systems of planning, finance, quality control, information management, governance and leadership within the organisation.

The purpose of Porter's value chain is to encourage a deeper consideration and understanding of the strategic potential of an organisation, having firstly understood how the value chain exists today.

Stop and think 5.6

If the value chain, or the supply chain, model is used and analysed from a *quantitative* perspective, it is possible to understand at which points in the operational flow a monetary value is gained.

If the value chain, or the supply chain, model is used and analysed from a *qualitative* perspective, it is possible to understand at which point in the operational flow the product or service gains perception of value perspective of the customer or consumer.

4.3 Benchmarking and gap analysis

Chapter 1 discussed the concept of using benchmarking as an approach to analyse the actual operational performance of an organisation measured and compared against the anticipated strategic performance. It was suggested that the differences between actual and anticipated performance needed further analysis, and this was referred to as gap analysis.

Gap analysis is an important method of enabling the people leading an organisation to determine which aspects of the operational flow, the resources and the capabilities are operating as intended, and which areas may need attention. They represent the gaps between was expected compared to what actually happened.

The benefits of benchmarking can include:

◆ the alignment of performance against strategic and operational goals and objectives

◆ the acceleration of management of change having recognised the need for such change

◆ the improvement of operational processes.

Lynch (2015) suggests that benchmarking should lead to more than a simple improvement in an organisation through the correction of the perceived gaps. He suggests that the real benefit is to use the benchmarking exercise as a means of enhancing overall competitive advantage within the wider operational environment. He argues that a natural sequence should follow as a result of a benchmarking exercise:

1. explore the results and analyse the reasons for the differences
2. redefine performance targets after discussion with key employees
3. redevelop the assets and systems of the organisation using the learning from the benchmarking exercise
4. develop new performance objectives for individuals and groups, changing expectations and attitudes to what is possible as a result of the learning from the benchmarking exercise.

The application of this type of cumulative approach enables the use of benchmarking in the assessment of strategic capability. This can then be aligned with the furtherance of competitive advantage through recognising where to change a process or strategy to drive increased efficiency and effectiveness within the organisation.

Test yourself 5.4

Clarify briefly the five primary activities of Porter's value chain analysis.

4.4 SWOT analysis

Chapter 3 considered the use of a SWOT analysis for the understanding of the *strengths* and *weaknesses* of the 'today' position and the perceived *opportunities* and *threats* of the 'future' as seen from that point.

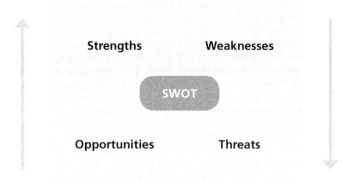

Figure 5.5 SWOT analysis

The application of this approach in the assessment of strategic capability should be apparent.

The resources of the organisation can be analysed to determine the respective strengths and weaknesses that exist. A deeper analysis will enable the organisation to understand its capabilities in the utilisation of its resources, and how these capabilities are perceived and demanded by the various stakeholders (its competencies).

As discussed in Chapter 3, completion of the SWOT analysis is in itself just the starting point of using this as an effective strategic tool – the real benefit comes from the recognition of how the strengths and weaknesses identified within the internal environment can be used to enhance the opportunities or thwart threats that are perceived within the external environment.

Case study 5.7

A recent SWOT analysis carried out at Plant plc included the following findings:

S   strength: the legal background of the newly appointed company secretary

W   weakness: reliance on historic terms of trade

O   opportunity: drive cashflow efficiency through tighter contractual terms with customers

T   threat: lengthy and costly legal action to combat potential breach of contract

A realignment of these findings allowed the directors of Plant to recognise that the legal skills of the new company secretary should be initially focused on developing new terms of trade, combating any threat moving forward and deriving the perceived cashflow opportunity. Through developing this in consultation with customers, Plant plc was able to drive significant efficiency and benefit across its supply chain.

A variation on this suggested by Weihrich (1982) was to invert the acronym, and therefore the analytical approach, to TOWS. This approach starts with a consideration of the external environment within which the organisation is attempting to achieve its strategic objectives, and then identifies the resources and capabilities required to operate within that environment. These can then be assessed against the actual strengths and weaknesses of the organisation at that point in time.

Similar scorecard, or matrix, approaches based around acronyms have been developed by other organisations and consultancy firms. An example is SOARR (situation, opportunity, action, result, reflect) which is used by a number of organisations. This is an example of how management tools and management thinking in themselves develop in an emergent manner. Many organisations will take some of the classic strategic tools but find that they do not quite meet their specific requirements and so adapt them accordingly. This is the lateral thinking that is required to help to develop successful organisational strategy.

Stop and think 5.7

Draw a simple SWOT analysis of the resources and capabilities of your current organisation. Try to identify three resources and three capabilities in each of the Strengths and Weaknesses boxes.

Then consider the impact these have upon Opportunities and Threats of your competitive market position.

4.5   The McKinsey 7S framework

The 7S framework is a strategy model developed by Tom Peters and Robert Waterman when working for the management consulting firm McKinsey. It is based around need to understand the alignment between seven core internal aspects of an organisation, the presumption being that such an understanding will help to deliver a strategic approach to the anticipated demands of the external environment. In our consideration of strategic capability, this model can help to provide significant depth in the identification of the alignment of resources and capabilities, which can then be translated into the competencies required to deliver strategic competitive advantage.

The 7 Ss are: structure, strategy, systems, skills, style, staff and shared values.

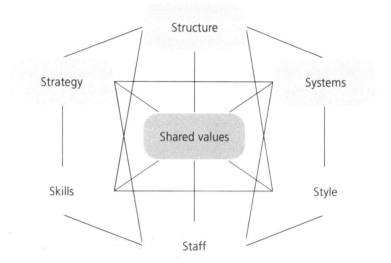

Figure 5.6 McKinsey 7S framework

The principle that sits behind the model is that each of the seven elements is constantly interacting with each of the other elements in the daily operation of an organisation. The elements are split into hard and soft elements.

Hard elements are easier to define and identify, and are largely determined by the strategic activities of the people within the organisation.

Soft elements are less tangible, are part of the culture of the organisation and are largely determined by the manner in which the people within the organisation interact and communicate.

Hard elements

◆   **Strategy**: the vision of achieving sustainable competitive advantage.
◆   **Structure**: the organisational hierarchy and lines of accountability.
◆   **Systems**: the activities, policies and procedures that enable day-to-day tasks to be completed.

Soft elements

◆ **Style**: the nature of leadership and the levels of empowerment as well as the channels of communication used by that leader.

◆ **Staff**: the mixture of employees and the combination of the capabilities.

◆ **Skills**: the specific competencies of each individual employee within the organisation.

◆ **Shared values**: the realisation of the culture and the general ethos of the organisation resulting from the perpetual and changing interaction of the other elements, sometimes referred to as goal congruence.

A practical method for the use within an organisation of the 7S model is to create a matrix which requires each cell to be completed in recognition of how resources and capabilities of the organisation can be utilised to achieve competitive advantage. Excel would be an ideal tool for this concept to be recorded and updated for management and trend reporting purposes.

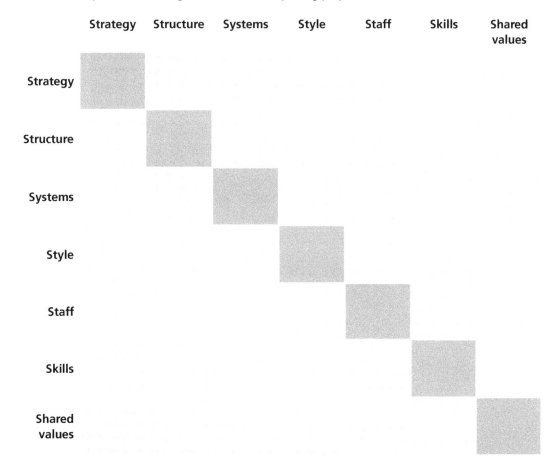

Figure 5.7 Using the 7S concept

Case study 5.8

GlaxoSmithKline (GSK) regularly reviews and adapts its strategy to match its values and priorities to the changing demography of its marketplace, in particular the increased longevity of people and the need for changing health support mechanisms and products.

Extract from GSK plc Annual Report and Financial Statements 2017:

'The healthcare industry is entering a period of significant change bringing opportunities and challenges. As life expectancy increases, demographic changes are both supporting market growth and contributing to pressures in the healthcare sector, particularly on pricing and access. While these challenges are not new for the industry, advances in science and technology are transforming the way scientists research diseases and are likely to improve how patients are diagnosed and treated in the future.

Our strategy is designed to respond to this changing environment: To bring differentiated, high-quality and needed healthcare products to as many people as possible, with our three global businesses, scientific and technical know-how, and talented people. Our new long-term priorities of Innovation, Performance and Trust will help us to deliver our strategy.'

5. Managing strategic capability

5.1   Developing strategic capabilities

The capabilities of an organisation are generally embedded within the routines of the organisation and are not always easy to define or document.

Take, for example, the ability of one organisation to bring a product to market faster than its competitors. This ability will be a combination of the abilities of the people and systems of that organisation and the resources that are at their disposal.

Capabilities are a link between resources and competencies, as discussed above, and shown clearly in Figure 5.1. It is important for an organisation to not just assume that such capabilities either exist or will develop out organisational input and therefore there is a need to consider how to nurture, maintain and develop the organisational capabilities that are required to fill the strategic objectives.

There are many different ways in which this can be approached, for example:

◆ An increase in capabilities could be achieved through the addition of new resources into the organisation, such as the recruitment of particular expertise and the sharing of that expertise amongst the current staff in that department.

◆ The development of brand-new capabilities within the organisation might be perceived through the use of a learning organisation type approach, and the innovative alignment of existing resources to produce a new capability. An example might be the realisation that a particular machine, currently used for an existing production process can be easily adapted to create a new added value dimension to a product. Alternatively, in the finance industry, the recruitment of an international tax planning expert could assist with the navigation of the complexity of corporate tax avoidance laws where both individuals and organisations may now be held directly accountable for using aggressive tax schemes.

◆ Additional capabilities could be aligned with the organisation through the type of strategic alliance discussed in Chapter 12 below.

5.2   The learning organisation – a reminder

Just a brief reminder of the concept of the learning organisation discussed in detail in Chapter 3. This approach to organisational structure and development is in itself a recognition of the ability of an organisation to evolve its resources and capabilities, through the recognition of individual capability and potential and the alignment of that with shared strategic thinking.

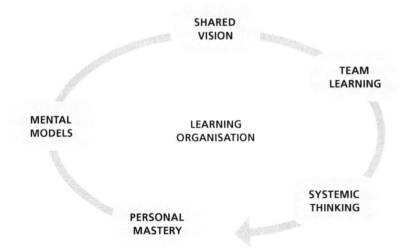

Figure 5.8 The learning organisation
((Senge, 2006) adapted by Mark Wearden)

The systemic thinking output of the learning organisation concept while in itself being a developed capability is also a competence that will be recognised by stakeholders from the ability of the organisation to behave in a proactive rather than reactive manner.

5.3 People as a resource (sometimes referred to as 'human capital')

People sit at the heart of the resource potential within organisation. This is clearly recognised through models such as the learning organisation which rely upon stretching of individuals to understand and reach for their personal potential.

An organisation can enhance and manage the strategic capability of individuals through:

◆ the development of a skills and knowledge requirement matrix, cross matching skills and knowledge of the individuals within the organisation with the skills and knowledge required to meet the competence requirements and expectations. This must not remain static and ongoing development and training is usually monitored and recorded within the HR department;

◆ targeted training and development of particular skills and a breadth of cross functional knowledge;

◆ the identification of 'rising stars' within an organisation through a comprehensive approach to succession planning. Rising stars will then become the go to person or champions or gurus to enhance the overall knowledge and specialism within the organisation as a whole as opposed to individuals operating in silos (not sharing);

◆ the recognition of individuality through effective leadership; and

◆ the development of a dynamic team environment.

People can also be a dangerous resource to rely upon if they:

◆ have too much autonomy or power which can be used to dominate decision-making;

◆ have an inappropriate attitude and approach to others which can lead to prejudicial behaviour, and the exclusion of people; or

◆ could cause substantive damage to the organisation, its capabilities and competencies through leaving and taking their knowledge with them, using their knowledge (e.g. in the use of IT) to disrupt the flow of a system, creating reputation damage by advertently or inadvertently disclosing corporate confidentiality.

Case study 5.9

Tesco recognises the vast number of people who are involved at every stage of its operational supply chain process, from supplier to customer.

Extract from Tesco plc Annual Report and Financial Statements 2018:

'As a leading retailer, our 440,000 colleagues serve around 80 million customers every week, in more than 6,800 stores and online.'

5.4 Money as a resource

Money is not just a resource in itself within every organisation, but also underpins the capability of the organisation to utilise its other resources, and the manner in which its competencies can be utilised to gain competitive advantage. The resource concept of money falls into three distinct categories:

◆ **Profitability**: the capability of the organisation to ensure that its income exceeds its costs

◆ **Wealth**: the creation of tangible and intangible wealth stakeholders of the organisation

◆ **Liquidity**: the realisation of cash from operational and funding activities to ensure that employees and creditors can be paid in full and on time

This requires the organisation to recognise that financial literacy is a core capability at differing levels of operation and is not just a director requirement:

◆ Intelligent analysis of the supply chain and the value chain, as discussed above requires the ability to assign monetary values aspect of the respective chains.

◆ Efficient and effective use of resources throughout the organisation will be better handled by people who understand the monetary value and significance of the resource that they are dealing with at the same time as being able to establish how spending and earning money will impact the current financial status reported (i.e. how liquidity works within the company and what subsequent effect any action may have on the assets and liabilities).

Money as a resource can create the ultimate risk to an organisation.

If there is insufficient working capital cash to pay creditors, they can force the closure of an organisation through the courts.

If stakeholders perceive that the monetary control within an organisation is inappropriate or inefficient, they may decide to withdraw their stake, not extend credit, refuse to continue to provide supplies, which could also lead the closure of the organisation.

Case study 5.10

Wal-Mart believes that its focus on the differing needs of its customer base has helped to drive its global success. It attributes this to a capabilities approach; it recruits, trains and encourages its workforce to hold and develop the capabilities required to satisfy its customers.

Adapted from 'Competing on capabilities', *Harvard Business Review*, **March/April 1992:**

What accounts for Wal-Mart's remarkable success? Most explanations focus on a few familiar and highly visible factors. The genius of founder

Sam Walton, who inspires his employees and has moulded a culture of service excellence; the 'greeters' who welcome customers at the door; the motivational power of allowing employees to own part of the business; the strategy of 'everyday low prices' that offers the customer a better deal and saves on merchandising and advertising costs. Economist also point to Wal-Mart's big stores, which offer economies of scale and a wider choice of merchandise.

The real secret of Wal-Mart's success lies deeper, in a set of strategic business decisions that transformed the company into a capabilities-based competitor with a relentless focus on satisfying the needs of customers.

Chapter summary

◆ This chapter differentiates between strategic capability and strategic competence, and it is important to understand the difference – *capability* being the potential to achieve an outcome and *competence* is having the ability to use the capabilities.

◆ Resources sit behind and feed the capabilities, and this helps to derive the strategy. The competence to deliver the strategy using the capabilities will drive competitive advantage.

◆ There is a need to be able to deal with the different attributes of tangible, intangible and human resources.

◆ Core competence is the ability to deliver, recognise and maximise the use of the available resources.

◆ Threshold capability is the ability to align organisational capabilities and competencies to deliver stakeholder value.

◆ Porter suggests that there are two types of competitive advantage – cost advantage and differentiation advantage.

◆ Barney identifies a range of competitive attributes using the acronym VRIO – value, rarity, inimitability and organisational support.

◆ Porter views the organisational supply chain to recognise the addition of value from a mixture of primary activities and support activities, suggesting that the correct alignment will drive margin for the organisation.

◆ The McKinsey 7S framework, comprising of hard and soft elements, is an example of a model that can be used to identify, understand and challenge different organisational capabilities and competencies.

◆ People and money are often recognised as the key resources required to drive competitive advantage and stakeholder value.

◆ The company secretary and governance professional needs to have a clear view of how and where tangible and intangible value is added within the organisational supply chain.

Part three

The impact of culture, governance and purpose on strategy

Introduction

Part one explored the foundations for our understanding of strategy and how it is developed, introducing the need for objective analysis of the current status and structure of an organisation ('today') and the vision of what it might look like to improve or adjust the operation ('future'). Part two challenged the organisation and the development process from the differing external micro and macro environments within which the organisation operates. Part three changes the perspective and looks at the organisation from the inside, considering culture, governance, purpose and ethics.

Overview

Chapter 6 explores the meaning and impact of different organisational cultures, thinking about how they develop and why they matter from a strategic perspective. Culture is recognised as being driven by, but also epitomising, the people working within the organisation, and that the manner in which these people, their behaviour and beliefs are aligned can form the basis for strategic success.

Chapter 7 considers governance from the perspective of the development of strategy, although these two dimensions are intrinsically linked. Those empowered with governance are expected to develop the strategies required to deliver value to the differing stakeholders of the organisation. We align these stakeholders with expectation, risk and control, and consider how together these can help to drive the reputation of an organisation.

Chapter 8 revisits the core drivers of strategy from Chapter 1, but now challenges them in the light of the different concepts that have been studied and considered. We need to be able to determine how and why the organisation exists and what it is trying to achieve – its purpose/vision.

Chapter 9 examines why people behave in the way they do. What is the rationale for their decisions, are they based upon a set of principles, rules or a code, internal policies and procedures or are they driven by the ever-changing circumstances of personal and organisational life? The accumulation of these corporate decisions and the perception of personal and corporate behaviour adds further to the corporate reputation. In today's world of environmental consciousness, we need to ensure we behave in a socially responsible manner.

Learning outcomes

At the end of this part, students will be able to:

◆ demonstrate a thorough understanding of the meaning and importance of culture within an organisation;

◆ understand the different types of culture models argued by Handy, Schein, Johnson and others;

◆ consider why there is a need for a breadth of cultural awareness in our local, national , multinational and multicultural business environment;

◆ understand and explain in detail the intrinsic relationship between governance and strategy;

◆ consider the alignment of strategy, risk and control as an essential part of governance;

◆ determine the needs and expectations of differing stakeholder groups, recognising the particular drive and expectations of shareholders;

◆ demonstrate an understanding of the different aspects of internal and external risk that are faced within an organisation;

◆ consider and analyse how the core aspects of the strategic journey – vision, mission, objectives and goals, contribute to and help to shape the purpose of the organisation;

◆ apply different models to the analysis of organisational purpose;

◆ understand the difference between principle-based ethics and situational-based ethics;

◆ consider how and why the growth of corporate social responsibility (CSR) has challenged organisations to search deep within themselves to protect and enhance their strategy and their business; and

◆ understand and demonstrate how culture, governance, purpose and ethics can be aligned strategically to enhance organisational reputation; and the risks of getting this wrong.

Chapter six
Strategy and organisational culture

Contents

1. Introduction

Accountants will often refer to a balance sheet as a snapshot, or a picture, of the finances of an organisation at a particular moment in time. In consideration of the development of strategy it is important that we are able to understand more than just the financial dimensions of an organisation at that moment in time.

It is necessary to understand why it is that the organisation behaves in the way that it behaves, why it is that the people interact in particular ways, and how the organisation interacts with its internal and external stakeholders (there is a detailed discussion of stakeholders in Chapter 7).

This is what is known as the *culture* of the organisation.

> Culture:
> – the arts and other expressions of human intellectual achievement
> – the ideas, customs, and social behaviour of a particular people or society

The dictionary definitions above suggest that the word 'culture' covers both tangible human output such as the creation of a piece of art or music, and also intangible aspects of human behaviour such as the growth of particular ways of living or behaving.

This chapter will explore how and why an understanding of the culture of an organisation, the snapshot of that organisation at a particular moment in time, our often referred to 'today' point, is fundamental in both the process and understanding of how to develop and challenge strategy.

A company secretary and governance professional will be required to be both part of, and at times apart from, the culture. As an employee of the organisation, they contribute to the culture, but the role will often require them to step back, mentally and/or physically, and consider how and why other people, and the organisation, are behaving in the way they are. The role requires significant objectivity, and the ability to understand and consider cultural drivers is a core skill to be developed in our own strategic development.

Case study 6.1

At BAE there is a clear view of the importance of its organisational culture, the tone from the top that aims to inspire the organisational ethos in satisfying stakeholder expectations.

Extract from BAE plc Annual Report and Financial Statements 2017:

'*Our culture*

As a company, we focus not simply on how much money we make but, more importantly, how we make money. The tone is set at the top and cascades throughout the organisation. We are proud of what we do and committed to serve and equip those that serve and protect us. We aim to inspire and excel in the work we do and the technology we develop. The management ethos is to work with customers in the spirit of partnership, striving to go the extra mile in the products we make and the service we offer, recognising that we must earn everything and are entitled to nothing.

We believe it is only by adopting these principles that we can win the backing of our stakeholders and the support of society at large.'

2. Culture and history

Consider this extract from the model of the strategic journey.

Figure 6.1 Operation of TODAY
© Mark Wearden

Our definition of what is happening 'today' is summed up in the operational circle where people are either:

◆   implementing the previously defined strategic tactics; or

◆   monitoring the results of that implementation; or

◆   making permitted adjustments within the currently permitted parameters of the operation of the organisation.

All three of these aspects are happening within the culture of every organisation at whichever moment in time we might choose to consider or observe it.

The parameters of the operational circle represent the working everyday culture of the organisation, the accumulated history of strategic thought, and the decisions that have been taken to the point at which we are considering the organisation. Part of the process of the development of strategy is to allow people within an organisation to fulfil the task requirement by using their own intellect, experience and intelligence to ensure that the organisation's strategic vision is being delivered.

We recognise that the forces of the macro environment are likely to challenge these parameters, but if we have developed our strategic plan effectively, the internal (micro) allowed parameters of decision making will enable people within a learning organisation (as discussed previously) to drive the organisation forward in alignment with the strategic vision of the future.

The point at which we analyse organisational culture can only ever be a consideration of the accumulation of wisdom and activity of those who have developed and operated the organisation from its original starting point to that very moment of analysis. To be able to understand the culture of an organisation requires us to consider its history.

2.1 History

Many organisations have long histories and their cultural drivers can stem back many years.

Case study 6.2

The Guinness Book of World Records suggests that the two oldest companies in the world still in existence are two Japanese hot spring hotels, one founded in 705 and the other in 718.

Often these cultural drivers are intrinsically linked with the beliefs of the original founders and have remained as a core part of the organisational ethos and are immediately recognised by a wide group of stakeholders. One negative aspect of this is that there can be conflicting visions between founders and directors and some organisations have been known to have issues when they have a dominant shareholder/owners – an example would be Rupert Murdoch and News International.

The following are examples of where the name and the culture associated with that name continue to this day.

Case study 6.3

In the UK, the John Lewis partnership was established in 1928 creating a different style of ownership of such a large organisation, the original cultural ideals of its founder, John Stephen Lewis, continue to this day.

In the United States of America, the Jim Beam bourbon company was founded in 1795.

In Italy, the Beretta gun company, founded in 1526, is recorded as the oldest manufacturing company in the world.

Barney (1986) explains that each organisation has a unique culture which has developed over the life of that organisation and is embedded in the history and heritage of the organisation and its employees. He suggests that culture is always difficult to describe, as its idiosyncratic nature is often taken for granted; this therefore makes it difficult to imitate.

The effective development of strategy requires an understanding of how an organisation behaves, and why it behaves in that way. This cultural understanding can be achieved by firstly considering the historical development of the organisation, the different forces that have impacted upon its behaviours, and secondly by considering how it aligns with the stereotypical models of culture (based on other organisations) that will be discussed in this chapter.

2.2 Organisational culture

If you look around you, in any organisation, what you see and breathe is the operating culture of that organisation at that moment in time.

It is suggested by Barney (1986) that culture is able to deliver a competitive advantage for an organisation and he defines culture as 'a complex set of values, beliefs, assumptions and symbols that define the way in which a firm conducts its business'. Further, that culture can improve efficiency through enabling appropriate focus on areas such as customers or innovation.

A frequently occurring definition of the word 'culture' with many different citations, is:

> 'the way we do things around here'.

This phrase is often used because it epitomises exactly what is meant by culture; people behave in a particular manner based around a number of different drivers and stimuli.

Our need, as we help to evolve the strategy, is to understand these drivers in a structured manner from different perspectives to help us to better analyse how the company behaves now, today, and our perception and vision of either how we would like those behaviours to evolve, or how those behaviours can underpin and be used to strengthen the strategic direction.

Consider the differing perspectives of culture from these organisational statements. What would you expect to find as you walked through their doors? If you have visited Tesco or John Lewis do you get this 'cultural feel'?

Case study 6.4

Differing perspectives of culture

GSK

'we aim to have a values-based culture by training people in the standards we expect, encouraging the reporting of any concerns and embedding our values into the way we measure employee performance.'

BAE

'we continue to build a culture where our senior leaders and employees are empowered to make the right decisions and to know where to go for help.'

TESCO

'inclusivity, and creating a culture where everyone feels welcome, remain integral to our business.'

JOHN LEWIS

'it is our culture of democratic vitality, created by all partners, acting as passionate co-owners, which will continue to set us apart from other businesses both now and in the future.'

Handy (1993) suggests that:

'in organisations there are deep-set beliefs about the way work should be organised, the way authority should be exercised, people rewarded, and people controlled ... (culture) is often about the degrees of formalisation required ... and the interaction of rules, procedures, and results ... all of these form part of the culture of an organisation'

Schein (2004) defines organisational culture as:

'the basic assumptions and beliefs that are shared by members of an organisation, that operate unconsciously, and define in a basic, taken-for-granted fashion an organisation's view of itself and its environment'

He further suggested (see Figure 6.2 opposite) that there are three distinct levels of organisational culture.

Underlying assumptions are held unconsciously by people working within the organisation. These assumptions implicitly guide the behaviour and opinions of employees for the majority of day-to-day operational activities.

Artefacts

Values

Underlying assumptions

Figure 6.2
((Schein, 2004) adapted by Mark Wearden)

Values are often promoted within an organisation, to epitomise what that organisation stands for. In reality there is often a gap between the values of the organisation and the individual values held by employees. However, these values allow an individual to decide how to tackle any situation or decision which is not resolved automatically through the underlying assumptions. The leaders of an organisation 'set the tone' and are ideally those who comply with the organisation's values, acting as inspirational employees. Acting with integrity should promote integrity in the people being managed which should then cascade down throughout the organisation.

Artefacts are the visible and tangible evidence of organisational culture. These include everything from the structure and layout of the workspace, to the written and spoken language within the organisation. In today's world this would include the way in which technology is expected to be used – for example, a company policy which allows people to use the internet for personal use while sitting at the desk.

As a company secretary and governance professional we are often required to deal with and understand the 'artefacts' of the organisation and then relate them to the present day context.

Stop and think 6.1

Take time to think about the organisation where you are currently working (or studying). How could you use Schein's threefold model to consider and identify the culture?

What are the underlying assumptions, the values and the artefacts that would define the culture and the human behaviours?

2.3 Strategic drift

Recall the differentiation between rational and emergent strategy discussed in Chapter 2. Johnson (2017) argues that much of emergent strategy is based upon incremental change which develops from cultural influences within an organisation. He further suggests that there is often a time gap between the development of the strategy and the changes within the environment. He refers to this as strategic drift and he recognises four distinct phases in the drift process. There is an example suggested here of how each phase might affect an organisation:

- ◆ **Incremental strategic change**: the small changes which occur during long periods of relative stability, where the external environment is changing slowly, and organisational strategy is able to adapt gradually without the need for more radical change.

    - Example: A manufacturing organisation (QWT) has implemented a new piece of control software to track efficiency in its people-controlled construction process, the strategic objective is to identify gaps in the process; it is estimated that two annual cycles will be required to fully identify and correct such gaps. During this two-year period there will be updates to the software, there will be changes of personnel, and there may be other customer and supplier influences, each of these are gradual and strategic direction will change incrementally with each of these influences.

- ◆ **Strategic drift**: occurs where micro and macro environmental changes restrict the ability of an organisation to amend its strategy. In this situation the organisation will continue on an incremental change path with an increasing gap developing between the planned strategic path and the surrounding environment.

    - Example: QWT fails to identify that its major competitors are replacing people-controlled construction processes with robotic processes and thus driving significant cost savings. QWT begin to lose significant customer orders to the competitors. They focus on trying to maximise efficiency in their current people-controlled process, but this has led to a significant drift away from the external competitive environment.

- ◆ **Flux** is caused by the gaps that have developed during the strategic drift stage, this can often cause significant periods of disagreement and complexity within an organisation. Different factions will be trying to find alternative methods to either change strategy or implement a radical environmental adaptation.

    - Example: QWT is a manufacturing business that started in 1942 and has gradually evolved. The current mixture of strategies, including the control software have been designed to help to gradually modernise the processes within the business and increase efficiency. Three of the five senior managers have spent their working lives within the business, gradually increasing their respective roles and responsibilities; the other two senior managers have been appointed within the last three years. The flux, as described by Johnson, can be imagined as the more recent managers wish to abandon the slow strategic journey and make immediate changes to retain their competitive edge, while the more traditional managers believe that it will 'all come right in the end'.

◆ **Transformation or death** is the result that naturally emanates from the stage of flux. Either there is an agreed resolution to realign the strategy with its external environment, or alternatively the strategy ceases to exist. In a worst-case scenario this might lead to the demise of the entire organisation.

– Example: An increasing number of customers begin to defect to the QWT competitors, giving those customers both a lower cost price and a more uniform product (due to the robotic production methods of the competitors). QWT are faced with the need for either a rapid and dramatic change to their business processes, or the risk of losing most or all of their customer base for this particular process. Whether this would cause the death of the business would depend on the material significance of this particular manufacturing process. The loss of customers and product can be both tangibly destructive through loss of sales and profit, but also, they can be intangibly destructive through the loss of reputation.

2.4 The influence of the past and the importance of recognising bias

To fully understand the culture of an organisation, it is essential to understand how an organisation has evolved and to be able to identify internal, micro, and macro forces that have resulted in the current structure, personnel and culture.

Such understanding requires significant consideration of the people who have been, and continue to be, involved with the organisation, their particular idiosyncrasies and the way they have chosen to shape and influence the culture of the business, both top-down and bottom-up.

Think back to the 'ladder of inference' introduced in Chapter 1, as developed by Argyris (1990). The 'ladder' was used to consider how the brain enables us to take any action, from the simplest decision to the most complex, with each individual brain moving through a series of steps based around sensory observation, with the assimilation of data and then the iterative sorting and selection which enable us to take a specific action. At the outset of each such process each brain will be influenced by the surrounding culture at that point and therefore inform and develop the culture further by the decision made or action taken.

The use of the 'inference' model suggests that the penultimate stage before we take any action or decision, combined with the result of the action or decision, will inform the earlier stage of 'data filtration', which allows us to retain and learn from what is perceived as relevant for our ongoing approach to life (our attitude).

This process can be described as the basis of prejudice or bias within the brain.

This prejudice is the basis of what has become known as natural or cognitive bias, and it is important to recognise the influence of this upon organisational culture. An Association of Chartered Certified Accountants (ACCA) publication 'Banishing Bias' (2017) recognises 12 frequent types of bias, as below – but different publications identify differing numbers of biases, with the extreme perhaps being the 'cognitive bias codex' (Manoogian, 2016) which identifies 180+ different biases!

Cognitive bias	Summary
Hindsight	Being wise after the event
Outcome	Results rather than origination
Confirmation	Selecting what agrees with our existing beliefs
Anchoring	Using a benchmark to judge
Availability	Not looking beyond the obvious
Groupthink	Fitting in with the crowd – 'when in Rome…'
Overconfidence	'We know better'
Recency	Not looking far enough back
Conjunction	Predefined linkage in our minds
Selectivity	Not looking beyond the obvious
Stereotyping	Box thinking
Blind-spot	Lack of 3600 vision

Table 6.1 Cognitive bias
((ACCA, 2017) adapted by Mark Wearden)

Given the objectivity required in the consideration of strategy it is important for a company secretary/ governance professional to be aware of the range of different cognitive biases, including their own, which will be affecting the development of strategy.

Stop and think 6.2

Be totally honest with yourself and consider your own cognitive biases. Use the list above and try to think of a scenario where each of them has applied to you in your own decision-making. Think further how your biases and decisions have influenced others around you, and ultimately the culture of your organisation.

3. Understanding culture

The values and beliefs of each individual manager and employee within an organisation will influence the strategic decision-making within that organisation. Each of us, as individuals, exist within a range of different cultural influences, therefore to understand the cultural conflict and cultural alignment that exist within an organisation it is important to consider the different frames of reference for those cultures, where they originate and their differing impacts.

Test yourself 6.1

Why is culture often identified as 'the way we do things around here'?

3.1 Cultural frames of reference

Johnson (2017) suggests that there are three main cultural frames that need to be taken into consideration to understand how and why an individual behaves in a particular way:

- **geographic**: mixture of national and regional influences
- **organisational field**: the sector of the industry with its differing professional influencers
- **organisation**: the intermix of subcultures and divisions within the organisation itself.

Geographic

It is recognised by many writers that people originating from different countries and regions may have significantly differing attitudes to work and authority. Hofstede (1980) identified the existence of cultural differences between the countries of southern and northern Europe during the years of the Roman Empire 2,000 years ago. He has been criticised for his 'whole country' approach which some say fails to recognise the significant cultural differences that exist between different regions within one individual country. However, Hofstede suggested that there are at least four key dimensions to take into consideration with regard to national culture:

- **The relationship with authority and the acceptance of inequality**: Hofstede identified the difference between the authoritarian management style in much of Asia with the more democratic approach in Australia.
- **The relationship between an individual and groups of people**: Hofstede contrasted the individualism of the US with the collectivism of South America.
- **The longevity of the vision**: Hofstede compared the shorter-term perspective of North America and Africa with the longer-term orientation of many Asian cultures.
- **The tolerance of uncertainty and ambiguity**: Hofstede suggested that while Chinese culture is generally pragmatic and accepting of uncertainty, Japanese culture is associated with a much higher intolerance of uncertainty.

Organisational field

The concept of an 'organisational field' describes any group of organisations that have frequent contact and relationships with each other, more so than with other organisations outside of that field, and therefore have developed a shared cultural approach. This can include particular sectors of industry (e.g. engineering, aerospace, retail) but might also refer to cross sectoral influencers (e.g. accountancy, law, finance).

Any one of these might be described as a professional field, but the reality is often a complex interweaving of different fields with each other. Johnson (2017) suggests that it is useful to consider three different types of concept with regard to cultural impact of an organisational field:

◆ **Categorisation**: the labelling of activities, products or services to identify societal impact – in technology we could differentiate the marketing and use of desk-based computers, laptop computers, tablets and increasingly advanced mobile phones.

◆ **Recipes**: a set of assumptions, norms and routines that are held in common, sometimes referred to as the 'shared wisdom' or 'best practice' for that field. In Chapter 7 we will discuss corporate governance, and it could be argued that the UK Corporate Governance Code is a strategic recipe in this context.

◆ **Legitimacy**: the institutionalisation of both categories and recipes across a period of time will lead to an assumption that people operating within the field should always follow these particular strategic routes. An example is the way that universities in the UK adapt and reflect their mutual approach to a diversity of degree courses and the attraction of students from an increasingly wider social and cultural background. In recent years this concept has been clearly evidenced by the gradual reduction in university entry-level expectations within all but the top universities.

Organisation

Schein (2004) suggests that organisational culture is:

> 'the basic assumptions and beliefs that are shared by members of an organisation, operate unconsciously and define in the basic taken-for-granted fashion an organisation's view of itself and its environment'.

This is epitomised by the phrase referred to above – 'the way we do things around here' – and is expanded in Figure 6.3. This suggests the constituent parts of the culture of an organisation are closely aligned to its strategic thinking.

◆ **Mission**
  - The underlying causes of the heartbeat of an organisation.
  - Those areas of strategic direction that are held closely and often with deep conviction.
  - The individual and collective focus on the underlying and core organisational purpose(s).

◆ **Methods**
  - The habits of the organisation, why certain tasks are carried out in certain ways (refer back to Chapter 5).

Figure 6.3 The culture of an organisation
© Mark Wearden

- − The communication infrastructure (or lack thereof).
- − The means of transforming inputs into outputs (refer back to Chapter 3).
◆ **Principles**
- − The hierarchical structure within the organisation and the flow of information to enable the fulfilment of tasks.
- − The strategic parameters and ethos that exist at any particular point in time.
- − The structure of interactions and communication with differing stakeholders.
◆ **Values**
- − The fundamental beliefs about humanity that pervade the organisation – e.g. individualism versus collectivism, authority versus democracy.
- − The ethical standards that employees are expected to adhere to.
- − The manner in which employees are expected to interact with each other and with stakeholders.

3.2 Subcultures

In anything other than a single person organisation there will be an interplay of the main cultural drivers with a range of differing subcultures. These might be based around the behaviour and expectations of different individuals, but will often be the result of different factions within the organisation and the creation of a diversity of aligned and conflicting 'fields'.

They might be based around different local, national and regional cultures within a larger multi-national organisation, but equally might be based around different internal departments and operational functions within the same office (e.g. there is often a different cultural approach between a sales team and a finance team).

Test yourself 6.2

Discuss briefly the alignment of assumptions, values and artefacts in organisational culture.

3.3   Models of culture

The culture of an organisation could be identified as the accumulation at any point in time of the different collection of people involved in the organisation at that moment, with their different biases and history working together within structure of the organisational biases (values) and history.

Culture will vary from organisation to organisation and will also vary between timeframes within the same organisation. However, there are certain generic culture patterns that can be identified across organisations, which are useful as a benchmark to assess an organisation. Such models, in theoretical consideration and in practical use, should always be a benchmark and not used as fixed framework to attempt to fit an organisation into a particular 'box'.

The following models, together with the others in this chapter, suggest differing generic routes that can be useful when assessing organisational culture.

Harrison and Handy: cultural types
In 1972, in the *Harvard Business Review*, Roger Harrison (Harrison, 1972) discussed the different aspects of character that exist within organisations identifying and differentiating between:

- **Power orientation**: the attempt to dominate the operating environment.
- **Role orientation**: a focus on legality, legitimacy and responsibility.
- **Task orientation**: the highest value always being the achieving of goals.
- **Person orientation**: serving the needs of members.

In 1993, Charles Handy (Handy, 1993) expanded these aspects of organisational culture and added a diagrammatic representation. These are now usually referred to as Harrison and Handy's cultural types, and are included in Figure 6.4 with some additional commentary and examples.

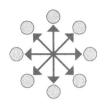

Power

- Control from the central power force extends throughout the organisation using key individuals
- All depends on relationships with the leader
- E.g. political organisations, entrepreneurial and specialised organisations

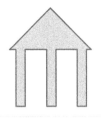

Role

- Strong organisational pillars which support the organisation – people and/or systems
- Structured and stable making change difficult
- E.g. banks, insurance companies, traditional manufacturing businesses

Task

- The network of people, roles and goals within an organisation working together but sometimes with loose connections
- Talent, energy, ambition tend to dominate
- E.g. consulting, advertising, research, high-tech

Person

- Boundaries exist to protect and provide an infrastructure for the people and their needs
- Personal freedom and mutual interest
- E.g. lawyers, medical practices, universities, organisations sharing space and facilities

Figure 6.4
((Handy, 1993) adapted by Mark Wearden)

Deal and Kennedy: organisational cultures
Terrence Deal and Allan Kennedy (1982) suggested that organisational culture was based around a set of six interlocked elements.

◆ **History**: sharing the narrative of the past.

◆ **Values and beliefs**: sharing what is important within the organisation.

◆ **Rituals and ceremonies**: the everyday habits of the organisation.

◆ **Stories**: the inherited tales of why things happen in the way they do.

◆ **Heroic figures**: previous and current charismatic leaders.

◆ **Cultural network**: the communication routes that enable people to find out what they need to know.

While studying and working with these elements across a variety of different types of organisation, Deal and Kennedy found that there were four distinct types of culture that kept re-occurring.

Figure 6.5
((Deal & Kennedy, 1982) adapted by Mark Wearden)

Their suggested structure of culture identification focuses on the interaction between the speed of feedback communication (in particular the iterative communication which allows change) and the level of strategic risk to the organisation and the individuals involved:

◆ **Macho, tough-guy culture**: people enjoy excitement and work hard to become organisational stars, recognising that this is an all or nothing approach which has little regard for teamwork or mutual support. If you succeed you are recognised, if you fail you are out. The entertainment and sporting sectors can be identified with this type of culture.

◆ **Process culture**: this sits at the other extreme from the macho culture, where no individual person, or individual action, is likely to have a recognised personal significant impact upon the success of the organisation. It will take an extended period of time to drive organisational change. Examples would be large retailers, banks, insurance companies and government departments.

◆ **Work and play hard culture**: the risks that are taken by employees are low but feedback on how well they are performing is almost immediate. An employee will be required to maintain a high energy performance, but will also be required to play a role as part of a team. Examples would be sales departments, fast food outlets and smaller retailers.

◆ **Bet-your-company culture**: the decisions are high risk, but the impact can be slow to materialise. Organisations may require significant capital investment to enable research and development and will require people to believe in the eventual outcome and build a team awareness and knowledge bank. Examples would be oil companies and pharmaceutical businesses.

This approach can be used to analyse and challenge culture within an organisation through developing appropriate questions alongside each of the four dimensions. As an example, long-term sustainability can be challenged by a single question against each of the above culture types:

◆   Is the future of the organisation safe in the hands of high profile, tough-guy individuals?

◆   Is the bureaucratic process too slow to enable the correction of errors, and the recognition of ultimately fatal consequences?

◆   Is the high energy involved in the work and play masking underlying poor performance by one or more individuals?

◆   Is the organisation able to react swiftly enough when the operating parameters (the odds) of the original 'bet' change significantly?

Johnson: the cultural web

The 'cultural web' was originally developed in 1992 by Johnson. It is offered as an alternative way of considering the current cultural paradigm of an organisation. They suggest that the recognition and understanding of the different drivers of the current paradigm will expose the rationale for the current culture and thus enable identification of aspects that might need to be changed as part of a strategic change programme. These are quite similar to, and build upon, the original aspects of culture identified by Deal and Kennedy.

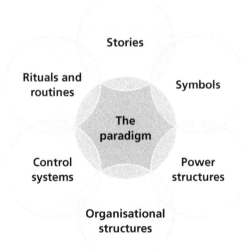

Figure 6.6 The cultural web
((Johnson, 2017) adapted by Mark Wearden)

◆   **Organisational structures**: the formal hierarchical lines as identified on an organisation chart, but also the written lines of communication and human interaction where influence is exerted in an attempt to achieve the desired strategic results.

◆ **Power structures**: the recognition that significant decisions are made by a defined number of individuals within any organisation, and it is these people who ultimately hold the power irrespective of any organisational structure. Sometimes such 'power' people can fall outside the formal organisational structure, such as an owner who is not regularly involved in the business, or a demanding shareholder.

◆ **Symbols**: the tangible visual presence of an organisation within its near and far environment. This can include logos, titles, types of car driven by executives, layout of offices, differing privileges for different levels within the hierarchy etc.

◆ **Stories**: how people, inside and outside the infrastructure, talk about the organisation. The myths and the realities of how the organisation has developed since its origin to today. Such stories can include the impact of internal and external events and also the mythologising of how certain individuals have had significant influence.

◆ **Rituals and routines**: the daily behaviour of people within the organisation to each other and to stakeholders. The expectations of how the organisation operates, the meeting structure, the level of freedom, potential time constraints, the pattern of a normal working day. In his work on motivation Herzberg (1964) would have defined this aspect as the hygiene factors.

◆ **Control systems**: the formal and informal methods of monitoring and maintaining people and systems throughout the organisation. Examples are financial systems, quality control systems, and will include methods of appraisals, remuneration reward and recognition. The introduction of whole organisation technology systems such as that provided by SAP, and the development of exception reporting within organisations, will have potentially increased the significance of this dimension.

Organisational culture has been seen as one of the reasons behind the financial crisis of 2007/08. Recent reports and corporate failures might suggest that not very much has really changed in the intervening period despite the best attempts of regulators and others.

Stop and think 6.3

Remember that all such models are being used to try to determine how and why an organisation, and its people, are behaving in a particular way and what is driving the culture of the organisation:

> **'the way things are being done around here'**

Consider your own working environment.

Take the time to apply the models to that environment and try to identify the core cultural drivers that surround you and your colleagues.

4. The importance of culture

This chapter has considered the importance of understanding how and why an organisation and its people behave in a particular way. As this is a text on the development of strategy, it is important that we consider culture from a historic and a strategic perspective. As has been suggested in earlier chapters, it is important to recognise that all effective strategic development and strategic initiatives have a base point from which they start. The development of strategy is the recognition of the need to change the status quo, and this may well include the challenge of trying to influence or change the organisational culture.

This next section will suggest some of the forces that organisational culture brings, and why we need to recognise its importance.

The culture is the lifeblood of the organisation, it helps us to identify how things happen, and how and why people behave in particular ways.

4.1 Dominant, strong and weak cultures

Dominant culture

It is sometimes possible to identify a *dominant culture* within an organisation, where it is clear that either a majority of employees, or the core focus of the organisation is driven by and moulded by an overriding, and often unchallenged, set of values. The various culture models identified above are designed to help to analyse the dominant culture which exists within an organisation and to attempt to understand why that culture exists.

Case study 6.5

Netflix is a well-known, successful company with a dominant culture. Instead of focusing on core values, Netflix set out what mattered and what the company expected in its people. There's no vacation policy, no travel policy, and no annual employee reviews. The result is a demand for self-sufficient employees who feel a responsibility to the company.

They are transparent about their company culture and acknowledge that such a demanding culture is not for everyone, but that it is necessary in order to be a ground-breaking, successful business.

Mullins (2016) suggested that there are differing reasons why an understanding and recognition of corporate culture is important – he argued that the following aspects build upon a consideration of behaviour within the workplace.

◆ **Work ethic**: how people behave and how people are treated.

◆ **Parameters of control**: how inappropriate behaviour, views and practices are controlled and corrected.

◆ **Performance and results**: how success is measured and how people are rewarded.

◆ **The evolution of leadership**: how momentum is maintained and who follows whom.

◆ **Differing beliefs**: how reality will always come to the foreground, even if organisational values are imposed, people's own beliefs will drive their behaviour.

Strong culture

A *strong culture* is defined by the core values being widely shared and held by a majority of the people within an organisation, and that these shared beliefs will drive the organisation forward.

In a study of companies with outstanding performance, Goldsmith and Clutterbuck (1997) observed:

> 'All of our case-study companies place great store on the development and dissemination of core values, namely the relatively few values that establish the cultural identity of the company and with which they expect all key people in the organisation to have instinctive empathy.'

They suggested that through such values the culture might:

◆ give people a sense of identity

◆ develop commitment

◆ guide and shape behaviour

◆ internalise control systems

◆ support and sustain decision making

◆ make communication and co-operation easier

◆ decrease ambiguity and align strategic purpose.

Weak culture

In a *weak culture* this will be reversed, and the minority will be always be striving to get their views and values heard within the overall operational structure. They tend to follow their own personal goals rather than those of the organisation.

Kotter and Heskett (1992) suggested that weak and unhealthy corporate cultures are derived from:

◆ individual entrepreneurship and/or luck

◆ an over dominant market position

◆ a lack of appropriately qualified or experienced managers

◆ increasing bureaucracy

◆ ignoring of external influences and forces

◆ management becoming insular or political

◆ an arrogant approach led by hubris.

Test yourself 6.3

Write one brief sentence to explain each of the four cultural types of organisation identified by Charles Handy, giving an example of each type.

4.2   Culture as a liability

A weak culture can become a liability to the strategic progress of an organisation and provide a barrier to change. Ultimately this can lead to the failure of a business.

When there is a disconnect between the presumed values of the organisation and those of the people involved, it is likely that the prevailing culture will have a destructive effect on present and future effectiveness. An organisation that is battling with its internal differences is likely to fail to respond appropriately to a changing external environment, and therefore the culture is preventing appropriate change.

In the global arena, the challenges faced by IBM and Kodak are often quoted as examples of cultures that failed to respond to technological changes in the external environment. In the UK marketplace, the demise or commercial decline of many high street retailers has been driven by their inability to respond to the changing habits and expectations of their consumers, in particular the rapid growth of online internet trading – examples would be Jessops, HMV and Maplin.

A strong culture can equally become a liability to strategic progress. An insistence on maintaining core cultural values that are widely shared within the organisation while failing to recognise that such values are out of step with a changing macro environment can lead to organisational destruction.

An example of this is the failure of many organisations to promote a wider diversity at all levels within the hierarchy, and in particular to fail to address the gender balance within senior management and board director roles. Many organisations have been forced to react to external pressures from the Financial Reporting Council (FRC) and others to address such issues of diversity when their previously strong cultures have consciously or unconsciously supported institutional bias and been insensitive to the wider social expectations.

Strong and weak cultures can be key points of leverage during a process of merger or acquisition. While the apparent mismatch would suggest that an organisation with a strong culture should be more easily able to acquire an organisation with a weak culture, it might be that the disparities within the weak culture provide both a financial and operational stumbling block to hamper a potentially successful merger or acquisition. It is important though, to recognise that there are a number of different ways in which the interaction between strong and weak cultures can be resolved.

Culture is always about people, their individual abilities, powers and weaknesses. It is ultimately the idiosyncratic nature of people that will drive strategic success or failure. Even Patty McCord from Netflix (Case study 6.5) eventually lost her role at the company through her insistence that the liberal atmosphere needed to dominate all aspects of the organisation and failed to recognise the need for a tighter structure in some areas given the rapid growth of the company.

4.3   The positive influence of culture on strategy

In 2006, Mark Fields, President of the Ford Motor Company was quoted as saying:

> 'culture eats strategy for breakfast'

by which he meant that culture will always have an intrinsically important impact upon the strategy of any business, and that it is impossible to consider the development of strategy without understanding the nature of the organisational culture of the immediate company and the individuals and other companies operating within the competitive sector and environment.

Prior to this, Grinyer and Spender (1979) had illustrated the enduring influence that culture has upon strategy and corporate performance, recognising that the need for cultural change (step 3 below) will often be required to successfully deliver sustainable strategic change. However, recognising that cultural change can be demanding (see section 5 below) he suggests that fundamental change to culture is more likely to be required through a significant external demand or force, whereas the improvement of immediate corporate performance should be achievable through either step 1 or step 2 in their model.

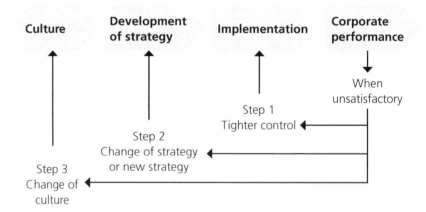

Figure 6.7
((Grinyer & Spender, 1979) adapted by Mark Wearden)

In respect of this model, Johnson (2017) suggests that:

> 'Even if people accept the need to change a culture's emphasis on the importance of conforming to established rules, routines and reporting relationships, they do not readily do so. It is a fallacy to assume a reasoned argument necessarily changes deeply embedded assumptions in collective experience built up over long periods of time.'

4.4 Culture Coalition Project

In 2016 the FRC together with other professional organisations, including ICSA: The Governance Institute and the Institute of Business Ethics, initiated a number of thought-leadership projects around the subject of corporate culture, under the generic title of the Culture Coalition Project. This resulted in a range of direct publications, but perhaps more importantly, as a result of this project, aspects of the importance of organisational culture are now recognised in and underpin a number of aspects of the 2018 UK Corporate Governance Code.

It is widely accepted that a core function of a board of directors is the development and oversight of the strategy direction and long-term sustainable strategic success of the organisations that they are empowered to govern. The following quotations from the FRC publication 'Corporate Culture and the Role of Boards' (2016) underline the significant importance of culture in the development of strategy.

> 'The strategy to achieve a company's purpose should reflect the values and culture of the company and should not be developed in isolation.'

> 'A healthy culture is a valuable asset, a source of competitive advantage and vital to the creation and protection of long-term value. It is the board's role to determine the purpose of the company and ensure that the company's values, strategy and business model are aligned to it.'

> 'Culture is not a separate item but there are elements of it in all discussions, decisions and actions.'

The report also identifies the following list of areas (among others) which require constant vigilance to ensure alignment of the strategy of the organisation with the culture of the organisation:

- silo thinking
- dominant chief executive
- leadership arrogance
- lack of openness to challenge
- lack of diversity
- hierarchical attitude.

5. Creating, sustaining and changing culture

5.1 The forces that create culture

This chapter has discussed at length a range of constituent aspects of the culture of an organisation. These aspects could be described as the forces that are shaping and creating the culture of the organisation.

The concept of shaping culture can be aligned to the concept of emergent strategy and Mintzberg's image (1987) of the potter shaping the strategy at their potter's wheel. The culture creates an image and an intent, but the shape will continually change depending upon the interaction of differing forces.

Culture is not and can never be something solid, fixed and unchangeable. Culture, at any point in any organisation, is the live interaction of a growing and changing accumulation of different forces. These are summarised in the matrix below and the impact and significance of many of the specific interactions will be discussed through the remainder of this text. This is not a finite model and hence the need for a question mark in each segment; specific challenges will vary between organisations.

Cultural force	Past	Present	Future
Purpose	– Vision and goals – Changes during evolution – ?	– Clarity of direct 'today' purpose – Sense-check of reality – ?	– Longevity of vision – Clarity of organisational focus – ?
People	– Original drivers – Charismatic leaders and managers – ?	– Key driving players – action and knowledge – Sources of power – ?	– Succession planning – Evolving skill-sets – ?
Product	– Market impact – Pattern of growth – ?	– Market strength – Reputation – ?	– Evolving customer requirements – Macro and micro environment impact – ?

Table 6.2 The forces of culture
© Mark Wearden

The suggestion here is that the culture we see around us today is the impact of the continuing forces of the past, the real forces of today and the perceived forces of the future. Specific culture is unique to each organisation at any specific point in its life-cycle, although we will be able to identify common trends and habits when that organisation is compared to others.

5.2 The need to develop and sustain culture

Culture needs constant attention and consideration by those leading the organisation.

As the organisation evolves, along either rational or emergent lines, it is important to recognise who is taking account of the changing cultural forces. It was suggested above, that if strategy is cerebrally and practically aligned with strategic change, then culture can be a force for good. If, however, there is a disconnect between culture and strategy, the organisational gaps will start to appear, and are likely to increase exponentially if not tackled early – hence strategic drift.

Recall Carter's organisational model. This could suggest that culture is best developed and sustained through a recognition of the power structures within an organisation, which he describes as being like the fault lines that run underneath the surface of the earth – constantly shifting with minimal impact until a larger shift takes place resulting in an earthquake.

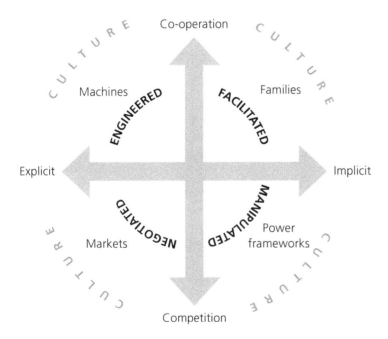

Figure 6.8
((Renaissance Management, 1999) adapted by Mark Wearden)

Carter's model illustrates a complexity of differing forces that need to be handled in the maintenance and evolution of culture. He illustrates the interaction that needs to exist between different types of approach within an organisation, and in particular the dynamic that has to be handled between power, markets, machines and the family concept of the people involved (after all much of our individual culture as human beings emerges from our experience of family).

Stop and think 6.4

Align the differing dynamics of Carter's model in Figure 6.8 above to your own organisation.

What are the key cultural driving forces 'today'?

Who are the key players – 'today'?

What is your role within such a framework?

5.3   The challenge of changing culture

The final two chapters of this text, Chapters 14 and 15, consider strategic change from the differing dimensions of process and people, and inevitably much of that strategic change is linked with the changing of culture within an organisation. The challenges of such cultural change in any organisation lie beyond the focused requirements of this Development of Strategy syllabus. However, it is important to briefly identify some of the aspects and techniques involved in such change. These are non-finite and non-exclusive starting points for the consideration of strategic change; students will be able to add many more from their own experience and thinking.

What is it that we might be trying to change?

◆   **Beliefs**: the changing of the mind of another person.

◆   **Behaviour**: the changing of the habits and practices of one or more people.

◆   **Focus**: the changing of strategic direction and drive.

How might we try to effect such change?

◆   **Direction**: the use of power to demand change.

◆   **Conformity**: human beings are not automatons and need reasons to comply.

◆   **Understanding**: this brings us back to the changing of beliefs.

Each organisation will need to consider its own need for, and route to, cultural change, in the same way that each organisation needs to determine its own strategic direction.

In their book *Nudge* (2008) Thaler and Sunstein suggest that change will often happen most effectively if started with a 'nudge', a small amount of pressure to help to move another person in a different direction. Their text includes some interesting thinking on how to best effect change, suggesting at the outset:

> 'To count as a mere nudge, any intervention must be easy. Nudges are not mandates. Putting the fruit at eye level within a supermarket or restaurant counts as a nudge. Banning junk food does not.'

As with all such approaches, they recognise the potential for the positive and negative use of the power of a nudge.

It would be reasonable to suggest that all culture change is only ever the desire of one or more individuals to alter the beliefs, behaviour and focus of one or more other individuals. Culture is very personal to people and to an organisation (a group of people).

Stop and think 6.5

When did you last manage to get someone to change their mind?

How did you achieve this?

What were the techniques that you used?

6. Organisational culture and national culture

Case study 6.6

Adapted from 'Managing Strategic Change' (Tichy, 1983)

The English Chairperson announced to the board meeting, 'it is now 12:30 and we must adjourn for lunch – it is important to eat at regular times and the restaurant will be waiting'.

The Eastern European finance director argued 'we are just in the middle of making a key decision, lunch and the restaurant can wait for us'.

The new Non-Executive Director from the Far East could not understand why food was not just available in the room so that the meeting could continue without interruption, and each person just eating what they personally required, as happened in his culture.

As the case study above suggests, cultural drivers extend beyond people and organisations. National culture has a significant influence on personal cultural norms. Research from Laurent (1983) found that national culture has a greater impact on employees than organisational culture. German employees working at an IBM factory in Munich are more likely to be influenced by German culture than by IBM culture.

Garratt (2010) believes that it is useful, if sometimes controversial, to be able to measure how and why national cultural differences are impacting upon an organisation stating:

'Having knowledge of the major national cultural dimensions on which your customers, strategic alliance partners, international suppliers, financiers and staff work makes for a more effective and efficient organisation.'

The importance of these geographic drivers has already been introduced in section 3 of this chapter, but we need to recognise that there are instances where cultures converge and instances where cultures continue to exhibit variance. In our multinational world of instant communication, it is important to recognise and respect the differences between such diverse cultural structures. Such alignment and difference can be exploited either deliberately or inadvertently as part of the political power-play of negotiation.

In his authoritative research on national cultural differences, Hofstede (1980) concluded that there were five major dimensions that exist within a national culture:

- **Power distance**: the extent to which power is distributed amongst different people and different hierarchical levels, and the ability for individuals to challenge each other and the structure.
- **Uncertainty avoidance**: the extent to which people feel threatened by unusual situations, and how they try to avoid them by living and working within the perceived rules.
- **Individualism versus collectivism**: the differing roles of individuals, families and network groups – recognising who looks after who within the organisational context.
- **Masculinity versus femininity**: the differing perspectives of, and beliefs about gender that exist within and between different national cultures.
- **Confucian dynamism**: does the organisation, and the society within which it is operating, exhibit a pragmatic future-oriented perspective which embraces change, or does it hold to historic conventional perspectives?

Hofstede's work was not accepted by all, and an alternative study was published by Trompenaars and Hampden-Turner (1998) concluding that people from different cultures vary in specific and predictable ways with each culture having its own thinking, values, beliefs and preferences. They summarised this by identifying seven different dimensions of cultural difference where they identified the dynamic that exists between different national cultures. A question has been assigned to each of these to focus on the real issue.

- **Universalism vs particularism**: do I obey, or can I interpret the rules?
- **Individualism vs communitarianism**: what comes first, me or the group?
- **Specific vs diffuse**: do we work to live, or do we live to work?
- **Neutral vs emotional**: am I allowed by others (and myself) to express my emotions?
- **Achievement vs ascription**: do others value me, or do they value the role that I am fulfilling?

◆ **Sequential vs synchronous time**: how many things can I do at once?

◆ **Internal vs external**: am I in control of my own destiny?

The following example from the motor industry illustrates well the need for culture alignment.

Case study 6.7

Adapted from *Strategic Intelligence* (Maccoby, 2017)

New United Motor Manufacturing Inc (NUMMI) was a joint venture of General Motors (GM) with Toyota established in Fremont, California in 1984. The venture took over a GM plant that had been shut down because of worker unrest and low productivity. NUMMI inherited the workforce and their combative union, but the Toyota manager transformed the plant to be comparable in productivity and quality to the wider Toyota business.

The Toyota culture was expressed at NUMMI in different ways, such as.

1. **Engineers at GM had previously used automation to cut costs; NUMMI used robots to do heavy lifting and make people's jobs easier. Technology was viewed as a tool which needed human wisdom to be effective.**

2. **Toyota exercised leadership at every level to create trust and facilitate learning in contrast to the previous GM hierarchical model.**

NUMMI demonstrated that workers would respond to a different cultural approach replacing hierarchy and autonomy with having the genuine potential to contribute to how their work was completed more effectively

Test yourself 6.4

Suggest briefly why 'organisational stories' are often seen to be important in the understanding of culture.

Chapter summary

◆ This chapter introduces and discusses in depth the nature and significance of organisational culture, often described as 'the way we do things around here'.

◆ In the development of strategy, it is fundamental to understand the culture of the organisation. It represents the framework from within which the strategy is devised and launched, and often the most challenging aspect of strategic change is the need for some aspect of cultural change.

◆ Culture is driven by and epitomises the people within the organisation, their minds, their opinions, their habits and their differing abilities to cope with change.

◆ Schein argues that culture starts with a collection of organisational assumptions which are then enhanced by the values of the individuals and the artefacts of the organisation, the tangible physical evidence of what is important – buildings, cars, management style etc.

◆ Handy argues that the culture within an organisation will fall into one of four structures – power, role, task or person, each with a slightly different drive and nuance.

◆ Johnson's cultural web identifies a range of aspects of organisational culture.

◆ These and other models that are described in the chapter are designed to help us understand what it is that drives the organisation from the inside, and therefore what it is that we might have to allow for in our development of strategy.

◆ The need, in today's multinational environment, to be cognisant of differing national cultures when devising strategy is briefly discussed.

◆ The company secretary and governance professional needs to have a very close awareness of the culture of the organisation. It will often help to explain people and organisational behaviour and can be a significant area for the objective professional to challenge.

Chapter seven
The governing body and strategy

Contents

1. Introduction

There is a Latin phrase '*Quis custodiet ipsos custodes*' which translates as 'who guards the guards?' or 'who watches the watchers?'. This phrase epitomises and challenges the different layers of governance within any organisation.

Most of today's governance has been a reactive response to fraud, corporate failure, misappropriation of funds and other human misdemeanours; an attempt to replace an errant guard, watcher or system, an attempt to place some sort of barrier around a perceived weakness in our corporate world.

The myth is that one scheme of governance is fit for all, that a codified structure will be seen to operate consistently. In the UK we have the principle of 'comply or explain' and this has served us well, but we (the professionals, the market, the media) have continually failed to recognise the diversity of human action, reaction and interaction which sits behind the uniqueness of each organisation; and thus, the need to allow governance codes to be written and interpreted in different ways.

When I am asked: 'What is effective governance?' I restrict myself to one simple answer:

> 'Effective governance is demonstrated through a governance structure within an organisation which is appropriate for it as an organisation, at this moment in its evolution and for the foreseeable future, within the expectations of its stakeholders.'

A company secretary or governance professional, at whatever level, will be involved in practical governance on a day-to-day, week-to-week basis. As suggested in earlier chapters, the role of the company secretary and governance professional is often to be able to stand back and take a view of what is happening within the organisation. This ability will then allow the imparting of objective, tactical advice as to how to move a people or operational situation forward, within the overarching strategic framework of the organisation, encompassing its culture, its objectives, its culture and its stakeholder expectations.

This chapter on the governing body and strategy requires students not just to consider the role of governance in the development of strategy and the driving of strategic change, but also to consider its relevance to them and their organisations. The objective is to help students to think about the reality rather than just the theory, to apply the concepts to their own experiences and to recognise that governance is an ongoing and constantly changing requirement, aligned with the strategic evolution of an organisation.

Strategy is a fundamental part of governance, but governance is also a fundamental part of strategy.

2. Corporate governance and strategy

2.1   The nature of corporate governance

Any structure which requires the use and control of the assets of a third party will require governance. Some sort of operating code (formal or informal) will need to be established which will set the structure for the utilisation of the assets, the parameters of operation, the perceived objectives, and the anticipated results.

Figure 7.1 Governance of assets
© Mark Wearden

◈   The owner of the assets needs governance assurance of correct usage – how do the owners 'hold the directors to account'?

◆ The manager of the assets needs governance parameters of expectation – what do the owners expect for allowing the use of their assets?

◆ The user of the assets needs governance related objectives – how do employees know about the vision and the mission?

In a commercial organisation the strategic expectation would normally be to maximise the long-term return to the owners and to enhance the value of the assets, and this is clearly defined for a limited company at the start of section 172 of the Companies Act 2006 (CA 2006):

> 'A director of a company must act in the way he considers, in good faith, would be most likely to promote the success of the company for the benefit of its members as a whole'.

The strategic objective must therefore be the promotion of success, that the beneficiaries should be the 'members as a whole' and that the directors are accountable for driving the organisation – and therefore are empowered with its governance. The concept of 'success' is open to interpretation and when this clause was being debated by the House of Lords it was suggested that success would normally mean the addition of 'value'. The problem is that the concept of 'value' will also mean very different things to different people.

The core strategic learning here is the need for clarity of what it is that an organisation is trying to achieve, before attempting to define the optimal approach to governance. What does it look like 'today', what do we hope will change in the 'future'?

The precise working out of governance principles in the UK, and the evolution of different codified approaches has been largely determined by regulator and governmental impetus focused around companies listed on the London Stock Exchange; such companies have a wide diversity of 'owners' and therefore there is a perceived need for the establishment of a generic standard for such companies.

The direct impact upon 'non-listed' organisations (private companies, state-controlled structures, third sector organisations and others) has been much slower to develop. Increasingly, having recognised the need for and/or the benefit of effective governance, many organisations that do not have a formal required code of practice have adopted and adapted an appropriate best practice code often being driven from focused regulations and requirements within their own sector.

The 'regulation' and 'oversight' of all matters pertaining to governance within the UK currently sits with the Financial Reporting Council (FRC) and they have undertaken frequent revisions of the UK Corporate Governance Code ('the Code') issued by Financial Reporting Council (FRC), the latest version being that issued in 2018, applicable from 1 January 2019. In addition to this main code, the FRC continually consider, review and publish guidance on all aspects of corporate governance behaviour and practice, and their 2018 Guidance on Board Effectiveness is a key document for concepts of both governance and strategy within the boardroom.

The adoption of the Code by the London Stock Exchange requires all companies with public share listings to apply the Code on a 'comply or explain' basis. If a company is not in compliance with the Code, it is required to explain why not in its annual report to its shareholders. The principle of compliance was extended to companies with shares listed on the Alternative Investment Market (AIM), with effect from September 2018, and they are required to either follow the Code, or alternatively state which code they are following. A new tier of large private companies have been required to comply with the Wates Principles since the start of 2019.

Case study 7.1

Extracts from UK Corporate Governance Code 2018:

'**Principle B: The board should establish the company's purpose, values and strategy, and satisfy itself that these and its culture are aligned. All directors must act with integrity, lead by example and promote the desired culture.'**

'**Provision 1: The board should assess the basis on which the company generates and preserves value over the long-term. It should describe in the annual report how opportunities and risk to the future success of the business have been considered and addressed, the sustainability of the company's business model and how its governance contributes to the delivery of its strategy.'**

2.2 The governance matrix

In the last chapter we considered the nature of corporate culture, and the differing aspects of the people driving that culture. It is the same people who ultimately drive the governance within any organisation. As the diagram in Figure 7.1 suggests, although the directors have the ultimate accountability for governance, and for the strategic direction, the working out of both the governance and the strategy is far more widely spread across the organisation.

Figure 7.2 Governance and operation
© Mark Wearden

There is always an interaction between the governance of an organisation and its operation. This may often involve the same people (e.g. the executive directors in a limited company) as the intersection in Figure 7.2 reflects, but there will also be others who sit in only one of the circles (non-executive directors (NEDs) within the governance circle and managers within the operational circle). It is suggested that the differentiation between these two circles is:

◆ *governance* involves responsibility and accountability for the satisfaction of stakeholder expectations; and

◆ *operational management* involves responsibility and accountability for the delivery of process.

The role of company secretary and governance professional will always sit in the intersection of the two circles, epitomising the need to be able to keep a tactical and strategic oversight on both governance and operation within the organisation, to ensure the people driving both aspects are 'playing within the rules'.

To understand the strategic significance of the governance matrix, we need to consider the differing powers of the key players, although this will differ in different types and size of organisation. In a stock-exchange listed company, it is unlikely that the shareholders will have any direct input into strategy, whereas in a private company it is more likely that owner directors will be fulfilling ownership, governance and operational roles on a daily basis. It is important to be able to differentiate between these roles from a development of strategy perspective, even if the roles are being fulfilled by the same people within an organisation.

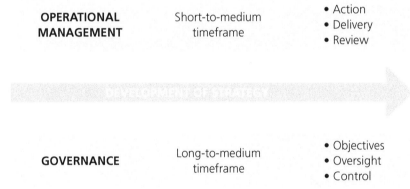

Figure 7.3 Governance timeframe
© Mark Wearden

◆ One of the largest differentiators is the timeframe involved: operational management will have responsibility and accountability (to those empowered with governance) for the short to medium term timeframe of strategy, the action required to fulfil the strategic objectives, the delivery of the perceived strategic outcomes, and a review of the effectiveness and sustainability of the required strategic approach.

◆   Those empowered with governance will have responsibility and accountability (to the ultimate owners) for the long to medium term timeframe, the establishment of strategic objectives, aligned with the identification of means of oversight and control to ensure that the ultimate strategic objectives are satisfied.

This matrix of governance and operational control and oversight can lead to confusion and conflict of who is accountable to whom. This is sometimes referred to as the principal and agent problem, and it is important to recognise the differing power and roles of each of the players:

◆   The *principal* establishes the objectives and the strategic direction and parameters.

◆   The *agent* works to deliver the objectives within the established strategic parameters.

The dilemma, as witnessed in many of the corporate scandals of recent years, is to establish whether directors and managers, as agents, are working simply on behalf of the principal, or also on behalf of their own interests as well. If the remuneration package of an agent is linked to the financial drivers of an organisation it might be in the best interests of the agent to ensure that such financial drivers maximise a personal return; and hence a potential conflict can arise.

While the requirements of the UK Companies Act are clear – the directors are required to act in the best interests of the 'members as a whole' – in the listed company environment the growth of shareholder activism, and the significance of the critical mass of shares held by institutional investors, brings a further challenge to the interaction of governance and strategy. Traditionally, in the UK, institutional investors have exerted influence through share transactions, to reflect their satisfaction or otherwise with the performance of a particular company. In the last ten years there has been a significant increase in the direct challenge emanating from activist institutional shareholders seeking to influence the strategic direction of companies, and further to control issues such as levels of remuneration of directors.

Case study 7.2

The example of the restructure of the governance at Aston Martin ahead of its flotation on the London Stock Exchange epitomises the problem with shareholder control and power. Where does the real power lie?

Adapted from 'Aston Martin gears up for better governance', FT.com, 10 September 2018 (www.ft.com/content/76b7e4f8-b4ff-11e8-bbc3-ccd7de085ffe):

Aston Martin does not yet make a people carrier. But it could do with a larger model if its new board members ever fancy a works outing.

On Monday, the luxury car group said eight new directors will join the

board on its planned stock market flotation, later this year. A former Coca-Cola executive who has served as a director of Royal Bank of Scotland, Vodafone and Wm Morrison will become non-executive chair. And another five new non-executives will join, bringing experience from J Sainsbury, InterContinental Hotels, Deutsche Bank, the Arab British Chambers of Commerce and Stern Business School.

Given the carmaker's seven bankruptcies under managers more right-foot heavy than FTSE, this injection of nous should be welcomed. The chief executive said as much, noting this is 'not a petrol head bunch of enthusiasts'. However, some of the worries over a listed Aston Martin are not so much to do with petrol, as with the previous private-equity-style ownership. They have suggested the car group's two majority owners could retain up to 75 per cent of the shares and sufficient board seats to prioritise their shorter-term financial interests, over those of new investors. The two main Private Equity firms both gain a new board representative, and retain some existing directors, which would take their post-flotation totals to two and four, respectively. That is less than the eight seats they currently share and proportionate to their reduced stake. But it will not give the new independent non-execs a majority – as required by the UK corporate governance code, and arguably any investor buying in at the float.

Aston Martin has committed to complying with the UK governance code within 12 months. So it will get to a position where a majority of directors are non-execs. Given it already has a prospective board of 14, though, including CEO and finance director, it is unlikely to want to do this by adding any more. That suggests the boardroom people carrier is to be fitted with a James Bond optional extra: an ejector seat, for at least one of the majority owner's incumbents.

As with so much of governance, there is no one right model or answer – it is incumbent upon each organisation to establish an effective matrix of governance and operational control to meet its own particular strategic objectives. Further, as one would expect within this strategy module, it is essential that the appropriateness of any governance structure is reviewed and updated frequently to recognise the changing nature of the drivers of today and the future.

2.3   Strategy, at the heart of governance

A core focus of effective governance is the alignment of strategy with risk and control as stated in Principle O of the UK Corporate Governance Code 2018:

> 'The board should establish procedures to manage risk, oversee the internal control framework, and determine the nature and extent of the principal risks the company is willing to take in order to achieve its long-term strategic objectives'.

This wording is very similar to that used within the 2016 Code, the only material difference being the addition of the words 'long-term' bringing this principle into alignment with the duties of directors included in section 172 of the CA 2006.

Figure 7.4 Strategy, risk and control
© Mark Wearden

This triangulation requires directors to step back from the internet world of immediacy and take time to reflect, consider, debate and challenge what is actually happening in their organisation, and the strategic changes required.

Those empowered with governance need to understand the strategic objectives of the organisation, the risks associated with the achievement of those objectives and how to then control and mitigate the identified risks.

The FRC further recognised the need for an enhanced strategic approach to board and committee deliberations in their 'Guidance on Risk Management, Internal Control and Related Financial and Business Reporting' (2014):

> 'effective development and delivery of a company's strategic objectives, its ability to seize new opportunities and to ensure its longer-term survival depend upon its identification, understanding of, and response to, the risks it faces' (section 1.4).

All of this aligns with the consideration in earlier chapters of the need to understand the realities of 'today' as the starting point for the development of our vision of the 'future'. The strategic governance requirement here is for directors, and others empowered with governance, to be able to recognise that all strategy is a leap into the unknown and therefore will involve at least a degree of risk. A common misconception is to perceive governance as simply the implementation of control, whereas the conception, driving and delivery of strategy with its associated risks sits at the very heart of governance.

Test yourself 7.1

Define the difference between the governance oversight of an organisation and the operational oversight of an organisation, suggesting which organisational roles might be involved in each.

Case study 7.3

Extract from 'Guidance on Board Effectiveness 2018', Financial Reporting Council, Section 11:

'An effective board defines the company's purpose and then sets a strategy to deliver it, underpinned by the values and behaviours that shape its culture and the way it conducts its business. It will be able to explain the main trends and factors affecting the long-term success and future viability of the company – for example technological change and environmental impacts – and how these and the company's principal risks and uncertainties have been addressed.'

2.4 Types of governance structure

The introduction of statutory duties for directors in the UK CA 2006 was seen by the law reformers as a radical shift within the UK corporate economy from a shareholder structure to a stakeholder structure. This is clear from the full version of section 172 of the Act.

Companies Act 2006 section 172

Duty to promote the success of the company

(a) A director of a company must act in the way s/he considers, in good faith, would be most likely to promote the success of the company for the benefit of its members as a whole, and in doing so have regard (amongst other matters) to–

(b) the likely consequences of any decision in the long term,

(c) the interests of the company's employees,

(d) the need to foster the company's business relationships with suppliers, customers and others,

(e) the impact of the company's operations on the community and the environment,

(f) the desirability of the company maintaining a reputation for high standards of business conduct, and

(g) the need to act fairly as between members of the company.

In section 3 below we will consider in more detail the identification and differing expectations of different stakeholder groups. In this section we will consider the more generic implications of the differences between a shareholder and a stakeholder model of governance.

The aspects identified below can be viewed as either positive or negative dependent upon the perspective that is taken, and the differing strategic expectations of people within an organisation. The type and size of organisation will significantly influence the core drivers in either model. This links back to our earlier considerations of the differing needs and expectations of stakeholders. It is important to be able to differentiate between the ownership model and the wider stakeholder model, and to ensure that the expectations of both groups are being met.

Shareholder Model of Governance	Stakeholder Model of Governance
The primary interest of shareholders is financial, and wealth is created for them through the organisation. They have a priority claim on the wealth of the organisation.	Wealth is created by and for a variety of different stakeholders, each of whom have a claim to an equitable proportion of the wealth of the organisation.
Investors are more likely to receive a focused higher rate of return through dividend and/or increase in share value.	The return to investors is likely to be diluted by the wider interests of differing stakeholders.
Shorter-term returns are likely to be important to maximise 'cash-in-hand' returns, in particular with the significant increase of short-term algorithmic investing.	A longer-term perspective can often be taken due to the nature of differing interests.
Focused decision making.	Slower decision making with wider stakeholder involvement.
Focused objectives.	Breadth of differing strategic objectives.
Focus on market return expectations and comparators.	Development of own levels of acceptable stakeholder returns.

Table 7.1 Types of governance
© Mark Wearden

Johnson et al. (2017) suggest the benefits and disadvantages of these two models of governance (see Table 7.2).

The shareholder model of corporate structure is dominant within the UK and US and areas that historically follow and replicate their organisational ideals. This model is usually controlled by a unitary board of directors, deciding company policy by consensus, acting on behalf of the shareholders.

The stakeholder model is found more widely in Germany and Japan and is often associated with differing control structures such as a two-tier board system incorporating a supervisory board and a management board.

Despite a previously apparent growing dominance of the UK/US single-tier (monistic) model of governance, since the 2007/08 financial crisis there has been an increasing interest in the potential benefits of a two-tier (dualistic) structure of governance, in particular the ability of lower-level management and workers to play a formal role within the governance structure. The choice of governance structure and the practical realisation of different systems has to be aligned with the expectations of different countries with regard to corporate culture and legal structure.

	Shareholder model	Stakeholder model
Benefits	For investors: – higher rate of return – reduced risk For the economy: – encouragement of entrepreneurship – encouragement of inward investment For management: – independence	For investors: – closer monitoring of management – longer-term decision horizons For stakeholders: – deterrent to high-risk decisions
Disadvantages	For investors: – difficult to monitor management For the economy: – risk of short termism – risk of senior management greed	For management: – potential interference – slower decision making – reduced independence For the economy: – reduced financing opportunities for growth

Table 7.2
((Johnson, 2017) adapted by Mark Weardon)

Stop and think 7.1

In the UK the political intent to enable worker participation around the board table, or to have worker representative directors, is in contradiction to the current director structure as determined under the CA 2006. Under the Act, each director acts as an independent director and is expected to bring their own professional and personal experience to the board table, rather than being seen as, or having any moral obligation to represent a particular group of shareholders.

A wider extension of the dualistic structure is known as a pluralistic structure, designed to enhance the input of a wide range of different stakeholders and lessen the control of managers. The governance structure of many Japanese companies includes a horizontal *keiretsu*, a system of interlocking governance involving a core ownership structure of a bank with different companies owning small portions of each other. A vertical *keiretsu* is an alternative model used to link and focus organisations at different levels within the same supply chain.

Governance	Monistic	Dualistic	Pluralistic
Purpose	Shareholder value	Stakeholder value	Stakeholder value
Principle	Unitary board and director controlled	Dual board control	Hierarchies of control
Practice	Capital market structure	Bank and large institution domination	Bank and large institution domination
Participation	Recognition through law	Underpinning social ethos	Driven through keiretsu structure

Table 7.3 A comparison of the three core governance structures
© Mark Wearden

Case study 7.4

Tesco is clear in its strategic governance objectives.

Extract from Tesco plc Annual Report and Financial Statements 2018:

'The core objective of the Board is to create and deliver the long-term success of the Company and long-term returns for shareholders. This requires the Board to set the Company's strategic aims, ensure that the necessary financial and human resource structures are in place to achieve the Company's objectives, provide oversight of management's performance in delivering against strategy on a day-to-day basis and set the Company's risk appetite. The Board is aware of its obligations to the Company's shareholders and other stakeholders and responds to their needs by transparent reporting and active engagement.'

3. Stakeholder expectations

Take another look at the detail of section 172 of CA 2006 as quoted above. There is specific reference to directors having a duty to consider the interests of different stakeholders in their strategic considerations of the promotion of success:

◆ **Members**: the shareholders, those who own the net assets of the company.
◆ **Employees**: those who give their time and effort to the operation of the company.
◆ **Suppliers and customers**: those who sell to and buy from the company.
◆ **Community and environment**: the wider societal expectations of the company.

The other required aspects concern the expected strategic approach that will be taken in satisfying the expectations of the stakeholders:

◆ **Long-term consequences**: the time dimension.

◆ **High standards of business conduct**: the ethics dimension.

◆ **Acting fairly between members**: the principle of share ownership.

These legal requirements surround the daily interaction of governance and operational management.

Test yourself 7.2

Suggest three differing dimensions of the shareholder and stakeholder models of governance.

3.1   Types of stakeholder

Figure 7.5 Governance stakeholders
© Mark Wearden

In corporate terms, a stakeholder is anyone who has an interest or concern in the business, is rightly expecting some form of return, response or action from the business, and if this is not received has the ability to disrupt the business in some manner.

◆ **Members**
  – In return for investing funds in ordinary shares they will obtain a voting right and the right to participation in any dividend or further share issue, together with the potential capital increase in the value of their share should they choose to sell it.

◆ **Employees**
  – In return for the input of their time, experience, knowledge and labour they will expect appropriate remuneration to be paid as agreed under their employment contract, together with safe working conditions, other potential workplace benefits, continuity of employment and, when appropriate, the opportunity for progression.

◆ **Suppliers and customers** (referred to as supply chain in Figure 7.5)
  - In return for providing reliable supplies to the business, suppliers will expect payment in accordance with agreed terms of their contract and have the potential for repeat orders and a continuity of supply.
  - In return for their purchase of products or services from the business, customers will expect satisfaction of their perceived expectations through the ability to 'consume' or 'resell' a safe and reliable product or service, in line with consumer law.
  - Banks and other providers of finance together with other contributors to the operation of a business would also fall under this 'supply-chain' category – in each case there will be an input from the stakeholder with an expected return of some sort in line with the contract agreed for the provision of finance.

◆ **Community and environment**
  - In return for the right to operate the business will need to comply with national and local laws and corporate social responsibility expectations – e.g. packaging and waste disposal, payment of taxation as required, minimisation of carbon and other emissions.

Stop and think 7.2

If shareholders decide to sell their shares, this can have significant market impact. The ability to disrupt strategy through voting can impact the strategic direction of a business.

If employees withdraw their labour or decide to 'work to rule', this can impact the strategic direction of a business.

The disruption of input by suppliers, or the refusal to buy by customers can impact the strategic direction of a business.

The refusal by a local or national authority to licence or issue approval for business operations can impact the strategic direction of a business.

Case study 7.5

BAE understand the need for governance to cover all aspects of the supply chain.

Extract from BAE plc Annual Report and Financial Statements 2017:

'We work with suppliers and their supply chains to provide fully compliant, cost effective equipment, goods, services and solutions. Our supplier relationships are often long term due to the length of our product lifecycles, so we aim to work with suppliers who share our values and who embrace standards of ethical behaviour consistent with our own.'

3.2   Stakeholder mapping

Stakeholders can be further classified as:

◆   **Internal**: owners and employees – those who have a close and dependent relationship with the business and a vested interest in its success

◆   **Market**: suppliers and customers – those who have a direct trading relationship with the business

◆   **External**: all other stakeholders of the business with either direct (e.g. banks) or indirect (e.g. government, environmental) relationships with and expectations from the business.

It is important for those empowered with governance to take into consideration the needs and expectations of the differing stakeholder groups, and this lies behind the introduction of the section 172 duty of the CA 2006. Further, since the start of 2019, directors of companies defined as 'large' under the Act are required to explain in their annual directors' report how they have fulfilled their requirements under this section and how they have actively considered the differing demands of their stakeholders. This level of transparency requires a core understanding by directors of their strategic direction as well as the differing and evolving needs of their stakeholders.

Lynch (2015) considers the primary and secondary expectations of these differing groups.

Stakeholder	Primary expectations	Secondary expectations
Owners (internal)	Financial return	Added value
Employees (internal)	Pay	Work satisfaction, training
Customers (market)	Supply of goods and services	Quality
Creditors (market)	Creditworthiness	Payment on time
Suppliers (market)	Payment	Long-term relationships
Community (external)	Safety and security	Contribution to community
Government (external)	Compliance	Improved competitiveness

Table 7.4
((Lynch, 2015) adapted by Mark Wearden)

The levels of power, influence and strategic impact of different stakeholder groups can be mapped to help to identify when and where a business needs to consider the potential impact of not satisfying the stakeholder expectations. Johnson (2017) suggested that the two core dynamics are the ability to disrupt and the levels of interest that the stakeholder would take in its 'stake'.

Stakeholder mapping	Low interest in the business	High interest in the business
Low power to disrupt the business	Minimal effort reqired by the organisation	Stakeholders must be kept informed
High power to disrupt the business	Stakeholders must be kept satisfied	These are the key players

Figure 7.5
((Lynch, 2017) adapted by Mark Wearden)

3.3   The politics of stakeholder power

The exercise of power reflects the ability of one or more individuals to persuade other people to follow different courses of action.

The strategic journey of an organisation can be significantly influenced by the forces of stakeholders and others. This is often referred to as the politics of power.

In any organisation, as time evolves, the power balance is likely to shift. In a fast moving organisation with many demanding stakeholders, this could mean frequent changes of strategic focus, which can lead to disruption and chaos. In a slower moving organisation the politics may still come to the fore from time to time and be far less likely to cause disruption.

Case study 7.6

At Tesco, the aim is to weave the governance into the organisational culture.

Extract from Tesco plc Annual Report and Financial Statements 2018:

'We are committed to maintaining high standards of corporate governance within Tesco. Over the last few years, we have worked hard to ensure that good governance is part of our way of thinking and working and underpins how we conduct ourselves every day.'

When undertaking a stakeholder mapping exercise, it is useful to look at and understand the origin and indicators of the differing powers that might be at play (see Table 7.6).

These aspects of power need to also be considered within the context of the type of organisation, and the stakeholder impact upon strategy. While most businesses exist somewhere in the middle between the two ends of the different dynamics, they are usually positioned more towards one end than the other.

Origin of power	Indicator of power
Position	Autocracy, right and ability to influence behaviour (e.g. seniority)
Resource	Control over a key required asset (e.g. raw materials)
Task	The awareness of how to complete a task (e.g. IT)
Expertise	Professional or other abilities (e.g. finance)
Information	Wider detail and understanding (e.g. why rather than what)
Vision	End-game understanding (e.g. 'the bigger picture')
Values	Moral character (e.g. personal ethics)
Argument	The ability to debate (e.g. persistency and focus)
Judgement	The power to decide (e.g. which route to take)

Table 7.5 Types of power
© Mark Wearden

Traditional		**Empowered**
Centralised		Devolved
Bureaucratic		Participative
Structured		Fluid

Figure 7.7 Power dynamic
© Mark Wearden

◆ At the *traditional* end of the dynamic it is much harder for a stakeholder to influence the strategic direction of an organisation, which is probably focused around a rational strategic approach.

◆ In a more *empowered* organisation, there is more likely to be an emergent and collective approach to strategic development and therefore a greater ability for stakeholder influence.

3.4 Stakeholders in non-commercial organisations

Many non-commercial organisations, for instance some public sector bodies, charities, co-operatives, and other social-based enterprises will often involve their stakeholders to a much greater extent than a commercial organisation. This can be a great source of strength but can also provide a significant restriction on strategic growth and direction. An organisation with multiple stakeholders can often find itself with too many people involved in the strategic and bureaucratic leadership of the organisation, or at least trying to influence that strategic direction.

Many of the stakeholder groups are similar to commercial organisations but the direct influence and understanding of what it means to be a member might be significantly different, and there are likely to be inherent conflicts of interest between the views of the individual member, the views of a group of members, and the views of the administrative function tasked with running the organisation:

◆   If the organisation is either structured as a limited company or a registered charity, those tasked with driving the strategic direction are likely to have clear governance expectations.

◆   When there is a less formal legal structure such as a club or association, it is much harder for those who are appointed as officers/committee members to fully understand the governance remit, and often the strategic drive is left to an executive team.

In a non-commercial structure, it is important to consider the objectives of each type of stakeholder:

◆   Who are the members?

◆   Who is the customer?

◆   Who are the suppliers?

◆   What are the expectations from the surrounding environment, both political and other?

Often, in a non-commercial structure an individual may be both a member, a customer, a supplier and an intrinsic stakeholder within the forces of the surrounding environment. This can create multiple conflicts for strategy and governance which are managed using a robust system of conflict management and often a conflicts register and accurate records of conflicted decisions made at board meetings.

Stop and think 7.3

Who are the stakeholders and what is their power? Consider and compare the following types of organisational structure:

1.   a large school in the centre of London

2.   a local charity running an end-of-life hospice for people with cancer

3.   a department of central government

4.   a professional membership organisation.

3.5   The need for stakeholder analysis

The importance of understanding and analysing different types of stakeholder groups when considering the governance of an organisation and its development of strategy should be clear from the various aspects discussed above.

To complete the earlier diagram, it is necessary to recognise the core forces that are continually impacting the organisation and its stakeholders.

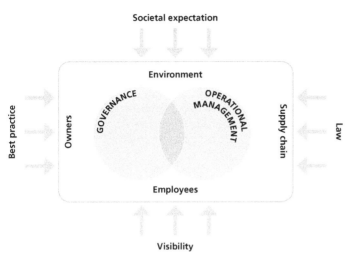

Figure 7.8 Governance forces
© Mark Wearden

◆ **The law** – UK, EU, worldwide – is the starting point and the benchmark for the political demands that underpin the structure of the society where an organisation is operating, and the limitations of those empowered with governance. *Resistance to this can result in civil or criminal court action against individuals and/or the organisation.*

◆ **Best practice** – codes, guidelines, customer expectations, 'what others do' – the perception of the organisation and its stakeholders as to the presumed behaviour of both the business and those empowered with its governance. *Resistance to this can result in reputational damage as well as potential damage to the relationship with any regulator.*

◆ **Societal expectation** – in a media driven world of instant communication the ever-changing expectations of wider society may often lead an organisation and its stakeholders to adapt both its governance and its strategy to be seen to be 'ticking the appropriate boxes'. *Resistance to this can result in media criticism of the organisation with resultant reputational damage.*

◆ **Visibility** – the perpetual dichotomy that exists between what we are willing and able to reveal about our organisation, its governance and its strategic direction. *Getting this wrong can result in substantive demands on time from those empowered with governance.*

Test yourself 7.3

Identify the input (stake) in an organisation and the differing output expectations of four different stakeholder groups.

4. Risk, reputation and strategy

In section 2 above and the considerations in earlier chapters, it was identified that risk is intrinsically linked with strategy. The minute we leave the safety of 'today', our known, and definable position, and head towards the unknown of the 'future', we are surrounded by risk. The only certainty that we have in life at any point is today. In our consideration of the relationship between governance and strategy, it is important that we define precisely what it is that we mean by risk in the context of strategy and how the governance structure can and should enable the recognition, analysis, understanding and control of such risk. The final aspect of this section and this chapter will include a brief consideration of the strategic significance of an organisation's reputation.

4.1   Risk management

'Risk' is a word with an immediate and very powerful meaning to an individual. The concept and consideration of risk has the ability to take a person from a predetermined path and lead them to behave in a manner that had previously seemed unlikely.

Although risk, as a single word in itself, can conjure up immediate understanding, we have become accustomed to attaching additional words to effectively use the word 'risk' as an adjective rather than a noun: risk assurance; risk mitigation; risk tolerance; risk activity; risk appetite.

At its simplest, risk can be defined as 'any circumstance with more than one possible outcome'.

If there is only one outcome, then the future is predetermined and therefore there is no risk. As soon as there are two or more possible outcomes from a given situation, we introduce an unknown future. Without thinking we often interchange the words risk and uncertainty to describe the same set of circumstances. The word 'risk' refers to a range of understandable and quantifiable outcomes, whereas the word 'uncertainty' suggests that although we can perceive a variety of outcomes, they are not quantifiable.

The basis of our understanding of the risk associated with any action is derived from the accumulation of knowledge and experience to that very moment in time when we are assessing such risk.

How we react is often referred to as wisdom – our ability to take everything that we have retained from the point of our birth to a particular moment of time, and our ability to use this knowledge to inform a specific judgement or action.

To achieve this concept of wisdom it is necessary to mentally, and/or physically, step back from any situation and allow the brain to assimilate what they are faced with and how our experience to date can inform our action or decision.

4.2 The meaning of risk appetite

Risk appetite is portrayed in the following momentum and plays an important role in how we develop strategy in different contexts.

Figure 7.9 Risk appetite
© Mark Wearden

A *risk-averse* person (or group of people) looks for certainty of outcome and is therefore prepared to sacrifice opportunities that might exist for change. Risk aversion can often lead to an intolerance of challenge and therefore an overreaction to any threat to the status quo. Facts are often preferred to theories; strategic breadth will be restricted.

A *risk-seeking* person (or group of people) accepts that life is full of options and uncertainty and such a person has confidence in using their abilities to counter whatever they may face. Threats that are seen by the risk-averse person are very often not even considered as threats by the risk-seeking person. Risk seeking can often lead to a dangerous dismissal of the realities that confront a person or organisation. Imagination is often preferred to facts; strategic breadth will be wide.

Risk capacity is the maximum level of risk that can be taken, and often that is required to be taken to achieve the intended strategic goals, but also might describe the difference between actual risk being taken and the higher or lower levels of tolerance.

Risk tolerance is required in the real world by both risk-averters and risk-seekers. It emerges from a different perspective to risk appetite and is best illustrated in the type of 'bubble chart' used by many organisations to consider their risk profile.

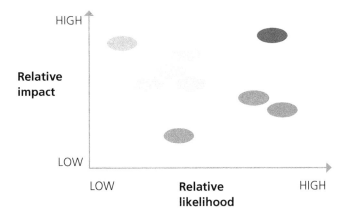

Figure 7.10 Risk tolerance
© Mark Wearden

Acceptable levels of tolerance are measured from the interaction of relative impact and relative likelihood and in most organisations (or people) there will be natural clusters of acceptability together with aspects that would be unacceptable in the case of a high:high result and would not be worth the effort in the case of a low:low result.

The plotting and acceptance of the risk, which is the real meaning of the word tolerance in this instance, allows a crossing of the tightrope and therefore progress.

A problem with a risk tolerance matrix is the origin of the criteria by which individual risks are judged, and therefore their position on the chart. These judgements have been made by the same people who have an end result in mind, and therefore their judgement may well be biased.

This problem of individual influence takes us just briefly into the realms of risk and ethics. In reality, people are often faced with options pertaining to risk, but which may have a dramatic impact upon the lives of others.

Case study 7.7

(Adapted from *The Trolley Problem* (Foot, 1978))

A runaway trolley is speeding out of control down a hill. The brakes do not work, so it cannot be slowed down. At the end of the track are five people who will be killed if the trolley hits them. The only choices the driver of the trolley has are:

1. **do nothing and kill five people; or**
2. **pull a lever that would result in the trolley shifting to another set of tracks in which one person who is unaware of the runaway trolley would be killed.**

As the driver what would you do – is it better to kill one person or five?

Two additional scenarios have been subsequently added to this dilemma:

If an individual observing the scenario had the ability to pull a similar lever and thus divert the trolley, would that then mean they assumed responsibility for the risks involved, and therefore the death of either the one or the five people?

An individual is observing the trolley from a bridge and realises that a heavy object thrown in front of the trolley could prevent the deaths. The only heavy object near enough is an overweight man also standing on the bridge. Should the observer try to throw the overweight man over the bridge to stop the trolley?

In his book *Risk Intelligence* (2012), Dylan Evans suggests that anyone involved in the assessment of risk (and that is all of us in our everyday lives) must develop the ability to gauge the limits of their own knowledge; to recognise the difference between the caution when we don't have sufficient information to make a judgement, and our confidence when we believe we do.

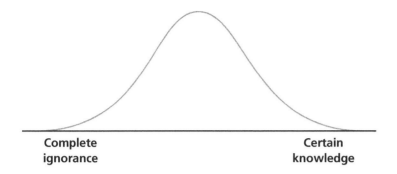

**Complete
ignorance**   **Certain
knowledge**

Figure 7.11 Risk intelligence

Evans suggests that the concept of 'risk intelligence' operates in the area that
exists between certain knowledge and complete ignorance, and that it is our
job to find our place along this momentum for each and every risk scenario
that we face.

Case study 7.8

**Tesco has a clear strategic view of what constitutes a principal risk to the
organisation.**

Extracts from Tesco plc Annual Report and Financial Statements 2018:

'**We have an established risk management process to identify, assess
and monitor the principal risks that we face as a business. We have
performed a robust review of those risks that we believe could seriously
affect the Group's performance, future prospects, reputation or its
ability to deliver against its priorities.**'

'**The risk management process relies on our assessment of the risk
likelihood and impact and on the development and monitoring of
appropriate internal controls.**'

'**As part of our risk management process, risks are reviewed as a top
down and bottom up activity at the Group and the business unit level.**'

4.3   Perspectives of different types of organisational risk

It is helpful to consider several different risk perspectives; this is not a finite or
restrictive list, but it indicates the breadth of consideration that is required, and
how these types of risk might be mitigated.

Financial risk
Any organisation is reliant upon its core infrastructure funding. This gearing
is usually a combination of shareholder (equity) funding combined with debt
(bank or similar).

Organisations that are high geared have higher debt than equity and face the risk of being unable to pay interest and or capital back to the lender. This can create significant direct reputational damage with the lender who will lose confidence in the organisation and/or its management.

Organisations that are low geared have higher equity than debt. If the shares are issued on a public market, the market value and reputation of the company is often based around the vagaries of market reaction to the various announcements that may be made by the company. There is an increasing expectation that such announcements (including the formal annual report) will include an alignment of strategy with the business model and the perceived risks, allowing investors and others to make their judgements.

Strategic risk mitigation comes through sound financial planning, ensuring long term funding is matched appropriately to long term assets. In a high geared company mitigation is to ensure appropriate levels of cash generation underpin the financial performance. In a low geared company mitigation comes from taking care in the timing and phraseology of public announcements.

Carillion would be an example of a company which, among other things, got its financial structure significantly wrong, using short-term cashflows to fund long term projects and vice versa.

Operational risk
Reputational damage can potentially affect both ends of the operational supply chain.

Customers buy and continue to buy based upon their perceived quality of the product or service and this will be closely aligned to the reputation of the company selling that product or service.

Customer-relationship management (CRM) systems, customer surveys and feedback and other such tools can be useful in mitigating the loss of reputation from a customer perspective.

The Volkswagen emissions falsification, or the Starbucks corporation tax coverage would be examples of reputational damage from a customer perspective.

Suppliers are often keen to be associated with a company which has a positive reputation, in particular with regard to regularity of payment within agreed terms, continuity of ordering, and structured logistics. Poor treatment of suppliers will lead to a loss of reputation. There is also another dimension to the supplier side, whereby a company can leave itself open to reputational damage if it fails to secure its supply base, and therefore is left unable to complete its production.

Sensible, calculated terms and a choice of potential suppliers can mitigate the reputational damage from both aspects.

A recent example would be Kentucky Fried Chicken who found it was unable to serve chicken for a few weeks in early 2018 as the company mishandled a strategic switch of logistics suppliers.

Competition risk

All organisations, even those who hold a tentative monopoly, face competition. If a product or service is selling and generating profit/wealth, then other organisations will see an opportunity to compete and try to gain a share in that market.

Reputational damage can arise from negative media reporting of the demise of a company's share of a market, and also from competitors letting it be known that an alternative exists. This can spiral out of control very quickly and will necessitate robust crisis management.

Mitigation can be in the form of assertive promotion or advertising, or a reliance on existing reputation.

An example of mitigation would be in reaction to the loss of food-retail market share by Tesco/Asda/Sainsbury to the newer overseas discounters who are infiltrating the retail market, such as Aldi/Lidl. The mitigation has seen pointed marketing campaigns asserting difference in quality, rather than just resorting to the direct price competition used by the discounters in their advertising.

Environment risk

A range of reputational risks could be aligned against many aspects of environmental risk.

A multinational organisation, with sites in many countries is potentially open to the reputational risk of using transfer pricing to aggressively minimise its taxation, ' fixing' its tax affairs.

The mitigation is to promote and adhere to clean, transparent operations – although agitators may still try to damage the reputation of the organisation, but this cannot work if there is nothing to hide.

An example would be the ongoing debates about the tax affairs of Apple, Amazon and other multinational corporates.

People risk

The reputational risks discussed above can be improved or worsened by the behaviour and words of the leaders (and employees) of an organisation.

The reputational risk from people arises, however, not just from the larger public declarations, but also from gossip and one-to-one conversations that take place between people – for example, 'what is said on the way home from work, or in the pub at night'.

Mitigation within an organisation comes from a firm policy on communication outside the organisation, and the development of a culture of joint ownership – people are likely to be far more careful when they are talking about an organisation for which they feel responsible and accountable. Ideally and particularly when there is a likelihood of adverse media, staff will be reminded how to handle approaches by telephone and electronic communications by reporters and to be careful about what is said in the public domain, even within the perceived safety of conversations in public places. In circumstances within the work place, staff are advised to make no comment and to refer the caller to a designated person such as the press officer or the chief executive officer (CEO).

Other reputational risks exist in this category such as allegations of people mistreatment (modern slavery or bribery being the areas of recent legal interest), but also outspoken leaders such as occurred with Ratner's jewellers historically (their CEO stating at an Institute of Directors (IoD) conference that 'money is made by selling rubbish products'; or more recently examples such as the personal reputation of Michael O'Leary being closely aligned to the reputation of Ryan Air, Mark Zuckerberg with Facebook and Elon Musk with Tesla.

Test yourself 7.4

Differentiate between risk appetite, risk tolerance and risk capacity.

4.4   Some different control tools for the management of risk

The following aspects of control contain only brief discussion and suggestions, based upon an assumption that these 'tools' will either already be in use within an organisation and need challenging, or have been part of previous learning and need considering from a practical and organisational perspective.

Key performance indicators
In many organisations, the transition and measurement of risk is designed around the use of *key performance indicators* (KPIs).

There are four core requirements to be able to use KPIs for the measurement, assessment and control of risk within an organisation:

◆   a closely defined set of measures – remember the first word is key
◆   accurate trusted data to ensure integrity
◆   measures that are strategically relevant
◆   indicators that have a forward impact – something will be done as a result of the measure.

A risk register
The variety and complexity of the risks faced by most organisations leads to the construction of a formal framework to allow them to list, categorise, and often weight the multiplicity of risks that face them.

It is common for this structure to be referred to as the risk *register* of the organisation, although such structures appear in many different shapes and sizes. To add organisational value, this needs to be a living and vibrant tool, rather than a formulaic and background compliance task.

The impetus for the creation of a risk register could derive from stakeholder expectation, but more usually will be created as a means of recording risks identified within an organisation, and then how they are controlled and mitigated.

The size and complexity of a risk register is usually based on the management level driving the initiative, the interest level of the person entrusted with the compilation, or alternatively by the availability of budget and/or technology for this purpose.

The current status of risks recorded on the risk register are often reported on a regular basis at the appropriate level of board or committee meetings.

A risk matrix

Some organisations will use a risk *matrix* structure to analyse the severity of a risk against its probability. This is often known as a 'red amber green' or 'traffic light' matrix to identify risk severity.

The advantages of such a matrix are that it is easy to develop and understand; and it creates a useful visual image of risk within the organisation.

The disadvantages of such a matrix are the lack of a timeframe; no concept of the volatility of risk; and no indication of the basis of the underlying data that has been used to generate the image.

Balanced scorecard

One of the many uses of a balanced scorecard is the oversight and control of risk. This tool will be discussed in detail in Chapter 13.

4.5 What are we trying to control?

On the basis that every organisation at any particular point in its existence will have its own particular mixture of risk, it is important to recognise that the tools briefly discussed above are only examples of the type of control structure that can be used by an organisation in its attempt to control the risks that it faces.

A quick reminder from earlier in the chapter of the alignment of strategy with risk and control as stated in Principle O of the UK Corporate Governance Code 2018:

> 'The board should establish procedures to manage risk, oversee the internal control framework, and determine the nature and extent of the principal risks the company is willing to take in order to achieve its long-term strategic objectives'.

The governance requirement is to establish and oversee a level of internal control to give directors an assurance that risk is being managed appropriately in line with the long-term strategic objectives of the organisation as far as realistically feasible. It is generally accepted that any such control process will include three dimensions:

- ◆ **Identification**: how do we know what the risks are and how frequently are we able to perceive new or different risks?
- ◆ **Evaluation**: the establishment of potential impact from the alignment of probability and materiality.
- ◆ **Mitigation**: the progress of measures taken to control and reduce potential impact while recognising that risk is still a necessary and intrinsic part of the strategic growth of any organisation.

4.6 Reputation management

Reputation can be defined as 'the beliefs or opinions that are generally held about someone or something'. This links back to the societal expectation forces discussed above. The reputation of an organisation or person is based around the (accurate or inaccurate) opinions held and developed by one or more other people. From a financial perspective, reputation is described as an intangible asset and equates to the amount that a person or an organisation is willing to pay above or below the accounting value.

Case study 7.9

In a charitable organisation such as Cancer Research UK, its reputation is fundamental to its ability to raise funds through donations.

Extract from Cancer Research UK Annual Report and Financial Statements 2017/2018:

**'*Reputation*
Events which may adversely affect our reputation and operations. This could include a serious data security breach (from a cyber-attack or non-compliance with GDPR), a serious fraud or an issue related to our fundraising practices. It could also include a significant health and safety or safeguarding incident or an incident relating to the integrity of our research programmes or patient trials.'**

Reputation management is an essential part of the strategic role of the Board of Directors; once a reputation is damaged, it can be time-consuming and expensive to turn it around. There is a need to regularly consider how the organisation is viewed by the diverse range of stakeholders discussed above. One means of achieving this is through market research.

John Kay (1993) suggests that reputation is the result of the creation and management of contracts and relationships within and around the organisation which add value. He suggests that there are three distinctive relational capabilities which allow an organisation to achieve competitive advantage.

- **Architecture**: the network of relational contracts both internal and external.
- **Reputation**: the assurance to stakeholders of quality through the interrelationship of experience, signalling, and promotion.
- **Innovation**: a perception of how far 'ahead of the game' a particular organisation is at any moment in time.

An important aspect of the strategic governance responsibility is to establish a means for directors to become aware of potential risks affecting the reputation of the organisation. Such risks might fall within one or more of the following categories:

- **Economic**: a change in consumer demand, or the reduction of sales through poor media reporting.

- ◆ **Natural**: an internal failure within the organisation which the directors have failed to consider, such as a gap in procedures.
- ◆ **Operational**: pursuance of unsafe practices, for instance with regard to health and safety.
- ◆ **People**: the perceived treatment of employees and others.
- ◆ **Governance**: the ethical dimensions and the values of the organisation.
- ◆ **Human**: the causing of damage or offence to an individual resulting in court or other public action.
- ◆ **Commercial blindness**: for example, the acceptance of a higher risk customer than usual to facilitate a higher fee.

CA 2006 requires directors to pursue long-term sustainability as a fundamental strategic objective. This is achieved through effective governance of an organisation. Reputation must always be at the forefront of the minds of those empowered with governance and all strategic developments that are being considered within an organisation need to be considered from the perspective of how they will enhance or detract from the reputation of the organisation.

Chapter summary

- ◆ This chapter looks at the relationship between strategy and governance, recognising that strategy will usually be initially formulated by the executive directors of the company and challenged by the wider unitary board of directors. As a combined force, this shows the practical link between strategy and governance.
- ◆ We have previously considered strategy as using the stakeholder assets to drive the business forward. Governance helps to provide a framework for the provision of the appropriate assurance on the use of those assets.
- ◆ The difference between governance and operation plays a key part in our strategic understanding – governance suggesting responsibility and accountability to stakeholders for devising a strategy, operation suggesting responsibility and accountability for actually getting the job done and delivering strategic objectives.
- ◆ The alignment of strategy, risk and control is at the centre of governance. What are we going to use the stakeholder assets for (strategy), what are the dangers in doing this (risk), how do we mitigate those risks (control)?
- ◆ There are subtle differences between a shareholder governance model, where the strategic focus tends to be shorter-term and financial, and a stakeholder governance model where the timeframe is usually longer, and the perceived outcomes can be much wider.
- ◆ There is a need to understand and map the differing expectations of different types of stakeholders; anyone putting a 'stake' into the organisation will be expecting some sort of return for that 'stake' and the strategy needs to be designed to ensure that is satisfied.

◆   The understanding of the different dimensions of risk – appetite, tolerance, capacity etc. – is essential when assessing the impact and control of strategy.

◆   A significant risk for any organisation, in today's fast-media world, is to enhance and maintain a positive reputation. This requires an awareness of the impact of any development of strategy.

◆   Anyone undertaking the role of company secretary and governance professional needs to ensure that they have a thorough understanding of the relationship between strategy and governance, and their role in ensuring appropriate probity and challenge to both dimensions.

Chapter eight
Expressing organisational purpose

Contents

1. Introduction

Chapter 5 considered the culture of the organisation and how it impacts upon the development of strategy; Chapter 6 then focused our thoughts on the governance process and the various forces that influence and impact those people who are empowered to govern and manage the organisation.

This chapter will bring the focus in closer and consider what really drives the strategic direction of an organisation, consolidating some of the structures discussed in earlier chapters that infiltrate and challenge the development of organisational strategy.

Case study 8.1

John Lewis has a different strategic and structural approach to all other large retailers in the UK – each employee of the organisation is a member of the partnership. Its strategy and structure is epitomised in its first Principle which states its organisational purpose.

'John Lewis Partnership: Principle 1 – Purpose

The Partnership's ultimate purpose is the happiness of all its members, through their worthwhile and satisfying employment in a successful business. Because the Partnership is owned in trust for its members, they share the responsibilities of ownership as well as its rewards – profit, knowledge and power.'

Case study 8.2

The longer-term stakeholder-centric view of purpose stated by Unilever makes an interesting contrast to the John Lewis people-centric approach.

Extract from Unilever Annual Report and Accounts 2017:

UNILEVER: OUR PURPOSE

'UNILEVER HAS A CLEAR PURPOSE – TO MAKE SUSTAINABLE LIVING COMMONPLACE. WE BELIEVE THIS IS THE BEST WAY TO DELIVER LONG-TERM SUSTAINABLE GROWTH.

As the pace of change accelerates in our markets, we are creating a stronger, simpler and more agile business. These changes will help us to deliver our Purpose and our Vision to grow our business, whilst decoupling our environmental footprint from our growth and increasing our positive social impact. However volatile and uncertain the world becomes Unilever's Purpose and Vision will remain because we believe that managing for the long term is the best way for us to grow. We are well placed to deliver long-term value through our strategy, category strategies and the Unilever Sustainable Living Plan (USLP), launched in 2010. These are supported by a transformational change agenda which combines our own actions with a stakeholder approach to external advocacy and public policy.'

Case study 8.3

Contrast both of these statements above with the simplicity of the Tesco statement based entirely around customer satisfaction.

Extract from Tesco website:

'Tesco: Our Core Purpose

"Serving shoppers a little better every day"'

Every organisation needs a purpose – that is why an organisation is formed in the first place, and why it continues to exist. One of our recurring themes is the centrality of people, with their diversity, their idiosyncrasies, and most importantly, their thought processes and behaviours. Purpose is formed by people, driven by people and delivered by people, and successful fulfilment of purpose is celebrated by people. Regrettably, it is also people who suffer when there is a lack of purpose, when the original purpose has not kept aligned with the changing organisation or world, or when the purpose proves to be supported by an ineffective or loss-making business model.

Stop and think 8.1

A limited company exists because of, and for, the delivery of success for its members (shareholders). This requires the company to have a purpose – a reason to exist.

A limited company can only be formally closed in one of two ways.

1.   If the purpose is not supported by an effective financial business model, and creditors are left unpaid, they can ask the courts to close the business.

2.   Alternatively, if the purpose of the company no longer exists, or has been satisfied, then the members can take a majority decision to close the company.

Consider two of the case studies above, John Lewis Partnership and Unilever – think about the different focal points and the different drivers, what would that look like from the inside of the organisation? Also think about the similarities.

How would you compare the two organisations?

There can be a lack of clarity in an organisation between vision and mission, between objective and goal, between strategy and objective, between goal and target. This is usually a question of local terminology, based around the individual or organisational interpretation and use of a particular term, to describe a particular aspect of their own purpose.

At the top of any perceived hierarchy we need to be able to understand the strategic vision, what is it that the leaders within the hierarchy are trying to achieve and what is the rationale behind that vision? The rationale might be defined as the mission of the organisation. Further, it is suggested that all other aspects of strategic definition flow from and are aligned to this clarity of difference between vision and mission. This will form part of the discussion in this chapter.

2. Strategy and organisational purpose

The purpose of any organisation needs to be understood at the outset of the strategic thinking and development process. If we do not understand the purpose, how can we devise an appropriate strategy? The purpose must be the fundamental reason why any organisation exists.

The question to be asked is not 'what do you do', but 'why do you do it'? As discussed in Chapter 6, this needs aligning with the question 'how do you do it?

An understanding of these three aspects of any organisation will enable a deeper understanding of the basis for all strategic thinking, it gives the starting point and the benchmark for the perceived strategic changes. Remember that the strategy will only ever be 'perceived' as our planning is derived within our minds and translated into projections and words, it is all part of our vision of the future.

A traditional view of commercial corporate purpose is the expectation that the directors will use the invested funds of shareholders and other creditors to generate profit on those investments. It is very money-centric, and all other aims, objectives and goals will be similarly money-centric. The problem with such a static perspective is that it fails to consider either people or time:

◆ *People* will always skew and personalise the focus, as each of us will have (at least) a slightly different vision of the future, and different personal goals which are not always aligned with the organisation's goal congruence.

◆ *Time* is a significant aspect of all strategic thinking. A declared purpose for today or tomorrow may have a reasonable chance of being realised in line with our personal current vision. A purpose for next week or next month will need to always have a number of 'ifs' or presumptions surrounding it because even the relatively near future is uncertain.

Organisational purpose has to be segregated and viewed from three different time dimensions. These are best defined through a series of questions to be posed by the strategist:

◆ **Past**
- What can we learn from the history of the organisation?
- Have there been previous definitions of purpose and strategy?
- What has been used to benchmark progress?
- How has success been measured and recognised?

◆ **Present**
- What are today's values?
- Is the prevailing culture likely to be oblivious to change, in need of change, or resistant to change?
- What are the restraining forces and parameters of today?
- How is success measured today?

◆ **Future**
- What needs to change, and why is there a need for change?
- Are the strategic views of different key players disparate or aligned?
- How far ahead can we realistically visualise?
- What will be the success measures of the future?

Stop and think 8.2

Try to answer the prior questions for your own organisation.

3. Elements of organisational purpose

A core strategic model was introduced in Chapter 1, which allows us to neatly categorise our strategic thinking around organisational purpose into a number of defined areas.

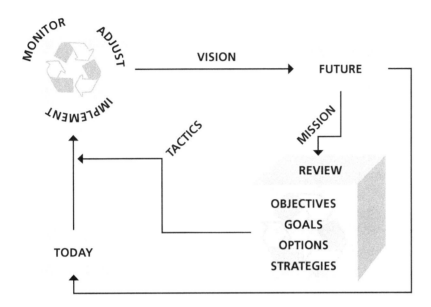

Figure 8.1 Strategy journey
© Mark Wearden

All of the aspects of our core strategy model contribute to a better understanding and recognition of organisational purpose.

3.1 Strategic vision – the tactical plan

The tactical plan, as illustrated in the top left-hand circle, describes what is happening now, 'today', in the operation of the business, at this very moment in time, in every organisation throughout the world. It emanates from the consideration of the 'future' that has taken place as part of the development of strategy and is the result of the tactics that are derived in the review process.

As we sit reading, studying and thinking about the development of strategy, the world is going on around us. Each person in each organisation is making their own individual contribution in their own individual way to the operation of the organisation. This is definable under three core functions and we all do all three without even thinking about it:

◆   **Implement**: fulfilling tasks that either we or others have defined as required to achieve the required and expected operational results.

◆   **Monitor results**: we have an immediate and short-term perspective of what we are doing, we can see the direct result of what we are implementing, and we can understand whether it is working as expected.

◆ **Adjust**: within the predefined parameters of the current tactical plan (in the diagram this is the perimeter of the circle) people are empowered to make adjustments to enable the task to be completed to allow the plan to be implemented. If we move beyond the perimeter of the current plan, we are changing the parameters of the current strategy. The strategy may then need adjusting to enable and approve a changed tactical plan.

This last stage, and the logic that sits behind this approach, looks and feels like a lengthy and time-consuming process, but this will depend on the enormity of the change, the potential impact of the strategy and the size and culture of the organisation.

Worked example 8.1

The tactical plan

1. **Implement**

    –   **I am currently writing this textbook within a set of parameters defined by ICSA: The Governance Institute, myself and other interested parties.**

2. **Monitor results**

    –   **As I type this text, I can see the words on the screen, and I am able to check levels of accuracy.**

3. **Adjust**

    –   **I can make immediate changes to spelling and grammar mistakes; I can rethink and adjust the tone and the structure.**

    –   **If I want to change the order of the syllabus, or the syllabus itself, I will hit the perimeter of the circles and the parameters of the current tactical plan and will need to consult with ICSA.**

    –   **If I decide I want to dramatically change the topic because it has become obsolete, or mostly irrelevant, then the purpose will need to be revisited and adjusted.**

Everything that sits outside the current tactical plan can be defined as part of the strategic vision of the organisation. It is different to what is already happening, to what has already been agreed as an operating parameter, and therefore it is part of the vision.

A dictionary definition of 'vision' is:

'The ability to think about or plan the future with imagination or wisdom'

Consider the potential global impact of the Amazon vision statement below and then benchmark it against some of the theories that follow.

Case study 8.4

Vision statement from the Amazon website:

'The Amazon vision

Our vision is to be earth's most customer centric company; to build a place where people can come to find and discover anything they might want to buy online.'

Bennis and Nanus (1985) suggest that 'vision' is 'a mental image of a possible and desirable future state of the organisation'. They consider that the forming, assembling and communication of this vision is a core role of an effective leader, suggesting further:

> 'Management of attention through vision is the creating of focus. Leaders are the most results-oriented individuals in the world and results get attention. Their visions or intentions are compelling and pull people towards them.'

Vision therefore needs to move the organisation beyond its current restrictions and parameters. This vision will feed the remainder of the strategic planning process and will both define and be defined by the organisational purpose. Without a vision, an organisation will become static and potentially complacent, believing that it has the answers in its current tactical plan and that it will be able to simply continue while the world around is constantly changing.

Lynch (2015) recommends that the concept of strategic organisational vision needs a wider consideration than that supported by Bennis and Nanus. His suggestion is:

> 'Vision is a challenging and imaginative picture of the future role and objectives of an organisation, significantly going beyond its current environment and competitive position'

We therefore have different dimensions and timeframes for the concept of vision:

◆   anything that changes the current tactical plan and its parameters

◆   something bold, big and challenging.

These are simply different ends of the same dynamic and both require equal consideration.

In summary, it is suggested that vision is a fundamental aspect of the development and challenging of strategy:

◆   It starts the process – there is an awareness of the need for change.

◆   It requires a challenge to the purpose – the organisation might be fulfilling the purpose today, but what about tomorrow?

◆   It challenges the existing perceived boundaries.

◆   It requires more than just an extension or replication of the current picture.

◆   It provides a challenge for the people involved, and this becomes an iterative process – the thinking individual will answer challenge with further challenge.

3.2 Strategic mission – the rationale

Organisational *vision* will identify a picture of the perceived outcome – *what does it look like*?

Organisational *mission* will define the rationale and the values – *why does it look like that*?

> *mission*
> – an important assignment given to a person or a group of people
> – a vocation or calling
> – a strongly felt aim, ambition or calling

Mission might be expressed in a single sentence of short inspiring and motivational ideals expressed in words

> 'To be a company that inspires and fulfils your curiosity' (Sony)

Or it might be a longer phrase with varying stakeholder aspirations:

> 'To delight our customers, employees and shareholders by relentlessly delivering the platform and technology advancements that become essential to the way we work and live' (Intel Corporation)

Maccoby (2017) discusses the need for an organisational mission to be emotionally driven, suggesting that it is the emotionally charged needs and values of the people involved in the process that need to be shaped into a motivational value system – this will give the mission an underlying drive and commitment from the core players. He suggests that there are six core aspects of human emotion that need to be considered in the shaping and development of *meaning* within organisational mission.

Dignity

Mastery   **Information**

Meaning

Survival   **Play**

Relatedness

Figure 8.2
((Maccoby, *Strategic Intelligence*, 2017) adapted by Mark Wearden)

- ◆ **Survival**: the basic human instinct of defence of oneself and one's group.
- ◆ **Relatedness**: the human need to interact and work with others.
- ◆ **Play**: the drive to explore and innovate.
- ◆ **Information**: the desire to understand and learn.
- ◆ **Dignity**: the need to feel a part of the whole and recognise our individual role.
- ◆ **Mastery**: the requirement to feel in control of at least part of what we do.

These emotional aspects of mission from Maccoby can be aligned with the concepts of motivation discussed by Maslow (1943) and the personal ego needs identified by Freud (1923).

Mission takes the organisational purpose from the brain to the heart. The concept of mission requires a belief in the perceived outcome:

- ◆ When perceived from an idealistic perspective, this can be seen to be driven by the ethics, values and beliefs of the individual and the group.
- ◆ In the cold, hard, world of business, the reality of mission might be driven by belief in the ability to succeed while putting to one side a more fundamentalist belief in the underlying ethics.

In either case there is a human need to clarify and write down organisational mission in a 'mission statement' with the external objective of declaring the organisational purpose to the world at large, and the internal objective of ensuring that employees have an understanding of the organisational mission and purpose.

Stop and think 8.3

Can you summarise the mission of your organisation in one sentence?

Lynch (2015) identifies five core traits that tend to sit within a mission statement:

- ◆ **The nature of the business**: what business are we in and what business should we be in?
- ◆ **A focus on the perceived needs of the customer or consumer**: what is it we are trying to satisfy?
- ◆ **The values and beliefs of the organisation**: what drives us?
- ◆ **An element of sustainable competitive advantage**: what gives us confidence in our viability?
- ◆ **The reasons for our existence**: what underpins our approach to life and business?

Johnson (2017) identifies the difference between internal and external role of a mission statement by suggesting an interaction between strategic drivers and the ethical stance of the organisation.

Ethical stance

Legal minimum   Ideological

Strategic drivers

Internal

Secretive   **Evangelical**

External

**Regulation
procedure**   **Politics**

Figure 8.3 The role of mission
((Johnson, 2017) adapted by Mark Wearden)

Notice the differentiation of the dynamics between the internal and the external
approach, the internal approach being derived from the internal human feelings,
the external approach being derived from perceived expectation.

Stop and think 8.4

**Consider why Johnson suggests these particular words in each of the
segments of his matrix.**

Argenti (1989) aligns his approach to mission statements with that of Johnson's
external perspective, and suggests that mission statements are more to do with
public relations (the image of the company that the directors wish to portray)
than with corporate strategic planning. He supports this view by suggesting that
it is easy for a mission statement to include a phrase such as 'we will enhance
the quality of our products', whereas it is difficult for a mission statement to
include a phrase such as 'we need to make savings to continue to be viable'. His
suggestion is that a mission statement, as a short, uplifting and motivational
statement can be a useful crafted output from the corporate planning process
but should not be an input into that process.

From his earlier research into 53 large and successful companies, Campbell
(1991) developed a tool known as the Ashridge Mission Model to both identify
and challenge the core drivers and rationale behind an organisation's mission.

◆   The purpose needs to describe why the company exists.

◆   The values need to describe what the company believes in, and who it is
     within the company that believes in this.

◆   The standards and behaviours need to identify how the company operates
     in order to maintain the values of the purpose.

◆   The strategy must be viewed, developed and driven holistically across
     the organisation recognising its competitive position and unique selling
     point (USP).

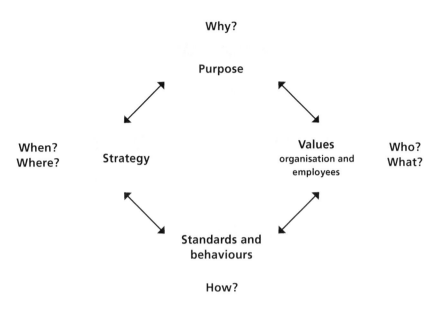

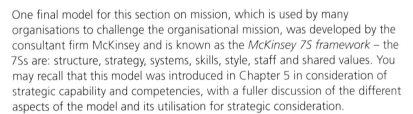

Figure 8.4 The Ashridge Mission Model

Stop and think 8.5

Think about your own organisation, how would you answer the questions which comprise the Ashridge Mission Model?

One final model for this section on mission, which is used by many organisations to challenge the organisational mission, was developed by the consultant firm McKinsey and is known as the *McKinsey 7S framework* – the 7Ss are: structure, strategy, systems, skills, style, staff and shared values. You may recall that this model was introduced in Chapter 5 in consideration of strategic capability and competencies, with a fuller discussion of the different aspects of the model and its utilisation for strategic consideration.

At the centre are the shared values of the organisation with the six surrounding factors being separated into *hard* and *soft* areas.

McKinsey recognised that the hard elements (strategy, structure and systems) are much easier to identify and manage compared to the softer elements (skills, staff and style), although the softer elements will be the foundation of the ethics of the organisation and its employees.

McKinsey suggests that all seven items need to have an equal weighting when being used to interpret different aspects of an organisation and its strategy, and this aligned approach would be required to challenge the mission and mission statement of any particular organisation.

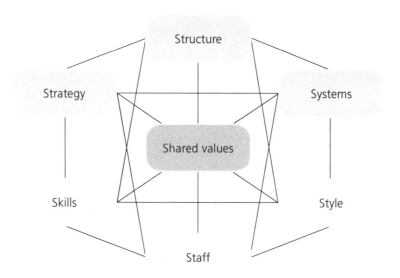

Figure 8.5 McKinsey 7S framework

Case study 8.5

The mission of Cancer Research UK shows a holistic approach to its objective of finding cures for all cancers.

Extract from the Strategy of Cancer Research UK (Cancer Research UK website):

'Our ambition is to bring forward the day when all cancers are cured, and our new strategy will help us make this a reality. We want survival in the UK to be among the best in the world. We're focusing our efforts in four key areas – working to help prevent cancer, diagnose it earlier, develop new treatments and optimise current treatments by personalising them and making them even more effective. In the coming years, we'll concentrate our research in these four areas to make a difference to people with cancer and their families.'

Stop and think 8.6

Imagine you are working in the corporate governance team within Cancer Research UK. How could you use the McKinsey 7S framework to interpret and challenge the statement in Case study 8.5 above?

3.3 Strategic objectives – intentions and actions

This chapter has so far explored:

◆ organisational vision will identify a picture of the perceived outcome – what does it look like?

◆ organisational mission will define the rationale and the values – why does it look like that?

These two aspects of organisational purpose could be described as being cerebral – they establish an image with its underlying values but make no attempt to suggest how strategically we might reach that point of vision or fulfil and maintain the values that we purport to hold. The next step required in our understanding and expression of the organisational purpose is the identification of the strategic objectives that will hold our strategic plan together and enable us to achieve the vision.

Test yourself 8.1

Differentiate between 'vision' and 'mission' within the development of strategy.

Chapter 1 defined *objectives* as 'a range of criteria which identify and clarify differing aspects of the vision and mission'.

We also defined *organisational* goals as 'specific and definable outcomes which enable identification of progress towards achieving the objectives and, if defined in such a manner, the achievement of the strategic intent'.

In many organisations, and many texts on strategy, the terms *goals* and *objectives* are used interchangeably. Mintzberg (1994) suggested that an 'objective' is a goal expressed in the form by which its attainment can be measured – e.g. a goal may be to cut costs, but the objective would be to reduce the overall budget by a certain percentage.

You will see that the difference between *objective* and *goal* is quite pedantic and subject to individual and/or organisational preference as to how each term is used. It is acceptable to use these terms interchangeably, but at times one may wish to clarify a particular aspect of the use of either term within the specific context.

The *strategic objectives* of an organisation take the vision and mission and attempt to place these into a series of organisational statements and outcomes. The existence of hierarchical development structure is suggested at the start of this chapter. We now need to place a practical and achievable reality upon the vaguer concepts of vision and mission.

3.4   Strategic alignment – taking a holistic view

The purpose of dividing the development of strategy into different, manageable sections is to help with the focus. Often these different aspects – vision, mission, objective, goals etc. – will be the responsibility of different people or teams within an organisation.

> 'Mark, can your team come up with a vision for our expectations from the new financial reporting system?'

This is fine, and works as a practical means of developing strategy, but it is crucial that there is also a holistic picture which aligns all of the different aspects. This can be a quite a high level such as that from BAE in Figure 8.6, and you will see how this gives the board a clear picture of the governance oversight required, but also probably helps to drive the internal culture of BAE.

Our vision

- To be the premier international defence, aerospace and security company

Our mission

- To provide a vital advantage to help our customers protect what really matters

Our strategy

- Maintain and grow our business in adjacent markets
- Develop and expand our international business
- Inspire and develop a diverse workforce to drive success
- Enhance financial performance and deliver sustainable growth in shareholder value

Our strategic priorities

Drive operational excellence

Continuously improve competitiveness and efficiency

Advance and further leverage our technology

Our values are Trusted, Innovative and Bold

Figure 8.6 BAE plc strategy alignment
((BAE plc Annual Report and Accounts, 2017) adapted by Mark Wearden)

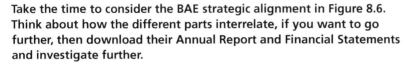

Stop and think 8.7

Take the time to consider the BAE strategic alignment in Figure 8.6. Think about how the different parts interrelate, if you want to go further, then download their Annual Report and Financial Statements and investigate further.

3.5 SMART thinking

One frequently used method of focusing on the specific attributes of the strategic objectives is the use of the acronym SMART:

> 'SMART thinking and SMART objectives lead to SMART results'

Interpretation of the letters will vary depending upon the writer, the tutor and the situation; the following are suggestive rather than prescriptive, and they should always be interpreted to best suit the particular situation with which one is faced, personal or organisational:

S – specific, special, significant, seismic

M – measurable, meaningful, motivational, massive

A – attainable, achievable, acceptable, action-based, accelerating

R – realistic, relevant, rational, rewarding

T – timely, traceable, testing, transforming

Like all such tools, the purpose is to provide a structure through which a series of criteria can be assessed, considered and challenged. A problem always arises when such a tool is used in a purely generic manner and not aligned with the particular circumstances and idiosyncrasies of an organisation and its individuals.

Stop and think 8.8

Use the SMART concept to identify the current objectives of your own role, then expand that to consider the SMART objectives of your organisation.

It is important to recognise that the strategic objectives of the organisation will not always be financial. Later in the text the use of key performance indicators (KPIs) will be considered in our attempt to measure strategic success, but it is worth noting now that Companies Act 2006 requires all companies other than small companies to discuss the financial and non-financial indicators of the organisation within their annual strategic report; these need to be SMART.

The increasing importance of the environmental stakeholder, as discussed in Chapter 7, and the need for organisations to consider their longer-term sustainability has led to the development of a concept known as the 'triple bottom line'. This suggests that an organisation should be looking at three core areas of strategic objective:

◆   financial performance

◆   addition of value to shareholders and stakeholders

◆   the impact of the organisation upon the economy, environment and society.

The interaction of all three of these areas is fundamentally important in maintaining a positive organisational reputation.

This has been taken to a further level by the International Integrated Reporting Council (IIRC) which actively encourages organisations to view their strategic objectives and produce their annual report and accounts in an integrated manner, ensuring that the different aspects of the report inter-relate and are not a series of isolated sections. Underpinning the IIRC concept is the identification of seven different forms of 'capital' within an organisation:

◆   financial

◆   manufactured

◆   intellectual

◆   human

◆   social

◆   relationship

◆   natural.

These 'capitals' are perceived as being used to generate differing levels of the same 'capitals' as the output of the organisation. This is illustrated by the IIRC in the model shown in Figure 8.7.

For the purposes of this text, the IIRC model is being used to illustrate that it is important to recognise that the objectives of any organisation will always be more than purely financial. It is unusual to find vision or mission statements stated in purely financial terms, so likewise it is necessary that the objectives and goals of an organisation cover a breadth of potential activity and outcome and not just the financial parameters.

Within the organisation itself, it is possible to identify objectives at different levels of the operation. The wider corporate objectives are likely to have a longer-term perspective, but these can be expanded into more specific and focused objectives for the operational control of an organisation on a day-to-day, week-to-week basis.

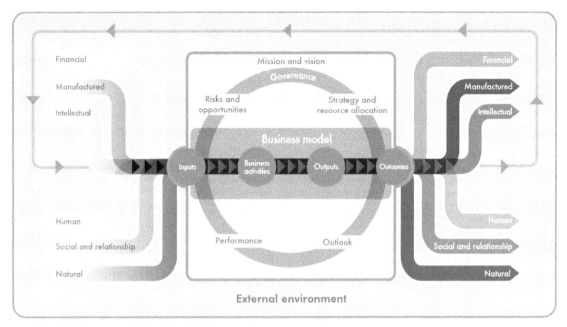

Figure 8.7 IIRC core model
© International Integrated Reporting Council

Case study 8.6

A company manufactures and sells a particular brand of alcoholic drink.

It establishes a strategic corporate objective to increase sales, with an operational goal being established of an increase of 10% within the next 12 months.

When this goal is considered against the seasonal pattern of sales, and the particular increase during televised national sporting events on the sales of alcoholic drinks, the company is able to establish a pattern of anticipated improvement where some months will have a much higher specific sales goal than others, but with the wider objective being the cumulative perceived increase of 10% across the year.

The identification of objectives is not always straightforward within an organisation and problems can often occur. These are usually based around confusion as to the ultimate vision, together with different interpretation of that vision and other priorities that are required to achieve success. Some examples of common problems that might be associated with the clarification and fulfilment of objectives are:

◆ multiple objectives that in themselves may be in conflict with each other – *an organisation needs to reduce staffing costs, but at the same time needs to recruit different areas of expertise*

◆ efficiency versus effectiveness – *manufacturing output on a particular machine might be increased by altering the speed of flow, but this in turn might result in a higher level of rejected products*

◆ constraint – *three aligned objectives all require additional funding, but there is only sufficient capital available to fund one of these objectives*

◆ the conflicting expectations and requirements of different stakeholders – *a common dilemma is the need to return funds to shareholders by way of dividend while also requiring the retention of funds for future investment in the organisation*

Test yourself 8.2

Suggest how Johnson differentiated between four different approaches to organisational mission in his alignment of strategic drivers and ethical stance.

3.6   Strategic alternatives – what could we do instead?

An organisation that applies itself to a serious consideration of the *objectives* that are required to fulfil the *vision* within the ethos of the *mission* will find that it will often generate many different alternative strategic methods and objectives to obtain the perceived end result.

This is important because there is almost always more than one way to achieve a desired vision, and it is important for the efficiency of an organisation that a number of strategic alternatives are generated which can then be assessed against a range of different criteria.

Berenschot (1998) suggested an approach, through the alignment of seven different forces, which could enable managers to consider and assess the different strategic alternatives that are available to them.

Figure 8.8
((Berenschot, 1998) adapted by Mark Wearden)

These can be interpreted as:

- **Necessity**: create a sense of urgency – something needs to happen.
- **Vision**: the creation of shareable images in people's minds.
- **Success**: don't leave the success to the end, ensure there are success measures along the route.
- **Spirit**: the driving force required to maintain the commitment.
- **Structures**: maintaining the essential underlying organisational support for people and functions.
- **Capacities**: involve the right people, with the right knowledge, skills and abilities.
- **Systems**: build an iterative system to maintain the communication process.

Test yourself 8.3

Briefly outline each of the six 'S' words used by McKinsey in its model to surround the seventh 'S' – shared values.

Redefining the tactical plan

This process of expressing organisational purpose through the defining of vision, mission, objectives and goals, and then the further challenging of the outcomes by the generation of alternative approaches, becomes a highly iterative process. This is illustrated in the right-hand side of Figure 8.1 in section three of this chapter.

The tactical plan of 'today' exists and is in operation. The purpose of understanding and defining organisational purpose is to recognise how the tactical plan needs to evolve.

Stop and think 8.9

Consider when you last witnessed a strategic outcome that was caused by insufficient iteration of strategic thinking. This lack of appropriate consideration is summarised well in the following anonymous quotation:

'There is a danger of drawing a mathematically precise line from an unwarranted assumption to a foregone conclusion.'

Test yourself 8.4

Differentiate between objective and goal in the following scenario:

When given his budget, Peter was tasked with saving £1.2 million of staffing costs in the next financial year, through a radical reduction of overtime and a realignment of his team. This was part of the organisational drive for greater efficiency and the retention of customers.

4. Statements of purpose – benefits and issues

Many organisations will use a much wider statement of purpose than a simple mission statement to align the different aspects of the strategic thinking process that has been discussed in this chapter. The rationale for the creation of such a statement is to ensure a clarity of communication both internally and externally, to ensure that all stakeholders have a clarity of understanding of the organisational purpose, and how it relates to their role within the organisation.

Lencioni (2002) identified three core principles that are useful when creating a wider statement of purpose:

◆ **Focus**: the statement needs to be used to focus the attention of the reader and to help to guide real decisions. Example: *Steve Jobs at Apple believed it to be fundamentally important to be able to say no to non-core activities and maintain focus on the core vision.*

◆ **Motivation**: the statement needs to motivate the employees, and those involved within the achievement of the strategic objectives, to give of their best at all times. Example: *Focus of the Apple vision of making computers available to everyone acted as a significant motivation in the early years of the company.*

◆ **Clarity**: any statement needs to be straightforward in its intent and its meaning leaving minimal room for interpretation by different individuals. Example: *The founder of Facebook, Mark Zuckerberg, has a very precise view of their organisational purpose – 'move fast, be bold, and be open'.*

Case study 8.7

The three principles above are well illustrated in the mission, vision and values statement of Coca-Cola, which brings a useful alignment to these differing aspects of strategic organisational purpose.

From www.coca-cola.co.uk/about-us/mission-vision-and-values:

'Mission, vision and values

The world is changing all around us. To continue to thrive as a business over the next 10 years and beyond, we must look ahead. Understanding the trends and forces that will shape our business in the future and moving swiftly will prepare us for what's to come. These are the declarations of our overall mission and goals and the values that guide us as a company and as individuals.

The Coca Cola Company Mission

Our mission is:

◆   To refresh the world in mind, body and spirit

◆   To inspire moments of optimism and happiness through our brands
    and actions

◆   To create value and make a difference.

The Coca Cola Company Vision

To achieve our mission, we have developed a set of goals, which we will
work with our bottlers to deliver:

◆   People: Inspiring each other to be the best we can be by providing
    a great place to work

◆   Portfolio: Offering the world a portfolio of drinks brands that
    anticipate and satisfy people's desires and needs

◆   Partners: Nurturing a winning network of partners and building
    mutual loyalty

◆   Planet: Being a responsible global citizen that makes a difference by
    helping to build and support sustainable communities

◆   Profit: Maximising long-term return to shareholders, while being
    mindful of our overall responsibilities

◆   Productivity: Being a highly effective, lean and fast-moving
    organisation.

The Coca Cola Company Values

Our shared values guide our actions and describe how we behave in the
world:

◆   Leadership: The courage to shape a better future

◆   Collaboration: Leverage collective genius

◆   Integrity: Be real

◆   Accountability: If it is to be, it's up to me

◆   Passion: Committed in heart and mind

◆   Diversity: As inclusive as our brands

◆   Quality: What we do, we do well'

Consider how these comprehensive statements from Coca Cola illustrate
the various principles that have been discussed in this chapter.

Chapter summary

◆ This chapter moves the focus of the development of strategy into the organisation itself, looking at some of the internal factors that drive strategic direction.

◆ As a company secretary and governance professional it is fundamental to understand the rationale for why an organisation exists – in simple terms this is its organisational purpose. The role requires us to ensure that purpose is expressed in a transparent and accessible manner, but also that it is used as a benchmark for the wide range of other strategic dimensions that we will be required to consider.

◆ We revisit the core strategic journey model from Chapter 1 and challenge the core drivers of vison and mission before considering how these more cerebral concepts align with the need to deliver practical and commercial results.

◆ The starting point is to consider not what we are doing within the organisation, but why we are doing it, and then align this with an understanding of how we do it. We need to ensure that organisational purpose is fully understood from the inside, to help us understand how others view us, and why.

◆ A number of different methods and models are introduced to help with the challenge, but one of the simplest is that from Ashridge suggesting four perspectives, which we aligned with the six question words: purpose (why?); values (who and what?); standards (how?); strategy (when and where?).

◆ The examples from BAE plc and from Coca-Cola provide useful real organisation views of strategic alignment.

◆ There is a need for SMART thinking to help plan and understand the strategic journey, but there are no preconceived words to apply to each letter in the acronym. Students need to determine what these should be for any given particular situation at a given point in time – 'today'.

◆ The various concepts discussed in this chapter might be usefully collated by an organisation into a 'statement of purpose'. The pre-emptive thinking required, and the production of an aligned 'statement' will be the responsibility of those within the organisations who are entrusted with the development of strategy but could well be part of the remit of the company secretary and governance professional.

Chapter nine
Business ethics and social responsibility

Contents

1. Introduction

Throughout the preceding chapters of this text it has been frequently concluded that, despite the most academic and intelligent business models and structures, the day-to-day behaviour within an organisation is driven by the people involved and their different characters, styles and beliefs. The study of ethics requires us to think about our role as an ethical professional, how that results from our perception and understanding of our own ethics, and how our behaviour and that of the world around us is perpetually influenced by the ethics of other people.

This chapter will consider the meaning of personal ethics, how it is transcribed into organisational behaviour, and how that same ethical behaviour is, and can be, perceived as having a wider influence through our corporate social responsibility (CSR).

There are many books on ethics, business ethics and financial ethics, and there has been a rapid growth in these books, particularly in the last 20 years. It is suggested that this reflects societal change from the post-war togetherness which dominated the way people viewed themselves in society 60 years ago, to the rampant individualism which is promoted and exploited by the media of the 21st century, and the impact of the instant communication age in which we now live.

An important aspect of the role of a company secretary or governance professional is to attempt to understand or to quantify why people within an organisation behave in different ways when seemingly trying to achieve the same strategic objective. This approach could be challenged as trying to 'place people within boxes', but we need to recognise that each individual is unique with their own upbringing, inherited values, formulated values, attitude and state of maturity. The success or failure of an organisation is driven by the bringing together of these diverse people.

Stop and think 9.1

To understand the ethics of others we need to understand our own ethics.

Before reading any further, write down some words which you would associate with your personal ethics.

2. The meaning of ethics

2.1 Ethics and decision making

Every time we make a decision and act in a way which affects someone else, we are making an ethical decision. This decision is based upon all of our learning to that point in our lifetime, and will be influenced by our principles and the situation within which we find ourselves. To understand ethics and our own ethical perspectives, we need to be faced with situations where we are required to make decisions. We then need to allow ourselves the time and space to step back and consider how and why we reached such decisions, and then review the impact. Although time does not always allow for this in a formalised manner, our inner reflections will continue to build our ethical approach to life around us.

We need to consider the real meaning of ethics and how and why it impacts our making of decisions. This is a fundamental requirement of strategy and change, within ourselves and within our organisations.

The dictionary definitions of this one small word allow us to consider the breadth of the three interrelated but different meanings, which will relate to our approach:

> *ethics*
> – the philosophical study of the moral value of human conduct and of the rules and principles that ought to govern it
> – a code of behaviour considered correct, especially that of a particular group, profession, or individual
> – the moral fitness of a decision, course of action etc.

The first definition of 'ethics' requires us to consider the word moral, and its definition reveals the nub of ethics and ethical behaviour – the paradoxes of good vs bad and right vs wrong:

> *moral*
> – concerned with or relating to human behaviour, especially the distinction between good and bad or right and wrong behaviour.

The strategic problem is apparent. While shaping our vision, we need to consider the ethical drivers of the people involved in the organisation. These drivers will be illustrated and driven by their own individual views and values. To make the challenge harder, our strategic perceptions then have to be viewed in the wider context of the multiplicity of ethical expectation of our organisation's internal and external stakeholders, in themselves just more people with their own differing views and values.

The second definition of 'ethics' differentiates between group, profession and individual, and this moves closer to the focus of our study of the development of strategy and our work as a company secretary or governance professional. In this role, we may often become involved in setting or helping to establish expected standards of corporate behaviour, not just in meetings but also within wider organisational contexts. Sometimes we will have to write or be expected to judge others against an Ethics Code – a set of expected norms which are expected to apply to all people within a particular organisation or grouping. The purpose of any such intended organisational norms is to act as a benchmark to allow us and others to compare the behaviour of ourselves, and others, against the perceived 'moral fitness' of the third dictionary definition.

Case study 9.1

Ethical options

As you walk out of a busy shop, your foot kicks a purse which is on the ground. You pick it up and it falls open, revealing a number of £20 notes inside – your cursory look suggests it contains a few hundred pounds. You look around but can see no evidence of anyone who might have dropped the purse. A person, with a sign saying 'homeless', is sitting begging for money outside the door of the shop – they have seen you pick up the purse and are watching with interest. What are your options and what do you do?

2.2   Virtue, expectation and rules

In his book *Ethicability* (2006) Roger Steare draws a useful distinction between three different moral philosophies. He discusses a *principled conscience* which is, in his words, effectively a moral DNA; this interrelates with our *social conscience*, what is right and wrong with regard to the way individuals behave towards each other within society; both of these consciences then need to exist within the context of *rule compliance* as dictated by those in authority within any particular societal grouping e.g. country, religion, company, profession, club etc.

An alternative approach is to draw a distinction between *principle ethics* and *situational ethics*, suggesting that the former leaves us little room for choice, whereas in the latter our response will be based upon the particular circumstances of the decision with which we are faced.

These are not new concepts and considerations. The word 'ethics' derives from the Greek word for character – *ethos*. Aristotle (384–322 BC) developed the thoughts of his predecessors Socrates and Plato by developing the view that the ethos was formed from a set of principles on how to live as a contributing member of a society run by politics. He recognised that this would differ between individuals, but held that there were certain absolute principles. This foundation of Aristotelian thought formed much of the ethical influence and norms within Western society for the next two thousand years.

St Thomas Aquinas (1225–1274) used the same principles to formulate the doctrines of the Roman Catholic Church as its influence began to spread worldwide, and many ethical doctrines of today still draw on these precepts.

René Descartes (1596–1650) continued this theme with his famous dictum: *cogito ergo sum – I think therefore I am*. His philosophical approach to the human being suggesting that it is our individual thinking, and therefore our individual reactions and decisions, which create the ethics which surround us. We should therefore not be surprised at the ethical conflicts which exist in a society of human beings all with the ability to *think*.

Immanuel Kant (1724–1804) developed this thinking further to suggest that moral law ought to be universal, but recognised that different circumstances (maxims) existed which inevitably meant that judgements needed to be made on an individual basis. Known as the categorical imperative, he summarised this in a variety of ways, including:

◆   'Act only according to that maxim whereby you can at the same time will that it should become a universal law.'

◆   'Act in such a way that you treat humanity, whether in your own person or in the person of any other, never merely as a means to an end, but always at the same time as an end.'

It becomes clear that when dealing with ethics, like much of our consideration of the development of strategy, we are dealing with something which never has only one correct answer. Any consideration of ethics and ethical thought processes will suggest options, opposing views and a greater or lesser acceptance of individualism.

It is not by chance that the underpinning legal duties of directors of limited companies, as defined under Companies Act 2006 (CA 2006), makes no reference to a collective (a board), but each of the seven required duties starts with 'A director ...'. The ethics of governance is based around the alignment of the ethics of individuals.

2.3   Integrity and reputation

Integrity sits at the heart of the ethical requirement of any human being, and in particular how we are expected to behave as professionals. As a company secretary and governance professional, this is a core trait that will be expected from us by others, by the law and by society.

integrity
- the quality of being honest and having strong moral principles
- the state of being whole and undivided.

The ethical behaviour that we portray is based upon the diversity of different inputs and forces that derive from our inherited traits, as moulded and matured through our life to this particular point in time. The requirement and expectation from a qualified, chartered professional is to have a proactive intent to do the right thing in the right way, and to not be knowingly involved in anything which might challenge or bring into question their personal integrity or the integrity of their organisation or profession (which could have a negative impact on reputation).

In our consideration of personal ethical behaviour, we need to link this concept of integrity to that of objectivity:

objectivity
- not being influenced by personal feelings or opinions in considering and representing facts.

Think about a core requirement for our development of effective strategy – the ability to always review and re-review the starting point, the 'today' position. The purpose of this is to allow us to develop an objective approach which will utilise our own integrity and wisdom at that very point of strategic consideration. Our personal ethical behaviour and beliefs will then iteratively enable us to develop personal integrity and a reputation for objectivity.

In Chapter 7 'reputation' was defined as:

'the beliefs or opinions that are generally held about someone or something'

and we linked this to the various societal forces (near and far) that had been discussed previously as affecting our strategic judgement.

Our reputation and that of our organisations is only ever based upon the ethical opinions and beliefs that are held and developed by others, each with their own diverse ethical opinions and beliefs.

Think back to the consideration of cognitive bias, in Chapter 6. As individuals, at any 'today' point in time, we have our own cognitive biases – these dictate not just the way that we behave, practically and ethically, but also the way in which we view other people and their behaviour and beliefs. Reputation could therefore be seen as the accumulation of the bias of others. We need to recognise that our biases can change rapidly through the influence of experience, events and other people. Think how often your opinions about a wide range of topics will have changed across your lifetime so far.

In today's internet and media infused world of immediacy, people's views can be swayed very quickly, and we need to be aware of this in our development of strategy. What might seem reasonable to expect from others today, might change very rapidly. Who knows the nature of the black swans that may impact our well-designed strategic route forward? There is no better example than national politics. Think about the world that surrounds you as you read this text, and then think back ten years – no-one could have predicted the political changes that we have seen in many countries.

Test yourself 9.1

Briefly suggest the difference between 'principle-based ethics' and 'situational-based ethics' at a personal level.

3. Business ethics in the development of strategy

The Institute of Business Ethics (IBE) suggest on its website (www.ibe.org.uk) that:

> 'Business ethics is the application of ethical values to business behaviour. Business ethics is relevant both to the conduct of individuals and to the conduct of the organisation as a whole. It applies to any and all aspects of business conduct, from boardroom strategies and how companies treat their employees and suppliers to sales techniques and accounting practices. Ethics goes beyond the legal requirements for a company and is, therefore, about discretionary decisions and behaviour guided by values.'

Stop and think 9.2

Think about the differences in these four ethical statements. What is each organisation trying to say, and what impact are they hoping for?

GSK website: www.gsk.com

'Everyone who works for or on behalf of GSK must abide by the law, but our code of conduct goes beyond that. It also establishes the standards and policies that help us meet the commitments of our heavily regulated industry and work as a high performing team. Our values and expectations help define us, build trust with society and direct us to do the right thing every day.'

TESCO website: www.tescoplc.com

'Our Code of Business Conduct is at the heart of how we run our business and is designed to help and protect us. It is important that we all understand the rules that we must follow, and the conduct that is expected of us, in order to look after our colleagues, do a great job for customers and protect our reputation.'

Coca-Cola website:
www.coca-colacompany.com

'At the Coca-Cola Company, we aim to lead by example and to learn from experience. We set high standards for our people at all levels and strive to consistently meet them. Our sound business principles and practices foster our strong, innovative and collaborative culture, which is committed to ethical behaviour, accountability and transparency We are guided by our established standards of corporate governance and ethics. We review our systems to ensure we achieve international best practices in terms of transparency and accountability.'

ICSA: The Governance Institute website:
www.icsa.org.uk

'The ICSA Code of Professional Ethics and Conduct comprises four core principles to which all Fellows, Associates, graduates, students and affiliated members registered with the UKRIAT Division of the Institute must adhere.

– integrity
– high standard of service and professional competence
– transparency
– professional behaviour'

3.1   The scope of business ethics

At any time within any organisation, the organisational business ethics, and therefore the reputation, can be seen to be a combination of:

◆   individual and combined values of all of the people involved

◆   the prevailing tone of the corporate culture

◆   codes of conduct that might apply across differing aspects of personal and organisational behaviour

◆   societal and internal and external stakeholder expectations

◆   local, national and international law.

Stanwick and Stanwick (2014) discuss how the ethical cycle within a business enables employees to understand who they are and to understand their strategic responsibilities from an ethical perspective. This cycle involves decisions being made with an ethical dimension, the results of such decisions being understood and then influencing the next time such a decision needs to be made. (Note the alignment here with the thinking of Argyris (1990) and the 'ladder of inference' discussed in Chapter 1.)

Stanwick and Stanwick further suggest that there are three core questions which need to be answered to enable an organisation to make and deliver effective ethical decisions within the wider business context:

◆   the individual needs to ask, 'Who am I?'

◆   the team or group needs to ask, 'Who are we?'

◆   the organisation needs to ask, 'Who is the company?'

Based on his research, the organisational theorist Nicolai Foss (1997) suggests:

'The decision-making process of all managers includes incorporating the goals and objectives of the firm into measurable evaluation points. Within the decision-making context, the decision-maker also needs to integrate ethical issues into the process. By being able to demonstrate its ethical virtues to its various stakeholders, firms incorporate ethical planning as part of the strategic planning process, and are then able to generate a positive reputation to the stakeholders'.

Constance Bagley (2003) devised a straightforward 'decision tree' which she published in the Harvard Business Review to encapsulate the core ethical questions at the heart of strategic decision-making. The importance of this 'tree' is that it illustrates that the ethical nature is not always straightforward – sometimes the ethical decision may not always be in the best interests of the organisation (identified by Bagley as maximising shareholder value).

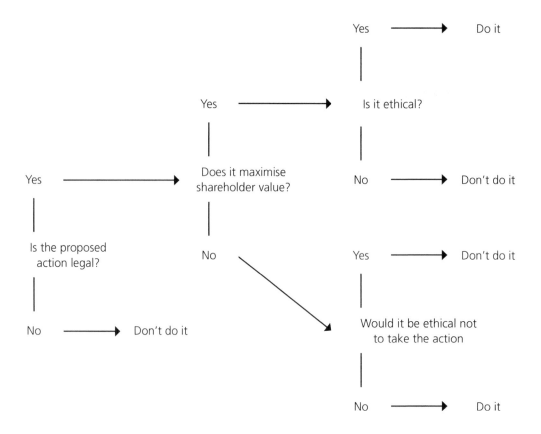

Figure 9.1 Decision tree
((Bagley, 2003) adapted by Mark Wearden)

3.2 Dimensions of ethics

Chryssides and Kaler (1996) suggest that the same two core dimensions of ethical behaviour that affect each individual – *principles* and *situation* – will also strongly influence the evolution of ethical norms within a business. They put forward five different views of business ethics:

◈ **Business is business**: the aims of an organisation are purely commercial and therefore the maximisation of the perceived expectations will outweigh any ethical dimension – *for example, the selling of goods with a known fault or danger might be perceived as acceptable under this view.*

◈ **Act consistently within the law**: it is accepted that the law is there to protect the greater good of all concerned and therefore should underpin ethical decision-making – *for example, faulty or dangerous goods would not be perceived as acceptable under this view, however that does not necessarily mean that such goods are for the greater benefit of the individual or for society.*

◈ **Good ethics mean good business**: this is sometimes known as the coincidence theory and there has been significant research to suggest that organisational sustainability is closely aligned with the perception by stakeholders of good business ethics – *for example, while it might be acceptable to manufacture and sell a particular product, if that product was deemed to be damaging to the reputation of the organisation it is likely that it would be withdrawn.*

◈ **Conventional morality**: the business will operate in line with the prevailing moral codes of the society within which it is based; there are a number of easily perceived problems with this view – *for example, such codes will evolve with the passage of time, codes will differ significantly within different geographic locations (e.g. bribery is accepted as a normal part of business in many parts of the world, while being deemed as unacceptable in other parts of the world).*

◈ **Universal morality**: people in the business world should maintain the same standards of ethical behaviour in business as they would in their private lives. This can be seen to be setting a high ethical standard. However, from the perspective of business sustainability, it would rely upon competitors following similar standards – *for example, strategic thinking is often aligned with the tactics developed to win a war; this raises an interesting challenge to the concept of universal morality and to the 'categorical imperative' of Kant referred to above.*

The important point for the strategist is that any business is only ever a collection of individuals. It is those people who will need to implement the strategy and achieve the objectives. It will be the individual or collective ethical views and perspectives of those people that will have recognised the need for strategic change, and they will expect you to develop strategies to align with their ethical beliefs and enable the strategic objectives to be achieved within the constraints of those same ethical dimensions.

Case study 9.2

Extract from BAE plc Annual Report and Financial Statements 2017:

'We aim to be a recognised leader in business conduct. This helps us to earn and maintain stakeholder trust and sustain business success. We consider it fundamental to maintain a culture focused on embedding responsible business behaviours. All employees are expected to act in accordance with the requirements of the Company's policies, including the Code of Conduct, at all times. As well as being the right thing to do, this reduces the risk of compliance failure and supports us in attracting and retaining high-calibre employees.'

3.3   The purpose of a code of ethics

The use of the word 'code', as in 'code of ethics', would, for most people, imply voluntary or expected compliance. However, the dictionary definition of the word code allows for the combination of principles (something with which we *might* comply) and rules (something with which we *must* comply). Although at times these might align, the human perspective might suggest differently. Therefore, we need to accept that the resultant document will inevitably include two complementary but necessarily different aspects of a code.

Firstly, there will be principles, standards and expected modes of conduct that the organisation, or the profession or sector, expects; these will include core beliefs and expectations of the organisation; together with behaviours expected from differing stakeholders. As an example, the John Lewis Partnership Responsible Sourcing Code states:

'Our aim is to build lasting relationships with suppliers, and we have always recognised that our responsibility extends to their employees and suppliers.'

Secondly, there may well be practical guidelines which could be as bold as a decision tree type approach – 'if this happens, what do I do' – or it could be a set of quite specific instructions. To continue the John Lewis example, the same Code states:

'Suppliers must complete fully documented risk assessments of their sites and accommodation provided, and regularly monitor risks posed to workers' health and safety.'

This latter area is very often the way in which aspects of bribery and or conflicts of interests are handled within an organisation.

The diagram below suggests the three key areas that are required to deliver an appropriate mix for our code, similar to the core drivers of our strategic thinking. In a code, we are trying to anticipate what might or might not happen in the future based on our understanding of today.

◆   The *structural* requirements will ensure alignment or compliance with the underlying and professional levels of conduct that are associated with our organisation, our sector, or our profession.

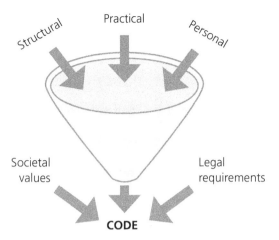

Figure 9.2 Creating an ethics code
© Mark Wearden

◆ The *practical* input will be a wide view of how the organisation, sector or profession expects people adhering to the code to behave.

◆ The *personal* section may well include specific examples illustrating how people are expected to behave, how they will be judged, and the potential organisational and personal consequences of non-compliance.

◆ The *pressures at the bottom*, the combination of *societal values* and *legal requirements* will affect style, impact and veracity of the eventual fate and/ or effectiveness of our code.

ICSA members are expected to adhere to the ICSA Code of Professional Ethics and Conduct. This comprises four core principles:

◆ **Integrity**
  – The quality of being honest and having strong moral principles. The term has been described judicially as connoting 'moral soundness, rectitude, and steady adherence to an ethical code'. It requires that members are impartial, independent and informed.

◆ **High standard of service/professional competence**
  – This should be delivered throughout one's working life. This involves an understanding of relevant technical, professional and business developments.

◆ **Transparency**
  – Members should be clear and open in their business and professional conduct.

◆ **Professional behaviour**
  – Members should act in a way which conforms to the relevant laws of the jurisdiction in which they are residing and/or undertaking business transactions and pay regard to all regulations which may have a bearing on their actions.

There are fuller details on the ICSA website, where each principle is expanded in more depth.

Stop and think 9.3

Consider the ICSA code of ethics, outlined above (and see the ICSA website where each principle is explained in more detail).

How do you measure up to this – today?

Have you ever been faced with an ethical dilemma where you have felt challenged as to how to make the right ethical decision?

Often in our role as a company secretary and governance professional we will be faced with such dilemmas, but also, we will witness others as they make their ethical decisions.

We might also be required at times to challenge others on the basis of their decision-making.

4. Corporate social responsibility as part of strategy

Corporate social responsibility (CSR) is aligned with a range of differing aspects of the life of an organisation:

◆   The impact that organisational decisions have on the world and on people.

◆   The ethical norms and behaviour that can or cannot be expected from any organisation, and then, at a deeper level, the behaviours that can be rightly expected from any particular organisation, within its own sector and context.

◆   The manner in which employees of the organisation are treated.

◆   The *ethics* and *ethos* which are expected throughout the organisation:

   –   *ethics* being the behavioural traits that are visible

   –   *ethos* being the ethical stance being taken by those who structure and oversee the culture within an organisation.

Test yourself 9.2

Suggest what is meant by the 'reputation' of an organisation and where it comes from.

Recognition of CSR by an organisation, in its fundamental form, is a commitment to contribute to economic development from within an ethical framework, while seeking to improve the quality of life for its employees and their families, the local community and society at large.

In practice, this often means the ability of an organisation to link its decision-making to a set of ethical values, while complying with legal requirements (health and safety considerations and requirements frequently being a key driver) while maintaining a respect for how, as an organisation it will or may affect the people within its wider stakeholder environment.

CSR, as an organisational concept, first appeared in the 1950s, initially in the US, with Howard Bowen raising the challenge of 'what responsibilities to society may businessmen reasonably be expected to assume?'. Since initial challenges such as this, CSR has seen a gradual growth of consideration across the world to the point where it has become an expected benchmark within organisational structure and reporting.

Since the CA 2006, the directors of all UK limited companies are required, as a duty, to ensure that their decision-making encompasses this wider environment; although not referred to as CSR, the linkage is clear. Corporate reporting requirements, enhanced in early 2019, require the directors' report, in all companies other than those deemed as small under the Act, to demonstrate to their members how they have fulfilled their duties under this section. Not only are directors required to behave with a wider stakeholder and CSR awareness, but they are required to explain and illustrate how they have done so.

Stop and think 9.4

UK Companies Act 2006 s172

Consider the CSR and underlying ethical principles of this core aspect of UK corporate law.

A director of a company must act in the way they consider, in good faith, would be most likely to promote the success of the company for the benefit of its members as a whole, and in doing so have regard (among other matters) to:

1. **the likely consequences of any decision in the long term;**
2. **the interests of the company's employees;**
3. **the need to foster the company's business relationships with suppliers, customers and others;**
4. **the impact of the company's operations on the community and the environment;**
5. **the desirability of the company maintaining a reputation for high standards of business conduct; and**
6. **the need to act fairly as between members of the company.**

CSR could be perceived as the obligation that any organisation has to develop and implement its strategy with a positive awareness of how that strategy is likely to affect society.

To achieve this, an organisation needs to have a wide and conscious awareness of the social issues and norms that are affecting society at any point in time. This does not mean that an organisation will only operate from an ethical or moral dimension if it has a heightened sense of CSR. It is likely that there will also be a competitive advantage to be gained from a perception by stakeholders that the organisation is operating in an ethical manner. The organisation will be seen as a good corporate citizen which chooses to do 'the right thing'.

4.1 Carroll's pyramid of CSR

The American management thinker, Archie Carroll (1991), places the concept of CSR into a pyramid framework to help businesses challenge and consider four distinct levels of responsibility that he argues are required to ensure that CSR is part of, rather than apart from, the wider business objectives.

Figure 9.3 Pyramid of CSR
((Carroll, 1991) adapted by Mark Wearden)

Carroll suggests that the following core attributes need to be associated with each responsibility.

◆   **Economic responsibilities**

  –   If an organisation is enabled or allowed to exist, in a formalised manner, within a society, then it has a responsibility back to that society.

  –   Society needs organisations that are profitable; within a democracy this then allows for the levying of taxation to generate funds to be used for the public good.

  –   Profits enable the direct reward of owners, but also allow reinvestment in the organisation to drive forward both the organisation and the stakeholder society that it is serving.

- Organisations that are not successful within their projected field of operation will eventually fail, and this will have a knock-on cost to society.

Legal responsibilities

- Any organisation needs to operate within the legal framework of the society where it exists.
- The laws reflect the accumulated operational (and sometimes ethical) principles of society and are there for the greater good and protection of society as a whole.
- It is important for an organisation to produce products or services that meet at least the minimum legal standards required for the protection of consumers.

Ethical responsibilities

- An organisation needs to develop its own ethics code – the way in which it expects its employees to behave.
- There needs to be some concept within an organisation of the moral and ethical norms that are acceptable to society – both generic and specific.
- An organisation needs to encourage its employees to be 'good corporate citizens'.

Philanthropic responsibilities

- This takes an organisation above the economic, legal and ethical and into a discretionary area where organisations may want to or may want to be seen to be 'giving back'.
- There is a fine line here between altruism (an unselfish concern for the welfare of others) and philanthropy (the performing of charitable or benevolent actions).
- The desire within an organisation, or within its leaders, to be seen to be going above and beyond for the greater good of others – there is a risk that this can both enhance and damage organisational reputation dependent on the views of others.
- Carroll uses the pyramidal structure to illustrate the gradual building of CSR within an organisation.
- The starting point is financial stability (going-concern, viability) and the requirement is to operate within the law. This can then enable the evolution of ethical and philanthropic practices in the belief that they will enhance the economic good (either tangibly or intangibly) and thus complete the circle.

Stop and think 9.5

How well would your organisation align with the concepts proposed by Carroll?

4.2 Taking an ethical stance

Every organisation will naturally take a slightly different stance on its approach to CSR. This will be based upon its current and historic culture, the views of the current employees (not always just at the senior level) and the stakeholder expectations (sometimes an organisation needs to be seen to be doing something related to CSR to keep its stakeholders satisfied, even if it is not a natural part of its culture).

Johnson et al. (2017) produced a matrix identifying a range of different CSR approaches with the dynamics that were driving them.

	Laissez-faire	Enlightened self-interest	Stakeholder interaction	Shaper of society
Rationale	Compliance, profit, taxation, employment	Good business	Triple-bottom line sustainability	Social and market change
Leadership required	Peripheral	Supportive	Champion	Visionary
Management required	Middle manager oversight	Effective systems of good practice	Led by directors with wide monitoring	Each individual
Mode and reputation	Defensive	Reactive	Proactive	Defining
Stakeholder relationships	Unilateral	Interactive	Partnership	Alliances

Table 9.1 CSR stances
((Johnson et al., 2017) adapted by Mark Wearden)

◆ **Laissez-faire**: the organisation just gets on with 'life-as normal' focused on driving profitability and shareholder value. Its CSR approach will be to achieve the minimum required to comply with regulation and expectation. The mode is defensive because the organisation will find reasons to avoid additional expenditure on CSR activities.

◆ **Enlightened self-interest**: the organisation recognises the commercial benefit of taking a positive CSR stance and in building greater sustainability into the supply chain. The mode is reactive because the organisation will be perceived as responding to CSR opportunities.

◆ **Stakeholder interaction**: the organisation recognises the benefit of working closely with its wider stakeholder community and has developed the ability to account for its operation and output from a triple-bottom line perspective (see below), or its equivalent. The mode is proactive because the organisation will be perceived as leading and opening CSR opportunities.

◆   **Shaper of society**: the organisation and/or its key leadership team are seen as visionaries who have the ability to influence social change. Such organisations will have an empowered workforce with each member expected to play their part within CSR. The mode is defining because the organisation will establish benchmarks and best practice for others.

Case study 9.3

Extract from 'How giving back can pay back', FT.com, 24 September 2018 (www.ft.com/content/70138010-a7c3-11e8-a1b6-f368d365bf0e)

'Social impact is spreading. Across the world, almost half as many people are creating start-ups with a primarily social or environmental purpose as those with a solely commercial aim, according to the Global Entrepreneurship Monitor, a multi-country study.

In the UK, almost 9 per cent of small and medium-sized businesses are social enterprises – meaning their aim is mainly social or environmental – while a further 22 per cent have some social or environmental goals, according to government data.

"For me, responsible business is far more than community involvement and 'programmes'," says David Grayson, emeritus professor of corporate responsibility at Cranfield School of Management.

It has been important to me to make sure that we're not just there to make money – there has to be a higher purpose Ashley Unitt, co-founder of NewVoiceMedia "It is about core business behaviour: how a business treats employees, customers and suppliers. So, it is much more about being a great place to work, treating customers well, taking responsibility for what is happening in its supply chain."

Community initiatives have their place, he suggests, as long as they are part of an overall strategy to take responsibility for a business's social, environmental and economic impact. Those that do it best are looking to have a positive effect rather than simply mitigating any negative repercussions of their business.'

4.3   The auditing of CSR

As with all aspects of organisational life, it is important for directors and others to be able to justify the approach taken to CSR with its inevitable use of stakeholder resources. Sometimes this is treated as a separate process referred to as a social audit. Increasingly there is a move towards a more holistic approach with all aspects of an organisation's activities being seen as part of its integrated approach, and therefore being scrutinised as part of the formal cyclical external and internal audit processes within the organisation.

As already briefly referenced, there has been a particular attempt to align the concept of a social audit with that of a financial audit and this has been variously referred to as the *triple bottom line* approach. This attempts to capture the essence of sustainability by measuring the impact of an organisation's activities on the world, this approach predates that of integrated reporting as discussed in Chapter 8 but can be seen to be attempting to achieve the same end result.

There is a recognition within the triple bottom line approach of the interdependence of people, the differing elements of society, and a range of different aspects that are required for the maintenance and sustenance of human existence.

Savitz and Weber (2006) suggest the following differentiation between the three different aspects of the triple bottom line.

Economic	Environmental	Social
Sales, profitability, return on investment	Air quality	Labour practices
Taxes paid	Water quality	Community impact
Monetary flows	Energy usage	Human rights
Jobs created	Waste produced	Product responsibility

Table 9.2
((Savitz & Weber, 2006) adapted by Mark Wearden)

Test yourself 9.3

What is meant by the acronym CSR and how is it demonstrated by an organisation?

Johnson et al. (2017) suggest that the areas within CSR that need to be reviewed and audited are differentiated into internal and external aspects:

◆ **Internal**: employee welfare, working conditions, job design, intellectual property.
◆ **External**: environmental, products, markets and marketing, suppliers, employment, community activity, human rights.

Although this split is slightly arbitrary, it can be seen that CSR concepts cover a broad range of stakeholder interests. In many instances there is an increasingly detailed legal expectation with regard to anticipated organisational action in areas previously referred to as CSR issues. This reflects societal change and an increasing expectation that many areas of organisational behaviour have moved from a social expectation to a legal requirement.

Examples of this would be:

◆ the variety of differing laws covering treatment of, and rights of employees
◆ the introduction into UK legislation of the Bribery Act 2010 and the Modern Slavery Act 2015.

Alongside these changes, for companies with shares listed and publicly traded on the London Stock Exchange (LSE) and the Alternative Investment Market (AIM) there is an ever-increasing expectation of transparency in their narrative reporting, as a fundamental part of their annual report and accounts. Aspects of CSR such as modern slavery, employee diversity, carbon and other emissions are required to be reported on a regular and comparative basis so that the company's approach to CSR is visible to all. Companies have responded to this in a plethora of different ways, at the one end there is a minimalist approach of boilerplate text, at the other end is a graphic and pictorial illustration of how the organisation is behaving as a 'good corporate citizen'. The style adopted will be driven either internally (the beliefs of the key players) or externally (the expectations of activist shareholder or stakeholders).

5. Sustainability as part of strategy

Take a quick look again at the extract from section 172 of the CA 2006 above and note that the first of the additional requirements under section 2 of the CA 2006 is for directors of a company to consider the long-term consequences of their decision-making, their strategy. This approach has been strengthened in recent years with the expectation that the traditional concept of going-concern (the ability of an organisation to meet its liabilities within the next 12 months) needs to be aligned more closely with an understanding and explanation by directors of the longer-term viability organisation. The latter is a reporting requirement for all except small and medium-size companies.

Although these tend to be largely financial concepts, when taken with the comments above about a triple bottom line thinking approach towards CSR, it can be seen how viability and sustainability are intrinsically linked. If we accept that a core principle of a CSR approach is the impact that an organisation is having upon the wider environment, then the stakeholder interest must be focused on the sustainability of such an approach. As with finance, a short-term, instant-win action might have an impact but will not be sustainable in the longer term.

Adrian Henriques (2004) has suggested that if we are to view sustainability as an intrinsic part of our organisational strategic thinking, then we need to have three different perspectives being held together at any one point in time, and being transparent to our stakeholders:

◆ **Economic sustainability**: do the figures add up?

◆ **Social sustainability**: who is impacted by our operational activities?

◆ **Environmental sustainability**: are we adding to or reducing the overall long-term viability of the environment within which our organisation operates?

It is worth re-considering the International Integrated Reporting Council (IIRC) diagram in Chapter 8 to help develop a holistic view of sustainability, from the six different 'capitals' that underpin the concept of integrated reporting.

As a simple means of differentiating between CSR and sustainability, it is suggested that:

◆ **Responsibility** = our accountability to and impact upon others.

◆ **Sustainability** = our accountability to and impact upon ourselves and others.

The incorporation of sustainability within the overall strategic thinking will bring a number of direct benefits, both tangible in terms of outcomes, and intangible in terms of the need for a developed strategic thinking and consideration:

◆ **Business protection**: through the reduction of risk of harm to the organisation and its direct and indirect stakeholders.

◆ **Business operation**: through a wider awareness of direct and indirect costs across a longer strategic time period.

◆ **Business growth**: widening of the breadth of strategic consideration will undoubtedly lead to the consideration of a greater range of opportunities.

◆ **Business reputation**: being known for a sustainable CSR approach.

Case study 9.4

Tesco has featured in a number of the earlier chapters of this text so you will have already built a picture in your mind about its approach to the different dimensions of strategy. Think about how Tesco's approach to sustainability aligns with the 'cognitive bias' towards Tesco that you have.

Extract from Tesco plc Annual Report 2018, p.6 and 16:

'A sustainable business

It is critically important that our business delivers growth, we do so in a way which is sustainable.

In October 2017, we published our Little Helps Plan, which sets out how we will:

1. create a business where colleagues can get on, whatever their background;

2. help our customers make healthier choices and enjoy good quality, sustainable products, at affordable prices; and

3. help make sure no food that could be eaten is wasted, anywhere in our supply chain

The Little Helps Plan outlines how Tesco works in partnership with others, including suppliers, NGOs, governments and other retailers, to make a positive contribution and work toward shared global ambitions. The plan builds on the progress we have made so far and covers three areas core to the long-term success of our business: people, products and places.

Accountability for the Little Helps Plan is led at an executive level by the Group Communications Director and at board level by the Group Chief Executive. The Corporate Responsibility Committee governs the plan.'

6. Social business and creating shared value

Alongside commercial business organisations, there has always been a strand of organisations that have been formed with the strategic drive and objectives of a more social based ethos.

In the UK and other European countries this has often resulted in a formal co-operative structure, the strategic objective being to create an equally shared value among the members of the organisation. These have very often been known as 'one person: one share: one vote' structures to delineate ethos of their membership.

Such social businesses are often referred to as 'non-profit' organisations. The latter is not strictly true, as the objective is still to realise financial gains rather than financial losses from the enterprise, however the utilisation of such financial gains is generally treated in a more equitable manner, based upon the originating constitution of the organisation.

Stop and think 9.6

Consider the real business meaning of the term 'not-for-profit'. An organisation will never have a strategic objective to make losses, so the drive must be for a different concept of 'profit' than that normally associated with the creation of financial wealth.

Since the financial crisis of 2007/08 there has been a growth of businesses defining themselves as either 'social businesses' or 'social enterprises' and they are perceived to have a more focused social ethos than normal commercial businesses, although of course they are covered by the same laws, regulations, codes and societal expectations as other commercial and third sector organisations. As with a co-operative structure, the genuine 'social' nature of such a business will be based around the principles included with in its constitution, and as exhibited by its leadership and its employees.

Such businesses can have a variety of social impacts, from the use of all profits to fund their desired causes, to allowing employees time to participate in charitable activities, to the deliberate employment of disadvantaged people, to the provision of urgent and immediate help to others.

From the perspective of a company secretary or governance professional, it is important to understand both the social nature and the legal constitution of such an organisation to ensure that appropriate governance standards and techniques are being adhered to.

The Nobel Peace Prize laureate Professor Muhammad Yunus (Social Business Earth, 2018) is credited with the expansion of thinking around social enterprise and defines a social business as follows:

> 'A non-dividend company that is created to address and solve a social problem.
>
> In a social business, the investors/owners can gradually recoup the money invested but cannot take any dividend beyond that point. The purpose of the investment is purely to achieve one or more social objectives through the operation of the company. No personal gain is desired by the investors. The company must cover all costs and be financially sustainable, while achieving the social objective in sectors such as healthcare, education, poverty, environment, housing, climate urgency etc. Once the original investment has been recouped by the investors, profit stays within the company to expand its outreach and increase the social impact.'

Test yourself 9.4

Differentiate between the 'laissez-faire' stance and the 'shaper of society' stance recognised by Johnson in consideration of CSR.

The organisation ClearlySo has a diagram which differentiates between four types of organisation.

Non-profit generating no revenues or profits	Combines commercial and social goals, but with emphasis on latter. Profits reinvested in community or company	Combines commercial and social goals. Investment would lead to equivalent increase in social impact	Profit maximising company. CSR and social impact considered an add-on to the core business agenda
Charity	**Social enterprise**	**Social business**	**For profit company**

Figure 9.4 Types of organisations
((ClearlySo) adapted by Mark Wearden)

In 2005 the UK government introduced the concept and legal structure of a community interest company (CIC). Such companies are differentiated by having to have a social mission as their core ethos, a clause in the constitution ensuring that the assets can only be used for a declared social mission, and a requirement that any net assets upon closure are transferred to a registered charitable organisation, nominated on the formation of the CIC. Although similar in many ways to a limited company, CICs have their own regulator at Companies House requiring a specific form of annual report in addition to the standard financial report and accounts.

Porter and Kramer (1991) produced a paper exploring the issue of non-financial goals and their alignment with competitive advantage and strategic management. They attempted to illustrate how the original core strategy models produced by Michael Porter could be adapted to take into account the social impact of the strategic choices being made through the recognition of negative and positive impacts that the organisation and its decisions have upon wider society.

An alternative approach is taken by David Hatherly (2013) who suggests that organisational accountability and reporting at the macroeconomic level needs to illustrate the relationship between production and consumption, while at the microeconomic level illustrate how an organisation is adding value through its strategy to its stakeholders. He further suggests that an organisation needs to be able to identify and account for a wider range of different measures with regard to its strategic direction including its use of working capital, its use and reliance upon intangible items, and the promises and prospects which underpin the longer-term sustainability and impact. He proposes that corporate reporting should be developed beyond the simplicity of a triple bottom line concept to include a wider accountability to a breadth of stakeholders, including society and the environment.

7. The role of individuals and managers

This chapter began with a consideration of the meaning and principles of ethics and ethical decision-making, and the impact that these have upon the development of strategy. It then widened the concept to consider the application of ethics within a social dimension in terms of the social responsibility and sustainability of our organisations.

Inevitably, we return to the reality that ethics and ethical decision-making is ultimately down to individuals, and therefore the direct impact of CSR will likewise be driven by individuals. When individuals are placed in any position of responsibility, such as becoming a manager or director, they may face a personal dilemma if their personal ethics is not in agreement with the actions and decisions that are expected of them within the organisation.

A person in such a position has a defined number of alternative actions:

◆   make the decision in line with the organisational expectations and live with the personal dilemma

◆   try to change the organisational expectations

◆   ensure that the differing views or opinions are documented as appropriate

◆   leave the business because of the clash of ethics

◆   if the organisation is perceived as going against legal or social norms, it might be necessary to consider whether to inform stakeholders and others through a whistleblowing approach.

Gary Hamel (2012) has written about using a 'values-based' approach to organisational leadership which he illustrated in a pyramid structure adapting the original Maslow 'hierarchy of needs' pyramid (Abraham Maslow). Hamel recognises that we only ever have a certain level of control and influence over the employees of an organisation, and that ultimately the values in the organisation will be based upon how people both respond and are seen to respond. An employee operating at the obedience level only will display very different attributes to an employee operating through a passion for the organisation.

This can significantly affect organisational ethics and therefore reputation – are we doing something, or behaving in a certain way, because we have to, or because we want to?

6 Passion

5 Creativity

4 Initiative

3 Expertise

2 Dilligence

1 Obedience

Figure 9.5 Hamel's pyramid (Hamel, 2012)

❖ **Aspects of behaviour that can be expected, controlled and commanded**
  – Level 1 Obedience: I turn up for work and do the intended job, if reluctantly.
  – Level 2 Diligence: I focus on the work and apply myself during working hours, but I'm happy to go home and forget about it.
  – Level 3 Expertise: I take personal responsibility for my own skills and abilities and feel satisfaction at being able to use them within a role.

❖ **Aspects of behaviour that can be aspired to but not commanded**
  – Level 4 Initiative: I take ownership for problem and try to find solutions.
  – Level 5 Creativity: I take time to think of better ways of doing something, using my brain to think outside of the immediate.
  – Level 6 Passion: I find real purpose in the work activities and environment, feeling fulfilled in the role that I have.

Case study 9.5

As an organisation based upon mutual benefit, the Co-op has been through a wide range of experiences in its attempts to survive in the cut-throat world of commercial retailing. A strategic vision of mutuality and core values seems to have been rediscovered by the chief executive officer (CEO).

Extracts from 'How to lead', FT.com, 12 August 2018 (www.ft.com/content/4da05e32-845e-11e8-96dd-fa565ec55929):

'Co-op Group's Steve Murrells has been discussing the reclaiming of core values within the organisation.

"We forgot what co-ops are all about, and that while you've got to have strong, successful businesses, you also have to do social good," says Mr Murrells. "We didn't focus on the things that make us different."

He is custodian of a group with an illustrious history. The Co-op developed from an organisation founded in 1844 by the Rochdale Pioneers, a group of ordinary people who wanted to provide reasonably priced groceries to working families. Many merchants adulterated flour with chalk and offered expensive credit terms. The pioneers offered them a stake in the business instead, with an annual dividend once they made enough money.

Today, Mr Murrells wants to offer a 21st century answer to the question: what is the point of the Co-op? "[It] is about the health of communities, the belief that the more successful we are commercially, the more good we can do in the local economy," he explains. Co-op customers can become members, which means 1 per cent of the money they spend is reinvested in community causes.

He is pushing its ethics further.

1.   The group is campaigning against modern slavery. It has recruited 20 former slaves, who had been trafficked into the UK and forced into prostitution or labour. Mr Murrells has written to every big business in the country asking them to do the same.

2.   It has moved into education, taking over state-run schools that convert to academies, which gives them greater freedom. It is investing £3.6m into its academies programme that will see the number of schools it runs through its Academy Trust increase from 12 at present to 40 in the next three years.

Mr Murrells wants to boost standards and offer many of the academy pupils an apprenticeship at the Co-op. "The young generation face a tougher life than their parents", he says.'

Chapter summary

◆ This chapter brings human behaviour into our consideration of the development of strategy, through a consideration of the meaning and impact of ethics and ethical behaviour. It does also discuss organisation ethics, but remember that this is only a collation of the ethics of two or more human beings working together within an organisation.

◆ There are a number of different approaches to understanding ethics, but there is a generally accepted split between principle-based ethical behaviour and situation-based ethical behaviour. In the former we follow rules or a code of conduct, in the latter we adapt our response to whatever it is that we are faced with.

◆ Throughout history people have recognised the frequent, apparent irrationality of human behaviour and tried to align this with different codes or ethical principles. The reality is that we all think we know how we would respond to an ethical decision, but we can never be absolutely sure until we have made that decision. We can analyse our own, or our organisation's ethical stance on a particular situation at the 'today' point, but we cannot be certain how we, or the organisation (them) would behave in the future.

◆ Our behaviour, ethical or otherwise, will lead to our personal reputation, and this will be based around the levels of integrity that others ascribe to us as an individual.

◆ The same concept works for an organisation, but on a larger scale and involving more people and hence the growth of the CSR movement – what can we expect from an organisation as an ethical norm?

◆ In our increasingly environmentally-conscious world, organisations have realised that by being seen to 'do the right thing in the right way' they can gain not just an improved reputation but also competitive advantage. Business ethics has thus become a key consideration in the development of strategy and the drive for sustainability.

◆ Ethics is an important strategic consideration for us as company secretaries or governance professionals, we will have our personal ethics, we will be surrounded by the perceived ethics of the organisation, but we will also have a code of professional ethics that we are expected to comply with. This is the way, from a professional perspective that we are expected to behave towards other people, and the objectivity that we are expected to bring to every situation with which we are faced.

Part four

Assessing alternative strategies

Introduction

Having examined in the first nine chapters the nature and purpose of strategy, together with the various different internal, micro and macro drivers, we now consider some specific strategic routes and options that might be available. There is a reassessment of the purpose and method of developing organisational strategy with an underpinning recognition that our aim must be to gain sustainable competitive advantage to enable stakeholder satisfaction, and how this can be achieved.

Overview

Chapter 10 identifies the different strategic options that are generally available to an organisation, recognising the need to be able to take a whole-business perspective, but also when required, to be able to drill down into more focused strategic business units. A number of core tools are introduced, such as the Ansoff matrix, the Boston Consulting Group (BCG) portfolio analysis matrix and concepts on internationalisation.

Chapter 11 examines three specific strategic pathways through which an organisation can be grown – organic development, acquisition and strategic alliance. The differing stakeholder aspects are considered together with the cultural and commercial implications of each approach.

Learning outcomes

At the end of this part, students will be able to:

◆ differentiate between short-term and long-term strategic choice;

◆ use the Ansoff matrix and the Porter strategic choice models to analyse differing market potential and how to progress it;

◆ consider the implications of a blue-ocean type approach to strategy;

◆ demonstrate the purpose of business process re-engineering;

◆ understand how and why the BCG portfolio matrix is a useful analysis tool;

◆ consider the impact and challenges of internationalisation;

◆ demonstrate the different advantages and disadvantages of the three core strategic pathways; and

◆ recognise the cultural and business impacts of an acquisition process and be able to compare this to a strategic alliance.

Chapter ten
Strategic choices

Contents

1. Introduction

In our consideration of the development of strategy we have already identified that there is very rarely, if ever, only one approach or strategic direction. Why?

Think back to our starting point and the generic strategy model that has been used throughout. (See Figure 10.1 on the next page.)

The iterations of *'objectives, goals, options, strategies'* on the right-hand side of the process illustrate the need for consideration of the alternatives available before deciding on the tactics, and then (strategically) changing the operation of the organisation. The mission to drive strategic change evolves from the understanding of *'today'* and the *vision* of the *'future'*. These considerations involve and require thought and imagination. Even if only one person is involved, that person will be able to imagine different scenarios for the *'future'*. These alternatives will increase when two or more people are involved in the thought process.

Every aspect of strategy that has been considered so far leads to the need for strategic choice:

- rational strategy requires identification of an optimal route to the perceived future;
- the concept of emergent strategy suggests that choices and alternatives will continuously appear as the organisation develops;

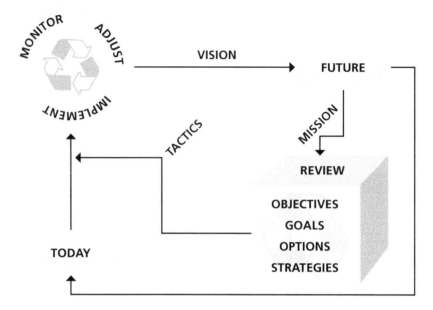

Figure 10.1 The strategic journey
© Mark Wearden

◆   changes in the external environment may require choices to be made to allow the organisation to adapt;

◆   the capabilities and competencies of the organisation and its people will expand or restrict our choices;

◆   the culture and the governance of the organisation will provide the framework for different options; and

◆   the ethical approach of the organisation and its individuals will help to focus our decisions.

In the world of the Fourth Industrial Revolution, we need to always be looking ahead and considering the rapid changes in the potential from technology, the black swan artificial intelligence that is waiting to challenge our strategy.

Case study 10.1

Extract from 'Which technologies will underpin the smart cities of the future?', FT.com, 10 September 2018 (www.ft.com/content/d181ef46-8f5c-11e8-9609-3d3b945e78cf):

'The world of dumb objects from rubbish bins to water pipes is about to become smart. We are on the brink of a communications revolution, with the potential impact almost as great as the introduction of mobile phones and the internet. Connectivity in 21st century societies will be completely different, says Rupert Pearce, chief executive of the satellite company Inmarsat. "We're moving from person-to-person voice centric networks, to machine-to-machine data centric networks."

In the so-called smart cities of the future, urban infrastructure will be interconnected; networked devices will be everywhere, from buses and cars to streetlamps, all linked to networks via the internet of things (IoT). Roads themselves will be online. Water and power grids will have smart sensors.

Plenty of real-life examples already exist. Seattle has a real-time rain prediction system called MinuteCast which anticipates precipitation at neighbourhood level and sends out flood warnings. The City of London has recently begun a programme to connect thousands of street lights to a mesh network (where individual lights act as nodes). This means greater ease of operation and that the lights will eventually form part of a network of sensors that can detect factors such as pollution. Many of the applications are surprising and hidden.

The consultancy Gartner predicts that there will 11.2bn devices connected by the end of this year and 20.4bn by the end of 2020. We are on the brink of a revolution with potential impact almost as great as mobiles and the internet.

When it comes to building the networks to power smart cities, not everywhere is equal, though. In the Middle East and Asia, cities are often being built from the ground up. This has considerable advantages. Fibre can be laid everywhere without disruption to traffic and businesses. Moreover, the city builders can take a strategic overview of what is needed, and existing legacy technologies do not need to be taken into account. In developed-world cities, incorporating "smartness" tends to be more piecemeal; the organisations that look after rubbish collection, for instance, will not necessarily be linked to those who look after transport. There is also the challenge of having to fit new digital infrastructure around existing buildings, underground lines and sewers.'

Stop and think 10.1

Does your strategy or that of your organisation allow for the very different choices that will need to be made in the future world of the internet of things?

2. The scope of strategic choice

At the outset of every strategic change, an organisation is faced with a plethora of different choices. Many of these options need considering, with the expectation of a rapid initial decision being made. Without change, we never progress beyond our understanding of the known point of 'today'. Even if we only consider our strategy from the internal perspective, we will find ourselves faced with many decisions to make. When we include the competing forces of the near and far environments, discussed earlier in the text, we will find a much wider level of potential change required.

If we start a new business, we will already have strategic ideas in our head, informed by our cognitive biases. We will have many preconceived notions as to our intended choices. Once we make an initial choice, to take the business in a particular direction, with the inevitable assumptions, expectations and requirements that will accompany that direction, we have started to limit our strategic choice.

This chapter will initially consider the theoretical scope of choice and consider a few underlying principles of how and why choices are made. It will then gradually widen the perspective in terms of both model and organisational potential, always seeking to find a way for the strategist to challenge their own preconceived notions and those of their colleagues.

Johnson (2017) suggest that there are three predominant areas of strategic choice an organisation needs to consider:

Figure 10.2 Strategic choice
((Johnson, 2017) adapted by Mark Wearden)

◆ *Business strategy* determines how an organisation has positioned itself in relation to its competitors.
◆ *Strategic direction* determines the products, industries and market sectors that the organisation intends to operate within.
◆ *Strategy methods* determine whether the organisation is acting in isolation or seeking some form of strategic alliance with one or more different but aligned organisations, this will be discussed in more detail later in the text.

The concept of strategic choice relates back to all of our previous 'today' considerations. We are faced at the outset of our development of strategy with a number of key questions. Even as the organisation develops and evolves, the underpinning concepts that sit behind these key questions will continue to create challenge. The concept of *emergent strategy* that we have already considered suggests that, unless we deliberately choose to take a different strategic direction, it is the emergence of external forces and extenuating circumstances (expected and unexpected, from the micro and macro environments, as discussed earlier in the text) which will force us to reconsider and adapt our original strategic choices.

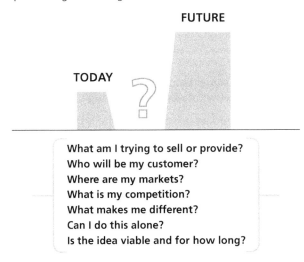

What am I trying to sell or provide?
Who will be my customer?
Where are my markets?
What is my competition?
What makes me different?
Can I do this alone?
Is the idea viable and for how long?

Figure 10.3 Strategic choices
© Mark Wearden

The questions in Figure 10.3 are not finite or exclusive. There are many other questions which might need to be added to the choices that we have to make as we develop our strategy. The scope of our strategic choice will be determined by the breadth of vision concerning the imagined future of the organisation, and ourselves.

3. Driving the business forward

What is clear is that we need to do something. If we are unable to make strategic choices, then we will be unable to pursue a strategy. The unknown nature of virtually everything beyond 'today' will require anticipated and unanticipated choice. This underlines the importance of the initial analysis that we take to understand the status quo of an organisation using many of the tools that have already been suggested in this text.

3.1 A whole-business approach

The concept of the development of strategy suggests that we wish to drive the business forward, rather than leaving it without clear and focused goals. Although we will discuss different options for different aspects of a growing business, it is important as company leaders (actual or perceived) that we understand the need to take an aligned approach to a complete business structure.

Company secretaries or governance professionals, while recognising the different aspirations of the individuals in the organisation and their respective sections or departments, are required to be able to consider and challenge the impact of strategic choices upon the whole business. Often, directors within a board meeting, or managers in a management meeting, hold strong and impassioned views based around their own beliefs and about the need for change and strategic momentum within an organisation.

Stop and think 10.2

The levers within a railway signal box, which operate and alter the tracks to allow a journey, is a good whole-business strategic choice analogy.

In the same way that we need a train to run on the right tracks, the organisational system only works as anticipated if the levers are set correctly.

3.2   Research and development

To achieve the necessary understanding of the organisation as it stands now in alignment with its future (strategic) potential will require a range of research and development activities. If we separate these two words through use of dictionary definitions, then the requirement becomes clearer.

Stop and think 10.3

Research
– a systematic investigation into materials and sources in order to establish facts and reach new conclusions

Development
– an event constituting a new stage in a changing situation

The development of strategy requires both of these activities to have been carried out to ensure that we are making informed choices. The nature of any successful business is that it will exist within a competitive environment, even charities and third sector organisations are in competition with each other to attract funding from within a finite pool of finance. We have considered competition from a number of different perspectives in the development of strategy, and it is fundamental that we understand the nature of the competitive environment within which we are operating before we make strategic choices.

Appropriate research into the competitive environment where we operate will allow us to challenge the internal drivers within our own organisation and will ensure that we are viewing the organisation within the context of the markets that are available for our products or services, and the position of other players within those markets.

To succeed in a world of competition it is necessary for an organisation to recognise how it can obtain competitive advantage, the means through which it creates value for its shareholders or stakeholders. This requires research into the competition to help to drive the development of the required changes within the organisation, to facilitate effective and efficient strategic change to enable it to meet its planned objectives and goals and to make it fit and agile for the future.

3.3 Strategic direction

A central strategic choice that needs to be made by every organisation is the direction in which it sees its future development and growth. There are only two variables to manipulate – products/services and customers. This recognition of the sharp end of the supply chain is fundamental in allowing the identification of the areas within which we need to refine our market research and strategic development, and ultimately our choices.

This concept was captured by Ansoff (1988) in his product/market grid, shown in its second stage of evolution in Figure 10.4 (his original version had lines separating each of the four quadrants, but he realised that the four different aspects were more malleable than can be indicated by a boxed matrix). In later research, he extended the concept to three dimensions to include *market geography*, *market need* and the *introduction of technology*.

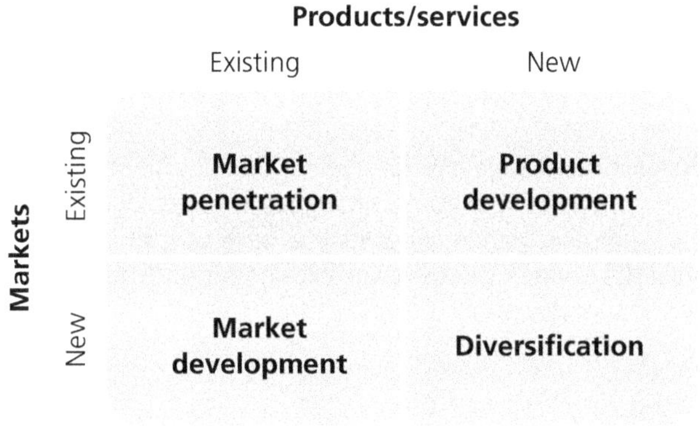

Products/services

	Existing	New
Markets Existing	**Market penetration**	**Product development**
Markets New	**Market development**	**Diversification**

Figure 10.4

((Ansoff, H. I., 1988) adapted by Mark Wearden)

◆ Market penetration suggests growth through the increase of the market share of the current product and market mix. This builds upon current strategic capabilities and is probably the most risk averse of the strategic directions that could be followed. The two core forces that may restrict this type of perceived growth are:

 – retaliation from competitors (wanting to capture a share of a proven successful market); and

 – legal restriction based around an acceptable concentration of market power. In the UK the Competition and Markets Authority (CMA) have the right to challenge, prevent or restrict any perceived monopolistic dominance. They have used this power on a number of occasions within the consumer retail market, requiring the closure of stores when one company is dominant.

Case study 10.2

In 2003 Morrisons plc was operating 119 supermarket stores across the UK. Their planned strategic expansion through the acquisition of the Safeway group which operated 449 UK stores was eventually approved by the then Office of Fair Trading. However, the approval was only on the basis that they were forced to close 52 stores where both companies operated outlets in direct competition for consumer footfall, within a defined geographic area.

◆ **Product development** suggests using the knowledge of the existing customer base and` markets to provide different, evolved or complementary products or services.

Case study 10.3

An example of product development would be the development of the iPad by Apple, where sales of a completely new concept were made readily to a marketplace that had already developed to sales of the iPod and iPhone.

◆ **Market development** suggests that there is an opportunity to take existing products or services into new markets. This would require significant pre-emptive market and consumer research, and possibly some product development to tailor the existing product to the particular expectations of the new market.

Case study 10.4

An example of market development would be when Sony introduced their PlayStation 2 games console. They radically reduced the price point of the earlier PlayStation 1 thus opening significant new market potential for an existing product, with the additional intangible benefit of building their brand reputation within a dramatically larger group of people.

◆ **Diversification** is undoubtedly the highest risk option from within the Ansoff matrix, requiring significant research and market intelligence in terms of both aspects of development. This type of diversification will often be narrowed through the recognition of opportunity:

  – Horizontal diversification takes place when an organisation sees the opportunity to develop a new or variant product and market it to the customers of its competitors. For example: after the successful introduction of the iPad tablet by Apple, and its reception by consumers, most other technology companies rapidly began to produce tablet style computer devices.

- Vertical diversification takes place when an organisation sees the opportunity to acquire either a new supplier or a new customer and therefore broaden its overall offering. For example: the China-based company Alibaba has grown its market presence through the frequent acquisition of direct suppliers of core commodities, and also the acquisition of delivery, payment and finance companies. This has led to a wide and deep breadth of commercial control within its operating market space.

- Concentric diversification takes place when an ostensibly new product (in reality closely related to a current product) is introduced by an organisation. For example: PepsiCo broadened its product line from soft drinks to a range of fast food franchises and snack foods. This often led to a mutuality of offering with the fast food franchises being used to sell the classic PepsiCo drinks ranges.

- Conglomerate diversification describes the situation where completely new and unrelated products are introduced by an organisation wishing to take advantage of its existing name and reputation. For example: Virgin Group is often held as an example of conglomerate diversification given the breadth of its different offerings and the breadth of its markets.

Stop and think 10.4

Have a look around the room where you are working or studying. Find an item that has been the result of diversification by its manufacturer. Think about the strategic decisions that would have needed to be taken to enable this diversification.

4. Business-level strategy

Business level strategy describes the development of strategy and the choices that take place within a defined business unit. This might be one individual business where one board of directors has responsibility for the governance (strategy, risk and control) of that single business.

It might also be one business within a much larger group of businesses, for example operating across the world in a range of different activities, sectors and markets. It is important for the decision-makers, those making the strategic choices, to recognise the boundary or parameter of the area of business that will be affected by their decisions.

In the case of being one business within a much larger business, the strategic decisions will need to be made from within the context of the particular business, but with the wider business aspects being considered as part of the micro environment.

4.1 Strategic business units

It is important to take a whole-business view, as mentioned above, when considering the choices to be made in the development of strategy. However, as an organisation increases in size, there is a need to recognise that some areas of the organisation will have a close **synergy** with other business units. This is particularly clear in a large group of companies combined under one holding company, where some subsidiaries will be naturally aligned, either through location or customer/supplier focus.

synergy
The alignment of assets or activities such that the combined result can deliver greater advantage than the separate parts.

It is common to refer to such a grouping as a *strategic business unit* (SBU) the classic definition being that an SBU is a fully functional unit of a business with its own vision and direction, operating as a separate unit but often still reliant upon the organisational centre for its ultimate direction. It is common for an SBU to have its own support infrastructure such as human resources, training and sometimes even finance. Not all SBUs are also defined as individual profit centres within an organisation – this will depend upon the corporate structure and culture of a particular organisation. It is likely to have its own specific policies and procedures (processes) however there may also be some more generic ones relevant to the organisation as a whole (for example, an ethics code of practice as discussed earlier in the text).

The purpose of creating formal SBUs within a large organisation is to allow focused and aligned strategy, and agility to react quickly in decision-making within a changing external environment.

Test yourself 10.1

Identify the four strategic choices for growth of the income streams of an organisation as suggested by Ansoff in his product/market grid.

4.2 Generic strategy options to gain competitive advantage

Michael Porter (2004) argues that there are three fundamental methods for an organisation to achieve competitive advantage, and that these require the organisation to take either offensive or defensive action to create a defendable strategic position. He argues that it either has to have structurally *lower costs* than its competitors or will be able to demonstrate to its customer base that its products or services are *differentiated* from those of its competition (in a positive way). In the latter case this will allow the charging of a higher price to represent the added value created for the customer by the differentiation, while maintaining the same cost base.

Porter further suggests that the business is able to *focus* its business and choose the scope of customers that it wishes to serve, this could be a particularly narrow segment where the strategic intention is to skim the top layer off a wider market, or it could be a strategy to dominate a particular segment of a market. Alternatively, business could adopt a broad scope and target customers with a new and much wider range of characteristics such as age, wealth or geography.

Porter illustrates these choices in the matrix in Figure 10.5.

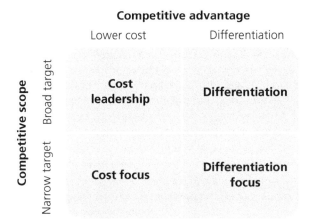

Figure 10.5 Generic strategic choices
((Porter, M., *Competitive Advantage*, 2004) adapted by Mark Wearden)

The top half of the model, with a *broad target* being held within the competitive scope, has two distinctive approaches to strategy – *cost leadership* and *differentiation*.

In the lower half of the model, with a *narrow target*, the emphasis turns to focus rather than explicit strategy and the dotted line of separation recognises the need for a combined focus on both *cost focus* and *differentiation focus*.

Cost leadership
There can only be one *cost leader* in any industry or sector, and the intent when pursuing this as a strategic choice is to become the lowest cost organisation within a particular area of activity while maintaining quality. It will require an aligned set of interrelated tactics including:

◆   a detailed understanding of all actual costs associated with the provision of a product or service – this will include the direct costs of production, but also a realistic assessment of the level of overhead cost that is absorbed in the production;

◆   a focus on cost reduction based upon historic performance within the organisation aligned with an understanding of the cost options available;

◆   the removal of unnecessary activities within the value chain;

◆   a focus on customers who will fund the supply chain on time and in full;

◆   a focus on quality of product or service to ensure a right-first-time delivery.

Johnson (2017) suggests that there are four key cost drivers that need to be taken into consideration:

◆   **Input costs**: in particular, by minimising the cost of labour and raw materials, cost advantage can be gained. This can be driven by ensuring, wherever possible, that the source of raw materials is located in close proximity to the point of production. Alternatively, the outsourcing of labour-intensive operations to countries with low labour costs can significantly reduce the input cost to a particular operation.

◆ **Economies of scale**: if high fixed costs are required to enable production to commence, the strategic choice must be to ensure the spreading of such costs across time and the maximum number of potential output units, rather than absorbing a disproportionate cost in the early stages of production. Economies of scale can also be achieved by having control over a critical mass of raw material suppliers within a particular market segment and therefore creating bulk purchasing power.

◆ **Experience**: is often a highly significant source of cost efficiency. The cumulative experience and knowledge of the people within the organisation can ensure efficiency within the production process. A person who knows what they are doing, and has already been through the learning curve, will operate more effectively and more efficiently. This is known as the learning curve effect.

◆ **Design**: a rational strategic approach can ensure efficiency is built into the core design of the product or process. This will require research and an understanding of the range of alternative materials that might be used to create the desired output; increasingly an enhanced use of technology is likely to enable much greater cost efficiency. A recent example is the introduction of 'all-in-one' desktop personal computers where the core processing unit is built into the monitor, giving the advantage of a desktop computer but with the flexibility of a laptop computer.

There are risks in pursuing such a focused strategy and there are a number of areas where cost leadership can fail, including:

◆ unjustified focus on the direct cost of one or more specific value chain activities, while ignoring or not realising the true underlying cost of other activities

◆ a restricted and insufficient supply base needing to be shared between all competitors

◆ easy imitation or replication of the cost strategy by competitors

◆ reductions being made in cost, by using cheaper supplies, to the detriment of quality.

Stop and think 10.5

Draw yourself a quick matrix of the advantages and disadvantages of taking a cost leadership approach. Think about your weekly or monthly shopping pattern – food, drink, clothes etc. Think of a business where cost leadership has worked and think of a business where it has made you think twice about quality.

Differentiation

The principle that underpins a differentiation strategy requires the development of one or more aspects of the product or service that are either unique or perceived by customers as being unique. This will enable the organisation to charge a price premium for the provision of that product or service. We are surrounded by examples of differentiation, often based upon brand name, sometimes supported by quality and reputation, but not always. In any supermarket a range of different 'cola' drinks will be on sale. These will vary from well-known brand names to supermarket own-brand to low-cost variants. The price (and sometimes the taste) is differentiated, but all continue to sell based upon personal consumer preference.

Johnson (2017) argues that there are three primary drivers of differentiation which an organisation ought to consider when pursuing this strategy – these can work in isolation or on a combined basis:

◆ **Product and service attributes**: the possibilities are virtually endless and only limited by the creativity of an organisation, with the objective to appeal to different consumer preference. This could be based around colour, design, size, speed, style, taste etc.

Case study 10.5

Apple continues to demonstrate market success with its focused range of products. It follows a development strategy of biennial new launch with purportedly new technologies, new designs, variations on style and improving consumer interface. In reality the changes are often minimal but are perceived to be adding value by the end consumer. The drive is in the 'must have the latest' psyche of the consumer and the market.

◆ **Customer relationships**: the manner in which the organisation deals with their customer which could include availability, speed of distribution, methods of payment or after sales service.

Case study 10.6

The rapid growth of different chains of coffee shops has been driven, arguably, more by the ambience and service that is received from different groups, than by a radical distinction between the types of coffee being served – although we will all have a taste preference.

◆ **Complements**: the perceived or actual receipt of additional products or service online, to enhance the value of the core purchase. An example would be the inclusion of software with certain phones and computers, differentiating them from less expensive alternatives.

The consumer perception could be linked to one or more of the following non-exclusive categories of differentiation:

Point of differentiation	Examples
Brand image	BMW cars
	Miele or Bosch for domestic appliances
	Shopping at Harrods rather than an alternative department store
Technology	BOSE headphones and sound equipment
Innovation	Apple computers, iPads and iPhones
Customer service	John Lewis department stores
Consumer preference	Buying a can of Coca-Cola or Pepsi-Cola rather than an own-brand alternative

Table 10.1 Points of differentiation
© Mark Wearden

The success of a differentiation strategy will be aligned to how well an organisation can identify and understand its strategic customer. This is not always clear to an organisation, and there may well be conflict. Does a leading daily newspaper view its core customer as the reader of the paper, or the advertiser? If the latter, the newspaper needs to ensure that the nature of the advertiser and the advertisements are likely to act as a positive differentiator for the reader of the newspaper; the sustainability of advertising income being intrinsically linked to customers continuing to buy the newspaper.

In an article in the Harvard Business Review, Garvin (1987) identified eight dimensions of differentiation quality:

◆ **Performance**: is it better than the competition?
◆ **Features**: does it have unique or unusual additional aspects?
◆ **Reliability**: will it outperform the competition?
◆ **Conformance**: does it comply with the law or required standards?
◆ **Durability**: will it last?
◆ **Serviceability**: if it breaks can it be repaired?
◆ **Aesthetics**: does it look, sound or feel better?
◆ **Perceived quality**: does the customer achieve a sense of satisfaction by acquiring this product or service?

These dimensions are clearly interlinked, but Garvin suggests that at least one has to be satisfied to attract a continuing customer base. Looked at from the other side, the strategic choices being made by the organisation need to ensure that one or more of these dimensions are deliberately built into the production process.

As with cost leadership, there are natural dangers of pursuing a very focused strategy of differentiation. These might include:

- too much differentiation with confusion for the customer
- too high a price premium
- easy imitation by competitors leading to dilution of brand value
- differing perceptions of the meaning of quality between buyers and sellers
- striving for a uniqueness that fails to bring sufficient added value.

Test yourself 10.2

Define the meaning of a strategic business unit.

Organisational focus

Alongside cost leadership and differentiation, Porter identified organisational focus as the third choice of generic strategy that is available to an organisation. His concept of focus assumes that the target within the scope is more defined, and narrower than those discussed in his previous two approaches to strategy. An organisation will tailor its product or service to one or more specific needs of the perceived customer.

Johnson (2017) gives useful examples of the two different types of focus strategy identified by Porter:

- *cost focus strategy*, such as that followed by Ryanair which targets price conscious travellers with no need for a connecting flight
- *differentiation focus strategy*, such as that followed by Belgian company Ecover which gains a price premium by targeting its ecological cleaning products at environmentally conscious consumers.

The choice of strategic focus requires an organisation to dedicate itself to achieving competitive edge by giving a better service to its target customers than that which is achieved by its competitors who are aiming for a broader customer base. Often an organisation following strategic focus is able to identify niche opportunities which have been left open by the breadth of coverage from its wider target competitors.

Johnson argues that a successful focus strategy depends upon at least one of the following three key factors:

- *identification of a distinct segment need* – is the perceived need genuine or imagined?
- *identification of distinct segment value chains* – will the value chain that leads to the focused product or service prevent easy imitation?
- *identification of a viable market segment* – are there sufficient customers to justify the strategy?

Porter is clear in his views that, under normal operating circumstances, an organisation should have clarity in the strategic choice that it makes between generic strategies. He suggests that:

◆   a cost leader will only add cost if it attempts to also differentiate its product or service;

◆   a differentiator will lose its point of difference if it fails to have clarity as to why its product or service is different; and

◆   a focus strategy can find its customer base eroded by being perceived as having lost its dedication or speciality.

However, there may be opportunities for a hybrid strategy, and part of the strategic choice is to recognise the time to move from one generic strategy to another. For example:

◆   The fast food chain McDonald's moved from its initial strategic positioning of product differentiation to combining this with a low-cost base. This was only achieved through size and dominance of its markets through the rapid multiplication of its outlets.

◆   Likewise, the major UK retailer Tesco has succeeded in being the largest UK retailer for over 25 years through a combination of all three of Porter's generic strategies being exercised jointly or individually in different product offerings or through recognition of local opportunities in specific store outlets.

4.3   Sustaining competitive advantage

We have already discussed many aspects of sustainability and viability with regard to the different dimensions of the development of strategy. The gaining of competitive advantage through any of the reasons discussed above can take significant organisational time and effort. A core part of the strategic choice being made by directors and managers must be to find a means to achieve a sustainable competitive advantage.

While it might be relatively straightforward to outwit the competition on a particular project or opportunity, it is strategically important to build a sustainable competitive position.

Chapter 5 referred to the following quotation from Arie de Geus in his book *The Living Company* (1999) – the process of learning that he identifies is a continual process within any organisation of developing options and making appropriate strategic choices to drive the sustainability: 'the ability to learn faster than our competitors … may be the only sustainable competitive advantage'.

The method required to build such sustainability will differ slightly dependent upon which of Porter's generic choices are chosen. There are many different tools available that an organisation is able to employ to help the process, and the following are just single suggestions from earlier in this text for each type of strategy.

Cost leadership can be monitored and controlled through the effective and ongoing use of a robust value chain analysis, as discussed in Chapter 5.

Differentiation can be monitored and controlled through a close understanding of different stakeholder expectations, through the effective and ongoing use of a stakeholder mapping exercise such as that discussed in Chapter 7.

Focus can be monitored and controlled through a robust understanding of the different options that are available to customers, and that might act in competition to the organisation, through the effective and ongoing use of a model such as that of the 'five forces' discussed in Chapter 4.

A *whole business approach* in a large and diverse organisation is likely to require a range of different strategic options and it is unlikely, in such an organisation, that one simple strategic choice will ever be sufficient.

Stop and think 10.6

Where does your organisation hold points of competitive advantage? Are they sustainable?

4.4   Business process re-engineering

Having taken the strategic choice recommended by Porter and decided upon how the organisation is to gain, or maintain, its competitive advantage within the marketplace, the management focus must be on how to design and implement the strategy to achieve the required objectives.

There are many different consultancy and advisory firms that have devised different methods for different companies, and throughout this book it has been commented that particular business models and concepts are rarely generic and will need adapting to suit the people and culture of a particular organisation.

One approach, popular in the 1990s, that has been used by many organisations (not always successfully) is that of business process re-engineering (BPR). This was the product of Hammer and Champy (1993) and was defined in their book *Re-engineering the Corporation: A Manifesto for Business Revolution*. As the title suggests, BPR requires a fundamental reconsideration in a radical redesign of organisational processes with the aim of achieving significant improvement in operation to enable the achievement of a particular set of strategic objectives. The ultimate aim is to increase efficiency within the organisation, and this could include all or one of cost control, product differentiation or specific customer focus.

The principles of BPR are underpinned by five rules:

◆ Strategy must be determined before any redesign takes place.

◆ The existing process-flow should be used as the basis for the redesign.

◆ The use of information technology should be optimised.

◆ The governance, culture and organisational structures must be aligned with the process-flow.

◆ People across the business need to understand and participate in the redesign –this is not just a top-down or bottom-up approach, but requires a whole-business involvement to ensure 'buy in'. A participative approach is known to be instrumental in capturing a positive commitment to making the changes happen.

The requirement of the last principle (the whole-business approach) identifies why many BPR projects have failed. There is a significant time and cost requirement from the organisation to run a BPR project, and often an organisation finds that it has insufficient project management skills or resources. Frequently, the day-to-day operational requirements of the ongoing business also mean that it is virtually impossible for people throughout the business to be deployed in a BPR project, leading to insufficient BPR focus and a tweaked continuation of the same processes rather than a focused re-engineering.

However, when implemented professionally, many of the principles that sit behind the concept of a BPR project can provide a useful challenge and learning to any organisation as it seeks to devise the optimal method to achieve its strategic objectives.

You will see from the Ford case below that there are many similarities between the BPR approach and the 'learning organisation' and 'systems thinking' approaches that have been discussed earlier in this text.

Case study 10.7

Ford undertook some research into their Accounts Payable process. They employed 500 people to manage and control the payment of their suppliers, and were certain that efficiencies could be realised – even more so when they discovered that Mazda managed the same process with 100 people.

In the first stage of their project, they found that each supplier payment required circa 14 separate actions within the team, based on processes that had evolved and been added to over time. Rather than make minor changes to the system to simplify the flow, they used a BPR approach combined with a new look at their use of information technology. They designed a totally new system flow which eliminated many of the previous stages and relied upon an initial single-entry point.

The new design enabled a 75% reduction in employees in the accounts payable department.

5. Corporate-level strategy and strategic models

The previous section considered the development of strategy at the business level which was defined as the development of the strategy and the choices that take place within a defined business unit. This section expands the focus to a wider corporate level consideration and introduces some alternative strategic models.

While this might be predominantly relevant to large corporations involving a number of different companies, even small businesses often evolve into organisations which contain a number of different business units requiring a more comprehensive approach.

Many of the tools discussed in the previous section are equally applicable at the corporate level. The differentiation between corporate level and business level is precisely where the operational boundary is drawn. *Business level* generally refers to a single business operating within a defined boundary. *Corporate level* refers to a number of businesses operating within a wider boundary.

This section will consider three alternative approaches to the development, analysis, challenge and understanding of corporate strategy:

◆ blue ocean strategy

◆ corporate parenting

◆ portfolio analysis and the Boston Consulting Group (BCG) approach.

Each of these, in themselves, may be applicable to many different scenarios, and also the principles that sit behind them can challenge all strategic thinking

Test yourself 10.3

Suggest how an organisation can obtain a cost leadership position, and the resultant advantages.

5.1 Blue ocean strategy

The concept of a blue ocean strategy evolved from the recognition that an organisation will often need to find a different approach to innovation. Kim and Mauborgne (2005) originated the term and proposed a different type of theoretical and practical approach to strategy built upon three underpinning principles:

◆ markets need to be analysed to find new opportunities

◆ value can be added by lowering costs and by raising prices

◆ innovative thoughts will come through a focus on the key elements that provoke new ways of thinking and acting.

Kim and Mauborgne argue that too much of current strategy is based around attempts to satisfy existing and historic perceptions of markets resulting in a fight for competitive advantage between rivals within these markets. They refer to these existing markets as the red oceans awash with the blood of the competitors who are seen as competing sharks.

They suggest that innovative organisations ought instead to be searching for and identifying the blue oceans that exist in today's marketplace. These blue oceans have untapped market space which demands creativity, and they offer the opportunity for highly profitable growth. In essence it is an encouragement to organisations to look beyond their existing markets in an entirely new and fresh way and find opportunities that will deliver a high-value return from the development of a new market offering that goes beyond the existing boundaries.

There is a recognition that the blue oceans need to coexist with the red oceans and that there will be the need to continue to develop strategies in existing markets while seeking out the higher value new and totally innovative opportunities that exist.

The blue ocean world sees strategists as entrepreneurs and suggests that traditional strategy tends to operate within the known, from customer and product perspectives, whereas strategic theories such as blue ocean encourage strategists to move their minds into the unknown and use their imagination.

Lynch (2015) identifies four dimensions of realising and deriving value from a blue ocean strategy:

- **Elimination**: the recognition of which aspects of the current red ocean are really important to customers, and which can be eliminated – *e.g. do we need excessive packing?*

- **Reduction**: the removal of overdesigned products and services that can take place within the red ocean without detrimental effect to existing products or customers – *e.g. do all mobile phones need to have complex technological features?*

- **Raising**: the need to improve features of current products and services to make them more attractive to customers – *e.g. are we more likely to buy a product if it contains a longer warranty in the price?*

- **Creation**: use of existing knowledge and abilities to create new value addition for both customers and the organisation itself – *e.g. when handled correctly, a move to more sustainable packaging can create a better approach to social responsibility and enhanced customer perception, combined with a reduced cost to the manufacturer.*

A note of caution

The reality of the blue ocean concept is, of course, that once the new creative product is being consumed on a regular basis, the laws of economics will take over and competition will arise (the sharks will be rapidly circling).

The classic example often used of a blue ocean strategy is that of the organisation Cirque du Soleil, which presented customers with a new and more ethical approach to entertainment, away from the more traditional form of circus. This concept has now been imitated by many others.

Other similar examples would be the original concept of iTunes by Apple; the introduction of the Nintendo Wii games machine; and the provision of real-time detailed online financial information by Bloomberg. All of these had their period of unique blue ocean presence and all now have a multiplicity of red ocean competition.

Stop and think 10.7

When was the last time you came across something unique and new to you? This was a blue ocean type of experience for you.

When was the last time your organisation tried to think this far outside of its current 'red ocean'?

5.2 Corporate parenting

Chapter 12 will discuss different types of corporate structure and their strategic appropriateness. While discussing corporate level strategy it is important to recognise that a diversified organisation with a number of different parts, subsidiaries, or SBUs, will require some level of centralised control. This is often referred to as *corporate parenting*.

The nature of organisational governance as discussed in Chapter 7 sits at the heart of the concept of corporate parenting. Every company has a top level board of directors who ultimately are accountable to the stakeholders for the use of the assets of the organisation and delivery of long-term value.

In a diversified organisational structure, each unit will have a substructure which enables it to fulfil its core strategic objective. However, there are a number of activities which might be more effectively and efficiently controlled through the centre, the corporate headquarters, or through corporate parenting. These could include strategic direction, boundaries of operational control, corporate ethics, human resources, legal services and often a centralised finance function.

Each organisation will ultimately find its own appropriate structure, and many large organisations will move from diversified to centralised structures, and back again in an attempt to find greater efficiency.

Case study 10.8

After its rescue by the UK government following the 2007 'financial crisis', RBS plc centralised many of its functions; a few years later it started to replicate functions within different sections, only to be followed again by another recentralisation – they are not alone in following this type of route.

There is no right answer, however Goold et al. (1994) identified five core activities through which a corporate parent can add value:

◆ **Envisioning**: the provision of a clear overall vision for each aspect of the organisation, enabling differentiation between different units while ensuring a comprehensive vision for the entire organisation.

◆ **Facilitating synergy**: the enabling of co-operation and sharing across different business units, often more visible in the centre than from the individual parts.

◆ **Coaching**: the development of business unit managers to encourage a shared vision and approach to the operation and to the ethos of the organisation as a whole.

◆ **Central services and resources**: the cost-efficient use of expertise from the centre.

◆ **Intervention**: where necessary, the alignment and correction of individual unit performance.

A note of caution

If not controlled correctly, corporate parenting can destroy value within an organisation through the addition of unnecessary central cost and bureaucratic complexity. There might also be the danger that a weak business unit is allowed to underperform through hidden compensation from an over-performing alternative business unit.

Test yourself 10.4

What are the five rules of the BPR principles of strategic change?

5.3 Portfolio analysis and the Boston Consulting Group approach

Portfolio analysis is a technique that has been developed by a number of strategic thinkers to help decision-makers consider the strategic options available to them and where best to build their organisation/business.

The 'portfolio' identifies the grouping together of a range of similarly performing products (or businesses in a more complex multi-sector organisation, such as a conglomerate organisational structure). The different strategic business units will have similar attributes and perform in a similar manner.

The principle for strategic growth is to recognise where a product or potential product will/might sit, and therefore its desirability as part of the whole portfolio – thereby recognising that most businesses will prosper most effectively through a strategically considered product mix. Different approaches tend to use a matrix structure to identify the different segments.

A popular and frequently used model was developed by the BCG (1979) and is widely recognised as a useful and challenging alignment of differently performing segments/units of a business.

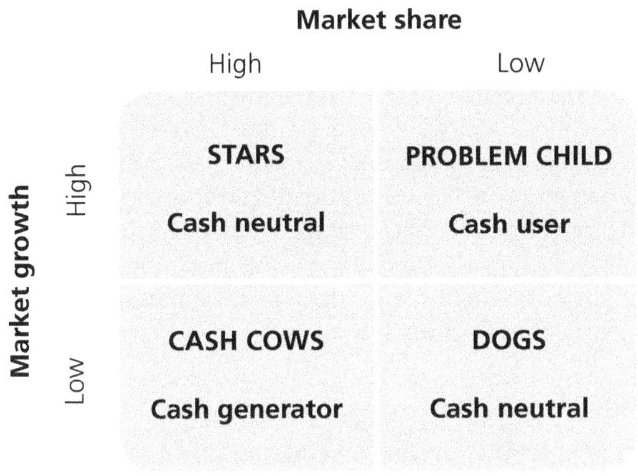

Market share

High   Low

Figure 10.6 BCG portfolio analysis matrix

◆ **Dogs – low market growth, low market share**: dogs have a low market share in a slow growth market. They will only be marginally profitable and therefore need monitoring and will be withdrawn when they become loss making (if not before) with a review being made of the opportunity cost of the resources being used. *They are cash neutral.*

◆ **Cash cows – low market growth, high market share**: cash cows are established products in a mature or maturing market, there is little if any further growth available in market share. They have established themselves as leaders (they could be niche or more general). They require only minimal further investment and are often the most profitable products within the portfolio, increased by market leadership and therefore greater economies of scale. Cash cows often fund the products that exist within the other quadrants of the matrix. *They are the core cash generators.*

◆ **Problem child – high market growth, low market share**: The problem child will compete in high growth markets but with low or relatively low market share. This will often include new products being launched into high growth markets which require high expenditure, but the intention being that such products will become either stars or cash cows. *They are users of cash within the organisation.*

◆ **Stars – high market growth, high market share**: Stars normally arise from a successful problem child becoming a market leader in a growth market, but with investment still being required to maintain the rate of growth and defend a leadership position. Initially stars are often only marginally profitable until they establish themselves and reach a more mature market position requiring less continued investment. *They are generally cash neutral.*

Examples from a high-street supermarket retailer might be:

◆ **Dogs**: the sale of batteries – necessary but not a core offering.

◆ **Cash cows**: a wide range of brand-name alcoholic and soft drinks.

◆ **Problem children**: inexpensive clothing designed for single-wear and then disposal.

◆ **Stars**: high-end ready prepared meal packages.

An initial analysis of a business using the BCG model will identify how and why the current product mix within the portfolio is performing and then help to identify the gaps for future strategic growth. Although such modelling can be used for a snapshot analysis, it is significantly more useful to monitor the movements of products within the portfolio across different time periods enabling development of a proactive rather than reactive strategic approach to business.

The benefit of the BCG model is to use it to both plot and monitor the movement of different products between the four segments and analyse how this aligns with the product lifecycle (anticipated and actual).

A note of caution

BCG matrix
The Boston Consulting Group matrix involving cash cows, dogs, problem children and stars.

Lynch (2015) identifies a number of difficulties with the **BCG matrix**:

◆ how to define market growth and an understanding of what is perceived as low or high

◆ a definition of the market in itself

◆ an understanding of what is meant by a relative market share and what it is based upon.

6. Internationalisation as a strategic option

In today's world of multinational corporations, underpinned by the immediacy of technological communication, it is natural for many organisations to consider internationalisation as a strategic choice for the expansion of their business:

◆ **International strategy** refers to the options that can be considered by an organisation when it wants to operate outside of its country of origin.

◆ **Global strategy** is a specific type of international strategy concerned with the co-ordination of geographically dispersed activities.

6.1   Drivers of Internationalisation

There are a wide range of pressures that affect the strategic consideration and success of internationalisation within an organisation including the barriers to trade, investment and migration that continue to exist between many countries.

There are a number of recognised forces which drive an organisation to consider internationalisation:

◆ **Market drivers**: The potential customer reach of taking a successful product or service to different countries. This needs handling with caution strategically as different countries operate from diverse cultural and behavioural positions. *An example was Tesco taking their business model to the US, acquiring a brand of stores, replicating their supply chain model and then failing because the US marketplace does not buy food items in the same manner as in the UK.*

◈ **Cost drivers**: operational costs could be reduced by operating internationally, particularly if an organisation is already sourcing input products from outside of the UK. Many of the fixed UK costs will not change and therefore the overhead can be spread over a wider market potential.

◈ **Government drivers**: government will often provide support and funding to enable companies to operate internationally. If used and targeted in an optimal manner, this can sometimes be the leverage that takes a company out of its home-based comfort zone and opens up new market potential.

◈ **Competition drivers**: the development and maintenance of competitive advantage might require an organisation to develop its markets. If it is dealing with international customers, then it is likely that it will need to also develop an international strategy.

◈ **Porter's diamond**: Michael Porter (1990) has introduced two core models to help strategists consider the potential for the internationalisation of their organisations. The first of these is the diamond model, which considers why some countries produce firms with sustained competitive advantages in some industries. He suggests that these four interacting factors will help an organisation to determine its optimal approach to internationalisation. (Porter's second model is discussed in section 6.2 below.)

Figure 10.7 Porter's diamond
((Porter, 1990) adapted by Mark Wearden)

◆ **Factor conditions**: what is it that goes into the making of a product/ service that can give a competitive advantage?

◆ **Demand conditions** within the original home market can help a company to become a more sophisticated operator when trading internationally.

◆ **Related and supporting industries** that are based in the same geographical locations can lead to cost and logistics advantage.

◆ **Firm strategy, structure and rivalry** in the domestic market will build a more resilient approach to trading internationally.

Case study 10.9

The four dimensions of distance

Adapted from an original *Harvard Business Review* article 'Distance Still Matters: The Hard Reality of Global Expansion' by Pankaj Ghemawat, September 2001:

Distance between two countries can manifest itself along four basic dimensions: cultural, administrative, geographic, and economic. The types of distance influence different businesses in different ways. Geographic distance, for instance, affects the costs of transportation and communications, so it is of particular importance to companies that deal with heavy or bulky products, or whose operations require a high degree of co-ordination among highly dispersed people or activities. Cultural distance, by contrast, affects consumers' product preferences. It is a crucial consideration for any consumer goods or media company, but it is much less important for a cement or steel business.

6.2   International strategies

The second structure developed by Porter is a matrix identifying the differing levels of international strategy that an organisation can consider.

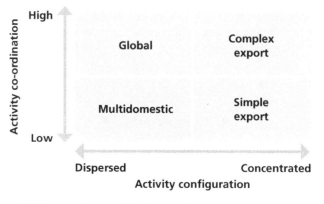

Figure 10.8 Porter – international strategies
((Porter, 1990) adapted by Mark Wearden)

- **Simple export**: the majority of activities remain concentrated in the domestic country of origin, with an approach being taken to generally export finished products with only marginally adapted international variants such as packaging and language. *For example: Microsoft products are available worldwide but only originate from a limited number of core Microsoft operations centres.*

- **Multi-domestic**: a range of activities are strategically placed outside of the domestic country of origin to maximise local efficiency and resources. Often local products are then produced locally within different international centres. *For example: Heinz will adapt its core product of Baked Beans to suit the eating habits of different markets.*

- **Complex export**: most activities are located in a single country, but that might not be the domestic country of origin. Marketing in particular is focused and co-ordinated to ensure that products and or services are driven into a linked range of appropriate destinations. *For example: many clothing brands which originated in the UK and are still perceived as being 'UK' are assembled within non-UK countries and then sold throughout the world.*

- **Global strategy**: this is the most mature of Porter's international strategies, with highly co-ordinated activities dispersed around different countries of the world, often producing replicated entire businesses in different countries, but sometimes locating different activities with countries offering the best cost advantage for that activity. *For example: Amazon are establishing fulfilment centres in many different countries throughout the world.*

Chapter summary

- This chapter recognises that the development of strategy will consist of a series of choices – some of these will be day-to-day and will be covered by the operational plan and the implement/monitor/adjust cycle, however many of the longer-term strategic choices will require a different and more considered approach.

- This chapter recognised that choice required the interaction of direction (where are we going), method (how are we getting there) and strategy (vision, mission etc.). Each of these three aspects requires choice from the organisation.

- The importance of understanding a whole-business approach was discussed, but also the need to sometimes dissect an organisation into SBUs, to allow a deeper and more aligned analysis of today's realities and the aspirational change of the future.

- The Ansoff matrix was introduced, with its approach comparison for new and existing products and markets and this led to Porter's strategic choice model recognising the two core routes of differentiation (doing something different to the competition) and cost leadership (doing something more profitably than the competition).

◆ The significance of and drive towards competitive advantage has been a core focus throughout this chapter, and in particular the need for this to be sustainable for the long-term.

◆ This chapter briefly considered the systems-based approach of BPR and its need to challenge what is happening, rather than just tweak it.

◆ This chapter introduced the idea of an alternative approach to strategic development such as blue ocean strategy, but with the need to recognise that this will often be a starting point for a more conventional market development. Anything is only new and unique until someone else enters the market with a variation or an alternative.

◆ This chapter introduced the important work from the BCG and their portfolio analysis matrix. The terminology and the method from this approach is often used in practical situations and theoretical discussions.

◆ The chapter ended with a consideration of the drivers of internationalisation and Porter's aligned but contrasting approaches.

◆ While all of these areas are an important part of the knowledge and application set of the company secretary and governance professional, the ability to be able step back and take a whole-business approach will be a genuine value that can be brought to the organisation and the board room. Successful strategy requires a perception of the whole and of the parts.

Chapter eleven
Strategy development

Contents

1. Introduction

Chapter 10 considered a range of strategic choices that need to be governed by the directors of a business. The principles that sit behind those choices were focused on differing options within an organisation that needed consideration, and a number of different models and options for the expansion of an organisation were introduced.

When an organisation has found a competitive advantage within a market, it is natural to want to exploit that to its maximum potential. This might not always be possible by remaining as a single organisational entity, even if as a group of companies. The required speed of growth to capitalise on the potential value addition might be too much for an organisation working in isolation within a market, and thus competitors would be allowed to take potential market share.

This chapter will initially consider a number of key drivers and restrictors of organic growth within an organisation. We will consider alternative strategic pathways through acquisition or alliance, with the opportunities and threats that are offered by these options. This will be followed by a review of some of the differing methods that can be used to evaluate and compare the strategic options available. The chapter ends with a reminder of the dangers of the human psyche and how our cognitive biases can lead our imagination into false assumptions.

Case study 11.1

WHSmith is a UK high street retailer focused on expansion through a particular strategic pathway to expand its offering internationally.

'WH Smith agrees deal', FT.com, 30 October 2018 (www.ft.com/content/350c5cca-dc12-11e8-9f04-38d397e6661c)

'UK retailer WH Smith has unveiled plans to buy US airport chain InMotion in a £155m deal to double its travel business, as part of a strategic shift amid declining high street sales.

The books, stationery and convenience retailer said on Tuesday it had agreed to acquire InMotion, the largest airport-based digital accessories retailer in North America. WH Smith said the deal marked a "significant step" in its international growth strategy and would provide it a springboard from which to move into the US, the world's largest travel retail market.

Stephen Clarke, chief executive, said "We intend to enter tenders for traditional airport retail. It gives us sufficient infrastructure in terms of head office and logistics, we can be serious contenders."

Mr Clarke said there was no interest in moving into duty free travel retail, however. "That's a very different market, it's dominated by massive players. There has been a lot of consolidation." The transaction increases still further the group's exposure to travel retail, which it defines as airports, train stations, motorway service areas and hospitals. The travel business has delivered more than 10 consecutive years of earnings growth and now generates two-thirds of the company's operating profit. It dilutes further the company's high street operation.

However, Mr Clarke said it was still a valuable part of the company. "There is no denying we are becoming more travel focused, but we still make more profit on the high street than we did in 2013. It doesn't have growth prospects, but it generates lots of cash."

Analysts at Peel Hunt wrote in a note that "strategically this is a great deal".'

Stop and think 11.1

Think about the strategic considerations that would have been in the minds of the directors of WH Smith plc as they debated this acquisition.

2. Strategic pathways

In the development of its strategy an organisation will need to assess its own abilities and potential within the perceived market place for its products and services. The scope of its business activities and of its competencies will have been determined. Its approach to risk will have been considered (risk aversion or risk seeking as discussed in Chapter 7). Its current portfolio mix will have been assessed against the size of the market. A range of other internal, micro and macro aspects of the strategic potential will have been considered.

2.1 Planning the route

There are a number of significant strategic decisions to be made, as shown in Figure 11.1.

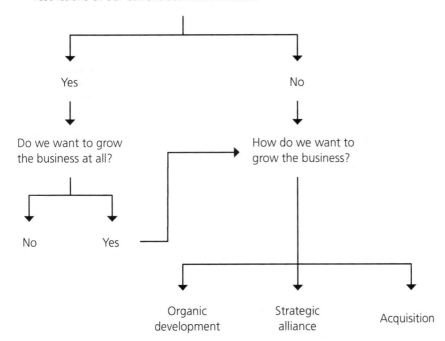

Figure 11.1 Strategic pathway questions
© Mark Wearden

Chapter 10 considered the type of strategic choices that need to be made by a business, focusing mostly on the type and nature of operational activity that can lead to market position and competitive advantage. The decisions being discussed in this chapter, the strategic pathways, add a different dimension requiring a business to consider the organisational method and route it wishes to take, from 'today' into the 'future', to enable it to achieve its strategic objectives through maximising the potential of its operational scope. The three core strategic pathways considered below are:

◆ organic growth
◆ acquisition
◆ strategic alliance.

	Advantages	Disadvantages
Organic growth	– lower risk – allows for ongoing learning – more control	– slow – lack of early knowledge – misreading of markets
Acquisition	– fast – buys presence, market share and expertise	– high cost – high risk, if wrong – lack of targets – problems with selling unwanted assets
Strategic alliance	– cheaper than acquisition – access to market knowledge – useful if an acquisition is impractical – a joint venture alliance can provide closer alliance and lock-out the competition	– possible lack of control – managerial differences

Table 11.1 A differentiation between alternative strategic pathways
((Thompson and Martin, 2005) adapted by Mark Wearden)

The snapshot of differentiation above gives a flavour of the optional strategic pathways that might be available to an organisation. Many planned acquisitions have ended up being a very slow process with multiple hurdles having to be jumped. In such circumstances the growth pathway can prove challenging, not least because it gives the competition time to regroup their resources.

Stop and think 11.2

Consider the differences between the strategic pathways above.

Before we consider each option in more detail, think about the 'people' difficulties that might be involved in each alternative.

2.2 Organic development

Organic development – sometimes referred to as internal development or a 'do-it-yourself' approach – is built around a strategic plan to grow a business through a strategic pathway of building upon and developing the existing capabilities of an organisation. As suggested above, this is probably the most risk averse of the three core strategic pathways, although it might take time to fully realise the strategic potential and objectives. An organisation following this approach will be in control of its own destiny (as far as it can feasibly be), working with the known strengths and weaknesses of its current infrastructure.

There are a number of key advantages of organic development, and it is suggested that these are the primary reason why many organisations will initially take this approach, to at least test the validity of their vision from a low risk dimension. Some advantages are:

- **Dealing with the known**: the current capabilities of the organisation can be maximised, and people involved in the process can be developed. There is more likely to be a united vision and a desire to achieve mutually agreed strategic objectives. This approach aligns closely with the concept of the learning organisation.

- **Staggered investment**: capital investment costs can be controlled across the period of development, and usually there can be a minimal initial cost required through using current excess capacity. This allows the organisation to test the marketplace with a minimum risk to its financial viability (and to maintain or build its reputation).

- **Minimised disruption**: the operational supply chain of the organisation can continue with minimal interruption to ensure continuity and continued revenue streams.

- **Self-reliance**: because organic growth relies upon the organisation itself, other than the need for an acceptable and suitable supply base there can be minimal reliance upon the particular skills and availability of any other organisation. A business that wishes to grow does not need to wait until a suitable partner becomes apparent in the marketplace.

- **Strategy focus**: the core strategic drivers of the organisation, vision, mission, objectives and goals can remain focused in line with the desires and expectations of the stakeholders of the organisation. The involvement of another organisation would be likely to require at least some variation in strategic vision and therefore strategic implementation.

- **Culture maintenance**: Chapter 6 considered organisational culture detail and it will be apparent that organic development will allow growth and new activities within the existing cultural environment. Culture change, or culture alignment between two different organisations can be time consuming and lead to a reduction in the core strategic focus.

Domino's Pizza Group UK has grown organically through maintaining product and service differentiation. It has also taken the opportunity to expand further through the acquiring of additional franchise territories and bringing its same UK differentiation to those territories.

organic development
Increase and improvement through the use of existing resources. This can apply to increase of business with existing customers and/or attraction of new customers for existing products and services.

Case study 11.2

Organic growth: Domino's Pizza Group plc

Adapted from the Domino's Pizza Group UK website: corporate. dominos.co.uk

The Domino's story began in 1960, when Tom and James Monaghan opened the first 'DomiNick's' store in Michigan, USA. A year later, Tom traded his car for his brother's share of the store and later renamed the business Domino's Pizza. The three dots on our logo represent the three stores that Tom originally planned to open. The business idea was simple; to deliver hot, freshly made pizzas in as quick a time as safely possible, while playing an active role in the local community. Through a little-known format now called franchising, Tom enabled other people to invest in opening their own store.

Since opening the first Domino's store in the UK in 1985, we now have over 1,000 stores across the country and more than 35,000 team members. Last year, we sold almost 90 million freshly handcrafted pizzas, including over 7 million of the UK's favourite, Pepperoni Passion. Domino's Pizza Group plc is the UK's leading pizza brand and a major player in the Republic of Ireland.

We hold the master franchise agreement to own, operate and franchise Domino's stores in the UK, the Republic of Ireland, Switzerland and Liechtenstein. In addition, we have a controlling stake in the holders of the Domino's master franchise agreements in Iceland, Norway and Sweden, as well as associate investments in Germany and Luxembourg.

As well as having great tasting pizzas, we're persistent in our pursuit of technology, helping to make our customers' lives that little bit easier. We work hard to make ordering quick and easy, putting customers in control. A tireless focus on learning drives continual improvement and ensures customers are always at the heart of all great innovation at Domino's.

We're driven by our brand purpose "to feed the power of possible, one pizza at a time". This desire to never stand still underpins the entrepreneurial spirit of our franchisees, our dedication to innovation and commitment to keeping promises. Together, it drives us to achieve our vision to be 'the number one pizza company in the world and in every neighbourhood'.

2.3 Acquisitions

This area is commonly known as mergers and acquisitions (M&A). In this text it is referred to simply as 'acquisitions' because in any such combination of organisations there is always a dominant party, and the directors or managers of one organisation will be exerting their strategic influence over the directors and managers of the other to entice a recommendation to the shareholders.

These activities frequently hit the media headlines, often because of the large amounts of money that are potentially involved, but also because of the increasing societal awareness and interest in the wider environmental and social impact of such combining of organisational strength.

Acquisitions activity tends to be cyclical within commercial markets, usually being driven by the ups and downs of different economic cycles, aligned with the differing focus of governments. The perceived view being that often such strategic pathways are driven more in the interest of the people directly involved (directors, managers and advisers) than necessarily in the interests of the shareholders or wider stakeholder group.

The following table clarifies the core terms involved in this strategic growth approach.

Merger	A reorganisation of the assets and the liabilities of two or more organisations who agree to join together and work together from a particular point in time. This could be partial or total alliance between the organisations. The practicalities of only needing one board of directors, one chief executive officer (CEO) and one chief financial officer (CFO) will challenge the genuine mutuality of the arrangement.
Acquisition	The buying of the share capital of one organisation by another organisation, allowing the acquirer to take complete control of the organisation it is acquiring. An intangible asset of 'goodwill' is created when the acquiring company pays more for its acquisition than the current balance sheet value of the company it is acquiring.
Horizontal acquisition	An organisation acquires another organisation in the same industry and stage of production to create a new single entity. In the UK, this type of acquisition is the most likely kind to be referred to the Competition and Markets Authority (CMA) if it is perceived that the newly enlarged organisation will have an unacceptable level of market dominance based on geography and/or product/service offering.
Vertical Acquisition	An organisation acquires another organisation in the same sector or industry but working at a different level in the supply chain. Therefore, this would usually involve the acquisition of either a direct supplier or a direct customer with the intent of reducing the number of links in the supply chain and ensuring greater operational continuity and enhanced supply chain agility.
Conglomerate acquisition	An organisation acquires another organisation in a different industry or sector to that of its core operations. The objective being the spreading of risk across a diversity of markets.

Table 11.2 Terms associated with acquisitions
© Mark Wearden

Case study 11.3

Adapted from 'Sports Direct acquires Evans Cycles', FT.com, 30 October 2018 (www.ft.com/content/144b62a4-dc5f-11e8-9f04-38d397e6661c)

Sports Direct, the UK sportswear retailer that acquired department store group House of Fraser in August, said it had bought Evans Cycles in a pre-pack deal for an undisclosed price. Mike Ashley, Sports Direct chief executive, said the company would only be able to keep around half the stores open stating 'Unfortunately, some stores will have to close'.

Evans, which traces its origins back to 1921, grew rapidly on the back of the UK's growing enthusiasm for cycling, fuelled by increasing uptake in the capital and by success at the Olympics and in road racing. It was bought by private equity firm ECI Partners for £80m in 2015 but ran into financial difficulties after rushing to expand outside its south-eastern heartland. Administrators PwC said a cash flow crunch had compounded weather-related trading problems suggesting:

'2018 has been a very difficult trading year for the business, in part due to the impact of the extended winter weather in the early part of the year and a lack of cash to invest in stores and develop the online platform. A combination of losses, the capital expenditure requirements and tightening credit has led to a liquidity crunch'.

When an acquisition has been made or is being considered as part of the strategic growth strategy, it is important to recognise the differing motives involved – strategic, financial and managerial:

◈   **Strategic motives for making an acquisition**

– An extension of the customer potential in terms of geography, products or markets.

– The consolidation of competitors within an industrial sector. This can reduce competition, enable the raising of prices to customers, increase efficiency through the sharing of common resources (such as head office facilities) and increase production efficiency.

– The combined capabilities of two organisations are likely to exceed and complement their individual potential.

– The development of new market opportunities may well arise from operating a larger organisation with greater financial strength and market coverage.

– The organisational synergy should lead to greater competitive advantage and strategic focus.

Case study 11.4

Facebook saw the opportunity to expand its offering through acquiring the successful technology and customer base of WhatsApp.

In 2014, Facebook acquired the mobile messenger service WhatsApp for $19 billion.

WhatsApp had been launched in 2009 by two former Yahoo employees and had grown a customer base of 420 million monthly users, with per-day volume at that time of circa 20 billion messages being sent each day.

Facebook had previously been pushing its own messenger service but with only limited success; this acquisition allowed it to immediately address a significant customer marketplace and build a direct alignment with its own existing product range.

◆ **Financial motives for making an acquisition**

 –   The alignment of assets and liabilities with different strengths and weaknesses into organisations can bring a greater combined financial strength. If a cash-rich company with a low tangible asset base is acquired by a company with high debt but also significant tangible assets, it should be apparent that the combination will produce a stronger balance sheet.

 –   Renewed balance sheet strength may prove a useful bargaining tool for the acquiring company in persuading the shareholders of the acquisition target to sell their shares.

 –   Greater financial efficiency can often be achieved through a combined revenue stream with an overall reduced cost base, although there may often be significant initial costs from an acquisition, such as redundancies or reorganisation costs.

 –   The market value of a firm rapidly enlarged through acquisition is likely to exceed the previous two separate market values, presuming there is a market and shareholder acceptance of the financial benefits of the acquisition.

 –   Tax advantages may be derived by a profitable organisation acquiring a less profitable, or loss-making organisation. This can be particularly beneficial when acquiring a company with historic tax losses as these can generally be offset against the taxable profit of the acquiring company depending on the tax rules of that jurisdiction.

 –   The opportunity for financial creativity in the structuring of acquisitions, within the remit of the law and of international financial standards, has led to the view that acquisitions can provide an interesting 'blackhole opportunity' for accountants to create 'reorganisation accruals'. This can give the ability for a company to spread the financial benefits of acquisition over time and give an impression of gradual strategic success.

- The potential to acquire an organisation for one or more core activities with the opportunity to sell other activities or assets that are not required, this is often referred to as asset stripping.

◆ **Managerial motives for making an acquisition**

- The personal ambition of directors and managers can often drive an acquisition. The likely benefits are the increased power, remuneration, job security or other benefits. It is worth recognising that often it can be the charisma and personal drive of a particular CEO or dominant leader that can make an acquisition successful.

- Hubris – the unfounded and exaggerated belief of an individual in their own ability. Often this is driven by their view of themselves as an agent controlling and gaming the assets of the shareholders, rather than necessarily as a steward of those assets. Their personal gain can be based around success criteria which does not necessarily lead to an increase in shareholder wealth. There is a prevailing view that the shareholders in an acquiring company will rarely see a short-term benefit; this may or may not be acceptable to the various parties involved in the process.

It will be clear from the above range of differing motives that an acquisition as a strategic pathway is not necessarily a clear and obvious route to success. It is the cultural mismatch of the organisations which will often have unforeseen financial cost, in terms of the time required for successful integration of the different operational substructures. Think back to the frequent common denominator of 'people' which has dominated our different considerations of the development of strategy. It is not surprising that the combination of two different organisations, with their own mix of people and ideas, and their own previous strategic directions, frequently fails to deliver the initial perceived strategic benefits.

◆ Potential advantages of an acquisition:

- rapid access to resources
- rapid access to an enlarged marketplace
- building of strength against the competition
- the effective restructure of an operating environment.

◆ Potential disadvantages of an acquisition:

- cultural mismatch
- managerial mismatch, in terms of both ambition and levels of salary
- enhanced and unwarranted power of individual managers or directors
- forced disposal of assets where market dominance is perceived by a government or regulator.

Johnson (2017) argues that there are four frequently occurring issues that will account for the success or failure of an acquisition:

◈   the addition of real or perceived value by the core stakeholders of the newly formed and enlarged organisation

◈   the gaining of the commitment of middle managers who are responsible for the operational success within the organisation

◈   the ability to realise tangible synergies at different levels

◈   the successful alignment of different cultures.

Due diligence

The initial research and analysis of a potential acquisition option as the preferred pathway to strategic development, is referred to as the 'due diligence' process. The importance of this stage should not be underestimated and requires the ability to take a holistic, objective and arm's-length perspective of the commercial, cultural, financial and operational opportunities (strengths, weaknesses, opportunities, threats) that may exist in both companies – and then how this might change through one company acquiring the other.

There is no one right method of undertaking due diligence, but it is clear that a number of generic considerations need to be considered, including:

◈   why is the potential acquisition available for sale?

◈   the current strategic position of the potential acquisition

◈   the current market standing and customer perception and reputation of the potential acquisition

◈   an understanding of current and previous business plans

◈   the soundness and integrity of the reported financial results of the potential acquisition, including the judgements that have been made in the reported figures (this would apply to both externally available and internal figures) together with market movements for a quoted company

◈   the culture and ethos of the organisation, including an understanding of the employee perception of the organisation

◈   are there any regulatory issues, unresolved complaints or impending litigation against the company being acquired?

In his book *Corporate financial management*, Arnold (2013) summarises four different perspectives of the acquisition process (see Table 11.3).

Although the focus for Arnold's table is the financial aspects of an acquisition, it is clear that there are many qualitative as well as quantitative dimensions which need to be taken into consideration.

2.4   Strategic alliances

A *strategic alliance* is formed when two or more organisations agree to share resources and activities in the pursuit of a common strategy. This is a popular method of strategic growth, enabling many of the benefits of the acquisition process, but without the negative aspects of trying artificially to completely align all operational and cultural aspects of the organisations. It does require trust and integrity between the various parties involved.

Synergy	Bargain buying	Managerial motives	Third party motives
The two firms together are worth more than the value of the firms apart. – $PV_{AB} = PV_A + PV_B + gains$ – Market power – Economies of scale – Internationalisation of transactions – Entry to new markets and industries – Tax advantages – Risk diversification.	Target can be purchased at a price below the present value of the target's future cash flow when in the hands of new management. – Elimination of inefficient and misguided management. – Under-valued shares: strong form or semi-strong form of stock market inefficiency.	– Empire building – Status – Power – Remuneration – Hubris – Survival: speedy growth strategy to reduce probability of being takeover target – Free cash flow: management prefer to use free cash flow in acquisitions rather than return it to shareholders.	– Advisers – At the insistence of customers or suppliers.

Table 11.3 Aspects of a corporate acquisition
((Arnold, 2013) adapted by Mark Wearden)

Johnson (2017) argues that the strategic drive for an alliance is likely to fall into one of two related but distinctive categories:

◆   **a collective strategy** requires a network of alliances to be built to compete against rival networks of alliances; *the example he gives is that of Microsoft gaining competitive success for its Xbox games console through the collective strength of its network of independent games developers, ensuring they have a stronger ecosystem than their rivals such as Sony and Nintendo.*

◆   **a collaborative advantage** requires a more effective managing of alliances than the competition; *in the example of Microsoft and its Xbox, it is not enough to have a stronger network than its rivals, but it needs to continuously be better at working within its network to ensure that the members continue to produce the best games.*

It is suggested that there are three main motives for the creation of a strategic alliance as the preferred strategic pathway:

◆   the rapid achievement of critical mass scale within a marketplace, leading to cost reduction and an improved customer offering;

◆   the complementarity of differing capabilities within the members of an alliance, ensuring a more holistic business and enhanced market coverage; and

◆   the learning potential from working closely with partners within an alliance without the need to change the underlying organisational structure or culture – although there will always be cultural implications for the people directly involved in the alliance. This has been the case in a number of the HP strategic alliances such as that discussed below.

Types of strategic alliance:

◆ A **customer end network** alliance will focus on either increasing the potential offering to existing customers of the individual partners or attempt to widen the potential customer base. This approach would use a tool such as the Ansoff matrix to analyse its potential. *An example of this was the initial alliance between Dixons retail group and Carphone Warehouse, although the end result of this alliance was Dixons acquiring the Carphone business.*

◆ A **supplier end network** alliance will seek to gain competitive edge in a marketplace by creating a critical mass requirement from a common supply base. *A current example of this would be the alliance that has been created between Tesco plc and Carrefour, the major French retail group.*

◆ A formal **partnership** can be formed with the individual organisations agreeing to work together within a partnership structure for a specific range of activities.

◆ A **joint-venture** is a legally recognised structure where two or more organisations remain independent and establish a newly created organisation that is jointly owned by the individual organisations, usually without specific asset or liability transfer, but to enable the development of a focused range of activities. Each organisation would financially account for its involvement on a net receipt, net contribution and net asset impact basis.

Case study 11.5

Adapted from HP.com news site:

HP and Foxconn announced a joint venture agreement to create a new line of cloud-optimized servers specifically targeting service providers who will continue to break new ground in search of both performance gains and cost reductions as they expand their cloud architecture implementations.

The changing needs of cloud computing require a new approach to server design that brings together cloud solutions expertise, quick customer response and volume manufacturing. Creating innovative servers and solutions has been a cornerstone of the relationship between Foxconn and HP for several decades and today's announcement further strengthens the partnership. Foxconn's ability to deliver superior value throughout the supply chain, together with HP's industry compute leadership and industry-recognized service and support, will deliver new world-class computing platforms by bringing high-density, easy-to-manage, cost-competitive solutions to market.

The president and chief executive officer at HP stated: 'This partnership reflects business model innovation in our server business, where the high-volume design and manufacturing expertise of Foxconn, combined with the compute and service leadership of HP, will enable us to deliver a game-changing offering in infrastructure economics.'

Advantages of strategic alliances:

◆   access to complementary resources without the need for substantive investment, *for example the alignment between retailers and banks to offer financial services to customers*;

◆   the sharing of risk and resource enabling individual organisations to reduce their risk exposure;

◆   the speed of access to market, an effective alliance can develop its offering rapidly and often without unnecessary bureaucratic delay, giving it competitive advantage; and

◆   reduced political and legal complications through working within a structure that does not require external authority approval.

Disadvantages of strategic alliances:

◆   the recognition of true cost to each party in the development and operating of the alliance;

◆   the risk of potential reputational damage through seeming to be associated with other non-alliance activities of a partner to the alliance;

◆   confusion amongst middle managers, or even directors, as to who they actually work for and who they report to, if they have two reporting lines defining which reporting line takes priority in which circumstances; and

◆   erosion of capabilities and competencies creating a situation where in-house abilities are diminished with a reliance on the strategic partner.

Stop and think 11.3

Look back at the various case examples included in this chapter. Make sure you understand the differences, advantages and disadvantages that distinguish between these different strategic growth pathways.

3. Evaluating strategic options

The optimal route to achieving the strategic vision in every organisation, and the realisation of the strategic objectives, will need to undergo evaluation. The first part of this chapter identified a number of potential pathways to achieving the desired market strength and gaining competitive advantage. Throughout this text, we continue to consider a breadth and diversity of options, methods, opinions and the means by which we might achieve a perceived change in the future; our development of strategy.

Many of the specific tools that are included throughout the other chapters of this text relate to different means of evaluating the strategic options that face us on a daily basis. The remainder of this chapter will consider a few additional tools, together with some generic concepts and principles which need to underpin the process of the evaluation of strategic options.

Test yourself 11.1

Suggest one advantage and one disadvantage of each of the three core strategic pathways.

A useful starting point for a strategic evaluation is to ensure that we have appropriately challenged the performance projections which take us from today into the future. We need to understand the basis of our belief that the future viability can be assured through the quantitative and qualitative measures that we are applying to our perceived achievement of objectives.

3.1   Key performance indicators

Key performance indicators (KPIs) were first discussed in Chapter 7 where it was suggested that they need to have three core dimensions – accuracy, materiality and forward impact. The effective use of KPIs can form an invaluable evaluation of how an organisation has previously delivered value and success (however those are defined) and can also then act as a useful benchmark for the potential strategic route to achieving objectives. If the future KPIs appear to be radically different than the historic KPIs, then serious questions ought to be asked. The use of KPIs will be discussed again in Chapters 11 and 13.

Behind the development of the correct KPIs, and always remembering that the first word is KEY, are a defined set of organisational *drivers*. These drivers need to enable us to evaluate both the current position of an organisation (and how it has reached that position) and its potential for achieving future success. In any organisation, no matter how complex it might appear, there are only ever a defined set of key drivers. A useful starting point for this is to define the relationship between the supply chain and the value chain as considered in Chapter 10.

The building of different *scenarios* is an important dimension of our ability to determine and evaluate potential success. There is always more than one way to achieve a strategic objective and it is important, as discussed in Chapter 10, that we are able to recognise how the alignment of different key drivers will allow the building of different scenarios and the determining of different KPIs.

The use of a *decision tree* while building different scenarios can help to clarify the mindset and the route. Throughout this text we have used a number of decision trees, such as Figure 11.1 above. The straight-line recognition of options that are available across the strategic pathway can help significantly with the evaluation of reality.

While plotting the route into the future, it is important to recognise that in addition to the key drivers there will be a number of *critical control* points along the route. An approach to the identification and challenge of these control points is discussed in section 6.3 of Chapter 13.

3.2 Key evaluation criteria

There are three fundamental challenges which need to be applied to every strategic option being considered within an organisation.

◆ **Suitability**: does the strategic option address the realities of the internal, micro and macro environment within which the organisation is operating? This requires:
  – an understanding of the mission and objectives of the strategy
  – use of a SWOT (strengths, weaknesses, opportunities and threats) analysis to identify the skills, competencies and resources that are available
  – an understanding of the culture of the organisation.

◆ **Acceptability**: does the strategic option meet the expectations of stakeholders, in particular with regard to potential risk and return? This requires an understanding of:
  – the levels of expected returns to differing stakeholder groups
  – the risk appetite and tolerance of the organisation and its stakeholders
  – the perceived synergy that will be driven by the achievement of the strategic objectives.

◆ **Feasibility**: will the proposed strategic option actually work in practice, in particular with regard to the availability of the resources required to deliver success? This requires:
  – the ability to drive sustainable change from both a process and people perspective
  – the availability of finance and other resources
  – the likelihood of gaining sustainable competitive advantage.

Test yourself 11.2

When might a strategic alliance be a useful pathway for strategic growth?

3.3 Real options

Real options are defined as the practical achievable options that are available to an organisation within its more generic strategic options. These are often based around concepts of timing:

◆ The commitment of resources may often require a *delay* in the strategic journey until the use of a resource can be justified without causing unnecessary damage to the ongoing operational environment.

◆ An organisation needs to understand the point at which a strategic option may need to be *abandoned* – this is often called an exit strategy. The strategic plan should have identified and formally defined and recorded this through the use of 'critical control point' analysis.

◆ The timing of the implementation of real options can be aligned to the different methods of moving between floors in a multi-storey building:

  – a lift will enable a rapid movement which ignores a number of in between stages

  – an escalator will require at least a passing of the different stages

  – a staircase will require a far more measured approach to the strategic implementation.

The advantage of taking a real-option approach to the development of strategy is to allow an organisation to act proactively when the strategy is not developing as planned, as opposed to having to be reactive.

3.4 Evaluation, caution and the human psyche

Rumelt (1980) suggested that there are four fundamental principles that are required when evaluating corporate strategy:

◆ **Consistency**: goals and policies should be aligned to ensure there is no distance or conflict between different divisions and different people.

◆ **Consonance**: strategy must be closely aligned with the external environment and able to adapt to environmental change.

◆ **Advantage**: there must always be an understanding of how competitive advantage can be created and maintained.

◆ **Feasibility**: the organisation must have the ability, the people and the motivation to carry out the strategy.

Johnson (2017) argues that a degree of caution is required in the process of strategic evaluation. His views align well with those of Rumelt above:

◆ the need to avoid conflict between people

◆ the need to ensure consistency between different elements of a strategy

◆ the need to ensure that the strategic options can be implemented in reality.

When evaluating strategic options, it is important to remember the different approaches that will be taken by different people and their individuality – for example, Chapter 1 introduced the concept of the 'ladder of inference' as developed by Argyris (1990). These concepts help us to understand the way in which we as human beings develop our individual attitudes and prejudices towards people and situations, and how we assess situations and make our decisions. The concept of the prejudice of the human psyche is the basis of what has become known as natural or cognitive bias, as discussed in Chapter 6.

Test yourself 11.3

What are the three core dimensions that are required of a KPI to ensure that it enables sound evaluation of a strategic pathway?

Chapter summary

◆ This chapter extends further the consideration of strategic choice, discussed in Chapter 10 and focuses on three potential strategic pathways for the growth and development of an organisation – organic growth, acquisition and strategic alliance.

◆ The underlying presumption is the need to find the optimal strategic route to maximise sustainable competitive advantage.

◆ *Organic growth* is perceived as the most risk-averse of the pathways, but that comes with the risk of a slow speed of growth unless the product competitive edge allows otherwise, or in some other way deters the competition from gaining market share.

◆ *Acquisitions* offer the chance to gain immediate differential, but can often be hampered by culture clashes. They may also be subject to market regulation to prevent undue dominance of a geographic or product market.

◆ It is important to be able to distinguish between the different types of acquisition and recognise the supply-chain relevance.

◆ The stakeholder and shareholder perspective of acquisitions, and the other strategic pathways, needs serious consideration with an understanding of tangible and intangible expectations.

◆ *Strategic alliances* can offer many of the benefits of an acquisition but without the formal alignment of all aspects of two or more organisations.

◆ The different strategic pathways need to be evaluated and this chapter reminds students of a number of previously discussed tools and methods that can be used for such evaluation, suggesting that each needs assessing against the three underlying criteria of suitability (does it address the strategic objectives?), acceptability (will it satisfy the stakeholder expectations?) and feasibility (will it actually work?).

◆ Anyone undertaking the role of a company secretary and governance professional needs to be able to differentiate between the optional strategic pathways for their organisation. It is important to be able to recommend appropriate tools to test and challenge whether a particular approach is optimal for achieving a sustainable competitive edge.

Part five

Implementing strategy

Introduction

The preceding 11 chapters have developed a breadth of
understanding about the nature of strategy and strategic thought.
We have challenged the development of strategy within the
differing contexts of the organisation itself and the external micro
and macro forces which affect our strategic journey. We kept
returning to the influence of the individual on every aspect of
the process of strategy. Part five will consider firstly the differing
structures that exist within organisations, and then how control
needs to be developed around the strategic process within those
organisational structures.

Overview

Chapter 12 will link our earlier understanding of systems and
culture to the differing forms of organisational structure that
exist within organisations. It will consider how the development
of the strategy will influence and help to mould the structure of
an organisation, and how the structure, with its restraints and its

opportunities, will help to mould the strategy. The chapter will also consider the organisational boundaries.

Chapter 13 establishes that control is a significant aspect of the development of strategy. The control needs to be for now ('today') but also the vision needs to consider how that control might need to change ('future'). The chapter will challenge control from the differing perspectives of analysis, audit, assessment and assurance, and will conclude with a brief consideration of using balanced scorecard approach to strategic thinking.

Learning outcomes

At the end of this part, students will be able to:

◆ understand and challenge the appropriateness of different types of organisational structures;

◆ challenge the relationship between structure, culture and systemic behaviour;

◆ demonstrate the iterative nature of the relationship between strategy and structure;

◆ consider whether, when and where we need strategic and organisational boundaries;

◆ demonstrate how and why control is required in developing strategy;

◆ consider the differences between qualitative and quantitative measures;

◆ demonstrate the difference between organisation efficiency and organisational effectiveness;

◆ consider how the use of metaphor can aid strategic thinking;

◆ challenge the need for analysis, audit, assessment and assurance; and

◆ demonstrate how to use a balanced scorecard approach in the development and challenge of appropriate organisational control.

Chapter twelve

Organisational structure and design

Contents

1. Introduction

Throughout this text and its exploration into the differing dynamics of strategy and how it is developed within organisations, it should be apparent that we return to two core themes:

- **People**: the collection of unique brains which individually and combined have the ability to envision and drive change.
- **Structure**: the types of organisational culture and systems which enable people to challenge what is happening today and underpin the perceived successes of the future.

At any point in time, we can freeze the operation of an organisation and examine its structure. In finance we can use a balance sheet as a snapshot to identify the underpinning financial infrastructure of an organisation, identifying its strengths and weaknesses. In our development of strategy, we need to similarly be able to step back and understand the operational structure: How are the people and their roles related to each other? How does the organisation work? How does it do whatever it is that it does?

This chapter will identify what is meant by *organisational structure* and consider a range of different types of structures which have often evolved from the traditional forms of the hierarchical and patriarchal behaviour that dominated society. We will also look at the emergence of different types of far more dynamic organisational structure, enabled through changes in societal attitude, the rapid growth in methods and models of communication and the dramatic impact of technology, often now referred to as the Fourth Industrial Revolution. The chapter will conclude with some thoughts about how to determine an optimal organisational structure for specific scenarios.

Case study 12.1

Tata Group operates a decentralised organisational structure which deliberately places significant responsibility in different companies within its group.

Extract from Tata Group website (www.tata.com/aboutus/sub_index/ Leadership-with-trust):

'Founded by Jamsetji Tata in 1868, the Tata group is a global enterprise headquartered in India, comprising over 100 independent operating companies. The group operates in more than 100 countries across six continents, with a mission "To improve the quality of life of the communities we serve globally, through long-term stakeholder value creation based on Leadership with Trust".

Each Tata company or enterprise operates independently under the guidance and supervision of its own board of directors and shareholders. There are 29 publicly-listed Tata enterprises. Many Tata companies have achieved global leadership in their businesses. Employing a diverse workforce in their operations, Tata companies have made significant local investments in different geographies. The Tata companies collectively employ over 695,000 people.

Going forward, Tata companies are building multinational businesses that seek to differentiate themselves through customer-centricity, innovation, entrepreneurship, trustworthiness and values-driven business operations, while balancing the interests of diverse stakeholders including shareholders, employees and civil society.'

2. The nature of organisational structure

The use of the word 'structure' is the reason we use the word 'organisation' to describe the manner in which we operate a business. Without an understanding of structure, we have no clarity of how the people within an organisation work, their differing roles, their lines of communication, their reporting lines, their areas of responsibility and accountability, the framework of relationships between the people and the various systems that enable the business to operate on a day-to-day basis, and also to evolve.

Think back to the supply-chain image of a business which we first used in Chapter 3.

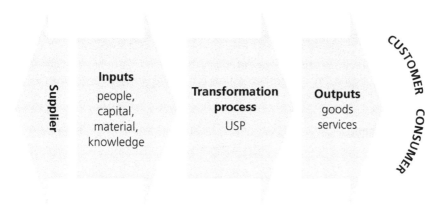

Figure 12.1 Supply chain
© Mark Wearden

Imagine the number of people involved within this chain, each with their individuality and their beliefs and objectives, but simultaneously each also having to play a role in the generation of business success. Without organisation and structure, this would simply not happen. There is no one right or correct organisational structure, there are as many different types of structure as there are types of organisation. The purpose of this chapter is to examine the different types of classic and emerging structures and consider how they help or hinder in our development of strategy.

The need for a company secretary and governance professional to be able to understand, analyse and challenge the structure of the organisation where they work is really important. The nature of the role itself should enable a cross-functional view of the organisation. Although one may be working within a specific secretarial, legal, finance department or similar, the role of that department covers the entirety of the organisation. Company secretaries and governance professionals will often find themselves in a privileged position to be able to step back and think:

◆ How does this organisation work?

◆ Why does this organisation work?

◆ Who makes the organisation work?

◆ What is the organisational structure?

The subject of organisational structure receives differing treatment and emphasis from academic writers, thinkers and practitioners. Johnson et al. (2017) suggest that the organisational structure can be seen as the 'skeleton' of the organisation which 'provides the basic framework on which everything else is built'. Drucker (1968) goes further by suggesting that the organisational structure is indispensable and the 'means for achieving the objectives and goals'. Carter (1999) discusses the structure as a 'framework of relationships', recognising the dangers of complexity and 'energy loss' where the structure has too many links.

We can re-use another image from Chapter 3 to ensure we take a systemic view. This illustrates the different aspects of the organisational structure that we need to understand to determine what is happening, think back to the alignment of this with business process re-engineering in Chapter 10. Without understanding the elements and the relationships we will not be able to determine whether our organisational structure is appropriate or not.

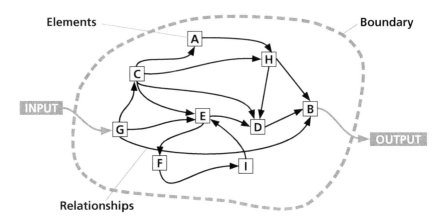

Figure 12.2 System structure
© Mark Wearden

Johnson et al. (2017) suggest that the structure is the manner of defining how and why an organisation works, and the systems are the mechanisms.

A more aligned approach would be to use the phrase 'organisational structure' to recognise that, in itself, the system is the structure which enables the organisation to survive.

Stop and think 12.1

Consider the human body as an organisation structure. We can define the how and why of the way in which the body works, and we can analyse the mechanisms, but the body as an organisational structure is a united whole which allows us to continue breathing and living on a daily basis.

Stop and think about your organisation, or any organisation, in this way.

There are a number of aspects within our initial analysis of organisational structure which need you to hold in your head both images used in this chapter – supply chain and system:

◆   How do the relationships work, where is the authority?
◆   What are the channels and the patterns of communication which enable the linkage between the different parts of the structure?

◆ How do we ensure that the structure is designed to enable the realisation of the strategic goals?

◆ How do we enable system change?

◆ What are the strategic drivers?

◆ Where in the structure is there an opportunity for the players (the people) to stop and think – about the organisation and about the maximising of individual potential?

2.1 Strategy and structure

If the structure is so fundamental to the success of an organisation, how does it relate to the strategy?

◆ Is a strategy required before developing a structure?

◆ Is a structure required before developing a strategy?

The correct answer: both are true in different circumstances.

The traditional view – strategy before structure – was supported by the American strategist Alfred Chandler (1962) and was based on research into how fifty leading US companies had developed their strategies in the early 20th century. His main conclusion was, that to be successful, a company needed to first develop strategy and then develop structure. He suggested this was the design which enables the administration of an organisation. His logic was clear and linear – having devised a strategy there is a need to determine what is required to deliver the vision, and this will lead to the required organisational structure.

Twenty years later a similar piece of research by James Brian Quinn (1980), again in the US, concluded that the organisational environment was changing rapidly, and that Chandler's conclusions needed placing within their historical context. Quinn argued that the strategy then structure model oversimplifies what is required and what actually happens within an organisation. He suggested that strategic change may need to happen incrementally (he called this logical incrementalism) and that the structure will be intertwined with the strategy through the life of an organisation, with both needing to lead and follow at different stages.

There is no right answer to this conundrum. Even if strategy is being defined at the outset of an organisation, or at a key turning point in its evolution, the people who are devising the strategy will themselves be based within a physical and mental structure. While their vision may be to change one or both of these structures, their status quo will influence their thinking. As strategy is developed, so the need for structural change will become clear as part of the enabling of that vision. However, the process of developing the strategy, and the breadth of the vision, may be restrained by the limitations of the structure.

The strategy needs to be designed to shape and deliver the vision as required by the stakeholders.

The structure needs to enable the delivery within the constraints of short-term and long-term viability and sustainability.

Stop and think 12.2

You should be able to see a clear linkage between this strategy/structure challenge and the discussion in Chapter 2 of the differences between rational and emergent strategy.

While form and logical thinking is required, the human reality is one of change and new ideas, so flexibility is often essential.

Consider also the influence of organisational culture as discussed in Chapter 6.

2.2 Elements of organisational structure

Before examining the differences between traditional and emerging forms of organisational structure, we need to briefly consider what it is that we are trying to address with the structure and therefore what elements need to co-exist.

Robbins and Judge (2016) describe organisational structure as being the manner in which the required business functions are formally divided, grouped and co-ordinated and suggest that there are six key elements that ought to be considered:

- **Specialisation**:
    - the subdivision of tasks within the organisation into separate jobs to make the most effective use of the differing skills of employees
    - the development of employees with specific skills which maximise their personal abilities
    - the building or organisational efficiency through the optimal focus of employees.

- **Departmentalisation**:
    - the grouping together of jobs to improve the efficiency and effectiveness of an operation
    - alignment of function, product, geography, process or customer can allow greater focus for a range of related jobs within a production process
    - the bringing together of related specialisations within a supply chain.

- **Chain of command**:
    - the hierarchical line of authority that runs from the top to the bottom of an organisation
    - clarification of levels of accountability and authority
    - unity of command suggest that each individual should only have one person to whom they report and are accountable.

- **Span of control**:
    - the number of people that any one person has who are accountable to them

- – the optimising of how many subordinates a manager can effectively and efficiently control
- – Robbins and Judge suggest that the greater the span of control the greater the cost effectiveness, with fewer expensive managers at each level.

◆ **Levels of centralisation**:

- – the degree to which decision-making is concentrated at a single point within an organisation
- – a centralised structure will imply that senior management make all or most of the decisions
- – a decentralised structure will imply that decision-making is delegated down throughout the organisation.

◆ **Formalisation**:

- – how the different jobs within the organisation are structured and formalised
- – the levels of discretion that are or are not given to the people carrying out the jobs
- – the impact and controlling nature of rules and regulations within an organisation.

Case study 12.2

Differing concepts of organisational efficiency:

◆ **Managerial efficiency: the ability of an organisation to meet its strategic goals.**

◆ **Allocational efficiency: the deployment of resources to achieve goals and create value.**

◆ **Productive efficiency: the output achieved in a period of time by employees working under managerial oversight.**

◆ **Resource efficiency: the use of organisational resources to achieve objectives and minimise waste.**

◆ **Process efficiency: the consumption of time, labour and cost by a process, relative to the organisational outputs.**

◆ **Cost efficiency: the understanding and alignment of required costs with output.**

Stop and think 12.3

How would you describe and illustrate your own use of time in terms of efficiency?

Test yourself 12.1

Suggest how the concept of emergent strategy relates to the debate between whether structure should come before strategy or vice versa.

3. Traditional structural forms

A clear and transparent organisational structure is important within any business, and a clarity of the lines of communication and accountability. Human resource research into delegation of tasks and the motivation of the individual shows clearly that for a human being it is important to know our position within any particular structure, and our relationship with the other aspects of the structure.

Transparency and clarity are required, for all to see within the organisation, and this is usually achieved by the drawing of an organisation chart, reflecting clearly the lines that exist between the different job functions and the levels of the hierarchy. Often the individual cells within such a diagram have the names of people rather than just the job function. An individual can feel motivated if they appear at the right level and with the anticipated lines of communication. There is a risk of demotivation if the chart reveals something unexpected.

This section will consider several types of traditional structure, each with an increasing complexity of both people and task; it will also consider structures which are more geared around the nature of the business requirement than the people, but nevertheless create the type of rigidity envisaged by Chandler.

In each of the different structures, three advantages and three disadvantages are included for that particular perspective, to demonstrate that each one of these types of structure is in itself highly flexible and will need adapting to suit a particular set of organisational circumstances and culture.

Stop and think 12.4

Before you continue and explore the different aspects of these traditional types of organisational structure, think about your own organisation and draw yourself a quick organisation chart. Identify your role; the immediate relationships and accountabilities; and how far removed you are (or not) from the 'seats of power'.

Then consider the origin of your organisation's structure, whether it is fit for purpose, or whether it needs to evolve to meet the challenges of the 21st century.

3.1   Simple structure

The majority of organisations across the world are small businesses and have a limited number of employees and also a limited range of activities. Even in such an organisation, it is important for people to know who is in charge. This type of organisation structure is usually quite flat with the business being run by a single owner manager, and with limited lines of hierarchy, as shown in Figure 12.3. Even if a supervisor was introduced into this structure, it would only add one additional line between the manager and the employees.

Figure 12.3 Simple structure

Advantages	Disadvantages
– clarity of accountability with decision-maker in regular contact with all employees	– the need for the manager to deal with every aspect of the business
– wide spans of control	– rigidity can prevent personal progression
– centralised authority	– focus on day-to-day rather than strategy

3.2   Functional structure

As an organisation expands and diversifies, it is usually necessary to expand the organisational structure and recruit people with specialist skills to act as a function head for different aspects of the organisation. The owner–manager is unlikely to be skilled, at an appropriate level, in all of the differing aspects of a growing business – for instance, finance, sales, production, engineering – and will often need to hire people with these skills to enable the business to continue on its growth curve.

Figure 12.4 illustrates a reasonably simple form of functional structure, but it is easy to imagine how this can expand initially horizontally and then vertically with increasing layers of hierarchy required as the business expands.

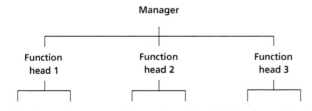

Figure 12.4 Functional structure

Advantages	Disadvantages
– flexibility and breadth of senior skills	– duplication of tasks, lack of centralisation
– focused decision-making structure	– differing values between functions
– opportunities for people progression	– short-termism – what is best for my function?

3.3   Divisional structure

Rather than using the business operational lines of the functional organisation structure, a divisional structure views the business as a series of products, services, geographical areas or something similar.

Whereas the functional structure requires specialists to oversee and manage the different aspects of business, the divisional structure is more likely to have a senior manager or director with significant control and oversight across the entire range of functions within a particular division.

In essence this might seem to be a much larger structure, but in reality, the concept and the requirement of either a functional or divisional structure will be based upon a particular business need, mode of operation and the anticipated customer or other stakeholder requirements. Figure 12.5 suggests what such a structure might look like, although this is a simple example to illustrate the idea.

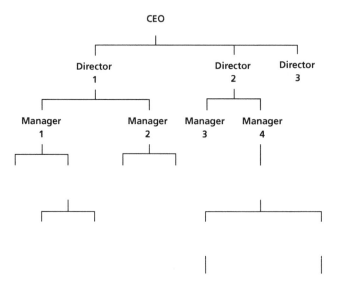

Figure 12.5 Divisional structure

Advantages	Disadvantages
– separation of strategic from operational	– loss of central control with short-term inter-division competitiveness
– responsiveness to the external environment	– expensive solution with duplication of function across divisions
– opportunities to 'grow' management skills and talent	– image and quality differentiation

It is worth noting that many listed companies will in effect operate a divisional structure with a holding company sitting at the top of the structure owning, either in whole or in part, the subsidiary and associated companies. There are two core types of such structure in operation, although obviously with many variants:

◆ The holding company and head office run a central services operation for all subsidiaries, giving a centralisation of functions such as finance and human resources. The cost of these functions is passed on as an overhead to each business based upon levels of requirement.

◆ The holding company simply acts as a forum for strategic thinking, boardroom and governance related activities. Each individual subsidiary being accountable for the operation and cost of its own administrative type requirements such as finance and human resources.

Many organisations will switch from one mode of operation to the other and back again in an effort to minimise cost and/or maximise efficiency.

3.4 Matrix structure

Many organisations find that using a matrix structure overcomes many of the problems that arise from some of the other purely hierarchical structures. The matrix structure combines the functional and divisional structures, often creating dual lines of accountability and a much greater communication cross-section (the horizontal dimension) across the different hierarchies (the vertical dimension).

In such structures there is often a separate head-office type function which offers cross-functional services to the remainder of the business. There is a recognition of the need for hierarchical reporting for ultimate accountability and developmental and progression opportunities. There is usually a more formalised communication structure operating across the different businesses, or different aspects of the same business.

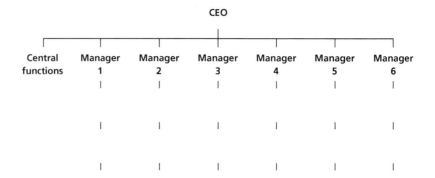

Figure 12.6 Matrix structure

Advantages	Disadvantages
– specialised skills can be used across divisions	– risk of power struggles across the senior team
– resources can be shared more easily leading to greater efficiency	– uncertainty about ultimate accountability – who do I really report to?
– flexibility can lead to removal of silo thinking and better personal opportunities	– hard-workers can become overburdened, and people can avoid accountability

Stop and think 12.5

Which of the above structural forms best represents the way in which your own organisation operates?

What are its strengths and weaknesses and how would you change it if you could?

3.5 Multinational and transnational structures

As discussed in Chapter 10, a company operating within an international or multinational context will be required to consider a wider range of structural operating parameters. The differences between national cultures, and the inherent expectations of employees, together with acceptability or otherwise of working practices will determine how such a company needs to be structured.

When an organisation is based in one country but buying from and/or selling to other countries, the structure can be largely based around what is acceptable within the 'home' country but making reputational allowances for the expectations of the international customers.

When an organisation is running operations in more than one country, there are a number of potential multinational structures that can be considered.

Figure 12.7 Multinational structures
((Bartlett and Ghoshal, 1998) adapted by Mark Wearden)

International divisions are stand-alone operations which, although run under the oversight and principles of the parent company, are not integrated into the core structure. This is often the starting point for a business when it is establishing its initial overseas operation and allows it to test the local potential and requirements without having to change the core 'home' structure. This is often used by organisations with large domestic markets such as the US or China when they establish smaller overseas operations. Usually such structures will draw upon 'head office' for many administrative and oversight functions.

Local subsidiaries will have a degree of autonomy in the overseas territory, particularly in customer-focused activities such as design, marketing and production. These structures are particularly useful where there is a need to be responsive to local regulations and culture. Legal, accountancy and other consultancy practices will often be established in this manner. This allows the building of a local reputation with a degree of autonomy from the main organisational structure, which in turn will not need changing to enable an effective subsidiary operation.

Global product divisions are the optimal structure when there is a financial benefit in establishing a particular business function (e.g. production, finance, help-desks) in one geographic territory, but with worldwide coverage for the organisation. The local responsiveness and independence are low because the function is established in that territory for sound economic reasons. The global co-ordination is high because the function will impact an entire organisation.

Transnational corporations require a challenging mix of local responsiveness, global co-ordination and the ability to drive strategic growth and innovation across a wide range of different geographic territories and cultures. In many ways this is similar to a matrix structure but spread across different countries. Bartlett and Ghoshal (1998) suggest that such structures have a number of core characteristics:

◆ Each national unit will operate independently as a source of ideas and capabilities for the whole corporation.

◆ National units achieve greater efficiency and economies of scale by being able to act as specialists for the entire corporation.

◆ The 'head office' will deliver success by establishing the independent role requirement of each business unit, but then underpin this with effective systems, relationships and culture across the units to ensure a cohesive approach. Ultimate strategic success for the group will often depend on the ability of 'head office' to effectively monitor and influence the business metrics (the key performance indicators (KPIs), working capital etc.) of all units while allowing for local culture requirements.

Case study 12.3

Consider how Unilever uses its central functions to drive its wide range of products and diversity on international customers.

Extract from Unilever Annual Report and Accounts 2017, p.9:

'Our business activities span a complex, global value chain. Starting with consumer insights, we track changing consumer sentiment through our 25 People Data Centres around the world. Through close collaboration between marketing and R&D, we use our insights to inform product development, leveraging our €900 million annual R&D spend.

We work with thousands of suppliers and spend around €34 billion on goods and services, including approximately €13 billion on ingredients and raw materials for our products. Our global manufacturing operations across more than 300 factories in 69 countries turn these materials into products.

Our products are then distributed via a network of more than 400 globally co-ordinated warehouses to 25 million retail stores, from large supermarkets, hypermarkets, wholesalers and cash and carry, to small convenience stores, as well as other fast-growing channels such as e-commerce, out-of-home and direct-to-consumer. We work in close partnership with customers to ensure our brands are always available and properly displayed.

Underlying our value chain is a set of defining strengths which set us apart from our competitors: our portfolio of global brands and local jewels; a presence in more than 190 countries with 58% of our turnover in emerging markets; deep distribution capability through ever more complex channels and a talent pool of local management – 70% of our leaders are local.'

Stop and think 12.6

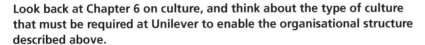

Look back at Chapter 6 on culture, and think about the type of culture that must be required at Unilever to enable the organisational structure described above.

3.6   Joint venture structure

A joint venture organisational structure, as already referred to as a form of strategic alliance, can take a range of different legal forms and can involve collaboration for a single particular purpose or for a wide range of business activities. The use of the word 'joint' implies two or more parties, and the structure is designed to enable each party to retain their individual autonomy while working together in a formal legal structure designed to achieve specific strategic objectives to add value to each participant party in the 'venture'.

Advantages	Disadvantages
– retention of individual autonomy and structure	– reporting and compliance may add to the administrative burden
– liability is limited to agreed contribution	– guarantees may exceed limited liability and increase potential costs
– reduces reputational damage	– risk of double taxation
– net accounting basis	

Case study 12.4

'Alibaba close to signing joint venture with Russian partners', James Kynge and Henry Foy, FT.com, 2 September 2018 (www.ft.com/content/faf2b934-ad41-11e8-94bd-cba20d67390c)

'Alibaba is in "advanced stage negotiations" to form a joint venture ecommerce company with Russian partners, as China's vision of a "digital silk road" across Eurasia takes shape. Russian officials and other people involved in the deal said Alibaba was close to agreeing a partnership with Russian internet company, Mail.ru, and the Russian Direct Investment Fund, the sovereign wealth fund. The involvement of RDIF indicates the level of official backing for the planned venture.'

3.7   Focused project structure

The final form of traditional structure which just needs a brief consideration is when an organisation establishes a formal internal structure for one specific purpose. The structure could take the form of any of the suggested structures above, depending on the size of the project, but it will always be aligned to the core strategic drive and under the oversight of the 'head office' operation.

Organisations such as civil engineering companies or film companies will commonly use such methods. The structure will be established to fulfil a set of focused criteria and strategic objectives and will then usually be dissolved when the objectives have been met.

Test yourself 12.2

Suggest the advantages and disadvantages of a matrix organisational structure.

4. Emerging structural forms

In the same way that emergent strategy almost inevitably builds upon rational strategy, so emerging structural forms build on and adapt the more traditional organisational structures discussed above. The emerging forms are reactive to the changes in societal expectations, globalisation and the ever-changing capabilities of technology.

4.1   Growth and change

While many organisations continue to operate very successfully using differing types of traditional organisational structure, adapting and evolving as required with their changing business requirements, the rapid change in societal expectation, transparency and the explosion in the use of internet and cloud-based technology requires us to consider the world as it is today, and how we can enable different types of organisational structure. Some of the drivers are identified in Figure 12.8.

Traditional		Empowered
Centralised		Devolved
Bureaucratic		Participative
Structured		Fluid

Figure 12.8 Drivers of structure
© Mark Wearden

- In a traditional structure we would expect to find a dominance of centralised and often bureaucratic control with clear lines of demarcation within a hierarchical structure.
- In an empowered structure we would expect to find devolved decision making at many different organisation levels, much greater participation and a far more fluid communication and accountability structure.

Lynch (2015) further identifies a number of environmental changes that have taken place which require this rethinking of organisational structure.

Early twentieth century	Early twenty-first century
– uneducated workers	– better education and at higher levels
– knowledge of simple engineering	– computer literacy and wider skills
– very early stages of technology	– complex, computer driven projects
– early concepts of management science and understanding of human behaviour	– sophisticated electronic engineering
– growing market expectations	– differing models of management and human behaviour researched and understood with greater overlap between differing hierarchical levels
– string separation between management and workforce	– radical growth in markets and market behaviour
	– ability to deal in intangibles (futures etc.)

Table 12.1
(Lynch, 2015) adapted by Mark Wearden)

4.2   Flexibility and innovation

Johnson et al. (2017) recognised three key challenges that 21st century organisations need to recognise and include within their business structures, business models and strategic thinking, and even these have evolved further since inclusion in their text:

◆   **The speed of change and increasing levels of uncertainty**: the ability of markets to react in an instant, and a change in perceived market values within seconds.

◆   **The importance of knowledge creation and sharing as a fundamental part of strategic success**: transparency is seen as a core stakeholder requirement.

◆   **An acceptance that markets recognise few geographic boundaries**: the evolution of multi-faith, multi-cultural societies requiring a wider appreciation and recognition of differing stakeholder expectations and levels of acceptability.

In more traditional structures, strategy and innovation were led from the top of the organisation, or through defined specialist functions. To enable organisational flexibility and the ability to respond rapidly and appropriately to stakeholder expectations, and to the required rate of technological response, organisations have had to learn to build flexible structures.

Atkinson (1984) developed a model of the flexible firm which required three dimensions of flexibility driven by market stagnation, job losses, economic uncertainty, technological change, and a reduction in the expected basic working hours of employees.

◆   **Functional flexibility**: the ability to redeploy employees quickly and smoothly between activities and tasks.

◆ **Numerical flexibility**: the ability to change the numbers of people required in line with the tasks being completed.

◆ **Financial flexibility**: the need for different methods of remunerating employees to enable the functional and numeric flexibility.

His model was an early recognition of the need for organisational structures to consider the tasks being undertaken by people other than the core group of employees.

Test yourself 12.3

What are the differences between an international division of a company and a transnational corporation?

4.3 Boundary-less organisations

The concept of a boundary-less organisation is of course in reality a misnomer. All organisations require some form of structure, not least to enable them to comply with laws, regulations and reporting requirements. The vision that emanates from the phrase boundary-less suggests unstructured chaos which clearly would not enable business success.

The term boundary-less instead suggests that while inevitable boundaries will have to exist, they can be significantly more flexible than in more traditional structures, with differing levels of people within the structure being given more autonomy to implement change and be accountable for such change.

The term boundary-less was first used in 1990 by Jack Welch, then chairman of the global corporation General Electric Corporation (GE), to describe his vision of a new organisational structure for GE. Since these early days the concept has been followed by many other global corporations, but also it has been used as an operating structure within many different sizes of business.

In *The Boundaryless Organisation* (1995) Askenas et al. explore further the idea of this concept. They suggest that what had been recognised by GE was:

> 'a social and economic revolution that is manifest in organisations as they shift from rigid to permeable organisational structures and processes'.

Through their consultancy work with GE and others, they recognised that the boundaryless concept was not a straight replacement for the more traditional and rigid forms of structure but was a recognition and flexing of the disconnections that existed across all organisational dynamics. They discuss four different dynamics which need to be flexible, either individually or jointly, and the strategic impacts that such an approach can drive within an organisation:

◆ **Vertical**: The hierarchical boundaries between people at different levels in the organisation. How can the CEO find out what the workshop engineer really thinks and vice versa?

◆ **Horizontal**: The silo boundaries that exist between different functions and departments. *The recognition of the internal chain impact (backwards and forwards) of decisions during the operational flow.*

◆ **External**: The micro-level boundaries that are placed between the organisation and its customers, suppliers and regulators. *By viewing them as external stakeholders we can treat them as an arms-length problem.*

◆ **Geographic**: The macro-level boundaries that exist between nations, cultures and markets. *An understanding of the need to behave differently within different cultures – one size does not fit all.*

A key conclusion was that the evolution of the boundaryless organisation aligns with the view ascribed to Mintzberg that the development of strategy needs to be based around emergent 'strategic thinking' rather than the more rational 'strategic planning'. Mintzberg (1994) suggested that:

> 'strategic thinking is what successful companies use to track changing social and economic trends, to assess their implications, to experiment with new ways of doing business, and to build on empirical experience. It is about synthesis. It involves intuition and creativity'.

Stop and think 12.7

How would you extend or open the boundaries of your organisation?

4.4 Modular structures and outsourcing

In his work discussed above, Atkinson (1984) had begun to explore the notion of a modular organisation structure, recognising the difference between core labour, peripheral labour and outsourced tasks.

Handy (1989) took this further and suggested that:

> 'While it may be convenient to have everyone around all of the time, having all your workforce's time at your command is an extravagant way of marshalling the necessary resources. It is cheaper to keep them outside the organisation ... and buy their services when you need them'.

He developed a simple 'shamrock' image to illustrate his point.

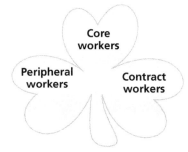

Figure 12.9 Handy's shamrock organisation

◆   The *core workers* are the full-time employees and provide a range of specialised professional, management and leadership functions across the organisation.

◆   The *peripheral workers* are part-time casual and freelance workers who are only utilised when the work requires them to be there. The ultimate form of this type of work is known as 'piece-work' where not only is the worker peripheral, but the remuneration is directly related to the output (e.g. a company growing and harvesting flowers in a field will often use casual labour being paid at a rate of £x per bunch forming a direct relationship between cost and productivity).

◆   The *contract workers* are outside of the core thrust of the firm and are paid for completion of certain routine tasks such as the overnight cleaning of premises, or at a different level the completion of a particular computer project.

In our rapidly changing labour markets, and the evolving people and organisation expectations of the Fourth Industrial Revolution we can see that the nature of the workforce as identified by Handy is altering. The concept of his mixture might well still be valid, but the nature of 'core workers' is changing to allow a more diversified and part-time workforce. This is further enhanced by the growth of the 'gig' economy with many people managing to work in two or more different roles, perhaps as a 'core worker' within one organisation, but then also as a 'peripheral worker' in another organisation. For example, a person with a part-time permanent core-worker role in a manufacturing business might also be delivering pizzas at night.

This is evolving even further, as discussed briefly in the next section.

4.5   Virtual structures

The rapid growth of technology and the ability to immediately communicate across the world has led to the growth of a totally different type of organisation. All of the prior organisational structures have the underlying assumption of a physical base where core operations are completed – even the emerging structures require the need to refer back to a tangible centre.

The virtual organisation structure is held together through partnership, collaboration, networking and increasingly the maximisation of the use of technology. Organisations such as Dell Computers, Nike and Reebok operate successful businesses without directly owning any of their own manufacturing facilities.

Internet communications have allowed the development of virtual organisations, where the leadership and administrative centre sits 'in the cloud' and although the thrust of the business might outsource manufactured products from tangible businesses, the organisational structure has only a 'net' existence.

Case study 12.5

Extracts from 'How to manage the gig economy's growing global jobs market', Sarah O'Connor, FT.com, 30 October 2018 (www.ft.com/content/5fe8991e-dc2a-11e8-8f50-cbae5495d92b)

'The gig economy is facilitating the rise of a global marketplace for online labour. For good or ill, this is a new strain of globalisation in its rawest form. When most people imagine the gig economy, they probably think of companies such as Uber or Deliveroo – apps that connect customers to nearby workers to do physical tasks like driving and delivery. It is easy to see why these companies have been in the limelight. They are vast and visible. Everyone can see how they have upended the traditional employment relationship.

But there is another type of gig economy platform that focuses on service sector work that is done remotely. Individuals and companies break up a job into a series of tasks or assignments – anything from data entry or translation to coding or copywriting. Workers, who can be anywhere in the world, place "bids" to do the work on offer. Think of eBay – but for human labour. This side of the gig economy, sometimes called the "human cloud", is growing apace. Plenty of people in developed countries find work on these sites, but it should not surprise anyone to learn that a sizeable chunk is going to the developing world where the cost of living is lower.

You can make a good case for the human cloud. It gives talented people in developing countries the opportunity to access global demand for their skills, when local markets are limited. The same might be true for people living in economically depressed regions of rich countries. This unlocks human potential that may otherwise be squandered. It also allows people to work from home – so long as they have the internet – in countries where poor infrastructure can mean gruelling commutes.

But there are dangers too.

◆ The first is inherent in any form of globalisation: workers in richer countries can find themselves undercut by competitors in poorer places. Online gig workers also reported long working hours, often overnight because of time zone differences. As freelancers, they have no employment protections.

◆ Governments will struggle to gather tax revenue from all this economic activity happening in people's bedrooms.

◆ Policymakers, too, have a chance to intervene to shape the future of this new world of work while it is in its infancy. The danger is that they are so busy grappling with the consequences of the last wave of globalisation that they fail to see the next one coming.'

5. Determining appropriate structures

Two things should be apparent from this exploration of different types of structure:

1. There is no one ideal structure that will definitely enable all organisations to achieve their strategic objectives.
2. It is important for every organisation to determine an optimal structure for its operations at any particular point in time, but to continually challenge and be aware of the need for flexibility and structural evolution when required.

This is not to suggest that an organisation needs its structure to exist in a state of constantly changing fluidity, but that those leading the organisation must ensure a process exists to keep relevant drivers of change on the radar, so that change can be proactive rather than reactive, a thought-through action rather than a knee-jerk reaction.

Handy (1993) argues that structural form results from the competing pressures of uniformity and diversity.

Uniformity	Diversity
– economies of scale	– differing stakeholder goals
– procedure interchangeability	– product differentiation
– control processes	– changing consumer demands
– homogeneity of products	– technological change
– specialisations	– need for experimentation
– central control	– decentralised control

Table 12.2 Handy's structural form

The core questions for an organisation to ask are identified by Lynch (2015) and align with the core questions that sit behind the development of strategy:

◆ What kind of organisation are we, and do we want to be anything different? *commercial, profit-making non-profit-making, charitable, co-operative, government etc.*
◆ Who are the influential stakeholders? *owners, directors, managers, employees, customers, suppliers, banks, environment etc.*
◆ What is our purpose? *vision, objectives, goals, success factors etc.*

This aligns with our earlier discussions of an extended supply chain.

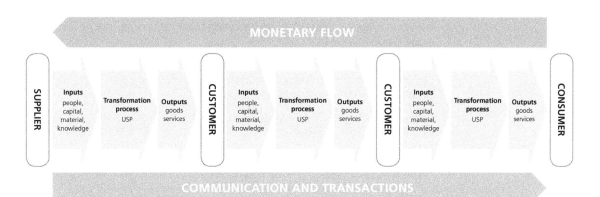

Figure 12.10 Supply chain flows
© Mark Wearden

◆ Where does our supply chain fit within the complete supply chain for our output?

◆ What influences us as an organisation?

◆ What type of structure do we need?

◆ What type of structure will be expected by our stakeholders?

Mintzberg (1979) proposed that there are four main environmental characteristics which influence the strategic appropriateness of different organisational structures. He suggested that these will result in six main types of organisational structure:

◆ entrepreneurial

◆ machine

◆ professional

◆ divisionalised

◆ innovative

◆ missionary.

Figure 12.11
((Mintzberg, H., 1979) adapted by Mark Wearden)

How do we know whether we are operating the most appropriate organisational structure?

Goold and Campbell (2002) proposed that there are nine different tests that we can apply to consider this question, based on our concept and perception of what is happening within an organisation.

Test	Basis
Market advantage	Does the structure enable strategic market focus?
Parenting advantage	Is the corporate centre adding value?
People	Is the potential of the employees maximised?
Feasibility	Are all legal and regulatory expectations recognised?
Specialised cultures	Is the input of specialists recognised and allowed for?
Difficult links	How does the structure enable communication challenge?
Redundant hierarchy	Are there too many layers of control?
Accountability	Are the lines of accountability transparent and clear?
Flexibility	How is a change in strategic drivers recognised and challenged?

Table 12.3
((Goold and Campbell) adapted by Mark Wearden)

Test yourself 12.4

What is meant by the concept of a boundary-less organisation?

Chapter summary

◈   This chapter examines a range of different types of organisational structure and form, considering their advantages and disadvantages, and challenging students to think about how and when each type might be appropriate.

◈   Organisation structure is intrinsically linked to the systems structure and the culture structure that exists within any organisation. The required structure may be leveraged to the supply-chain position or the stakeholder expectations.

◈   It is important for every organisation to determine whether strategy comes before structure or structure before strategy. The reality is that this will almost always be a moving emphasis and an iterative process.

◆　It is important to recognise the core, more traditional types of structural form to enable them to be challenged and re-considered in the light of today's emerging and often technology-driven structural forms.

◆　Multinational and transnational structural forms will require a number of particular dimensions to be satisfied to enable national and cultural compliance and expectations.

◆　The concept of a boundary-less organisation needs to be understood and considered to enable a challenge to be levied at the more traditional closed-boundary structures. It is also important to consider how boundaries can still be maintained in today's internet and cloud-driven world of technology.

◆　The company secretary and governance professional needs to be able to stand back and consider the structural form of their organisation; how it influences behaviour and culture; its strengths and weaknesses from a 'today' position; and how it could, should or must change to enable the achievement of the strategic objectives and the realisation of the vision.

Chapter thirteen
Strategic control and performance management

Contents

1. Introduction

The 12 previous chapters of this text have built a cumulative picture covering a breadth of dimensions that are required for an organisation to develop and deliver strategy. The role of people and their thought processes have a core focus at every stage. Even in today's developing world of artificial intelligence there is a strong reliance on the cognitive ability of the people behind the programming, the people behind the process design and the people who review the ultimate outcomes and conclusions of an unimaginable number of iterative loops.

In the final two chapters of the text, Chapters 14 and 15, we will be considering a number of the drivers, dynamics and restraints of strategic change – both process and people.

This chapter will review:

◆ how we should interpret and understand the outcomes of our various considerations of strategy

◆ how we should control, review and sometimes pre-empt the process of strategic change; the risks we perceive during the change; and the ultimate impact of that change

◆ how we need to take a holistic view of the process when monitoring and assessing the entire process of the development of strategy

◆ how we can gauge the efficiency and the effectiveness of our strategy

◆ how we need to interpret all aspects of the process from different perspectives.

Case study 13.1

Extract from Unilever plc Annual Report and Financial Statements 2017:

'C4G, our largest organisational change programme in more than a decade, was fully implemented during 2017 with the benefits to be realised progressively during 2018 and 2019. C4G encourages and equips people to adopt an owner's mindset by giving them more control through a simplified organisational and reward structure. An owner's mindset means more ownership and collaboration, clarity of purpose, more test and learn, embracing failure to gain insight, and an obsession with customers and consumers – ultimately driving long-term value creation and financial rewards for our employees. This mindset hands teams in local markets responsibility for business results. They are encouraged to treat resources as if they were their own, helping ensure we maintain the highest levels of efficiency.'

2. Strategy, risk and control

In Chapter 7 during the consideration of governance we introduced a model aligning strategy, risk and control based on Principle O of the 2018 UK Corporate Governance Code:

'The board should establish procedures to manage risk, oversee the internal control framework, and determine the nature and extent of the principal risks the company is willing to take in order to achieve its long-term strategic objectives'.

Figure 13.1 Strategy, risk and control
© Mark Wearden

This alignment needs directors and strategic decision-makers to step back from the immediate demands of the business operation and take time to reflect, consider, debate and challenge the strategic objectives that they are aiming to fulfil. The principles around this suggest that a strategic plan is required to change from the status quo:

◆ **Strategy: setting the direction**

   – There will inevitably be significant risks on all sides.

◆ **Risk: the dangers along the route**

   – Different players need to consider the risks and impact, and then implement measures of control to protect the stakeholder assets and deliver sustainable value.

◆ **Control: intelligent parameters**

   – Control therefore sits as a fundamental aspect of strategy:

      – We need to understand where we are heading – the strategic vision.

      – We need to determine the dangers of the change – the perceived risks.

      – We need to understand the drivers of success – the required control parameters.

It is important for organisations to develop appropriate methods and tools to enable the ongoing monitoring of the various strategies that will be taking place simultaneously, and to find a way of alerting themselves when the journey is moving outside the perceived parameters. In our age of increasing transparency, it is essential that the results of the monitoring at various stages are recorded and reported. This helps with the analysis of gaps, but also can act as an audit trail of action if the organisation and its directors and officers are challenged.

The basis of emergent strategy is that there will be the need to react and change the original plans, but the purpose of monitoring and control and its subsequent reporting is to attempt to ensure that this is done in a considered manner rather than through a reaction to the perpetual changes in the internal, micro and macro environment.

We will split this into four perspectives within the structure of this chapter, as shown in Figure 13.2.

◆ **Analysis**: methods to understand what is happening and why (section 4 on performance and effectiveness).

◆ **Audit**: oversight and professional review and reporting of what has happened (section 5 on the nature of management control).

◆ **Assessment**: the alignment of the differing **levers of control** (section 6 on strategic control, concept and models).

◆ **Assurance**: our accountability to stakeholders (section 7 on using a balanced scorecard).

levers of control
The understanding that the alignment of the choices that we make will influence the outcome of the future and of our strategy. In simple form, a light switch is a lever of control – we determine whether the light is on or off.

Figure 13.2 Control logic
© Mark Wearden

3. Implementation of strategy

We have considered in detail the differing aspects and interaction of today and the future. To place our control logic into context requires us to revisit this concept. Remember that the 'strategic journey' model reflects time as a perpetually moving dimension. Your 'today' point has already moved forward from when you started to read these chapters. As the 'future' is reached, it becomes the today point.

Control therefore can only ever realistically be implemented based on our knowledge of today, in anticipation of the future. This is the purpose of risk analysis, the assessment of today aligned with what might happen within a forecasted scenario.

As we move from today into the unknown, we will encounter risks; some of these will be the risks that we have perceived might occur, and some will be unexpected. In both cases the decisions we make will be based upon our analysis of today, as we are required to react to the apparent risk, danger or a change in the external or internal environment.

Every day we are implementing strategy, in our personal lives and within our organisations. Life is lived in the operational circle where we are either implementing, monitoring or adjusting. This is what each of us spends our life doing.

The control measure for the actions of ourselves, and others, is the perimeter of that circle, and that exists as a direct result of previous strategic considerations. That perimeter has been set as a boundary within which we and others are able to take a measure of control for our daily actions.

Case study 13.2

We go to catch a train to work, but find it has been cancelled, so we take the bus instead; we can control this, the perimeter is the expectation from our employer that we will get to work.

We are asked to prepare a board paper on control of risk – we will have our own ideas, but the length of the paper, the type of language we use, the format or house-style of the paper will be part of the organisational perimeter. We can structure ideas within that format, but to move outside that format would require the strategic intervention of someone else, unless we are prepared to take the risk of challenging the status quo and suggesting that the perimeter of operation has been wrongly set.

These might seem simplistic concepts, but that is the most effective way to consider the development of effective and efficient strategic control.

Stop and think 13.1

Key learning: we are surrounded by a perimeter of expected control

Perimeter – dictionary definition:

'a continuous line forming the boundary of a closed figure'

◆ Think about your next 24 hours – business and personal.

◆ What are the measures that will restrict and control your actions and behaviour?

◆ Consider the strategic processes that have taken place in the past to establish the perimeters which are now restricting your actions.

4. Performance and effectiveness – concepts, issues and approaches

4.1   Taking an analysis perspective

Strategic control requires an analytical understanding of the status quo within an organisation, both at the outset of the strategy and at the point where objectives appear to have been realised.

Our development of strategy has enabled us to derive objectives and goals which have been turned into actual tasks for us and others to complete. The word 'performance' is used to describe the actual working out on a perpetual basis of that strategic intent. As all strategy exists in the unknown of the future, we need to be able to analyse, assess and measure how the actual performance compares to the strategic perception. Two phrases are frequently interchanged to achieve this, but it is important for the company secretary and governance professional to be able to differentiate between these:

◆ **Organisational effectiveness**: does the performance enable the realisation of the organisation's strategic goals?

◆ **Organisational efficiency**: has the performance made optimal use of the stakeholder resources in the implementation of the strategic plan?

We need to further consider how we are going to assess both the effectiveness and the efficiency, as both of these concepts can be considered and measured from qualitative and quantitative perspectives:

◆ **Qualitative**: a consideration of performance from the collection and consideration of narrative data (human views and opinions) – often referred to as a subjective approach.

◆ **Quantitative**: a consideration of performance from the collection and consideration of numerical data – often referred to as an objective approach.

Case study 13.3

Consider how you would differentiate between effectiveness and efficiency when describing the chaos that occurred on the opening day of Heathrow Terminal 5.

Terminal 5 at Heathrow airport was conceived as one of the most technologically advanced airport terminals in the world, but the opening day for the new £4.3 billion investment was generally considered to be disastrous, despite many people praising the magnificence of the new building. The new baggage facility was capable of handling 12,000 bags an hour, but by early afternoon there were long queues of people waiting as long as two-and-a-half hours for their luggage, and a backlog of 15,000 bags. Thirty-four short-haul and domestic flights were cancelled.

It was accepted that there were serious problems with staff familiarisation with the terminal, its layout and its equipment – one passenger who was trying to find the departure lounge commented that he had been given 'six different directions by six different people'. Twenty-eight out of 275 lifts were not working. Staff had problems finding sufficient car-park spaces and had trouble getting through the new enhanced security systems. During the first five days of operation, more than 23,000 bags were misplaced, and 500 flights were cancelled losing British Airways around £16 million.

The late Peter Drucker is quoted as having said 'you can't manage what you can't measure'. The problem with this quote is that it is too often interpreted as suggesting that all control needs to be quantitative, and people often rely on an organisation's accounting system and figures to provide control data. Think back to our many earlier discussions on strategic drivers, the numeric (quantitative) measures were only ever a small part of the overall strategic vision. They may support and justify some of the risks that can be taken to achieve the strategic objectives, but they are rarely, if ever, the strategic goals or objectives in themselves.

In the assessment of any organisation, it is important to understand:

◆   how to measure and assess performance and behaviour

◆   the different levels at which such performance and behaviour can be measured

◆   what is going to change as a result of having made the measurement and assessment.

This raises some core questions:

◆   How is the effectiveness and the efficiency of the organisation going to be controlled?

◆   What comparative criteria and benchmarks are going to be applied?

◆   What is going to be measured and when?

◆   At what level within the organisation will such measures be taken?

Test yourself 13.1

Differentiate between strategy, risk and control in the context of strategic control and performance management.

4.2   Areas to evaluate and measure

Evaluation of performance will need to be related to the original drivers of the strategy:

◆   Were there certain specific objectives or goals which needed to be met?

◆   Was there a particular manner in which such objectives or goals needed to be met?

◆   Were there other criteria which the strategy presumed would be delivered?

At the high level, this could be separated into:

◆   **Financial measures**

–   Profitability – has the performance delivered the anticipated return in line with the projected benchmark or target?

–   Liquidity – has the performance delivered the anticipated liquidity?

–   Wealth – has the performance delivered the anticipated longer-term wealth for shareholders and stakeholders?

◆ **Productivity measures**

- People – is the existing human resource being used to enable individuals to work to their full potential?

- Product – is the product or service in line with the organisational and stakeholder quality and performance expectations?

- Resources – are all resources being utilised at their optimal level?

There is no generic answer as to what specifically needs to be measured or when it needs to be measured. Each organisation will need to determine its own appropriate measures from within its own business model. Although by way of an example, companies are required to report their annual financial figures within a formalised 'financial reporting' structure governed by accounting standards, the internal financial measurements of control will vary greatly between organisations.

Stop and think 13.2

What is meant by profit or margin?

At its most straightforward, this should mean excess of income over expenditure, and it should be a useful financial control measure – but it all depends at what level this is being measured and understood by any particular organisation.

There is no standard definition of the following terms, so there can be confusion if any are being applied as a control measure without the full understanding of all interested parties – gross profit, operating profit, net profit, operating margin, contribution, etc.

The confusion is further compounded by the introduction of acronyms such as EBITDA – earnings before interest, tax, depreciation and amortisation – much used by analysts and journalists and supposedly a measure that is comparable between companies, but each aspect is highly subjective:

1. **Earnings – do we mean just the revenue stream?**

2. **Interest – is this net interest paid or gross interest paid?**

3. **Tax – do we mean the tax paid in the year, or the tax accrual for the year?**

4. **Depreciation and amortisation – even with the fair value reporting standard, the assessment of 'fair' is a very individualistic concept within each company.**

The development of control within any organisation requires measures to be developed which are in themselves:

◆ Effective: they deliver meaningful awareness of operational performance which can influence future strategy.

◆ Efficient: they are understood by all users and are based on easily obtainable and accurate data.

Think about how this looks from the Porter value-chain perspective – where do we need to put the analysis so that we understand actual and imminent deviation from the strategic plan?

Figure 13.3
((Porter, 1980) adapted by Mark Wearden)

4.3 Goals

If we are setting strategic goals, then these should be a clear way of measuring both progress along the strategic path and ultimate success. This is referred to as an output measure. Its usefulness as a control measure will depend on the clarity and precision of individual goals.

Stop and think 13.3

Consider the level of precision with which the following goals could be assessed:

1. **our goal is to increase our sales**
2. **our goal is to improve our operating margin through increased sales**
3. **our goal is to generate a cash surplus of at least £80million in the next 12 months**
4. **our goal is to help others through running a socially sustainable business.**

In his text *Organisational Theory and Design*, Richard Daft (2013) argues that sometimes organisational goals may be in conflict with each other. He suggests the following goals as an example:

◆   profitability
◆   market share

◆ growth
◆ product quality
◆ social responsibility.

It would be easy to imagine a scenario where *market share* was *growing* and delivering an increasing *profit*, but only through a reduction of standards and hence *product quality* resulting in a reduction in *social responsibility* through the distribution of unfit products.

In the development of strategy, it is important that the goals are aligned with each other with a clear recognition of mutual impact.

4.4 Resources

An alternative approach to organisational control is to consider how effectively the stakeholder resources are being used. This is referred to as an input measure and assumes that an organisation will derive success through maximising the efficient use of the resources that it is feeding into its transformation process.

A useful way to consider this is to think back to the reporting expectations of the International Integrated Reporting Council (IIRC) discussed in Chapter 8 and represented in their reporting model. The reporting organisation is required to consider the inputs into its system and then reflect on how its business model has transformed those resources into outputs.

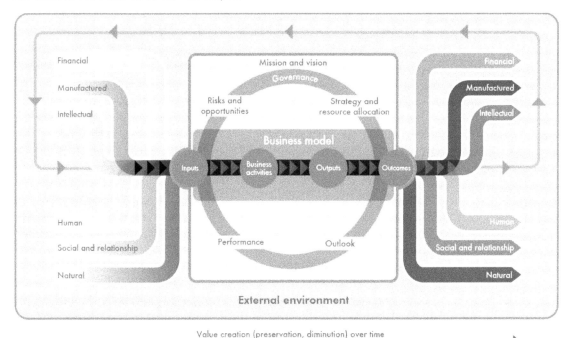

Figure 13.4 IIRC reporting framework
© International Integrated Reporting Council

The IIRC core objective is one of sustainability requiring the organisation to demonstrate that it is holistically delivering more than it consumes, but the principle is a useful way of considering resources as a control measure.

4.5   Stakeholder influence

Dependent on the organisation's structure, the goals and objectives may be set by differing stakeholders, with clear measures of control built in to their expectations and based around their anticipated return on their 'stake'.

Daft (2013) researched the impact of the following stakeholder expectations as measures of effectiveness, finding that organisations sometimes experienced difficulty in satisfying all seven stakeholder expectations at the same time, requiring the strategist to consider prioritisation for the anticipated performance of the organisation.

Stakeholder	Effectiveness criteria
Owners	Financial return
Employees	Worker satisfaction, pay, supervision
Customers	Quality of goods and services
Creditors	Creditworthiness
Community	Contribution to community affairs
Suppliers	Satisfactory transactions
Government	Compliance with laws and regulation

It should be clear from this section that the criteria which determine effectiveness and efficiency may differ greatly from organisation to organisation, driven by the particular mix of stakeholder expectation and management abilities. Transparency and accurate and timely reporting are essential to deliver sustainability.

Case study 13.4

In 2008, issues were raised about higher than average mortality rates in patients admitted as emergencies to Stafford Hospital. A subsequent investigation suggested that inappropriate cost-cutting had been made in certain areas of the hospital, in an attempt to meet budgets and deliver financial efficiency, with a lack of transparency as to the real potential impact of such measures.

An independent government commission report into this case concluded that it would be unsafe to directly align the perceived high levels of mortality and the financial cost-cutting, although the report did comment on an attempt by the hospital trust to save £10 million in 2006/07:

'The board decided this saving could only be achieved through cutting staffing levels which were already insufficient'.

5. The nature of management control

5.1   Taking an audit perspective

The concept and the need for audit underpins what we are trying to achieve in our ability to understand and control performance. The origin of the word is the Latin word '*audire*' which has a breadth of different meanings. At its simplest it means to '*hear*', but it also means to '*listen*', and more importantly it means to '*understand*'. The alignment of these three requirements – hear, listen and understand – requires us to assess the data and information with which we are presented. We need to have confidence in the integrity of that data and information to the point where we are content that we are dealing with certainty. This will at least partly be based around our judgement of the integrity of the originating source of the data, and the level of bias that is associated with the judgement we make.

5.2   Control methods

In Chapter 3 we discussed the concept of systems thinking and the need to be able to view an organisation as a system, with its interaction and relationship between the different elements working within the organisational boundary. We need to consider this from two related but different dimensions to consider how we insert control into the system.

◈   **Internal awareness**: in what is known as a *single-loop system*, there is a straight iteration around the system, the control sits as part of the problem solving and is built into the system itself. For example:

  – a machine will automatically switch off if certain criteria are not fulfilled

  – a strategy has a goal requiring delivery of a certain volume, production ceases when that volume is met.

Figure 13.5 Single-loop learning
© Mark Wearden

◈   **External awareness**: however, in a *double-loop system*, and this type of system will usually involve many more than just two loops (iterations), there is an external sense-check built into the system which is required before it is allowed to continue. For example:

  – a machine recognises that certain criteria are not fulfilled, and alerts the operator who can then decide whether to proceed or not

  – a strategy has a goal requiring delivery of a certain volume, when that volume is met, the operational team are required to consider whether there is commercial benefit in producing a higher volume.

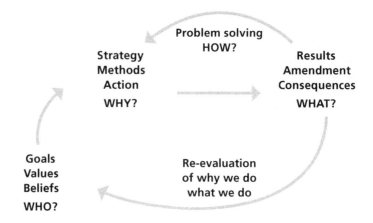

Figure 13.6 Double-loop learning
© Mark Wearden

5.3   Organisational metaphors

In his book *Creative Problem Solving* Robert Flood (1991) suggests the use of a number of different metaphors to help us to understand a range of different types of control and behaviour that exist within our organisational systems. In our age of technology, we take systems for granted at many levels, often without thinking about the implications.

It can be useful to find alternative methods of standing back and reviewing the type of organisational control system that we are relying upon. Flood's metaphors, or you own metaphors, can help you and others to challenge what is happening around them.

> metaphor
> – A figure of speech in which a word or phrase is applied to an object or action to which it is not literally applicable.
> – A thing regarded as representative or symbolic of something else.

Flood argues that each of the five metaphors below will help us to consider the type of qualities that we may be looking for when we start to examine systems more deeply in a business context. Flood is not suggesting that this is an exclusive list, but rather that the variations generated by these thoughts will help us to stretch our brains more laterally to enable a wider understanding.

MACHINE metaphor
◆   Flood describes this as a 'closed system' single-loop view.
◆   Organisational examples (from Flood): the armed forces, fast food chains.

There are predefined inputs and outputs.

A machine is designed to work, you push the button and it operates, in a continuous and repetitive manner, to deliver one or more pre-defined outcomes.

There is a strong reliance on the efficiency of the parts of the machine, which simply need replacing when they wear out or fail. The control can be built in as part of the system.

ORGANIC metaphor

- Flood describes this as an 'open system' double-loop view.
- Organisational examples (from Flood): most industrial businesses.

The inputs can be determined, but the outputs will evolve.

This represents a direct challenge to the machine view particularly when one or more of the 'parts' of the machine is a person. Motivation theories and human resource thinking clearly illustrate that people do not easily comply with a machine philosophy, not least because different brains react in different ways to the same set of stimuli. The parts of the system are likely to regenerate and rethink themselves to ensure continuity. The organic system within such organisations needs to allow for a range of objective controls.

BRAIN metaphor

- Flood uses the word 'neurocybernetic' rather than 'brain' and suggests this is a particular category of 'open system' with a keen focus on 'viability'.
- Organisation examples (from Flood): autonomous work groups, innovative industrial firms, consultancy firms.

The inputs can be manipulated to ensure that the outputs are delivered, but the outputs themselves are likely to also be manipulated. The human brain is itself seen as a control system, which will reactively and proactively bring about changes to the operation of the system. As with the brain, the system needs to have the ability to teach itself to learn and build its own methods of controls, based upon objective external stimuli.

CULTURE metaphor

- Flood uses the word 'culture' as a metaphor for the unspoken, familiar ways of thinking and acting in all organisations.
- Organisational examples (from Flood): high-technology firms, competitive individualism, machine-like military structures.

The inputs may be selected based upon the culture criteria, then the engine of the organisation will operate in a manner dictated by the beliefs, practices and evolving norms of the organisation. Firms in identical markets can behave very differently based upon the underlying culture. Bower's phrase 'The way we do things around here' (1966) has been used by many to epitomise the meaning of culture, and from a systems perspective, emphasises the need to understand the 'connections between the parts' discussed in our previous consideration of systems.

A reconsideration of the impact of culture, in particular its effect on corporate governance needs to be considered as discussed in Chapters 6 and 7. In a recent Financial Reporting Council (FRC) report 'Corporate Culture and The Role of Boards' (2016), the opening paragraph suggests:

'There needs to be a concerted effort to improve trust in the motivations and integrity of business. Rules and sanctions clearly have their place but will not on their own deliver productive behaviours over the long-term. This report looks at the increasing importance which corporate culture plays in determining long-term business and economic success'

POLITICAL metaphor
◆   Flood uses the 'political' metaphor to describe the pursuit of power by individuals and the impact this has on organisational relationships.
◆   Organisational examples (from Flood): all organisations show examples of political activity.

It is interesting to consider why Flood uses the metaphor of 'political' as a separate system structure, when clearly even he recognises that it exists within all systems where people are involved. The reason for the separation in thought is to consider how the 'political' systems at play frequently influence, damage and drive the effectiveness of the other four metaphorical systems. The influence of the individual will ultimately drive success. The politics can skew the control output and communication to others.

Stop and think 13.4

Look at the headlines in today's business pages and find your own case example for one or more of these metaphors.

Consider the meaning of the words being used, consider the controls that should be in place within the reported organisations, and consider how and why the journalist has taken a particular stance on the story.

Determine where the real control lies within the organisation.

5.4 Leadership and control

The assertion here is that effective control in the strategic thinking process needs to be aligned with achieving the right balance in the governance process. What matters for control is the real impact of the type of governance which can realistically and practically oversee the running of any size and type of organisation on a periodic basis.

The governance 'balance' will differ within every organisation and will continue to vary as the external environment, the organisation and the people evolve. Control sits as part of the strategic or formal framework which creates the 'balance', and together with the triangulation of strategy, risk and control we need to consider the organisation's reputation.

If the reputation of an organisation is one of efficiency, then one would expect to find effective control. If an organisation is known for its poor standards and inefficiency of operation, then one would expect to find poor and inadequate controls and a negative reputation.

The structure requires a challenging balance of differing leadership skills:

◆   Experienced players: people who understand what they are dealing with.

◆   Lateral thinkers: people who have the ability to think beyond the obvious.

◆   Intelligent listeners: people who will audit (hear, listen, understand) the views of others.

◆   Determined challengers: people who are prepared to formulate and ask the difficult questions.

◆   Independent unbiased and objective leaders with certain specific and relevant knowledge and skill sets (this is often the expectation of non-executive director (NEDs)).

◆   Leaders who are prepared to lead the process as effective leaders of committees and boards (chair).

Simons (1994) argues that to really understand whether we have appropriate and effective controls around and within our strategic thinking and the emanating risks, we need to understand the differing levers of control within an organisation. These, like an optimal 'balance', will differ between organisations, but there are a number of generic concepts that can be applied:

◆   **Beliefs**

–   These are the core values within an organisation.

–   There is the need to understand how and why value is created, so where the controls need to be placed.

–   There is the need to understand the human relationships within the organisation and the differing communication methods and systems – how do people know what they are meant to be doing?

◆   **Boundaries**

–   Every organisation will have its 'current' pre-defined limits and parameters.

–   The strategic boundaries will define the journey and need for appropriate control measures.

–   The implementation of control, and the autocratic or consultative approach to compliance will have particular significance when boundaries are broken – how do people know if they have taken too much initiative?

◆   **People interaction**

–   The people interactivity requires a system thinking approach to be able to visualise how the organisation actually works.

–   The difference between what is happening and what should be happening can require a gap analysis approach.

–   This will often be aligned to the power culture that exists – and the identification of who makes the core decisions – how do we people know who has the power and authority to make decisions?

◆   **Feedback monitoring**

- There is the need to understand what happens when a control system alarm is activated – who does what, how and why.

- There is no point in having diagnostic controls that are just ignored – 'Oh don't worry, that alarm often goes off'.

- There needs to be an assurance that feedback is taken seriously – how do people know when to deliver feedback and who they should deliver it to?

5.5 Power and control

Traditional autocratic organisations would restrict power and control to those in positions of seniority. As the theory and practice of organisational behaviour has evolved, so has the growth of empowerment at differing levels within organisations. There has been a wide recognition that control can often be most effective when used directly at the source of the problem, or change that is required, rather than waiting for a reactive response after the event.

The importance of having clarity of where the control lies is clear from the following dispute.

Case study 13.5

Extract from FT.com, 7 November 2018 (www.ft.com/content/23ba0376-e2ae-11e8-8e70-5e22a430c1ad)

'Contracts signed between the Post Office and sub-postmasters showed an "imbalance" of power, a court heard on Wednesday, as a legal fight involving the government-owned company got under way. The trial at the High Court in London centres on the Post Office's Horizon computer system, which a group of 550 current and former sub-postmasters claim caused accounting discrepancies relating to business transactions for which they were wrongly held responsible.

They allege that problems with the software led to accusations of theft, fraud and false accounting against sub-postmasters by the Post Office, with some individuals prosecuted or forced into bankruptcy after they were told to repay thousands of pounds linked to the accounting errors. A small number of sub-postmasters went to jail.'

5.6 Structure and control

The growth of enterprise resource planning (ERP) systems, such as that provided by the company SAP, and similar levels of advanced technology within many organisations has led to a different level of expectation around control. ERP systems are structured to place direct control, with sometimes significant room for interpretation, within the hands of the different people using the system across an organisation.

The end results will be quantitative and financial and monitored through audit and risk control structures, but the level of control allowed by such software structures is designed to deliver more effective end-to-end control within an organisation on an immediate rather than a retrospective basis.

Historic 'legacy' systems delivered control data at the end of an operational cycle – *an audit firm realises after completing an audit that the time consumed has not been fully recovered in the fee being charged.*

An ERP system allows ongoing control – *the same audit firm realises early in the audit process that time is being consumed faster than anticipated and can either adjust accordingly or renegotiate the fee with the client.*

The nature of data capture and data efficiency can lead to different perspectives and problems of structure and control as suggested in the next case example.

Case study 13.6

Extract from FT.com, 1 November 2018 (www.ft.com/content/7adbdb04-c1be-11e8-84cd-9e601db069b8)

'Ever since employees began clocking in and out on punch cards, companies have captured data on their workers. Now, new workplace technologies – from smart badges that track office interactions, to sensors monitoring truck drivers' performance – are generating mountains of data on workers. But while this can increase safety and efficiency, some worry it could also result in unfair or abusive practices. "It can cut both ways," says Jeremias Prassl, Oxford university associate professor of law. He cites the wristbands that track the movement of workers shifting packages around a warehouse. "If it plots the most efficient line for you, that's good. But if the same algorithm bullies workers into working extra hard, that's bad." Moreover, as in the case of consumer data, a lack of clarity hangs over the question of who owns workplace data and what is being done with it. Some argue that giving workers more control over their data could bolster their negotiating power on conditions and pay rates.'

Test yourself 13.2

Suggest the meaning of and identify an organisation, or type of organisation, which could be aligned with the metaphors of a) machine-control, and b) brain-control.

6. Strategic control, concept and models

6.1   Aligning control with strategy – taking an assessment perspective

A question that is often asked about control in many organisations and situations is 'why does it matter?'. The reason is that we are all accountable to someone. Within any organisation, we will be required to deliver effective control and governance to give assurance to our stakeholders that the levels of control are appropriate.

The FRC (2014) suggests that:

> 'The board should establish the tone for risk management and internal controls ...'

> 'The board should identify what assurance it requires and, where there are gaps, how these should be addressed'

At the top of any organisation, listed company, private company, third sector organisation, charity, etc., those empowered with the governance have to establish the appropriate levels of control to deliver stakeholder assurance. This cannot be formulaic, generic or simply a box-ticking approach. As discussed in Chapter 7, governance needs to be focused and relevant to each individual organisation. There will need to be a cost–benefit justification for governance activity – *through this method we deliver this for the stakeholders*.

Throughout our process of the development of strategy, we will have developed an appreciation of stakeholder expectations, and in the same way that our route and risks will have been influenced by differing forces, stakeholder expectations will also change.

The use of a double-loop learning control structure as referred to above allows us to build a far more effective control structure. It will build the people dynamic into the control structure and ensures that every aspect of control is sense-checked against the goals, values and beliefs of the people – the need to understand why they behave and react in the way that they do.

A traditional single feedback loop would move through three stages in a one-way loop.

Figure 13.7 Control 1
((Dess et al., 2014) adapted by Mark Wearden)

Dess et al. (2014) suggest that a more effective control structure is delivered by a realignment of these three core aspects of the development of strategy.

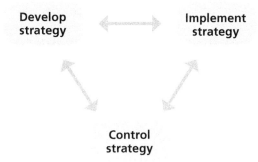

Figure 13.8 Control 2
((Dess et al., 2014) adapted by Mark Wearden)

◆   The linkage between *development* and *control* relies upon appropriate levels of information – is the organisation 'doing the right things'?

◆   The linkage between *implementation* and *control* relies upon the behaviour of the people within the organisation – is the organisation 'doing things right'?

The informational and behavioural aspects of strategic control are both required but are not sufficient within themselves. This control structure itself sits within the micro and macro environments referred to earlier in the text.

Effective control will only come from periodic and regular challenge and review of the strategic environment to ensure that the strategic direction and parameters are still relevant. This requires a continuous process of monitoring, reviewing and testing (together with the reporting of those results to the control structure on a timely basis), and the development of appropriate tools to enable this to happen.

6.2 Different types of control process

Simons (1995) suggested that there are four main characteristics that are required from an effective control system:

◆   A focus on and capture of the constantly changing informational demands of senior managers and their potential strategic importance.

◆   A recognition that control information must be important enough to demand frequent and regular attention from operating managers at all organisational levels.

◆   The need to interpret, discuss and challenge the generated data and information in face-to-face meetings between differing levels of an organisational hierarchy.

◆   The control system itself should be seen as a key catalyst for the ongoing debate about the validity of underlying data, assumptions and plans.

The common denominator in Simons' view is the need for people within an organisation at differing levels to take an active role through the challenging of all aspects of the strategy process – development, implementation and delivery of goals. The organisation needs to develop the right questions, it is impossible to be prescriptive here, but the creative use of the core six question words can provide a useful starting point for the company secretary and governance professional.

Who	can make changes to process?
	provides the data and information?
	can we trust?
What	do we need to review?
	are we trying to prove?
	do we hope to see?
When	should we collect the data?
	do we need an answer?
	can we make a strategic change?
Where	do we need to look?
	do we expect problems?
	should we place the controls?
How	do we distinguish fact and fiction?
	do we prioritise stakeholder expectations?
	do we maintain viability?
Why	do we need to introduce control measures?
	is our system structured in this way?
	do we believe we have the right questions and control measures?

Table 13.1 Core control questions
© Mark Wearden

6.3   HACCP

The use of a hazard analysis and critical control points (HACCP) approach is prevalent particularly within the food sector, but has useful control principles for other organisations. In the food sector, it is an industry expectation and is seen as a systematic and preventive approach to food safety, in particular the isolation of contamination from biological, chemical and physical hazards that might exist within the production process.

The control is a double-loop iterative approach requiring:

◆   An analysis and understanding of all stages in a production process.

◆   The identification of critical control points – where are the points where damage and risk are likely to occur and where might this affect the quality of the food and the process?

- The establishment of crucial limits and parameters – acceptable levels of tolerance.
- The establishment of monitoring procedures and reporting of those results.
- The establishment of the corrective actions required when a risk moves outside its tolerance levels.
- The establishment of a verification level to ensure that the HACCP process in itself is robust and iterative, recognising that the critical control points might change.
- The building of records for corporate history and a **due diligence defence** (if required).

due diligence defence
The investigation or exercise of care that a reasonable business or person is expected to take before entering into an agreement or contract with another business or person.

The concept and cerebral process that sits behind HACCP is a useful approach to a control process for any organisation to consider:

- What does the system look like?
- Where can it go wrong?
- What can we do about it, and what are we going to do about it?
- How do we recognise when the parameters change?

6.4 Gap analysis

The concept of gap analysis was first referred to in Chapter 1 using the example in Figure 13.9. At the outset of our consideration of the development of strategy, we recognised that our strategic projections of the route from A to B are unlikely to be accurate. There will be different influences and forces long the route which will deliver variations upon the expected path.

We need to know why the route differed – the high point variants are as important as the low point variants to enhance our wider understanding.

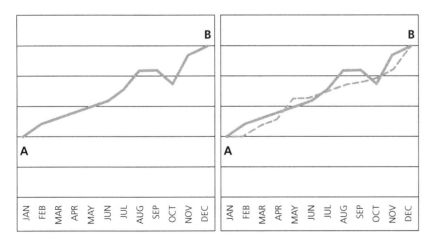

Figure 13.9 Benchmarking and gap analysis
© Mark Wearden

The left-hand graph illustrates an anticipated movement from A to B across a one-year period. The right-hand graph reflects the position looked at retrospectively having arrived at point B. The objective has been achieved, but the route has been different. Benchmarking forms the basis of gap analysis, sometimes called exception analysis or exception reporting, enabling analysis of the cause of all differences.

Gap analysis is one of the most powerful control tools as long as it is embedded into the structure and culture and the system and does not wait until the end of the process before being considered. If we know the future is likely to differ from our expectations, then intelligent control will require us to understand the key drivers of the original projection and then to be able to judge, through our analysis of the gap(s), how and why these have changed the anticipated path. If these are seen as part of a double-loop control system, then we will be able to use our understanding of what has happened to influence our development of strategy.

Worked example 13.1

QWERTY plc is a multinational financial technology organisation with a head office in London and a financial year end of 31 December.

◆ **Each year the finance team are tasked in August with producing a financial budget for the following financial year. This is a projection running from January (four months ahead) to December (16 months ahead).**

◆ **Given the nature of the business and its macro-economic drivers, the finance team recognises the illusory nature of its projections – they could, in reality, use their spreadsheet to justify a very wide range of potential outcomes and staging positions across the 12-month period.**

◆ **They have developed a sophisticated weighted model based around a defined set of core macro drivers which they map at the close of each London Stock Exchange (LSE) trading day – UK and US base rates, FTSE350 and NYSE spread rate movements, UK and US inflation; five and ten-year sterling and US dollar LIBOR.**

◆ **The 12-month figures produced in August for the following January to December are known as the budget.**

◆ **In December the core drivers are adjusted for the original budget – this is called projection 2. Similarly, every month new projections are derived, and a new projection produced.**

◆ **The model has shown that by September, the year-end position can be reflected with strong accuracy and allow a 'safe' projection to investors.**

◆ **The process of gap analysis is used each time the projection is redrawn to enhance the company's market knowledge and understanding.**

◆ They recognise that they may still be subject to another financial crisis, or other major macro-economic disaster, but believe that their gap awareness will ensure their longer-term viability.

6.5 Key performance indicators as a measure of control

In many organisations the transition and measurement of risk is designed around the use of key performance indicators (KPIs) as the measures of control.

This subject deserves a wider consideration by the company secretary and governance professional than is included in this section. It is sufficient here to suggest that there are four core requirements to be able to use KPIs for measurement, assessment and control:

◆ The word KEY is fundamental – there should only ever be a closely defined set of measures which are agreed by all affected parties.

◆ A KPI must be based upon accurate and reliable data and information to ensure integrity and trust of the reports being generated.

◆ The business measurement aspect covered by a KPI must be relevant to the core strategic drive of the organisation, and not used just as a confidence booster.

◆ A KPI must have a forward impact – there is no point in purely measuring the past, without being able to use that knowledge to help to drive the strategy, mitigate the risk and/or implement more effective control.

Case study 13.7

GSK has a closely defined set of KPIs which covers all core aspects of its business. Consider how each of its 'indicators' aligns with the four key requirements suggested above.

Extract from GSK plc Annual Report and Financial Statements 2017:

'We have identified ten operating Key Performance Indicators (KPIs) to track progress against our new long-term priorities:

◆ *Innovation*: innovation sales, pipeline value and progress

◆ *Performance*: turnover, profit, cash flow, market share, top talent in key roles

◆ *Trust*: supply service levels, employee engagement, corporate reputation

Here we provide performance data for the operating KPIs we are reporting externally. Due to commercial sensitivities, we are not planning to publish data for all operating KPIs.

The Remuneration policy used to reward the performance of our executives includes measures linked to our KPIs.'

In the case study above, note the different emphasis of the KPIs – there is an interesting mixture of financial and non-financial, quantitative and qualitative. Note also the clear alignment between the performance against these KPIs and the director remuneration policy.

6.6 Ownership and control

Refer back to the different models of organisational structure discussed in Chapter 12. The purpose of such structures is ultimately to understand the different lines of responsibility and accountability that exist within an organisation.

The reality of a corporate structure is that it is owned by its shareholders. The directors have a legal duty to drive success and value through the strategy for the benefit of the owners.

Caveat 1: you already know from your awareness of the UK Companies Act 2006 section 172 that directors have a wider stakeholder duty in addition to their focused shareholder duty.

Caveat 2: differing strengths and requirements of other stakeholders will drive differing expectations of control.

A company where the long-term funding is split 50:50 between shareholder funds and other external lines of credit in effect has two different ownership groups, with potentially equal demand rights, but also potentially differing expectations of control.

◆ The shareholders may be focused on longer-term success, happy to sacrifice short-term profit for longer-term share value – their measures of control would be based around market-perception, market value of shares and company reputation.

◆ The external financial providers would require tighter control measures on a shorter-term basis to ensure that the organisation is able to fulfil its contractual obligations and to ensure that profitability was at a level to generate sufficient free cash to both pay interest and reduce capital.

In the development of strategy, the differing layers of control need to be fully understood to enable the strategic drivers, goals and objectives to be aligned with the differing stakeholder expectations.

Test yourself 13.3

Suggest why gap analysis is a useful tool when implementing a control process.

7. The balanced scorecard as a strategic control method

7.1 Taking an assurance perspective

This chapter has considered many aspects of the strategic control of an organisation and the need to understand, interpret and challenge the operational performance. Having identified the breadth of the requirement, we should be clear in our need to use an optimal combination of quantitative and qualitative measures. Be aware that the external reporting requirements of most organisations will lead time-pressed directors and management to focus on the quantitative, and in particular financial measures – the company secretary and governance professional is often required to bring an objective lead in the challenge for alternative perspectives to be taken.

The danger of a focused financial approach had long since been recognised by academics and practitioners alike, together with the need to devise different methods to enable the capture and consideration of wider data perspectives.

7.2 The balanced scorecard

Writing in the *Harvard Business Review*, Kaplan and Norton (1992) first developed the concept of the *balanced scorecard*. A balanced scorecard approach is in common usage in many organisations and is usually a derivation of the original work of Kaplan and Norton.

Principles of the balanced scorecard
Strategic thinking requires us to challenge the quantitative nature of financial thinking with other qualitative aspects of organisation dynamics and culture. The balanced scorecard takes a structured approach which requires us to consider our organisation today and then the strategic changes envisaged from a number of formalised perspectives. The original model uses the following four perspectives, but it is important to find the right perspectives for the particular idiosyncrasies and drivers of any organisation:

◆ **Customer perspective**
   – What do our customers think of us? Why do they buy from us? Will they continue to buy from us? Etc.

◆ **Internal business perspective**
   – What do we look like from the inside? Are we efficient? What do our employees say about us? What does our culture look like?

◆ **Innovation and learning perspective**
   – What does our 'today' point look like? Is it always changing? Has it stayed still for too long? When did we last change the way we do things? How seriously are we taking the technological challenges of the next 10–20 years?

◆   **Financial perspective**

–   How robust is our financial infrastructure? What could make us fail (one aspect going wrong, or a concatenation of aspects)? Do our key players have their respective fingers on the financial pulse of the organisation?

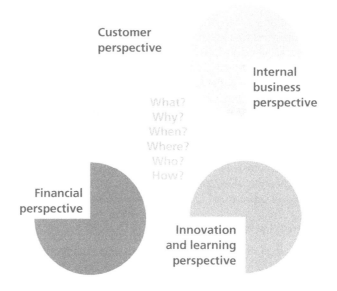

Figure 13.10 Balanced scorecard
((Kaplan and Norton, 1992) adapted by Mark Wearden)

To build an effective analysis of a range of different potential future scenarios, it is important to understand and identify the key parameters that are likely to change in the future, and how these parameters interact with each other. This requires us to take the concepts of changeability and predictability into a third dimension.

We need to rethink what we are trying to achieve from a control perspective.

Evolution of the balanced scorecard
Many organisations have evolved the original balanced scorecard concept to a bespoke tool for their own particular drivers and business dynamics. This is the right use of such tools, as long as the analytical differentiation originally perceived by Kaplan and Norton is maintained. Their four perspectives were designed to ensure a holistic analysis of an organisation. It is the analytical questions that dig deep into each perspective that will derive the real control value. We need to be able to freeze 'today' and analyse it from different dimensions, and at the same time we need to be able to take our visions of the 'future' and attempt to also analyse those from a similar range of dimensions.

Tesco plc originally created a more complex approach to the balanced scorecard – the Tesco wheel – which involve d a wide range of different internal and external performance measures. This was changed in 2016 to reflect six core strategic dimensions:

- grow sales
- deliver profit
- improve operating cashflow
- customers recommend us and come back time and again
- colleagues recommend us as a great place to work and shop
- we build trusted partnerships.

As with many companies these dimensions, derived from a balanced scorecard approach, are now used as the KPIs in the narrative reporting.

Barclays Bank plc used a similar approach, but with five key dimensions:

- **Customer and client**: we are the 'go-to' for our customers and clients.
- **Colleague**: our colleagues are fully engaged; we create a diverse and inclusive environment where colleagues can fulfil their potential.
- **Citizenship**: we positively impact the communities in which we operate.
- **Conduct**: our products and services are designed and distributed to meet client needs; we act with integrity in everything we do.
- **Company**: we create sustainable returns above the cost of equity; we understand and effectively manage our risks, and continuously improve control.

7.3   Alternative approaches

Results and determinants framework

The *results and determinants framework* was proposed by Fitzgerald and Moon in 1991 to illustrate the difference between organisational results and organisational determinants. The result enabling control of performance and the determinants enabling control of the rationale behind the performance.

- **Results**
  - financial performance at all levels
  - competitive positioning and market alignment.
- **Determinants**
  - quality
  - flexibility
  - resource utilisation
  - innovation.

European quality framework management model

An alternative approach is the *European quality framework management* (EQFM) model for business excellence which suggests that organisational performance can be measured and controlled through a wide awareness of:

- satisfied people
- satisfied customers
- a positive impact upon wider society.

Enablers			Results	
Leadership	People	Processes	People results	Business results
	Strategy	Products	Customer results	
	Partners and resources	Services	Society results	

Table 13.2 The EQFM model

The model is applied within an organisation through the development of appropriate KPIs for each of the categories.

7.4   Aligning a scorecard with strategy and structure

We are able to draw a number of conclusions and control lessons from the various aspects considered in this chapter:

◆ **Control lesson 1**:
  – Make sure the control is being considered in the light of the latest possible analysis of data, information and knowledge.
◆ **Control lesson 2**:
  – The control of risk, and the protection of the strategic objectives, long and short-term, has to happen at a re-analysed 'today' point, based upon the operational realities of the day-to-day progress along the route from today to the future.
◆ **Control lesson 3**:
  – As far as possible, try to understand the mindset of the people involved in the control process.
  – What are their beliefs? Why do they behave in the way they behave?
◆ **Control lesson 4**:
  – Identify the levers that are required to deliver the anticipated result from the strategy and the aligned financial thinking.
  – Further, make sure you know the optimal alignment of these levers, and the impact if one is incorrectly positioned.
◆ **Control lesson 5**:
  – Make sure you have the optimal data and information.
  – Ensure you have a healthy scepticism.
  – Align the various levers of control.
  – Remember that assurance relies on integrity.

Test yourself 13.4

What are the original four perspectives suggested by Kaplan and Norton in their balanced scorecard model?

Chapter summary

◆   This chapter partially reflects upon the wide range of different approaches that have been considered in the development of strategy and challenges students to consider how we can control the process, the strategic journey from the realities of 'today' into the unknown of the 'future'.

◆   Control is positioned as part of the governance expectation and triangulation of strategy–risk–control. The control is required because of the risks that are inevitably being taken to achieve the strategic vision and objectives.

◆   A fourfold approach is suggested to control – analysis, audit, assessment and assurance.

◆   Analysis requires a clarity of understanding of what is happening now, and what the vision requires. There are four suggested dimensions which are interrelated – effectiveness, efficiency, qualitative, quantitative. The chapter suggests the need to ensure an organisation does not just concentrate on the quantitative for its development of strategy.

◆   Audit requires a clarity of understanding of the data and information that surrounds us. Remember that the word audit means to hear, to listen and to understand. This requires the auditor to be prepared to challenge to the point where all three meanings are satisfied; this will require a double-loop learning approach rather than just a single-loop approach.

◆   The use of metaphors is recommended to enable an objective view of the organisation and its people to be developed.

◆   Assessment requires us to be able to ask the right questions, and to find different methods of challenging the people, the process and the organisational culture.

◆   Assurance is a fundamental requirement in the development of strategy. Those developing the strategy need to firstly provide assurance to the owners of the assets that their assets are being used to fulfil the strategic objectives in order to preserve and enhance value. Secondly, there is also a need to provide assurance to those using the assets that they are working within the expected boundaries. Thirdly, there needs to be an assurance that appropriate levels of control exist to protect the assets and allow the operational boundaries to be reviewed as new dimensions and forces emerge.

◆   The balanced scorecard is positioned as an important tool, both in itself and in its concept, to guide and challenge a breadth of whole-business thinking.

◆   The company secretary and governance professional needs to have a keen awareness and understanding of the control measures that are used throughout the organisation. The privileged breadth of the role allows a virtually unparalleled ability to witness, consider and challenge the interaction of the control structure.

Part six

Managing change

Introduction

The final part of this text's consideration of the development of strategy centres around strategy as a change process. Strategy and change are closely related, the difference being that strategy requires change, but change does not always require strategy. The intention throughout this text is to consider how to develop strategy and therefore how to anticipate and plan the type of change that is required to move from the realities of today to the vision of the future. Change is looked at from two different, but closely related, dynamics – process and people.

Overview

Chapter 14 looks at the process of change and considers the distinction and different impact of an evolutionary approach and a revolutionary approach. We need to understand the boundaries of the change system that we are operating within, and then determine how, if and when it is appropriate to create a planned and structured change to achieve our strategic objectives.

Chapter 15 considers a range of aspects of the people dynamic of change. We recognise that change needs people as the drivers and enablers, but also that people need change to allow them and their organisations to evolve. The chapter introduces different approaches to the human resistance to change and considers the impact of differing leadership and communication approaches.

Learning outcomes

At the end of this part, students will be able to:

◆ identify the change process that is required as part of the delivery of strategic objectives;

◆ understand the difference between evolutionary change and revolutionary change;

◆ demonstrate the different forces that drive and restrain change;

◆ consider the impact of different approaches to change – on the process and on the people;

◆ understand the need for effective change leadership;

◆ consider the role and purpose of a change agent;

◆ demonstrate the use of the 'Johari window' to identify communication breakdown; and

◆ understand the nature of human resistance to change and demonstrate how different researchers have provided tools to help us deal with this.

Chapter fourteen
Managing strategic change – the process dynamic

Contents

1. Introduction

The final section of the syllabus, in the last two chapters of this text, are about the management of change. In many ways we conclude our study of the development of strategy by recognising that change lies at the very heart of all strategy.

The reason that we need to move from 'today' into the 'future' is to enable change. In our consideration of strategy, we have to recognise that 'today' is a constantly moving dimension, that time does not stand still and that what we are seeking to achieve is the ability to influence the nature, dimensions and impact of the inevitable changes that will take place.

These two chapters look at this from two different but closely related perspectives:

◆ This chapter (14) will consider the 'process dynamic' of strategic change – why it happens, why it is required and the ability to place this into context within the strategic journey.

◆ The next chapter (15) will consider the 'people dynamic' of strategic change – the differing leadership roles, the ability to overcome the natural human resistance to change, and a number of final theories which neatly tie together the entire syllabus.

2. The cause of and need for change

2.1   Elements of change

Understanding what we mean by change
We need to understand that:

◆   we participate in change, but we can also be the originators of change

◆   we can be the recipients of change, but we also have the ability to recognise change.

Think about this from a strategic perspective.

We are always positioned at the starting position of 'today' where we have the ability to identify and understand personal and organisational reality, we can recognise what has changed since we last assessed a particular situation (or person). At the same time, we have the ability to visualise a different 'future' and the strategic changes that we believe are necessary to deliver that vision. We then also can become the implementors and the initiators and drivers of the change that we perceive as being necessary.

What do we really mean by a 'strategic' change?

A classic starting point would be 'a change in the direction and scope of an organisation over the long term' (Johnson et al. (2017)), but this would suggest that all strategic change is deliberate and planned to have a lasting impact. This denies a significant amount of what we have studied within this text, in particular the ongoing shorter term social and political processes through which an organisation will decide the ultimate long-term scope. As considered in a number of chapters the reality is always a mixture of rational, considered and proactive strategy, combined with emergent and often reactive strategic decisions.

Stop and think 14.1

Take the time to remember and write down a few facts about yourself ten years ago.

Could you have imagined yourself now at this precise point, studying this subject?

Could you have imagined how different the world of today is from that of ten years ago?

Then, from a strategic perspective, what can we genuinely predict for where we or the world will be in ten years from now?

Recognition and awareness of change
It is often suggested that the volatility, uncertainty, complexity and ambiguity of today's world requires a constant awareness of the implicit and explicit changes

that impact upon us. The period since the early 1970s has been described as an age of discontinuity underpinned by economic change. Beyond this we are moving into the age of the Fourth Industrial Revolution, bringing a dual challenge of increasing speed in electronic communication and rapid growth in the potential future use of artificial intelligence impacting upon all aspects of life as we know it today.

These are of course only a few of the symptoms which underpin the macro changes within our environment. It has been said that strategic change was easier to plan for in the past where it was assumed the future would be more of a simple extrapolation from the past. This is disputed here. In reality, whenever we stop and consider our strategy, the past which has already happened is much easier to assimilate in our minds than the future which is unknown and yet to come.

Today's 21st century reality is that of instant communication, and therefore the risk of instant reaction. It could be argued that this creates a more reactive and therefore emergent approach to strategy. As we saw in Chapter 7, there is an increasing governance creep within organisations to try to help those who run the organisation to take a step back and still operate from a rational perspective, while recognising the need to be able to amend the vision, based upon each new emergence. This is underpinned by a stakeholder requirement for increased transparency, understanding and integrity from those running an organisation.

Pressure points and requirement

Aside from the recognition that change is a perpetual requirement, throughout the life-cycle of any organisation there will be points which bring a particular pressure for change. These are represented in the following diagram and show that each such pressure will have an impact upon the whole rather than just standing in isolation. The need therefore is for an organisation to think holistically about the strategic impact of all change.

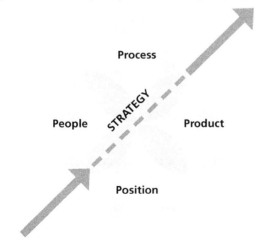

Figure 14.1 Pressure points
© Mark Wearden

◆ Process: the need to adapt and amend the core operational function of the organisation.

◆ Product: the need to ensure that the output of the organisation continues to meet the changing demands of the customer, both internal and external.

◆ Position: the need for a constant awareness of the strategic and economic positioning of the organisation against its competition.

◆ People: the need to include the right people in the right way within all change processes; this will be discussed further in Chapter 15.

Kaufman et al. (2003) suggest in their book *Strategic Planning for Success* that the biggest single mistake that is often made in managing and creating strategic change is the attempt to implement a change too quickly, without the appropriate buy-in from stakeholders, and without integrating the change with everything else that is going on in the organisation at that point.

They further suggest that 'it is probably better to be conservative during the first initiation, rather than to be too aggressive'. A core recognition of theirs being that:

'change is a process and not an event'.

Kaufman et al. discuss the need for us to be able to visualise a range of changing paradigms, across many aspects of an organisation. Further, we need to consider the likely strategic impact that these changes will have upon people who are already often struggling to manage their daily operational tasks within an acceleration of change in their own professional and personal lives. They introduce three levels of change:

◆ **Mega level**: changes involving a long-term perspective, including future generations and their survival, self-sufficiency and their overall quality-of-life. It is recognised that change at this level is complex, as it is required to deal with a range of relationships across the underlying systems that we are able to influence. This type of change is described as being 'holistic, profound and deep'. *For example, a company is acquired by a different, perhaps overseas owner – e.g. when Jaguar Land-Rover became part of Tata Group this was a mega-level change.*

◆ **Macro level**: changes involving the inputs and outputs of the main organisational system, affecting and being affected by a wide range of different external stakeholders. *For example, a company changes its production lines from manual to robotic.*

◆ **Micro level**: changes to the key results and performance indicators which can be achieved by individuals, teams and processes within an organisation. *For example, a company needs to drive higher profitability to meet increasing wage costs.*

Strategically these differing levels can work in both directions, with the micro ultimately affecting the mega level and vice versa.

2.2   Circumstances of change

Martin (2001) suggested that there are four differing ways in which change can be recognised and controlled within an organisation, shown in his change matrix.

Figure 14.2 The change matrix
((Martin, 2001) adapted by Mark Wearden)

This is a useful matrix to consider when we are trying to identify the type of change that we are faced with in an organisation, and we have added a related scenario for each dimension of the model.

◆   Change that comes as a **surprise** is by its nature unplanned, but the organisation is able to adapt to the emerging requirement. *Scenario: If a small customer of an organisation goes into liquidation, owing a small amount of money, then the organisation is able to adapt to this unexpected event.*

◆   Change that can be considered as a **crisis** is unplanned and then has a potentially fracturing impact upon the organisation. *Scenario: If a larger customer of the organisation goes into an unexpected liquidation owing a significant amount of money, then the organisation will be at least partially fractured and have to manage a potential liquidity gap.*

◆   Change that is described as **incremental** results from the building of small, planned changes in the gradual evolution of the organisation. *Scenario: There is concern over the potential future liquidity of a significant customer, there is no immediate panic, but the organisation is able to either reduce the funds outstanding from the customer or balance the material significance of the customer by developing a wider customer base. The organisation will adjust its financial projections.*

◆   Change that is described by Martin as **strategic** is a result of planning but has a fundamental impact upon the organisation. This is described as fracturing because it requires potentially significant change in process and people. *Scenario: An organisation has become reliant upon one major customer who has required a dedicated supply. The organisation recognises the risk of this situation and begins to implement a plan to increase both product range and customer range. The strategic fracturing* *would be reflected by the changes required in organisational structure to enable such growth, and also possibly the risk of losing the existing major customer who enjoys their position of exclusive supply.*

Stop and think 14.2

Think back to changes that have happened within your organisation during the past 12 months.

Align them with the four dimensions from Martin above.

2.3 Organisational drivers and forces of change

In their book *Exploring Strategic Change*, Balogun and Hope Hailey (2004) extended the concepts considered by Martin to suggest more radical ways in which the differing types of change might be managed. In many ways this is looking at the same concepts but from a different perspective, but they take the concept further in terms of how the organisation needs to recognise and deal with the changes. The reality being that in any organisation change will be driven from two different perspectives:

◆ **Evolution**: steady incremental change envisaged by Johnson and others, building through a gradual strategic approach and enabling the organisation to develop and adapt with rare transformational changes.

◆ **Revolution**: the occasional 'big bang' which will require significant structural reorganisation (fracturing).

Extent of change

	Realignment	Transformation
Big bang	**Reconstruction**	**Revolution**
Incremental	**Adaptation**	**Evolution**

(Nature of change)

Figure 14.3 Types of change
((Balogun & Hope-Hailey, 2004) adapted by Mark Wearden)

Test yourself 14.1

Distinguish between process change at the mega level, the macro level and the micro level as suggested by Kaufman.

Case study 14.1

WPP plc is a useful example of a company where the strategic journey has changed from *evolution* to *revolution*.

WPP plc was founded as Wire and Plastic Products plc in 1971, manufacturing wire shopping baskets. In 1985, Martin Sorrell bought a controlling stake in the organisation and WPP plc evolved across subsequent years to become a leading multinational advertising and public relations company.

The strategic journey was not always straightforward, with the group buying and selling a number of different types of organisation, but always with a strategic focus on its ability to communicate the potential of differing organisations and products to a multinational marketplace.

The company and its leader, Sir Martin Sorrell, were intrinsically linked in the minds of all stakeholders.

On 14 April 2018, Sir Martin Sorrell retired from the company for personal reasons which have not yet been fully explained. However, his employment contract with WPP placed very little restriction on his future activities, and this enabled him to rapidly acquire another business and return to the forefront of the advertising industry in direct competition with his previous employer, WPP.

Imagine the strategic considerations that are now taking place around the board table of WPP plc.

Stop and think 14.3

How and why have WPP been so successful?

3. Understanding the context and process of change

Balogun and Hope Hailey (2004) suggest that all organisational change needs to be considered within eight differing contexts. Not all of these will apply in all instances, but the strategist will need to ensure that they have been considered when developing a programme of change. We have provided suggested questions for the strategist against each of the eight contexts:

- **Time**: How urgent is the change? Is there time for lengthy consideration or is there the need for immediate action?
- **Scope**: Will the change impact the entire organisation, or initially only a small part?
- **Preservation**: Does everything need to change?

◆ **Diversity**: Have sufficient different and relevant opinions been explored?

◆ **Capability**: Are the people within the organisation able to deliver the required change or are new people or external consultants required?

◆ **Capacity**: Does the organisation have sufficient accessible resources, in particular financial, to implement the required change?

◆ **Readiness**: Has the appropriate level of preparation been undertaken?

◆ **Power**: Where does the power lie to drive the perceived change, is it dependent upon one or more people acting appropriately?

Alongside these eight areas, it should be clear that the specific type and context of the organisation will have a significant influence on any change programme. As an example, there may often be a legal context that needs to be considered in the implementation of change.

There will be a significant difference between the process of change within a small privately-owned business compared to managing change within a large multinational listed company which has more formal requirements to adhere to. We could also recognise other types of organisation where change management will require different considerations, for instance a charity or a government department where the drivers and influencers may be far less commercial.

3.1   Internal and external drivers of change

To enable us to manage change effectively, from a process perspective, we need to understand at which point the organisation as a system is being pressured to change and therefore both the originating cause and the potential impact of the need for change.

Tichy (1983) identified four main triggers for strategic change:

◆ **Environment**: the need to adapt to differing economic conditions, legislation and new or changing competition.

◆ **Business relationships**: the need for frequent review of customer and supplier impact and their respective competence.

◆ **Technology**: the need to decide how rapidly, or otherwise, to follow and lead the technological revolution (this is probably even more applicable 35 years after Tichy came to his conclusions).

◆ **People**: the recognition of how it can sometimes only require one person to change the organisation and also require the organisation to change.

Nine years later, Kanter et al. (1992) recognised the influence of the environment but suggested that two different dynamics existed to drive real strategic change within organisations:

◆ **Life-cycle differences**: nature of change in consumer demand at the ultimate end of all supply chains, intrinsically linked to the changes in individual people's expectations.

◆ **Political power changes**: largely within an organisation, as individuals and stakeholders compete for the ability to make and implement strategic decisions to suit their own particular ambitions and vision.

Stop and think 14.4

Consider the government politics of today – evaluate how they currently impact upon your organisation.

Then take the strategic view and try to analyse the many different ways in which political change could affect your organisation.

Test yourself 14.2

Write down the eight differing contexts of organisational change identified by Balogun and Hope Hailey.

In a fuller study, Robbins and Judge (2016) regrouped the external environmental forces of change into six categories, as shown in Figure 14.4.

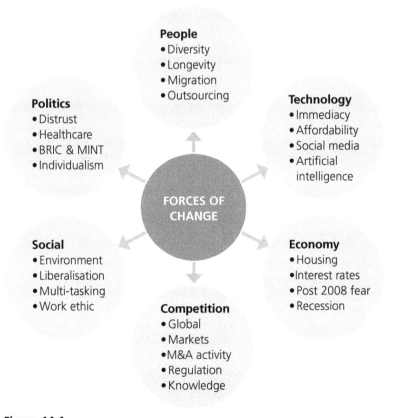

People
- Diversity
- Longevity
- Migration
- Outsourcing

Politics
- Distrust
- Healthcare
- BRIC & MINT
- Individualism

Technology
- Immediacy
- Affordability
- Social media
- Artificial intelligence

FORCES OF CHANGE

Social
- Environment
- Liberalisation
- Multi-tasking
- Work ethic

Economy
- Housing
- Interest rates
- Post 2008 fear
- Recession

Competition
- Global
- Markets
- M&A activity
- Regulation
- Knowledge

Figure 14.4
((Robbins & Judge, 2016) adapted by Mark Wearden)

- ◈ **People**: a significant single issue with regard to people is increased longevity and therefore an ageing workforce with an expectation to be required to be working longer, and to have benefits (retirement income of some kind) for a markedly longer period of time.

- ◈ **Technology**: many describe the current age as being one of the Fourth Industrial Revolution, and the potential impact of this has to be considered when planning any sort of strategic change. The Fourth Industrial Revolution is evidenced by a fusion of technologies that is rapidly blurring the lines of distinction that previously existed between the physical, the digital and the biological.

- ◈ **Economy**: the financial crisis of 2008 has had a significantly longer strategic impact upon the world economy than originally expected – most major world economies continue to dip in and out of a state of recession, interest rates have remained unusually low and there is an organisational and personal reluctance to diminish cash reserves ('just in case').

- ◈ **Competition**: all organisations now operate within a global market, driven not least by the immediacy of knowledge that is available through the internet.

- ◈ **Social**: people are often influenced by and contribute to social media networking; we have seen allegations of vote rigging in major elections, and the development of world leaders being willing to use social media to influence actual news, and 'fake news'. In terms of social strategic change, the growing awareness of environmental issues has led to a greater demand and expectation that action will be taken by governments, companies and individuals.

- ◈ **Politics**: some of the moves referred to above have led to a much greater distrust and challenge than politicians have been accustomed to. The traditional economies of the world are being challenged by the rapidly developing size and significance, the differing political beliefs and economies, and the challenging cultures and expectations of the BRIC (Brazil, Russia, India, China) and the MINT (Mexico, Indonesia, Nigeria, Turkey) economies.

If you take all of these models together – Tichy, Kanter and Robbins – you have a wide, if not exclusive, range of perspectives of the forces that really affect organisational change from a generic perspective. Highlighting all three of these models together also re-emphasises that your study of strategy, and your implementation of strategic change within your own life and that of your organisation(s), always needs to be placed into specific context, and in particular the forces that are either requiring or influencing the change that has been identified or the 'today' problems that are being challenged.

Case study 14.2

In 2005, Shell plc entered a strategic supply chain transformation programme to boost production, the searching for and extraction of oil and gas (referred to by Shell as an 'upstream' activity) and to increase its income from its refining activities (referred to by Shell as a 'downstream' activity).

Using the mantra 'More upstream, profitable downstream', Shell embarked upon its change programme through an enhanced use of information technology, but also by implementing a series of global, standardised operating procedures impacting more than 80 Shell operating units. From the start it was recognised that the changes needed to be mandatory to gain the strategic growth required. The main message of the change team was that simpler, standard processes across all countries and regions, which would benefit Shell globally, would take priority over any local and individual needs. Every aspect of the global business was moved to centralised distribution networks.

3.2 Lewin – force-field analysis

The work of the psychologist Kurt Lewin (1951) provides a simple methodology to help in our consideration of change. He researched the forces that restrain desired change within organisations and contrasted these with the forces that drive the desired change. His theory of force-field analysis argues that restraining forces need to be reduced to enable the desirable change to happen naturally; this requires a mapping of both dimensions.

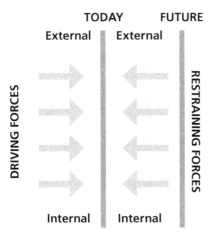

Figure 14.5 Force-field analysis
((Lewin, 1951) adapted by Mark Wearden)

This is a practical interpretation of what is intended by Lewin in terms of mapping, analysing and understanding the driving and restraining forces.

The model recognises that we are on a journey from today into the future and that the driving forces will be a mixture of external and internal forces that want to influence the strategic direction, however there is an equal likelihood that there will be external and internal forces that are restraining the strategic change that is required.

Lewin's concept is that by understanding these forces we are able to offset the restraining forces by use of the driving forces. In concept this is not radically different to the practical use of a SWOT (strengths, weaknesses, opportunities and threats) analysis discussed in Chapter 3.

Stop and think 14.5

What are the driving and restraining forces that affect your organisation?

What are the driving and restraining forces that prevent you from having a better work/life balance?

3.3 Culture change

In Chapter 6 we considered a range of different models of organisational culture, together with the various forces and drivers that impact upon these models. When we are planning strategic change, it is essential that we consider the impact of such change upon the varying aspects of culture within the organisation. Of course, it might be that the strategic change required is in itself a change of culture.

In their book Managing Change for Competitive Success and based upon their research across four different sectors of commercial life – car manufacture, book publishing, merchant banking, life assurance – Pettigrew and Whipp (1991) recognised that a number of core factors were at play in the management of cultural change, as shown in Figure 14.6.

These five factors inter-relate, and effective strategic change requires an understanding of the impact of all five:

◆ **Environmental assessment**: strategic change always needs to be placed within the setting of the organisational environment – macro and micro. Environmental understanding has to be part of the 'learning' concept of the organisation so that all players understand its significance – it is not a specialist function.

◆ **Leading change**: leadership will be driven by and drive the context of strategic change and requires the ability to recognise and link the differing skills of a wide group of players and stakeholders.

◆ **Strategy and operation**: an organisation can be viewed as a complete entity in itself. Although strategy making might be a focused task, it only becomes relevant as it impacts the operation of the organisation, as the vision starts to be realised.

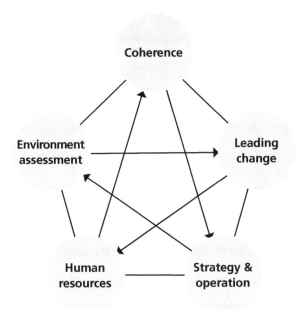

Figure 14.6
((Pettigrew & Whipp, 1991) adapted by Mark Wearden)

◆ **Human resources as assets and liabilities**: strategic change requires the effective oversight and control of the strengths and weaknesses of people and their often seemingly irrational behaviour. Competitive performance can often be optimised with the alignment of knowledge, skills and attitudes within an organisation.

◆ **Coherence in the management of change**: whatever happens has to make sense within the context of the other four factors; a vision must be realistic; the people within the organisation have their current mix of skills, behaviours, values and biases; the organisation already has an existing mode of operation and culture. The strategic change needs to be characterised by consistency, consonance, advantage and feasibility.

Test yourself 14.3

Describe the difference between the 'driving forces' and the 'restraining forces' in Lewin's theory of force-field analysis.

3.4 Economic and political change

Unless an organisation is prepared to be entirely reactive to economic and political change, it is necessary to create a deliberate radar to recognise, assess and understand the likely impact of external forces upon the strategy of the organisation. Throughout this text we have included a number of models such as PESTEL (political, economic, socio-cultural, technological, environmental and legal) and scenario planning, with continual reference to the impact of economic and political forces.

Successful strategic change requires an organisation to track such forces by capturing the relevant intelligence and movements of these aspects of the macro environment through different scenarios.

Case study 14.3

Santander, the Spanish banking group, took a decision in 2008 to establish a stronghold in the UK banking sector, recognising the opportunities that might be available after the reputational damage suffered by (and need for UK government cash injections of) the major UK banks following the 2007 'financial crisis'. Santander acquired a portfolio of historic UK financial institutions including Abbey National, Bradford & Bingley and Alliance & Leicester.

Santander recognised that the legacy that existed within its newly acquired subsidiaries was one of a lack of change, a lack of evolutionary vision and an inability to grow organically and capture new opportunities. The decision was taken to unify the acquisitions under the Santander brand in an attempt to break the ingrained culture and process and to enable the creation of a strong retail bank in the UK market.

This was achieved through a fast-track, systems-led banking model to bring clarity, efficiency and best practice. The newly appointed chief executive officer (CEO) of Santander UK drove a focus on ensuring that all stakeholders understood the value of change and the need to embrace the new methods – this was a revolution rather than an evolution.

In January 2010, Santander UK was officially launched, and by 2013 it had become one of the UK's leading retail banks and one of the largest providers of savings and mortgages.

3.5 Stakeholder communication

This short section is simply a reminder, in the context of process change, that stakeholders need to be aware of and be able to anticipate likely strategic changes within the organisation where they hold a stake. Remind yourself of the core stakeholder groups discussed in Chapter 3 section 4.4 – owners, employees, customers, other supply chain stakeholders. It is essential, other than in instances of extreme confidentiality, or the risk of unacceptable market disclosure, that these stakeholders have an awareness of the potential impact of strategic change upon their respective stakes in the organisation.

Stop and think 14.6

How well is change communicated to the stakeholders of your organisation?

Try to measure it against some SMART objectives.

3.6 Risk and reputation

A reminder from Chapter 7 of the intrinsic relationship between strategy, risk and control. As soon as we move away from the known position to implement or deliver the change required to achieve the strategic vision, we enter into the risk territory of new and emerging challenges, where the various forces already discussed can impact upon our organisation, and our planned strategic route.

It is important to remember that we never take this journey in isolation or without others taking an interest in what is happening. A focus of our strategic thinking throughout this text has been that we exist in a state of competition, needing to gain or maintain competitive advantage, and therefore our competitors, and our stakeholders, will want to know what we are doing, and why we are being successful. Hence the close interlinking of risk and reputation.

All change brings risk; part of the strategic planning of every change needs to be an assessment of the risks involved, together with the perceived impact (positive or negative) on our reputation as and when the change succeeds or fails.

The Financial Reporting Council (FRC) guidance on risk suggests:

> 'the board should establish the tone for risk management and internal control and put in place appropriate systems to enable it to meet its responsibilities effectively'.

There is a recognition that this will vary significantly with the size, diversity and complexity of a particular organisation. There is also recognition that it is the responsibility of the directors and officers of a company to identify the level and nature of the assurance that it requires, and to ensure that appropriate people are in place to deliver such assurance.

To recognise the reputational impact, the organisation will need to have implemented a structured system to enable:

- identification of the nature and extent of the risks, including principal risks, facing or being taken by the company, which are regarded as necessary, desirable or acceptable;
- an understanding of the likelihood of the risks concerned materialising, and their potential impact;
- the ability to reduce the likelihood of the risks materialising by mitigation and possible application of sourcing further resources;
- how such risks are being monitored and controlled, with an awareness of the appropriateness of the control processes; and

◆ an iterative process for the reporting on a periodic basis from the control level to the governance level.

Test yourself 14.4

Try to recall the relevance of the five change factors identified by Pettigrew and Whipp.

Chapter summary

◆ This chapter considers the need for organisational process to change as part of the development of strategy, recognising that the process requirements of the past will have been different from those of today, and the process dynamics of today in turn will be different from those required in the future.

◆ It is necessary to understand the pressure points that will affect our strategy – summarised as process, product, position and people.

◆ Kaufman argues that we need to consider three levels of process change – mega, macro and micro. These can be seen as our different boundaries of strategic influence.

◆ There is an important distinction to be made between change which results from a measured evolutionary approach, and that which results from either deliberate or unexpected revolution.

◆ A core model for analysing the forces of change comes from Lewin in his force field analysis with its dynamic between driving forces and restraining forces.

◆ The company secretary and governance professional will often be a key player in the documenting and oversight of differing aspects of process change. There will be the need to understand the rationale behind the change, the approach being taken to change and the perceived impact on different stakeholders. The evidence required to support this has become more important since the changes to the Companies Act 2006 now requiring all but small companies to explain how directors have approached section 172, and the impact on stakeholders of any resultant drive to create sustainable value.

Chapter fifteen

Managing strategic change – the people dynamic

Contents

1. Introduction

> 'It must be remembered that there is nothing more difficult to take in hand, more perilous to conduct, or more uncertain in its success, than to take the lead in the introduction of a new order of things. Because the innovator has for enemies all those who have done well under the old conditions, and lukewarm defenders in those who may do well under the new'.

> Machiavelli (1532)

Leadership of change has never been easy.

If we need to make a direct change to something within our own direct control then that can often be relatively straightforward, but as soon as other people are involved, and may need to be persuaded of the need for change, we have a problem. In his *Hierarchy of needs*, Abraham Maslow (1943) suggested that before we can reach a sense of personal fulfilment, we need to go through the stage where we develop a self-respect and enjoy the esteem and plaudit of others. Freud (1923) had already identified this as what he called the 'ego', that part of each individual which enables us to think highly of ourselves.

A leader of change must firstly be comfortable with their own 'ego', but then the problem comes when they have to interact and work with the plethora of different 'egos' that surround them.

Change relies on people, people also rely on change.

Throughout this text and its consideration of the many different aspects of the development of strategy, we have continually returned to the theme of people, their influence, their opinions, their impetus, their requirement, their differing understanding of 'today', and their differing vision of the 'future'.

It is deliberate and appropriate that the last chapter of the study text is a further challenge and reminder of the strengths, weaknesses, opportunities and threats (SWOT) that are offered by people throughout the strategic journey, from initiation to completion. This chapter will be a combination of reminders, revision, additional models and further challenge.

2. Roles in the change process

In Chapter 3 we discussed the roles of a number of different people in the development of strategy and the initiation of strategic change. In this chapter we will consider the same people, and the same groups of people, but now we will focus on the direct roles and involvement that they have in the actual change process. It is people who must have the courage to leave the safety of 'today', be appropriately prepared for the change that is ahead of them, be ready to reconcile how things have changed when they reach the 'future', and, of course, recognise that the future has now become 'today', and so a new strategic iteration begins.

While as a company secretary and governance professional we will be required to consider this objectively, from our position as an objective observer and challenger, the reality will be we will always look at it from our role as a participant. While it is easy to recognise the need for change in situations and in other people, Peter Senge (2006) offers a better challenge, which is the need for us to recognise that:

> 'Change starts with me'.

2.1　Leadership of change

We have already discussed extensively the need for effective leadership within the operation of any organisation, within the development of strategy, and therefore inevitably in the leadership of strategic change. Here is a quick reminder of two different but complementary types of change leadership:

◆　**Transformational leadership**: The leader will focus on the building of the strategic vision, the creation of identity and empowerment and the development of an appropriate culture (refer back to Chapter 6). The original inspiring entrepreneur behind an organisation is often a transformational leader, such as Steve Jobs at Apple. The people and organisational impact of a key charismatic individual is always clear for all stakeholders to see, but so is the gap created when that personalised driving force is no longer part of the organisation, particularly if much of the operational driving force relies upon it.

◆　**Transactional leadership**: The leader is generally more concerned with making sure that the operational flow is appropriate to enable the strategy to be achieved, the term transaction referring to the motivation of followers by exchanging reward for performance. The leadership at RBS plc leading up to the 2007 'financial crisis' was clearly transactional – the bank was seen as a series of high-profile operations with significant levels of reward for success. Problems occur in the longer term if strategic vision is unachievable or based on the hubris of one or more key individuals.

The leadership of strategic change requires a combination of both transformational and transactional leadership, in the same way that it requires both autocratic and participative leadership. The sign of a truly successful strategic leader is their ability to use a range of leadership styles in the ever-changing world around them, in an attempt to satisfy differing stakeholder expectations.

We could conceivably link these two styles of leadership to our earlier considerations in Chapter 7 of the governance of an organisation and how this differs from the operation of an organisation. As a principle, governance could be perceived as more of a transformational style of leadership, gradually driving difference and change, whereas the operation of the organisation on a day-to-day week to week basis might require a more transactional leadership style.

Case study 15.1

Adapted from CGMA (Chartered Global Management Accountant) TOOL, 'How to Develop a Strategy Map' (www.cgma.org):

Human capital is the economic value an organisation derives from:

◆ **application of knowledge**

◆ **collaboration and**

◆ **engaged individuals.**

Managed well, human capital is an enormous source of value that comes from committed individuals making informed decisions on service, quality, effectiveness, creativity, goal alignment and productivity.

The leader's use of power when dealing with other people
The role of leader implies that there are followers, and therefore that the leader in some way or other is in a position of power with regard to the followers. We discussed this from one perspective in consideration of Covey's concept of principal centred leadership (1992) but we need to go a bit further than that when we are thinking about the use and potential abuse of power in our leadership.

Covey suggests that there are three core types of power which are exerted by leaders:

◈ Coercive power: the follower is concerned or afraid of what will happen if they do not follow the expectations of the leader (often based around fear of punishment or revenge).

◆ Utility power: the follower fulfils the requirement in the expectation of some form of reward, the leader has something that they want, tangible or intangible (often based around remuneration or benefits).

◆ Legitimate power: the follower has a trust and respect in the leader and their objectives (often based around respect and belief).

To see easy examples of these three different types of power in daily operation, it is only necessary to open the pages of a daily newspaper and look at interactions between different politicians within any political party, and the different approaches to leadership, and to the leadership of their party.

Type of power	Leadership change words
Position	'I am in charge'
Resource	'I have what you need'
Difficult decisions	'I know this isn't easy, but…'
Honesty	'Sorry, I got that wrong'
Expert	'I have many years of experience'
Information	'How can I help you?'
Vision	'Can you see the bigger picture?'
Argument	'I have done the research'
Values	'I need you to believe in this'

Table 15.1 Types of power
© Mark Wearden

Stop and think 15.1

Think about the *types of power* in the above table.

How have such types of power been operated over you in the past, or still in the present?

How do you operate from a power perspective?

If you take the different perspectives of power included in the last exercise and think about the suggested 'leadership change words', the impact of these words will be entirely dependent upon the character and behaviour of the leader themselves, their tone of voice and above all the manner in which they deliver their change leadership. It is easy to see how power can be abused, and we will reconsider this matrix later in this chapter when we consider the human resistance to change.

Test yourself 15.1

Differentiate between transformational leadership and transactional leadership.

2.2   Identifying the change agents

A change agent is a person, or people, who are able or required to use their particular abilities (and/or knowledge) or position to effect change within an organisation.

A useful way to think about the impact that a change agent can have is to think back to experiments in the chemistry laboratory at school. We have all come across the concept of the use of a catalyst, a substance which changes the rate of a reaction – different catalysts will cause different reactions and the level of catalyst required will depend upon the substances that one is expecting to react with each other.

In this way, a change agent within an organisation will be acting as the catalyst to enable, speed up or slow down, the strategic change required. A change agent may have a significant role within the strategic change itself, or may be someone who is able to remain entirely objective. In either case, this person will need to wear a number of different hats and always be able to bring clarity and objectivity to the strategic change as it takes place.

Case study 15.2

Adapted from Investors In People, 2016:

Investors In People is a Community Interest Company founded in 1991, originally as a government project, which leads the drive for better leadership and better workplaces. The company describes itself as 'the change agents' and strives to help organisations understand and improve the way that they manage their people.

Investors In People sees its role as an agent for positive change, supporting leaders to create high-performance cultures with smart objectives, making work a more rewarding experience for everyone. It is passionate about unlocking the potential of the individual.

The company suggests that in order to be successful in enabling organisational change, a change agent will:

1. **understand the benefits the changes will bring and have the patience to take the longer-term perspective**
2. **remain close to the human side of change, understanding why people behave and react the way they do**
3. **balance emotional intelligence with a relentless focus on the bottom line, always remembering that results matter**

4.   **embody the change and be prepared to take risks**
5.   **open the process of change to ensure all people involved have the chance to incorporate their knowledge**
6.   **remember what's great about the business already, very rarely strategy about entirely removing the stability of the today position**

2.3 Using the team and building momentum

Einstein suggested that we 'should not listen to the person who has the answers but listen to the person who has the questions'.

This is a good maxim for ensuring that the team is always involved within strategic change. Chapter 3 discussed the concept of a learning organisation: the bringing together of the individual brains to react and interact which enables an organisation to bring lasting and effective strategic change.

Each individual person is limited by their knowledge, experience parameters and particular paradigm at any point in time. It therefore makes sense to recognise the need to involve, at differing levels, all people affected by any perceived strategic change.

The specific study of teamwork lies outside the scope of this text. However, the work carried out by Belbin (1985) is important in this context. His model of the core roles required for a team to operate effectively could easily be transliterated and used as the roles required to ensure successful strategic change within an organisation.

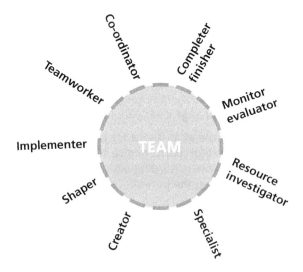

Figure 15.1
((Belbin, 1985) adapted by Wearden)

By recognising that strategy is a perpetual process, combining the rational and the emergent, we can realise that the development of strategy, and the driving of strategic change within organisations requires a range of different human skills and abilities. Although we all contain the potential to deliver each of these requirements, it is unlikely that any one of us will be able to fulfil all such requirements at the same time. Hence the importance of bringing teams together within the context of strategic change.

2.4   Using external leverage

In Section 2.2 on change agents above, it was recognised that an objective mindset is important in delivering strategic change within an organisation and that this can sometimes be delivered most effectively by a person or people external to the organisation. An organisation will often employ external consultants to help in the formulation of the strategy or plan and then to facilitate the change process required – this might also be a reason for recruiting new non-executive directors (NEDs).

A consultant is able to operate outside of the organisational culture and bring a dispassionate view to that process, and sometimes there is additional leverage brought to the process by a person who is not subsumed within the politics of the organisation and has no apparent conflict of interest.

Chapter 7 discussed the differing stakeholders within an organisation, and their role within strategic change. Sometimes it is their stake and their requirement that is the driver of change, and it could be that strategies are developed around the vision of one or more stakeholders. Stakeholders such as the government, investors, banks, customers and suppliers can have a significant influence upon the need for strategic change and may themselves try to play a part in the leadership of that change.

As highlighted throughout this text, an important aspect of the role of the company secretary and governance professional is always to find an objective position and be able to understand both sides of an argument.

Stop and think 15.2

Consider the advantages and disadvantages of using an external agent to drive strategic change within an organisation. For example:

1.   **objectivity versus subjectivity**

2.   **ownership versus remoteness**

3.   **involvement versus detachment.**

In his recent book, Nassim Nicholas Taleb (2018) suggests that it is only people who have 'skin in the game' who are able to genuinely deliver long-lasting strategic change and results.

Consider how to reconcile this with the benefits of using external leverage.

3. Managing effective change strategically

3.1 Communication techniques

Communication is an essential part of managing effective strategic change. As soon as more than one person is involved, there is the need to consider how a message is best communicated and through the most appropriate channel according to the person or group receiving the message.

Communication is always a two-way process – transmitter and receiver.

While the technical communication process itself may not involve any direct change, as soon as individuals are involved, the problem of the variety of differing individual interpretation and understanding is introduced. Chapter 1 considered the Argyris (1990) 'ladder of inference' and the judgemental and prejudicial iterations that take place within each individual human brain based around the particular alignment of experience at any moment in time.

> 'What I believe I am saying to you is not necessarily the same as what you think you are hearing from me.'

This disconnect applies in all forms of communication, and an important strategic consideration for the person transmitting is how to ensure optimal receiving of not just the communication, but also the intention and the meaning of the words being used.

We have emphasised the importance of the involvement of a wide range of different people within all aspects of the development of strategy and the delivery of strategic change. A significant part of any strategic plan must also be how that plan is communicated, knowing that a listener will create their own meaning and interpretation (based on their own experience and knowledge).

When to communicate and what to communicate needs to be built into every strategic plan. There is no ideal time, other than to ensure that every effort has been made to communicate to relevant parties ahead of the need for their involvement within the anticipated strategic change; and further to attempt to ensure that those being communicated to have understood the really salient facts and requirements.

We live in an age where electronic methods increasingly dominate our communication. When developing strategy, it is essential to stop and think about the most appropriate method of communication.

An over-riding comment on all methods is to consider the time factor involved. How quickly do you need someone to understand and react to something?

The word communication delivers in excess of 200,000 options in a book search on Amazon, and you can guarantee that each of these books will have its own version of the strengths and weaknesses of different communication methods and models. This text includes just one model for your consideration in terms of strategic communication: the Johari window. By considering the implications of this model, it should be possible to at least reduce the number of potential communication errors.

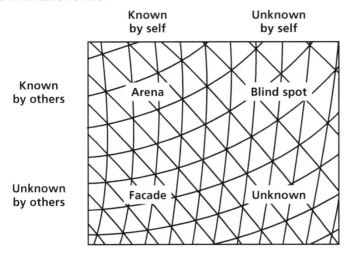

Figure 15.2 The Johari window
((Luft and Ingham, 1955) adapted by Mark Wearden)

This model was developed by Joseph Luft and Harry Ingham in 1955, and by plotting the dimensions of the known and the unknown with that of ourselves and others it helps us to identify, consider and challenge where the disconnect happens in our communication with others.

◈ **Arena**: an area where there is open communication between all individuals concerned; subjects can be openly challenged as all parties have a good understanding and knowledge – e.g. me, as an accountant talking to another accountant about balance sheets.

◈ **Blind spot**: an area where we, as a communicator, need to seek additional knowledge from other people to ensure that we have a full understanding and thus enable better communication – e.g. a human resources (HR) manager asking me, as an accountant, for tax advice without having given me any specific details.

◈ **Façade**: sometimes called the hidden area, can allow us, as a communicator, to dominate the decision-making and potentially abuse our leadership power; the objective must be to help others understand to enable better communication – e.g. me, as an accountant talking to the HR manager about the details of a balance sheet I have been studying.

◈ **Unknown**: an area of uncertainty where all parties have limited or no real knowledge or information and therefore there is the risk of incorrect decision-making; the objective is clear – better knowledge and information through research or the introduction of additional people, this might be a good example of where an external consultant could play a useful role in the strategic change process – e.g. me, as an accountant talking with the HR manager about how we might mend the plumbing, a subject neither of us know anything about.

Stop and think 15.3

Company 1 and Company 2 are undertaking the same strategic change process.

They have analysed the existing knowledge within their project teams and the Johari diagrams below represent the knowledge levels within each company.

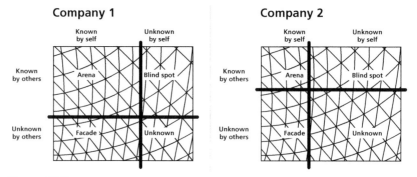

Figure 15.3

Imagine the difference that would exist between the communication process in each company and the likely outcomes during the strategic change process.

3.2   Methods for managing change

The following approaches will be useful in different communication circumstances; these might be separate strategic change processes, or different approaches may be required during the same strategic change process.

Earlier in the text we considered the use of 'power' and its ability to have a strategic impact. The following section suggests the type of language that might have a powerful strategic impact. As examples they are neither prescriptive or exclusive.

As you read them, consider the impact and how it is likely to be received by other people. How could you use these methods to ensure success in driving a strategic change process?

In section 5 below we will consider the human resistance that may follow each of the suggested 'opening statements'.

◆   **Education**: The process of facilitating learning is an important part of the communication process in the management of change; its effectiveness will be largely based around the culture of the organisation and the readiness of the learners to accept the process. If we take the Johari window as an example of the gaps, then there will always be areas where people need to learn. Those who lead the change process need to identify good teachers for this process, recognising that they themselves might not be the best at this task.

- – Opening statement: 'welcome to today's learning workshop, it is important that you understand the changes that have been made to this process'.

◆ **Participation**: When people are able to participate in different stages of strategic change, they are far more likely to become part of the change rather than reject it. There is a risk that people will find change solutions based around current practice and culture rather than be prepared to consider alternative approaches. It is also not always possible to involve people in the early stages of strategic change planning in order to maintain confidentiality.

- – Opening statement: 'we would like you to consider the changes that we hope to make and how they might impact upon your working day'.

◆ **Facilitation**: It is important that one or more people within a change project team have specific responsibility for facilitating differing communication processes. When understanding is just assumed people are often left unaware of the real organisational expectations.

- – Opening statement: 'don't worry, you will find out what you need to know at the right time'.

◆ **Support**: Part of the strategic change plan should be to identify and communicate the different stages of the process where it is important to garner support from all key people. As with participation, the sooner people are involved in a process, and the importance of their role is explained and understood, the sooner they are likely to participate fully within the change process.

- – Opening statement: 'please could you think about the suggested changes, so we can understand your concerns in advance'.

◆ **Ownership**: This is a keyword which is often misused by consultants and others 'we need to give the people ownership'. While of course the approach is right, people will take more care and consideration over something that they believe they own, the concept often fails to realise the remoteness with which many people view their work in comparison to their personal life. The real benefit of an 'ownership' approach will come from a culture of inclusion within an organisation as discussed in Chapter 6.

- – Opening statement: 'this is your part of the business and it is important that you take ownership for what is happening in your section'.

◆ **Negotiation**: The concept of negotiation as part of the change communication process can be useful if treated professionally. A natural human reaction to a perceived change can be 'what's in it for me?'. Negotiation, when used intelligently can help to plan both sides of a change process identifying pre-emptively the benefits that can be gained (tangible or intangible) by people participating fully within the perceived changed environment.

- – Opening statement: 'if you try this new approach you should find that it takes you about two hours less per week'.

◆ **Force**: It may be necessary at times to give people no choice but to co-operate with a change, and therefore insist they fulfil the requirements. It is a dangerous precept upon which to base any change as human nature is resistant to force, and natural instincts will begin to rebel. It could be that this becomes a breaking point with an organisation requiring a change of personnel.

  – Opening statement: 'if you don't follow these new methods the consequences should be obvious to you'.

◆ **Manipulation and coercion**: Manipulation suggests attempting to get people to do something different by not giving them all the facts, or potentially making the situation appear better than it actually is. Coercion is a more extreme form of manipulation, where change is imposed through power often through the use of threat.

  – Opening statement: 'if you make these changes in the way you do the job you will find that life becomes easier for you; of course we could always find somebody else to do this role instead and find you a different role'.

Test yourself 15.2

What are the four different communication dimensions identified in the Johari window?

4. Levers for strategic change

Recall the idea that the optimal alignment of strategic drivers is similar to operating the control levers within a railway signal box to ensure the strategic changes are driven through the system in the most appropriate and safe manner.

How do we keep the strategy on track? In front of us we have a set of strategic levers. Imagine that at each identified breakpoint within the development of our strategy, we have the ability to switch the levers to decide which direction the strategy will take.

We are in control. Having understood the system and the various forces, we have to decide the optimal route to take in the strategic change programme, and which levers (or tactics) to operate. This sounds like a purely mechanical task, but of course at every stage in our system we have the behaviour of people to take into consideration.

Senge (2006) would recognise this as a learning organisation approach with the person, or people, with the authority to switch the levers, having taken the time to recognise the systemic implications of the underlying environmental and people forces that will influence the success of the strategy.

The type of levers being referred to could be:

◆ time intelligence
◆ removing presumption
◆ change of routines and operations
◆ change of expected outcomes.

4.1   Time intelligence

Time will always play a significant part in the management of strategic change. As a resource, time is both restricted (there are only 24 hours in each day) and needs utilising (if you fail to use today's time, you cannot move it forward into tomorrow).

A significant part of the leadership role is determining the optimal time to operate the levers of change. Sometimes this may be dictated by the need for completion of a project by a particular time; sometimes there may be an urgency and with a short and defined timescale; sometimes the availability of people will dictate the timeframe; sometimes the leader needs to determine the timing for the different stages of the strategic change. The deadlines will often be set by the stakeholders and therefore have a direct influence on our efficiency and our effectiveness.

Case study 15.3

Changing timescales can have a significant impact upon a strategic change project. A good example is the mega-project of the new east–west London railway, Crossrail.

Extract from article in Financial Times, 3 September 2018 (www.ft.com/content/83dc0786-acfd-11e8-89a1-e5de165fa619):

'Crossrail opening pushed back to next autumn in blow to TfL

The opening of Crossrail, London's new £15bn east-west railway, will be delayed until at least next autumn (2019), dealing a significant blow to Transport for London. Crossrail said it would miss its target of opening the central section of the line in December 2018. Services through the centre of the city would not begin until late next year. Trains on the service are already operating between Shenfield and Liverpool Street in east London and between Paddington mainline station and Hayes & Harlington in west London. The central section between Paddington and Abbey Wood had been scheduled to open before the end of this year.

This is likely to delay the profitable opening of the entire line, from Reading in the west to Shenfield in the east, beyond the planned completion date in December 2019. Crossrail said the delay was needed for "final infrastructure and extensive testing", even though TfL had claimed as recently as July that the project was 93 per cent complete and on track to open in December. According to

people close to the project, there are unfinished building works at Whitechapel and Farringdon stations, and there have been delays in testing the communication between trains and signalling.

A spokesperson for the Mayor of London said the postponement was "disappointing" but added: "This has been a 10-year construction project and is one of the most complex engineering schemes ever undertaken. It is essential that a safe and reliable railway operates from day one, and this has to be the top priority."'

4.2   Removing presumption

There is often the need to pull a lever to change the paradigms of long-standing, taken-for-granted presumptions about the way an organisation has to operate. We naturally become familiar with a known manner of operating and often presume firstly that certain operations happen in a particular way ('we do this because we have always done it'). To change this lever will require a participatory route, the opening of people's minds, and the willingness to think laterally about what actually happens and what needs to happen within an organisation, or a subset process within the organisation.

4.3   Change of routines and operations

The complexity of large multinational organisations, and even the level of complexity that often develops within smaller organisations, means that people are used to operating levers within the system at a particular time and in a particular way. Often these routines can be perceived as the basis of core competence and competitive advantage, but such routines can prove a difficult lever to shift when seeking strategic change. An important part of the strategic planning process is to identify and map these routines, and the people who are closely associated with them. This will allow the appropriate challenge, education and communication to ensure that the operation of all such levers is fully understood before any change is implemented.

4.4   Change of expected outcomes

We have recognised throughout this text the inevitable interplay of rational strategy and emergent strategy. It is therefore intrinsic that the strategic change process is specifically designed to allow for regular reassessment of the intended process based around emergent outcomes. There is a risk that the end objective is never achieved, and therefore a disciplined focus on time and the setting of clear targets and expectations is essential.

Worked example 15.1

XYZ is an important supplier to a major UK retailer. It had been agreed at the top level of XYZ that the IT system will be updated to enable the retailer to access live information. This was a 15-month project with all costs being covered by XYZ. There have been a number of emergent challenges:

1.   It is now month nine of the project – the system design and implementation are one month behind the time plan of the original strategic change programme.

2.   The recently appointed new senior buyer at the retailer has requested a change to the dynamics of the required live information and insists the retailer needs to see it by the end of month 12. XYZ estimates this will add 15% to the cost of the project.

3.   A companywide IT project at XYZ as identified the need to change part of the core operating system of the business, this will have a further time impact on the retailer's project.

4.   The executive board of XYZ has signed a supply agreement with a different additional retailer, where the live information requirement is similar, but not the same, requiring a further change to the original programme.

The head of IT at XYZ is concerned that the live information programme will never be completed due to conflicting emergent challenges.

5. Managing human resistance to change

This text has referred a number of times to the natural human resistance to change throughout our discussion of the development of strategy. This resistance will affect the planning and design of the strategic change programme, the consideration of differing forces within the macro and micro environments, the culture of the organisation and the management of strategic change.

The final two sections of this chapter will consider some of the reasons for this resistance and how to overcome – although also recognising that resistance can at times be positive as a challenge to preconceived notions of required change – and to ensure that all options have been considered. The effective operation of an organisation will require consistency and can rarely sustain perpetual change.

The risk of a line of robotic, unchallenging automatons is that the opportunity for improvement and challenge and feedback never occurs.

The advantage of a line of human, challenging people is the imagination of their brains and the ability to stimulate debate about what is actually required.

5.1 Explicit and overt resistance

In some ways this is the easiest type of resistance to deal with, the problem will be clear, it will be possible to debate the rights and wrongs of the situation and a solution can be found, although not always on a win-win basis.

This could be a threat by a workforce to go on strike if certain aspects of the change process are not amended, or alternatively the directors of a company refusing to change strategic direction so as not to appear weak.

5.2 Implicit, subtle and deferred resistance

This type of resistance is not always easy to identify and may take time to come to the surface of an organisation. While a change might initially appear to have been accepted, there could be underlying issues which ultimately may cause longer term organisational damage.

This can be evidenced by reduced motivation and increasing inefficiency within a workplace, the risk of mistakes being made and a reduction in operating margin efficiency, where the decline is only gradual, and the organisation fails to recognise that the decline is aligned with a strategic change that has been made in the past.

5.3 Five stages of grief

Work undertaken by the Swiss-American psychiatrist Elisabeth Kubler-Ross has identified that there are five different stages of grief within the human resistance process, giving an insight into how people are able to cope with change or loss.

Stage	Emotion	Behaviour
1	Denial	– initial shock – expectation change, or bad news, will go away – apathy and withdrawal – attempt to rationalise the perceived change
2	Anger	– irritation, jealousy and resentment – putting the blame on other people – 'shooting the messenger' – attempt to sabotage the perceived change
3	Bargaining	– trying to move away from the problem – setting of compensatory goals – considering different scenarios – attempt to negotiate a way out of the perceived change

4	Depression	– the truth is finally sinking in
		– feelings of helplessness and being misunderstood
		– loss of control
		– attempt to withdraw or hide from the perceived change
5	Acceptance	– acceptance of reality
		– recognition of the grief process
		– ability to discuss with others
		– attempt to find the positives of the perceived change

Table 15.2
((Kubler-Ross & Kessler, 2014) adapted by Mark Wearden)

5.4 Ten reasons for resistance

Rosabeth Moss Kanter (1992) identified through her research and work with a wide range of different organisations that there are ten basic reasons for resistance. These could be cross-related to the Kubler-Ross grief model to provide further depth of analysis as to why organisational change is often difficult.

The reason for resistance (Kanter et al.)	The human fear (Wearden)
Loss of control	'Who is going to do that now?'
Excess uncertainty	'I don't know what I'm doing'
Surprise, surprise!	'I don't have time to think and react rationally'
Everything seems different	'I'm happy doing what I do'
Loss of face	'What will other people think?'
Concerns about competence	'Do I have the ability to do this?'
More work	'This will just mean that I have more to do'
Ripple effects	'Who knows where this will end'
Past resentments	'Well this didn't work last time did it?'
Sometimes the threat is real	'If I don't succeed, I will lose my job'

Table 15.3
((Kanter, Stein, & Jick, 1992) adapted by Mark Wearden)

5.5 Using emotional intelligence

emotional intelligence
  – The capacity to be aware of, control, and express one's emotions, and to handle interpersonal relationships judiciously and empathetically.

The daily work of the company secretary and governance professional requires an ability to use emotional intelligence. Thus, we return briefly to the change methods identified in section 3.2 of this chapter, but this time with an additional identification of a positive and negative response to each opening sentence.

Education: 'welcome to today's lesson, it is important that you understand the changes that have been made to this process'

Positive response	Negative response
'I love being challenged with new information'	'I can't see what is wrong with the current process'

Participation: 'we would like you to consider the changes that are about to be made and how they might impact upon your working day'

Positive response	Negative response
'I'm really pleased to be involved in this change'	'I expect it will just mean more work'

Facilitation: 'don't worry you will find out what you need to know at the right time'

Positive response	Negative response
'I trust you to keep me informed as necessary'	'I don't suppose it'll make a difference anyway'

Support: 'please could you think about the suggested changes, so we can understand your concerns in advance'

Positive response	Negative response
'I've already given this some consideration and ...'	'I don't want anything to do with this change'

Ownership: 'this is your part of the business and it is important that you take ownership for what is happening in your section'

Positive response	Negative response
'I'm keen to make sure that we operate effectively and efficiently'	'I don't see why it is my fault'

Negotiation: 'if you try this new approach you should find that it takes you about two hours less per week'

Positive response	Negative response
'I am really pleased with that because I need to spend more time on the risk register'	'I'll believe that when it happens'

Force: 'if you don't follow these new methods the consequences should be obvious to you'

Positive response	Negative response
'I will make sure that the changes work first time, don't worry'	'I thought it would come to this'

Manipulation and coercion: 'if you make these changes in the way you do the job you will find that life becomes easier for you, of course we could always find somebody else to do this role instead and find you a different role'

Positive response	Negative response
'I'm happy to work with you to make sure this happens in the best interests of the organisation'	'I'll start looking for a new job now then'

It is recognised that the above scenarios suggest focused ends of the response scale, but these are based upon reality and experience. It is important to recognise the divergent responses to change that are made and, as part of the management of strategic change to have pre-emptively considered the likely responses and how you will deal with them. This can require significant emotional intelligence.

Test yourself 15.3

How many of Kanter's ten reasons for human resistance to change can you remember?

6. Managing strategic change effectively

This final section will very briefly consider four change models together with some final thoughts on how to use the people dynamic to manage strategic change.

6.1 Mintzberg – change cube

Mintzberg (2008) uses the rigid and fixed model of a cube to encapsulate all of the 'bits and pieces' that he identifies in managing strategic change.

The strength is that it requires us to think in three dimensions.

The weakness is that it is another model which assumes regularity and a precise shape.

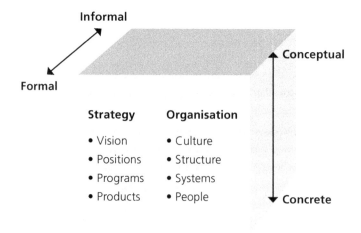

Figure 15.4 Mintzberg change cube
((Mintzberg, Ahlstrand & Lampel, 2008) adapted by Mark Wearden)

The organisation and its strategy need to be considered on two different dynamics: formal to informal; and conceptual to concrete (or tangible). The differing aspects of strategy and organisation are deliberately listed in a way which moves from conceptual to concrete. To use this cube in practice it would be possible, through research discussion and analysis, to identify the conflicts that would exist between these different dimensions within an organisation.

The strength of the Mintzberg model is that rational or emergent strategy will affect the entire cube, and it can be a useful, arm's-length paradigm of an organisation.

Stop and think 15.4

Consider how you would portray your organisation within this the Mintzberg change cube.

What are the dynamics that exist between formal and informal strategy, and between concrete and conceptual strategy – and then likewise with the organisational activities?

6.2   Beer et al. – six steps to effective change

An article in the Harvard Business Review from Beer et al. (1990) suggests a bottom-up approach to effective change within an organisation.

This model sees strategic change being driven by initially helping people develop a shared diagnosis and understanding what is actually wrong in the organisation, and what can and must be improved. The language used throughout the model suggests momentum in action, with words such as develop, foster, revitalise and institutionalise.

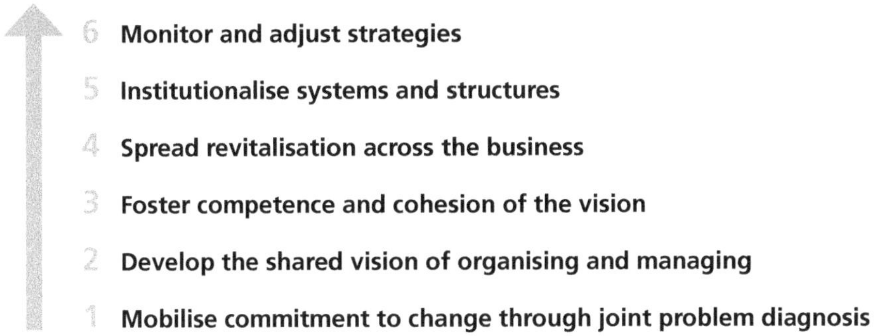

6 Monitor and adjust strategies
5 Institutionalise systems and structures
4 Spread revitalisation across the business
3 Foster competence and cohesion of the vision
2 Develop the shared vision of organising and managing
1 Mobilise commitment to change through joint problem diagnosis

Figure 15.5
((Beer et al., 1990) adapted by Mark Wearden)

The model recognises that having gained a groundswell of support and understanding across the critical mass of people within the organisation that a momentum can be developed which will help to drive strategic change to the point where it then becomes monitored and adjusted.

There is an alignment here with that of the learning organisation, and the need to regularly re-evaluate perceived strategies in the light of emergent forces.

6.3 Kotter – eight stages of change

In contrast to Beer et al., the change model suggested by Kotter (1995) is more of a top-down approach although commonly illustrated as shown in Figure 15.6.

Establish a sense of urgency
Form a leading team
Create a vision
Communicate the vision
Empower and involve others
Create short-term wins
Implement and consolidate
Institutionalise change

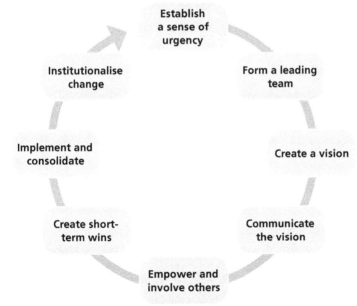

Figure 15.6
((Kotter, 1995) adapted by Mark Wearden)

Although the language and many of the concepts are familiar, the work undertaken by Kotter suggested that the optimal process of strategic change was one being driven from the top by establishing the sense of urgency and then forming a strategic change team. Interestingly, the endpoint becomes similar to that of Beer et al. in the need for change to be institutionalised.

In the words of this text, and the underpinning core model that runs throughout this text, there is a recognition that having reached the 'future' (in terms of strategic vision) this now becomes the 'today' point. It is from here that we need to launch the next set of strategies.

6.4 Pettigrew and Whipp – five factors theory revisited

Finally, just a brief re-visitation to the work of Pettigrew and Whipp (1991), discussed in the previous chapter, as a reminder of the five different areas that they suggest have to underpin the management of strategic change, irrespective of whichever people model is adopted, or more likely adapted.

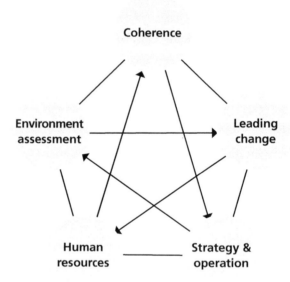

Figure 15.7 Pettigrew and Whipp five factors

6.5 Developing a change programme

It should be clear from the various approaches to change discussed in this and the previous chapter, that both process and people are essential to the successful development of strategy. A strategic change programme will need to incorporate an interconnected underlined recognition of all dimensions pertaining to process and people. All organisations from the smallest to the largest operate as a holistic whole and the only way to ensure a successful transition from 'today' to the 'future' is to incorporate and fully understand the breadth and depth of the challenges offered by process and people.

Test yourself 15.4

What are Kotter's eight stages of change?

6.6   Keeping a finger on the pulse

A final and reiterated reminder: all strategic change will be triggered initially by either a rational or emergent perceived need to change one or more aspects of 'today'.

If rational, the vision is likely to be more defined than if it is emergent.

As human beings, the measurement of our pulse, reflecting the control of the flow of blood through our body by our heart, is used by doctors to monitor and control our state of health.

Whoever has accountability for managing the delivery of strategic change within an organisation will be required to find the equivalent of the organisational pulse to enable them to stimulate, monitor, manage, challenge and control the successful development of strategy.

Chapter summary

◆   This chapter recognises that change relies on people, but also that people rely on change. We all have a vision of how today could be different, that is change. Our organisations are always trying to maintain or gain competitive advantage in a diverse and changing market. This often requires them to change, but such change is only ever driven by us, the people.

◆   It is important to be able to distinguish between transformational leadership (building the vision) and transactional leadership (driving the physical changes).

◆   The use of power by leaders will evidence their abilities as a change leader, but also will drive the organisational culture. Autocratic leader – hierarchical culture; participative leader – participative culture. Change leaders need to think about both of these sides of the human response to their enthusiasm, requests or instructions.

◆   Change agents can prove to be a useful objective force in the implementation of change, but it could also be argued that they are not directly involved so will not drive strategic change with the same sense of mission.

◆   The people dynamic of change requires the ability to communicate effectively and efficiently within the parameters of available resources and human behaviour patterns. Using the Johari window, we suggested that there were four differing and merging aspects of communication between people – the arena, the blind spot, the risk of façade, and the unknown.

◆ Different approaches to helping people come to terms with change and the change process were introduced, thinking about drive and impact.

◆ It was recognised that human beings are naturally resistant to change. We considered this, and how to lead change despite it, using findings and research from Kubler-Ross, Kanter, Kotter and others.

◆ The development of strategy involves the planning of change, and that will involve people. As a company secretary and governance professional we need to recognise and challenge the people dynamic that is involved in strategic change within our organisation. We have the privilege of a role which will often give us access to, and vision of, the entire organisation, we can see the actual impact and visualise the potential impact. Our professionalism and approach can give us the opportunity to take an objective and challenging perspective, and we should be prepared to use that to challenge others as and when appropriate.

Appendix

Company and organisation glossary

Company/ organisation	Brief introduction	Chapter references
Alibaba Group Holding Limited	A Chinese multinational conglomerate business specialising in e-commerce, retail, internet and technology www.alibabagroup.com	12
Amazon Inc	An American multinational technology company focusing on e-ecommerce, cloud computing and artificial intelligence. www.amazon.com	8
Apple Inc	An American multinational technology company that designs, develops and sells consumer electronics, computer software and online services. www.apple.com	10
Aston Martin Lagonda Global Holdings plc	A British independent manufacturer of luxury cars. www.astonmartin.com	7
BAE Systems plc	A British multinational defence, security and aerospace company. BAE Systems plc (BAE) develops advanced defence technology to protect people and national security and to keep critical information and infrastructure secure. BAE provides a useful example of a group with a core strategic focus, defence, but whose portfolio of products and range of skills has evolved across many years, while maintaining the same core focus. The company was formed in 1999 by the merger of Marconi Electronics, General Electric Company and British Aerospace, extending its market range but maintaining the core strategic focus on multinational defence, security and aerospace. It is the biggest manufacturer in Britain. www.baesystems.com	1, 2, 3, 5, 6, 7, 8, 9

Company/ organisation	Brief introduction	Chapter references
BP plc	A British multinational oil and gas company, one of the world's major seven oil and gas companies. www.bp.com	4
Cancer Research UK	The world's largest cancer charity dedicated to saving lives through research. It focuses on laboratory work to find new approaches to treating cancer. In 1923 the charity pioneered radiotherapy and started the era of chemotherapy in the 1940s and have subsequently led on many cancer treatment initiatives. Cancer Research UK's vision has been consistent throughout its existence. www.cancerresearchuk.org	1, 3, 7, 8
The Coca-Cola Company	An American manufacturer, retailer and marketer of non-alcoholic beverage concentrates and syrups. www.coca-colacompany.com	8, 9
Co-operative Group Limited	A British organisation operating in food retail, insurance, funeral services, legal services and life planning. In existence since 1844, The Co-op trades with a social commitment and a mutual ownership and trading structure. www.co-operative.coop	9
Crossrail Limited	A British company established in 2001 to build the new railway that will become known as the Elizabeth Line when it opens through central London. It is a wholly owned subsidiary of Transport for London. www.crossrail.co.uk	15
Domino's Pizza Group plc	A British company holding the exclusive master franchise rights for Domino's Pizza to own, operate and franchise branches in the UK, Ireland (and certain other territories). www.corporate.dominos.co.uk	11
Ford Motor Company	An American multinational manufacturer of cars and other vehicles. www.ford.com	10
GlaxoSmithKline plc (GSK)	A British science-led global healthcare company operating through three businesses with the common aim of improving health. In 2017 the company invested £3.9 billion in research and development to bring new medicines, vaccines and consumer healthcare products to patients, payers and consumers. The company has a scientific clarity in the alignment of the different aspects of its strategic vision. www.gsk.com	1, 4, 6, 9,13

Company/ organisation	Brief introduction	Chapter references
Hewlett-Packard Company (HP)	An American multinational information technology company. www.hp.com	11
John Lewis Partnership	The UK's largest employee owned business owning two retail brand names – John Lewis and Waitrose – owned in Trust by circa 84,000 partners. www.johnlewispartnership.co.uk	6, 8, 9
Wm Morrison Supermarkets plc (Morrisons)	The fourth largest chain of UK supermarket retailers, operating circa 500 stores and an online home delivery service. Its business is mostly food and grocery, but unlike other major retailers the retailer sources and processes most of its fresh food offering through its own manufacturing facilities. www.morrisons-corporate.com	10
Netflix	An American media-services provider. www.netflix.com	6
D S Smith plc	A British company operating as a leading global manufacturer of sustainable corrugated case materials and speciality papers. www.dssmith.com	5
Tata Group	An Indian multinational conglomerate holding company operating globally in many sectors. www.tata.com	12
Tesco plc	The largest of the UK retailers and has held that position for many years. The problem with being the leader in a sector is maintaining competitive advantage. In recent times, Tesco has suffered from increasing competition and challenge which has had a direct impact on the necessity to reassess the alignment of its six strategic drivers in its response to external challenges and market forces. Tesco's strategy is clear: 'be different, be cost effective and be innovative'. www.tescoplc.com	1, 2, 3, 4, 5, 6, 7, 8, 9
Unilever plc	A British company operating worldwide in fast moving consumer goods. Its core sectors are personal care, home care, foods and refreshments. www.unilever.com	8, 12, 13

Test yourself answers

Chapter 1

Test yourself 1.1

Clarify the relationship between knowledge, capability and strategy.

Clegg, Schweitzer, Whittle & Pitelis (2017) suggest that:

Knowledge + Capability = Strategy

Knowledge is required to enable a human being to be able to imagine a future state of affairs together with the ability to visualise how one might obtain that future state.

Capability is the power and ability to get things done, to be able to implement ideas, visions and plans.

Strategy is the long-term vision for the direction of an organisation requiring the knowledge to imagine a structure that is different from 'today', and the capability to do something about it.

Test yourself 1.2

Suggest three significant differences between the strategic dimensions of 'today' and 'future'.

1. 'Today' is a fixed and known point in time.

   'Future' is imprecise and unknown, being anything beyond the 'today' point.

2. 'Today' exists because of the decisions that have already been made.

   'Future' will be a result of 'today' + future decisions (as yet unknown).

3. We can analyse a wide range of aspects of 'today'.

   We can only ever imagine an analysis of the 'future', although we can use our strategic vision to analyse how we might like it to look.

Test yourself 1.3

Why is it important to establish benchmarks as part of the development of strategy?

As we plan and develop strategy, we anticipate that boundaries, parameters and routes may need to change to enable the realisation of our objectives. We need to benchmark our anticipation of the required changes by plotting the changes on a graph, producing a numeric projection, or creating a description.

The importance of benchmarking in the development of strategy is to enable an understanding of why reality is almost always different from anticipation. This is often referred to as gap analysis or exception analysis.

Test yourself 1.4

Write a short sentence about each of Mintzberg's five aspects of strategy (the 5Ps).

◆ **Plan** – The plan gives a direction or course of action, attempting to define a route to get from here to there.

◆ **Pattern** – The pattern describes a manner of behaving across a period of time recognising that human beings generally like to work and behave in a comfortable and familiar way.

◆ **Position** – The position within strategic planning suggests that there is a right time and right place.

◆ **Perspective** – The perspective recognises that strategy does not just happen by chance and that the people charged with the development of strategy must be able to look at the organisation and its strategy from one or more perspectives.

◆ **Ploy** – The ploy suggests that strategy may often be a deliberate and intended move to thwart the competition and maintain a competitive edge.

Chapter 2

Test yourself 2.1

Identify the four methods suggested by Ansoff that can be used to identify the success or failure of a strategy.

◆ **Economic**: have resources been used effectively to create the planned outputs of the organisation, has the strategy delivered the required economic profitability, or other numeric measure?

◆ **Non-economic**: have the expectations of the differing stakeholders been satisfied?

◆ **Self-renewal**: has the strategy contributed to the ongoing life and sustainability of the organisation?

◆ **Flexibility**: has the strategy allowed sufficient latitude to enable real-world change?

Test yourself 2.2

Briefly define what is meant by 'rational strategy' and give an example.

A rational strategy will contain conscious choices that have been made concerning the length of the strategic plan, the levels of risk, and the perceived opportunities and threats.

For example, when Nintendo launched the 'Nintendo GameCube' the company had determined its strategy to build upon its earlier games consoles, it laid an upgrade path for customers illustrating the advances offered by the new technology, and had fixed a higher price point based upon its perception of what the customer would be willing to pay.

Test yourself 2.3

Briefly define what is meant by 'emergent strategy' and give an example.

An emergent strategy will occur when an intended rational strategy comes under the influence of unexpected external (or internal) forces, and the strategic plan requires change to enable the achievement of the strategic objectives.

To return to the example in Test yourself 2.2, within a few weeks of Nintendo having launched its 'Nintendo GameCube', Sony released its new PlayStation. Sony picked a price point below that of the newly released Nintendo games console. To preserve its marketplace and continue to attract its customers, the original Nintendo strategy had to change – the company reduced their price point to just below that of the Sony machine, and gave software discount vouchers to anyone who had already purchased the GameCube at the original higher price (this was emergent strategy, as it diverged from the original rational plan).

Test yourself 2.4

Suggest the relationship that exists between complexity and chaos in strategic planning.

Complexity is based around the understanding that any organisation exists on a day-to-day basis due to the interaction of the many different aspects of the systems that are operating within that organisation. Systems theory suggests that complexity is not usually due to the different attributes that exist within a structure, but linked to the relationships between the attributes.

Chaos recognises that while an organisation can be structured and defined, the irrationality of human behaviour can always introduce the risk of chaos. Lorenz talked about the 'butterfly effect' – the recognition that a small move or change in one part of a system can have a much larger impact elsewhere.

Chapter 3

Test yourself 3.1

Suggest why Adair's threefold action-centred leadership model is useful in the driving forward of strategy.

Adair suggested that effective leadership comes at the centre of the recognition of:

◆ individual: the need of each person

◆ group: the aligned needs of the mixture of different people within a team

◆ task: the requirements for the team of individuals to fulfil the strategic task.

He suggests that every leadership decision will emanate from one of these three aspects, and the effective leader will be able to take decisions to ensure that all three perspectives are taken into consideration and satisfied appropriately.

Test yourself 3.2

Identify the six skills that Schoemaker suggests are needed for successful strategic leadership.

Schoemaker suggests that an effective strategic leader requires the ability to fulfil each of the following as and when appropriate during the development and leadership of strategic change.

◆ The ability to ANTICIPATE through watching out for changes in the intended path or the surrounding environment.

◆ The need to be prepared to CHALLENGE the plan, the people and one's own views.

◆ The time to INTERPRET what is actually happening or changing and why.

◆ The strength to DECIDE and therefore drive momentum, you cannot just think about something for ever.

◆ The recognition of how and where different aspects of the strategy ALIGN and can therefore drive change and outcome.

◆ The wisdom to LEARN from the process and to therefore be prepared to change.

Test yourself 3.3

A pharmaceutical company employs a team of expert scientists to create a new drug. Suggest briefly why this team, jointly or individually, might appear in each of the four aspects of a SWOT analysis.

◆ **Strength**: the technical ability, expertise and knowledge of the individuals is clearly a value-adding strength to the company.

◆ **Weakness**: the knowledge of the individuals is limited to what they know at this time, and this might not be sufficient for the required research.

◆ **Opportunity**: if the scientists are aligned and the strategy progresses well, the team may be able to drive competitive advantage for the company.

◆ **Threat**: if the company is reliant on one or more of these individuals, what happens if they leave to work for a competitor?

Test yourself 3.4

Give three reasons why the particular skills of a company secretary and governance professional can make a significant contribution in the development of strategy.

◆ A knowledge of the whole business, its legal structure, its operating parameters and an understanding of the regulatory requirements of the various operating environments.

◆ A knowledge and understanding of the directors of the business, their personalities, their ability to work together, their individual and united strengths and weaknesses.

◆ The ability to use professional training and personal ethics to take an unbiased and holistic view of a strategic plan, with the ability to be prepared to challenge when necessary.

Chapter 4

Test yourself 4.1

Identify the difference between environmental, technological and human influence on strategic thinking.

Environmental influence will require the strategic thinker to consider the use of natural and other resources in the strategy being developed. Thinking is likely to be influenced by corporate social responsibility (CSR) expectations.

Technological influence requires the strategic thinker to firstly ensure that the strategic plan is making use of known technology, but secondly that the plan is adaptable enough to allow for current areas of technological development such as artificial intelligence.

Human influence requires the strategic thinker to be aware of the influence of individual behaviour, the impact of teamwork and the overall culture of their organisation; on the basis that any organisation is only ever a collection of human beings.

Test yourself 4.2

Discuss briefly the impact of each of the factors of a PESTEL analysis.

◆ **Political** factors recognise the impact of the decision of government(s) on the organisation.

◆ **Economic** factors consider the 'macro' impact on quantitative measures within the organisation such as interest rates and exchange rates.

◆ **Socio-cultural** factors require the strategic thinker to consider megatrends such as increased human longevity, or wealth distribution.

◆ **Technological** factors, and the continuing changing world of automation, requires an organisation to determine whether it leads or lags – will it be the first to try innovative technology, or will it wait until it is tried and tested.

◆ **Environmental** factors will help an organisation to consider not just its own sustainability, but also the stewardship of the wider environment within which the organisation operates.

◆ **Legal** factors require an organisation to understand the breadth and depth of the legislation pertaining to its operational environment, but also to consider the underlying legal trends such as an increased focus on the personal accountability of leaders.

Test yourself 4.3

Suggest briefly why it is important to consider, at an early stage of the development of strategy, the position of an organisation on the economics dynamic.

Strategic planning requires an understanding of where an organisation sits in comparison to its competition. If it is at the monopolistic end of the economics dynamic it will be able to influence or 'make' prices. If it is at the perfect competition end, it will be a 'price taker'. Most organisations, or rather their products/services, are somewhere along the dynamic. It is important for the strategic planner to recognise where the product/service currently sits and which direction it is moving in.

Test yourself 4.4

Write one short question that you could use with an organisation to identify the impact of each of Porter's five forces.

◆ **Competition**: where is your organisation currently placed – price maker or price taker?

◆ **Suppliers**: how reliant are you on one or more suppliers – who holds the power?

◆ **Customers**: does your customer have a choice of supplier, or are you core to their success?

◆ **Entrants**: who might be able to take some, or all, of your market-share?

◆ **Products**: what might a customer or consumer use instead of your product?

Chapter 5

Test yourself 5.1

Differentiate between a strategic capability and a strategic competence, giving an example in each case.

Strategic capability is the potential that exists within an organisation to achieve an outcome; it has the appropriate mixture of resources available. *Example: Company G has a good mixture of people skills, sufficient cash and other resources and a strategic plan to create a new product and the capability to create competitive edge in a market place.*

Strategic competence is the understanding of how to use the organisation capabilities to drive a successful strategic outcome. *Example: To turn its capabilities into competence, Company G needs to have the appropriate leadership, drive and determination to align the resources in the fulfilment of the strategic objectives.*

Test yourself 5.2

Identify two different types of competitive advantage.

Michael Porter described two basic types of competitive advantage:

- *cost* advantage is where an organisation is able to deliver a greater level of profitability and financial benefit than its competitors
- *differentiation* advantage is where an organisation is able to deliver a product or service that is distinct from that of its competitors.

Test yourself 5.3

Summarise briefly the four different aspects of a VRIO framework.

- The **value** of the resources and capabilities of an organisation will be determined by the ability of the organisation to deal with the opportunities and threats that exist and provide a perceived value to stakeholders.
- The **rarity** of the resources and capabilities of an organisation will deter or prevent competition.
- The **inimitability** of the resources and capabilities of an organisation will prevent the competition from copying the success.
- The **organisational** support offered by the organisation can be a differentiator and can enhance competitive advantage.

Test yourself 5.4

Clarify briefly the five primary activities of Porter's value chain analysis.

- **Inbound logistics**: The receipt, storage, stock control and transportation of the material resources required for the business operation.

◆ **Operations**: The transformation of the raw materials into the final product or service, including manufacturing, packaging, testing and quality control.

◆ **Outbound logistics**: The storage and stock control of finished products together with the transportation of these products to the customer; in the case of a service rather than a product this process would include the means and location of the delivery of the service.

◆ **Marketing and sales**: The means through which consumers and customers are made aware of the product or service and are able to purchase it, including the selling process itself, the administration of the sales and associated advertising.

◆ **Service**: The enhancement addition of value to a product or service, such as installation, repair, training, spares or ongoing support and consultation.

Chapter 6

Test yourself 6.1

Why is culture often identified as 'the way we do things around here'?

This phrase is a popular definition of what is meant by the phrase organisational culture because it captures the core essence of what culture is about:

◆ WAY and DO: the manner in which something is done within an organisation.

◆ WE: the people who operate the organisation.

◆ HERE: culture is specific to an organisation or a situation.

Test yourself 6.2

Discuss briefly the alignment of assumptions, values and artefacts in organisational culture.

Schein suggested that there are three distinct levels of organisational culture:

◆ **Underlying assumptions** are held unconsciously by people working within the organisation and guide the behaviour and opinions of employees during day-to-day operational activities.

◆ **Values** represent what an organisation stands for. There is often a gap between the values of the organisation and the individual values held by employees. The combination of values allow an individual to decide how to make decisions which are not resolved through the underlying assumptions.

◆ **Artefacts** are the visible and tangible evidence of organisational culture, including the structure and layout of the workspace and the written and spoken language used within an organisation.

Test yourself 6.3

Write one brief sentence to explain each of the four cultural types of organisation identified by Charles Handy, giving an example of each type.

◆ **Power**: the culture and behaviour is controlled from the centre by the leader – example: political organisations.

◆ **Role**: the culture relies upon the interaction of a number of key roles or pillars – example: traditional manufacturing businesses.

◆ **Task**: the culture works through the network of people and their roles and goals – example: technology and marketing firms.

◆ **Person**: people are allowed freedom of expression within organisational boundaries – example: law firms and universities.

Test yourself 6.4

Suggest briefly why 'organisational stories' are often seen to be important in the understanding of culture.

Culture is about people, and people are about their accumulated knowledge and wisdom. This will include a received or experienced rationale as to why something happens in the way that it does.

In his consideration of the 'cultural web', Johnson suggests that the myths and the realities of how the organisation has developed since its origin to today form an important part of how and why the organisation continues to exist. Such stories can include the impact of internal and external events, and also the mythologising of how certain individuals have had significant influence.

Chapter 7

Test yourself 7.1

Define the difference between the governance oversight of an organisation and the operational oversight of an organisation, suggesting which organisational roles might be involved in each.

Governance oversight is the accountability for the satisfaction of stakeholder expectations. The board of directors are directly accountable to the shareholders and stakeholders for the governance, but its effectiveness will be determined by the understanding and actions of people throughout an organisation. Non-executive directors (NEDs) have a particular focused governance role with no operational involvement.

Operational oversight is the accountability for the delivery of successful business process transforming inputs into saleable outputs. Executive directors and management are accountable to the board of directors for the running of the operation. Executive directors have both a governance and an operational accountability.

Test yourself 7.2

Suggest three differing dimensions of the shareholder and stakeholder models of governance.

Shareholder model of governance:

1. focus on financial return for investors
2. likely to focus on shorter-term
3. perceived success driven by market reputation as well as by the direct success of the organisation itself.

Stakeholder model of governance:

1. differing stakeholders will have differing value output expectations
2. likely to hold a longer-term focus
3. the organisation will help to determine the acceptable output success levels.

Test yourself 7.3

Identify the input (stake) in an organisation and the differing output expectations of four different stakeholder groups.

Shareholders (*owners*) will input their own money into the organisation and will expect a return through dividend and/or an increase in the value of their shares.

Employees give their time and expertise to an organisation and in return will expect remuneration, sustainability of employment and other benefits as appropriate within different organisations.

Customers will buy from the company, paying for the receipt of goods or services; in return they will expect quality, safety and that the product or service at least matches their expectations.

Local and national government will provide the right to operate and the legal and economic infrastructure; in return they will expect compliance with laws and the payment of taxes as appropriate.

Test yourself 7.4

Differentiate between risk appetite, risk tolerance and risk capacity.

Risk appetite defines the approach of an organisation to risk. Where do they sit on the spectrum that exists between risk-aversion and risk-seeking? How hungry are they to risk the assets of the organisation?

Risk tolerance defines the lower and upper level of risk that can be taken by an organisation, irrespective of its risk appetite. The tolerance suggests the limits beyond which it would be dangerous for an organisation to go under normal operating conditions.

Risk capacity is the maximum level of risk that can be taken, and often that is required to be taken to achieve the intended strategic goals, but also might describe the difference between actual risk being taken and the higher or lower levels of tolerance.

Chapter 8

Test yourself 8.1

Differentiate between 'vision' and 'mission' within the development of strategy.

◆   Vision creates and identifies a picture of the perceived strategic outcome – what does it look like?

◆   Mission explains and defines the rationale and the values that sit behind the vision – why does it look like that?

Test yourself 8.2

Suggest how Johnson differentiated between four different approaches to organisational mission in his alignment of strategic drivers and ethical stance.

Ethical stance

	Legal minimum	Ideological
Internal	Secretive	Evangelical
External	Regulation procedure	Politics

(Strategic drivers — vertical axis)

◆   **Secretive** – keep it to yourself

◆   **Evangelical** – spread the word

◆   **Regulation** – keep others happy

◆   **Politics** – trying to satisfy all of the people all of the time

Test yourself 8.3

Briefly outline each of the six 'S' words used by McKinsey in its model to surround the seventh 'S' – shared values.

◆   **Strategy** – where are we going?

◆   **Structure** – what does the organisation look like?

◆   **Systems** – how do the resources work together?

◆   **Style** – what gives us a competitive edge?

◆   **Staff** – have we got the right people?

◆   **Skills** – have we got the right skills?

Test yourself 8.4

Differentiate between objective and goal in the following scenario:

When given his budget, Peter was tasked with saving £1.2 million of staffing costs in the next financial year, through a radical reduction of overtime and a realignment of his team. This was part of the organisational drive for greater efficiency and the retention of customers.

◆ The *objective* is at the organisational level – greater efficiency and customer retention. This might be achieved in a number of different ways.

◆ The *goal* is the focused saving of £1.2million – this will either be achieved or not.

Chapter 9

Test yourself 9.1

Briefly suggest the difference between 'principle-based ethics' and 'situational-based ethics' at a personal level.

Principle-based ethics defines the way that we behave as an individual based around our personal beliefs and principles. These might come from religious or other 'rule-based' principles, or just be based around the principles that we develop ourselves as we go through life. This might be called our personal moral DNA.

Situational-based ethics suggests that the way we behave and the decisions we make will be based more upon the particular circumstances that surround us, than on a set of immutable principles.

Most human beings operate at both levels throughout their lives. We build a set of principles, but these are challenged and evolve through different situational experiences.

Test yourself 9.2

Suggest what is meant by the 'reputation' of an organisation and where it comes from.

Reputation is defined as the beliefs or opinions that are generally held about someone or something.

As *reputation* is based on the views of others – the reputation of an organisation will be based around the views of its various stakeholders; these of course may differ dependent upon the stakeholder expectation and perspective.

Generally an organisation that is held to have a good reputation will be maximising how it satisfies its stakeholder expectations, but in particular the way in which the organisation behaves towards its employees and how they in turn behave towards people across all aspects of the organisational supply chain.

Test yourself 9.3

What is meant by the acronym CSR and how is it demonstrated by an organisation?

CSR stands for corporate social responsibility.

It can be defined as the obligation that any organisation has to develop and implement its strategy with a positive awareness of how that strategy is likely to affect society. To achieve this, an organisation needs to have a wide and conscious awareness of the social issues and norms that are affecting society at any point in time.

Test yourself 9.4

Differentiate between the 'laissez-faire' stance and the 'shaper of society' stance recognised by Johnson in consideration of CSR.

In a 'laissez-faire' stance, an organisation will just get on with its 'life-as normal', focused on driving profitability and shareholder value. Its CSR approach will be to achieve the minimum required to comply with regulation and expectation. The mode is defensive because the organisation will find reasons to avoid additional expenditure on CSR activities.

In a 'shaper of society' stance, an organisation and/or its key leadership team will be seen as visionaries who have the ability to influence social change. Such organisations will have an empowered workforce with each member expected to play their part within CSR. The mode is defining because the organisation will establish benchmarks and best practice for others.

Chapter 10

Test yourself 10.1

Identify the four strategic choices for growth of the income streams of an organisation as suggested by Ansoff in his product/ market grid.

◆ **Market penetration** suggests growth through the increase of the market share of the current product and market mix. This builds upon current strategic capabilities and is probably the most risk averse of the strategic directions that could be followed.

◆ **Product development** suggests using the knowledge of the existing customer base and` markets to provide different, evolved, or complementary products or services.

◆ **Market development** suggests that there is an opportunity to take existing products or services into new markets. This would require significant pre-emptive research, and possibly some product development to tailor the existing product to the particular expectations of the new market.

◆   **Diversification** is undoubtedly the highest risk option from within the Ansoff matrix, requiring significant research and market intelligence in terms of both aspects of development.

Products/services

	Existing	New
Existing	**Market penetration**	**Product development**
New	**Market development**	**Diversification**

Markets

Test yourself 10.2

Define the meaning of a strategic business unit.

A strategic business unit (SBU) is a fully functional unit of a business with its own vision and direction, operating as a separate unit but often still reliant upon the organisational centre for its ultimate direction. It is common for an SBU to have its own support infrastructure, such as human resources, training and sometimes even finance. Not all SBUs are also defined as individual profit centres within an organisation – this will depend upon the corporate structure and culture of a particular organisation.

Test yourself 10.3

Suggest how an organisation can obtain a cost leadership position, and the resultant advantages.

Cost leadership will require an aligned set of interrelated tactics, including:

◆   a detailed understanding of all true costs associated with the provision of a product or service – this will include the direct costs of production, but also a realistic assessment of the level of overhead cost that is absorbed in the production

◆   a focus on cost reduction based upon historic performance within the organisation aligned with an understanding of the cost options available

◆   the removal of unnecessary activities within the value chain

◆   a focus on customers who will fund the supply chain on time and in full

◆   a focus on quality of product or service to ensure a right-first-time delivery.

Cost leadership enables an organisation to price its product or services competitively and gain competitive advantage.

Test yourself 10.4

What are the five rules of the BPR principles of strategic change?

The principles of business process re-engineering (BPR) are underpinned by five rules:

1.   Strategy must be determined before any redesign takes place.
2.   The existing process-flow should be used as the basis for the redesign.
3.   The use of information technology should be optimised.
4.   The governance, culture and organisational structures must be aligned with the process-flow.
5.   People across the business need to understand and participate in the redesign – this is not just a top-down or bottom-up approach, but requires a whole-business involvement.

Chapter 11

Test yourself 11.1

Define the difference between a vertical acquisition and a horizontal acquisition.

◆   **Vertical acquisition**: An organisation acquires another organisation in the same sector or industry but working at a different level in the supply chain. Therefore, this would usually involve the acquisition of either a direct supplier or a direct customer with the intent of reducing the number of links in the supply chain and ensuring greater continuity and agility.

◆   **Horizontal acquisition**: An organisation acquires another organisation in the same industry and stage of production to create a new single entity. This type of acquisition is the most likely kind to be referred to the competition and markets authority if it is perceived that the newly enlarged organisation will have an unacceptable level of market dominance.

Test yourself 11.2

Suggest one advantage and one disadvantage of each of the three core strategic pathways.

◆   **Organic growth**:
  –   advantage – low risk
  –   disadvantage – slower to implement.

◆   **Acquisition**:
  –   advantage – immediate market presence
  –   disadvantage – potentially high cost and high risk.

◆   **Strategic alliance**:
  –   advantage – lower cost gaining of market share and knowledge
  –   disadvantage – lack of control.

Test yourself 11.3

When might a strategic alliance be a useful pathway for strategic growth?

Strategic alliances can be a useful option when there is a need for:

◆   the rapid achievement of critical mass scale within a marketplace, leading to cost reduction and an improved customer offering

◆   the complementarity of differing capabilities within the members of an alliance, ensuring a more holistic business and market coverage

◆   the learning potential from working closely with partners within an alliance without change to underlying organisational structure or culture.

Test yourself 11.4

What are the three core dimensions that are required of a KPI to ensure that it enables sound evaluation of a strategic pathway?

◆   **Accurate**: it is based upon sound core data rather than one or more judgements or skewed opinions.

◆   **Material**: it is a measurement of a fundamental operational or strategic driver of the organisation.

◆   **Forward impact**: having derived the measurement the organisation will use it to challenge what is happening and, if required, amend the strategy or the operation – it is not just a tick-box measure.

Chapter 12

Test yourself 12.1

Suggest how the concept of emergent strategy relates to the debate between whether structure should come before strategy or vice versa.

The concept of *emergent strategy* suggests that an organisation will need to be prepared to 'mould' its predefined *rational strategy* as the organisation and its strategic plan are influenced by internal and external forces.

If a structure is used to define the strategic plan, then the emergence of structural change (people, environment etc.) is likely to require change to the strategic plan.

If a strategic plan is used to define an organisational structure, then the emergence of challenge and force on the strategy (changing perspectives of the market or of stakeholders) is likely to require changes to the operational structure.

Test yourself 12.2

Suggest the advantages and disadvantages of a matrix organisational structure.

Advantages of a matrix organisational structure:

◆   specialised skills can be used across divisions

◆   resources can be shared more easily leading to greater efficiency

◆   flexibility can lead to removal of silo thinking and better personal opportunities.

Disadvantages of a matrix organisational structure:

◆   risk of power struggles across the senior team

◆   uncertainty about ultimate accountability – who do I really report to?

◆   hard-workers can become overburdened, and the 'work-shy' can hide more easily.

Test yourself 12.3

What are the differences between an international division of a company and a transnational corporation?

An *international division* will be a stand-alone operation which, although run under the oversight and principles of a parent company, will not be integrated into the core structure. This is often the starting point where a business is establishing its initial overseas operation and can test the local potential and requirements without having to change the core 'home' structure. It can be used by organisations with large domestic markets such as the US or China when they establish smaller overseas operations. Usually such structures will draw upon 'head office' for many administrative and oversight functions.

A *transnational corporation* offers a challenging mix of local responsiveness, global co-ordination and the ability to drive strategic growth and innovation across a wide range of different geographic territories and cultures. In many ways this is similar to a matrix structure but spread across different countries. Bartlett and Ghoshal (1998) suggest that such structures have a number of core characteristics:

◆   Each national unit will operate independently as a source of ideas and capabilities for the whole corporation.

◆   National units achieve greater efficiency and economies of scale by being able to act as specialists for the entire corporation.

◆   The 'head office' will deliver success by establishing the independent role requirement of each business unit, but then underpin this with effective systems, relationships and culture across the units to ensure a cohesive approach. Ultimate strategic success for the group will often depend on the ability of 'head office' to effectively monitor and influence the business metrics (the key performance indicators (KPIs), working capital etc.) of all units while allowing for local culture requirements.

Test yourself 12.4

What is meant by the concept of a boundary-less organisation?

The term *boundary-less* organisation suggests that while certain parameters of operation (based around stakeholder expectations) will have to exist, this type of structure can be significantly more flexible than more traditional models, with differing levels of people within the structure being given more autonomy to implement change and be accountable for such change. The term boundary-less was first used in 1990 by Jack Welch, then chairman of the global corporation General Electric Corporation (GE), to describe his vision of a new organisational structure for GE. Since those early days, the concept has been followed by many other global corporations, but also as an operating structure within many different sizes of business.

Chapter 13

Test yourself 13.1

Differentiate between strategy, risk and control in the context of strategic control and performance management.

The purpose of a strategic plan is to enable required change from the current position to the vision – *strategy: setting the direction*.

As all strategy is based in the unknown future, inevitably risk is being created – *risk: the dangers along the route*.

The people within the organisation need to understand and challenge risk at different levels and implement measures of control as they see best – *control: intelligent parameters*:

◆ We need to understand where we are heading – the *strategic vision*.
◆ We need to determine the dangers of the change – the perceived *risks*.
◆ We need to understand the drivers of success – the required *control* parameters.

It is important for directors and managers to develop appropriate methods and tools to enable the monitoring of the various strategies that will be taking place simultaneously and to find a way of alerting themselves when the journey is moving outside the perceived parameters.

Test yourself 13.2

Suggest the meaning of and identify an organisation, or type of organisation, which could be aligned with the metaphors of each of a) machine-control, and b) brain-control.

a)   Machine-control: A machine is designed to work, you push the button and it operates, in a continuous and repetitive manner, to deliver one or more pre-defined outcomes. There is a strong reliance on the efficiency of the parts of the machine, which simply need replacing when they wear out or fail. The control can be built in as part of the system. *An example would be a fast-food outlet such as McDonalds.*

b) Brain-control: The inputs can be manipulated to ensure that the outputs are delivered, but the outputs themselves are likely to also be manipulated. The human brain is itself seen as a control system, which will reactively and proactively bring about changes to the operation of the system. As with the brain, the system needs to have the ability to teach itself to learn and build its own methods of controls, based upon objective external stimuli. *An example would be a marketing or advertising firm relying on the creative output of different people.*

Test yourself 13.3

Suggest why gap analysis is a useful tool when implementing a control process.

Gap analysis is one of the most powerful control tools as long as it is embedded into the structure and the system and does not wait until the end of the journey before being considered. If we know that the future is likely to differ from our expectations, then sensible control will require us to understand the key drivers of the original projection and then to be able to judge, through our analysis of the gap(s), how and why these have changed the anticipated path.

Test yourself 13.4

What are the original four perspectives suggested by Kaplan and Norton in their balanced scorecard model?

- ◆ **Customer perspective**: What do our customers think of us? Why do they buy from us? Will they continue to buy from us? Etc.

- ◆ **Internal business perspective**: What do we look like from the inside? Are we efficient? What do our employees say about us? What does our culture look like?

- ◆ **Innovation and learning perspective**: What does our 'today' point look like? Is it always changing? Has it stayed still for too long? When did we last change the way we do things? How seriously are we taking the technological challenges of the next 10–20 years?

- ◆ **Financial perspective**: How robust is our financial infrastructure? What could make us fail (one aspect going wrong, or a concatenation of aspects)? Do our key players have their respective fingers on the financial pulse of the organisation?

Chapter 14

Test yourself 14.1

Distinguish between process change at the mega-level, the macro-level and the micro-level as suggested by Kaufman.

◆ **Mega level**: changes involving a long-term perspective, including future generations and their survival, self-sufficiency and their overall quality-of-life. They recognise that change at this level is complex as it is required to deal with a range of relationships across the different subsystems that we are able to influence. They describe this type of change as being 'holistic, profound and deep'.

◆ **Macro level**: changes involving the inputs and outputs of the main organisational system, affecting and being affected by a wide range of different stakeholders.

◆ **Micro level**: changes to the key results and performance indicators can be achieved by individuals, teams and processes within an organisation.

Test yourself 14.2

Write down the eight differing contexts of organisational change identified by Balogun and Hope Hailey.

◆ **Time**: how urgent is the change – is the time the lengthy consideration or is there the need for immediate action?

◆ **Scope**: will the change impact the entire organisation will initially only a small part?

◆ **Preservation**: does everything need to change?

◆ **Diversity**: have sufficient different opinions been explored?

◆ **Capability**: are the people within the organisation able to deliver the required change or are new people or external consultants required?

◆ **Capacity**: does the organisation have sufficient resources, in particular financial, to implement the required change?

◆ **Readiness**: has the appropriate level of preparation been undertaken?

◆ **Power**: where does the power lie to drive the perceived change, is it dependent upon one or more people acting appropriately?

Test yourself 14.3

Describe the difference between the 'driving forces' and the 'restraining forces' in Lewin's theory of force-field analysis.

Lewin's theory of force-field analysis, as a means of understanding the strategic change process, recognises that we are on a journey from 'today' into the 'future':

◆ the *driving forces* will be a mixture of external and internal forces that want to influence the strategic direction – stakeholders, systems, market potential etc.

◆ the *restraining forces* will be a mixture of external and internal forces that want to prevent change – competitors, markets, legislation etc.

Lewin's concept is that by understanding both sets of forces we are able to offset the restraining forces through intelligent use of the driving forces.

Test yourself 14.4

Try to recall the relevance of the five change factors identified by Pettigrew and Whipp.

◆ **Environmental assessment**: strategic change always needs to be placed within the setting of the organisational environment – macro and micro, environmental understanding has to be part of the 'learning' concept of the organisation so that all players understand its significance – it is not a specialist function.

◆ **Leading change**: leadership will be driven by and drive the context of strategic change and requires the ability to recognise and link the differing skills of a wide group of players and stakeholders.

◆ **Strategy and operation**: an organisation is a complete entity, although strategy making might be a focused task, it only becomes relevant as it impacts the operation of the organisation, as the vision starts to be realised.

◆ **Human resources as assets and liabilities**: strategic change requires the effective oversight and control of the strengths and weaknesses of people. Competitive performance can often be aligned to the optimal alignment of knowledge, skills and attitudes within an organisation.

◆ **Coherence in the management of change**: whatever happens has to make sense within the context of the other four factors; a vision must be realistic; the people are who they are, with their existing skills etc.; the organisation will have an existing mode of operation. The strategic change needs to be characterised by consistency, consonance, advantage and feasibility.

Chapter 15

Test yourself 15.1

Differentiate between transformational leadership and transactional leadership.

◆ **Transformational leadership**: The leader will focus on the building of the strategic vision, the creation of identity and empowerment and the development of an appropriate culture. The original inspiring entrepreneur behind an organisation is often a transformational leader.

◆ **Transactional leadership**: The leader is generally more concerned with making sure that the operational flow is appropriate to enable the strategy to be achieved, the term transaction referring to the motivation of followers by exchanging reward for performance.

Test yourself 15.2

What are the four different communication dimensions identified in the Johari window?

◆ **Arena**: an area where there is open communication between all individuals concerned, subjects can be openly challenged as all parties have a good understanding and knowledge.

◆ **Blind spot**: an area where we, as a communicator, need to seek additional knowledge from other people to ensure that we have a full understanding and thus enable better communication.

◆ **Façade**: sometimes called the hidden area, can allow us, as a communicator, to dominate the decision-making and potentially abuse our leadership power; the objective must be to help others understand to enable better communication.

◆ **Unknown**: an area of uncertainty where all parties have limited or no real knowledge or information and therefore there is the risk of incorrect decision-making; the objective is clear – better knowledge and information through research or the introduction of additional people.

Test yourself 15.3

How many of Kanter's ten reasons for human resistance to change can you remember?

1. Loss of control.
2. Excess uncertainty.
3. Surprise, surprise.
4. Everything seems different.
5. Loss of face.
6. Concerns about competence.
7. More work.
8. Ripple effects.
9. Past resentments.
10. Sometimes the threat is real.

Test yourself 15.4

What are Kotter's eight stages of change?

1. Establish a sense of urgency.
2. Form a leading team.
3. Create a vision.
4. Communicate the vision.
5. Empower and involve others.
6. Create short-term wins.
7. Implement and consolidate.
8. Institutionalise change.

Directory of resources

Further reading

- Ansoff & MacDonnel, *Implanting strategic management*
- Argyris, *Overcoming Organizational Defenses: Facilitating Organizational Learning*
- Arnold, *Corporate Financial Management*
- Clegg et al., *Strategy: Theory and Practice*
- Evans, *Risk Intelligence: How to Live with Uncertainty*
- Johnson et al., *Exploring Strategy*
- Lynch, *Strategic Management*
- Maccoby, *Strategic Intelligence: Conceptual Tools for Leading Change*
- Martin & Riel, *Creating Great Choices: A Leader's Guide to Integrative Thinking*
- Ringland, *Scenario planning: Managing for the Future*
- Robbins & Judge, *Organizational Behaviour, Global Edition*
- Spender, *Business Strategy: Managing Uncertainty, Opportunity, and Enterprise*
- Stanwick & Stanwick, *Understanding Business Ethics*
- Taleb, *The Black Swan: The Impact of the Highly Improbable*

Glossary

Actions – The steps that are required to be undertaken to enable the achievement of goals and objectives.

BCG matrix – The Boston Consulting Group matrix involving cash cows, dogs, problem children and stars.

Companies Act – UK Companies Act 2006 together with its subsequent amendments. The phrase may also incorporate earlier UK Companies Act legislation.

Company – Formal usage: a limited liability company formed under Companies Act legislation. Informal usage: any structured organisation.

Control – A step or measure taken or implemented to attempt to reduce or mitigate perceived risks or uncertainties.

Critical mass – Holding a controlling or majority share or influence in any market, product or service.

Due diligence defence – The investigation or exercise of care that a reasonable business or person is expected to take before entering into an agreement or contract with another business or person.

Gap analysis – The comparison of actual performance or events with projected or desired performance or events. The analysis is required to understand the gap between actual and projected/desired.

Goals – Specific and definable outcomes which enable identification of progress towards achieving the objectives and, if defined in such a manner, the achievement of the strategic intent: it is often useful to consider a goal as something tangible which is either achieved (scored) or not.

Hubris – Excessive pride or self-confidence.

Iteration – A repetition of a process or action, usually to either clarify a previous outcome or to apply a slightly different set of criteria to be able to assess the impact of a change.

Levers of control – The understanding that the alignment of the choices that we make will influence the outcome of the future and of our strategy. In simple form, a light switch is a lever of control – we determine whether the light is on or off.

Market – A group of customers with similar needs who are prepared to compete with each other for the satisfaction of that need.

Mission – The ethos, beliefs and values which enable the forming of a vision.

Objectives – A range of criteria which identify and clarify differing aspects of the vision and mission–objectives are often aligned with the acronym SMART.

Organic development – Increase and improvement through the use of existing resources. This can apply to increase of business with existing customers and/or attraction of new customers for existing products and services.

Organisation – Formal usage: a group of people with a particular purpose and focus. Informal usage: used interchangeably with the word company.

Paradigm – The perspective, view or vision held by one or more human brains at any particular point in time.

Planning – The bringing together of objectives, goals and actions in a cohesive and comprehensive manner to enable the realisation of the vision while maintaining the ethos of the mission.

Power – The ability of an individual or organisation to persuade, induce or coerce others into following a certain course of action.

Resource – A source or a supply from which a benefit can be produced.

Review – A process by which any aspect of the strategic journey is considered to enable an evaluation of progress and/or fulfilment: a plan will often include a pre-emptive review process to ensure that progress is considered at key points.

Risk – Any situation or decision where there is more than one possible outcome, and such outcomes can be visualised and ranked against likely probability.

Stakeholder – A person or organisation that has an interest or involvement (a stake) in another organisation and can both affect or be affected by that organisation.

Strategy – The combining of knowledge and capability in the perception of a future outcome.

Success – Notionally, the achievement of goals and objectives, the fulfilment of the plan, the realisation of the strategic vision; however, the concept of success must always be aligned with the particular expectations of the person or persons who are assessing whether or not the strategy, plan, objectives or goals have been achieved.

Synergy – The alignment of assets or activities such that the combined result can deliver greater advantage than the separate parts.

Uncertainty – Any situation or decision where there is more than one possible outcome, but it is not possible to visualise all possible outcomes.

Values – Beliefs and principles which drive our decision making, our opinions and our attitudes.

Vision – The ability of the human brain to imagine something different from a current situation.

Index

Lightning Source UK Ltd.
Milton Keynes UK
UKHW051304080922
408547UK00019B/197